PRAISE

LAST BOAT OUT
OF SHANGHAI

"Beautifully crafted, carefully researched . . . *Last Boat Out of Shanghai* is an engaging work of high-quality popular history. It has things to offer not just to general readers with little knowledge about the city's intriguing past, but even to specialists. . . . Ms. Zia lets us eavesdrop on the conversations in 'hushed voices' of several people whose childhoods are brought vividly to life. . . . *Last Boat Out of Shanghai* is so good I'll certainly need to add it to the syllabus for my class. That means something else will have to go—or my students will simply have four hundred more pages of fascinating reading."

—JEFFREY N. WASSERSTROM, *The Wall Street Journal*

"The dramatic story of four young people who were among the thousands fleeing China after 1949's Communist revolution. Eye-opening." —*People*

"A deftly woven, deeply moving chronicle of the extraordinary ordeals of four ordinary Chinese in a world torn by war and fractured by ideology . . . a fascinating read as an intimate family memoir, as well as a missing chapter of modern history finally coming to light . . .

What makes the Shanghai story unique . . . is that we didn't really know the story. Except in some films and novels that make passing references to this episode of Chinese history—often as a nostalgic backdrop, equivalent to a crowd scene in cinematic terms—the real human cost of the massive exodus has remained a mystery. Official records, if any, are suppressed, and research in this area has been sketchy. In this sense, Helen Zia's new book, *Last Boat Out of Shanghai: The Epic Story of the Chinese Who Fled Mao's Revolution* . . . fills a gap in our collective memory."   —*San Francisco Chronicle*

"A compelling account of the millions who fled Shanghai as the People's Liberation Army closed in . . . [The] stories are compelling and told in depth, with plenty of Old Shanghai detail to bring them to life."   —*Financial Times*

"Blending the personal with pivotal world history, Zia succeeds in creating a universal, timeless story. . . . Gathered, analyzed, and distilled with insight and meticulous documentation, Zia's book gives voice to a history almost lost."   —*The Christian Science Monitor*

"In this enthralling, heartfelt narrative, journalist [Helen Zia] tells the stories of four people during the 1949 mass exodus from Shanghai following China's Communist takeover. . . . Vivid and well researched, Zia's engrossing work brings this tumultuous period to life."   —*Publishers Weekly* (starred review)

"A compelling history . . . The stories of these refugees offer a window into Chinese culture, family life, and the history of this tumultuous period, resulting in a beautiful and emotional work that should be essential reading for those interested in twentieth-century Chinese history."   —*Library Journal* (starred review)

"Engaging . . . [Zia sheds] light on the depth and nuance that coverage of refugees needs but frequently lacks. . . . Background research is seamlessly woven into the narratives, resulting in an illuminating and highly readable volume that will appeal to a wide range of readers."
—*Booklist*

"An absorbing history of a refugee crisis that mirrors current events . . . vividly chronicles the lives of several individuals . . . With captivating detail, the author reconstructs the tense 'panic to flee' that engulfed the nation." —*Kirkus Reviews*

"Zia crafts intimate portraits of individuals as they navigate World War II, the Chinese Civil War, the agonizing choice of whether to stay and where to go, and, ultimately, life as immigrants. In doing so, she sheds light on an underreported mass migration which radically altered the landscape of China and the world. . . . Zia skillfully weaves . . . four biographies, inserting historical context along the way. The effect is a work that feels at once rigorous and personal. . . . The call for a more nuanced understanding of Chinese identity—both within and outside of China—is one of the most important takeaways from the book." —*Hong Kong Review of Books*

"In *Last Boat Out of Shanghai*, Helen Zia provides the wide lens of history and an intimate focus on four young individuals facing the personal torment of leaving China, as well as family members. Meticulously researched with a scholar's acumen, the pages unfold with the harrowing suspense of a novel. Zia's portraits are compassionate and heartbreaking, and they are, ultimately, the universal story of many families who leave their homeland as refugees and find less-than-welcoming circumstances on the other side. I read with a personal hunger to know the political and personal exigencies that led to those now-or-never decisions, for they mirror the story of my own mother, who left on virtually the last boat out of Shanghai."

—AMY TAN, *New York Times* bestselling
author of *The Joy Luck Club*

"Helen Zia's new book is a true tale of wartime savagery and difficult moral choices. Rich in sweep and detail, this compelling saga is a Chinese *Dr. Zhivago*. Enjoy a great historical read: Take the *Last Boat Out of Shanghai*."

—JAMES BRADLEY, *New York Times* bestselling
author of *Flags of Our Fathers*

"I have long been an admirer of Helen Zia's writing and scholarship, but *Last Boat Out of Shanghai* is at a whole new level. It's a true page-turner, which isn't something that's often said about nonfiction. Zia has proven once again that history is something that happens to real people. Money, chance, fate, and destiny play their parts too. I stayed up late reading night after night, because I wanted to know what would happen to Benny, Ho, Bing, Annuo, and their friends and families. We all know that real life is stranger than fiction. An action that on the surface looks like a good one can send you down a disastrous path, while sometimes a mistake can bring triumph. These are choices that refugees around the world continue to make, which helps to make this book relevant in addition to being such a compelling good read."

—LISA SEE, *New York Times* bestselling author of
The Tea Girl of Hummingbird Lane

"Gripping, magisterial, ambitious, and intimate, *Last Boat Out of Shanghai* not only depicts a cataclysmic century as it was lived and felt by four very different people, it keeps you on the edge of your seat the whole way. What a tour de force! I could not put it down."

—GISH JEN, author of *The Girl at the
Baggage Claim: Explaining the East-West Culture Gap*

"*Last Boat Out of Shanghai* is an impeccably researched and beautifully crafted account of the dramatic events surrounding the Communist takeover of China's largest and most cosmopolitan city. Tracing the fate of four fascinating families, Helen Zia offers a warmly human perspective on one of the most wrenching political transitions of the twentieth century. This book is a genuine pleasure to read, with much to inform and interest the general public and China specialists alike."

—ELIZABETH J. PERRY, Henry Rosovsky Professor
of Government at Harvard University and
director of the Harvard-Yenching Institute

"War, foreign occupation, revolution, counterrevolution, exile, and new lives: the worst and best times of a remarkable population from China who became Americans. Helen Zia tells their stories with clarity, understanding, and empathy. . . . Unforgettable and moving."

—GORDON H. CHANG, professor of history and
Olive H. Palmer Professor in Humanities, Stanford University

"Much has been written by and about the diaspora from war-ravaged Europe during World War II, but accounts of those who fled China's postwar turbulence are rare. Helen Zia remedies this lack in a book that makes the experience of those who fled Asia's most vibrant city both accessible and emotionally compelling. *Last Boat Out of Shanghai* deftly weaves together the stories of Chinese displaced by political turmoil into a mosaic that celebrates human determination, resilience, and ingenuity."

—STELLA DONG, author of
Shanghai: The Rise and Fall of a Decadent City

BY HELEN ZIA

LAST BOAT OUT OF SHANGHAI:
THE EPIC STORY OF THE CHINESE
WHO FLED MAO'S REVOLUTION

ASIAN AMERICAN DREAMS:
THE EMERGENCE OF
AN AMERICAN PEOPLE

MY COUNTRY VERSUS ME
(WITH WEN HO LEE)

LAST BOAT OUT OF
SHANGHAI

LAST BOAT OUT
OF SHANGHAI

....

THE
EPIC STORY OF
THE CHINESE
WHO FLED
MAO'S
REVOLUTION

....

HELEN ZIA

BALLANTINE BOOKS
NEW YORK

Last Boat Out of Shanghai is a work of nonfiction.
Some names and identifying details have been changed.

2020 Ballantine Books Trade Paperback Edition

Copyright © 2019 by Helen Zia
Map copyright © 2019 by David Lindroth Inc.

All rights reserved.

Published in the United States by Ballantine Books,
an imprint of Random House, a division of
Penguin Random House LLC, New York.

BALLANTINE and the HOUSE colophon are registered
trademarks of Penguin Random House LLC.

Originally published in hardcover in the United States
by Ballantine Books, an imprint of Random House,
a division of Penguin Random House LLC, in 2019.

LIBRARY OF CONGRESS CATALOGING-IN-PUBLICATION DATA
NAMES: Zia, Helen, author.
TITLE: Last boat out of Shanghai: the epic story of the Chinese
who fled Mao's revolution / Helen Zia.
DESCRIPTION: New York: Ballantine Books, [2019] | Includes
bibliographical references and index.
IDENTIFIERS: LCCN 2018036197 | ISBN 9780345522337
(paperback) | ISBN 9780525618867 (ebook)
SUBJECTS: LCSH: China—History—Civil War, 1945–1949—
Refugees. | Political refugees—China—History—20th century. |
Chinese—Foreign countries—History—20th century. | China—
Emigration and immigration—History—20th century. |
Shanghai (China)—History—20th century.
CLASSIFICATION: LCC DS777.542 .Z53 2019 | DDC 951.04/2—dc23
LC record available at https//lccn.loc.gov/2018036197

Printed in the United States of America on acid-free paper

randomhousebooks.com

68975

Book design by Barbara M. Bachman

To all refugees from crises amok;
To the compassionate who strive
Toward a world where no one must flee to survive;
To the memory of my mother, who inspired this book.

Running away is one of our nation's characteristics. We are very good at it. The best strategy for getting out of a bad situation is to run away. It may be the only way you can save yourself. If you don't follow this rule, you end up suffering.

The two characters 逃难 "*tao nan*" mean "*running away from difficulty.*" When transposed, it is 难逃 "*nan tao*" and means "*difficult to run away.*" Looking back at those who tried to run away by plane or train or ship, many ended up getting killed in accidents. It was indeed difficult for them to run away.

—EXCERPT TRANSLATED FROM *LUN YU* [*The Analects Fortnightly*], CHINA'S LEADING LITERARY MAGAZINE, IN ITS "SPECIAL ISSUE ON RUNNING AWAY," MARCH 16, 1949

CONTENTS

PART THREE: EXODUS   *195*

PART FOUR: WAR'S LONG SHADOW   *277*

A NOTE ON
NAMES

ANYONE WHO DELVES INTO CHINA, ITS PEOPLE AND HISTORY, soon discovers that, over the years, there have been an assortment of imperfect methods used to render the nonalphabetic Chinese language into English and other "romanized" languages. Most systems have been phonetic—that is, words have been transliterated based on the sounds in Chinese. This is problematic since pronunciation of words can vary to the point of their being unrecognizable from one Chinese dialect to the next. My surname, *Zia*, for example, is a common Chinese name that was transliterated using the system dominant in early 1900s Shanghai and based on its dialect. With different romanization methods and dialects in play, the alphabetic spelling can be *Hsieh*, *Hsia*, *Sieh*, *Sie*, *Jie*, and more. In today's China, it would be *Xie* using pinyin, the official standard in China and widely accepted by most universities around the world, including in the United States.

During the period covered by this book, from the 1920s to the 1960s, various romanization systems have been in use. Furthermore, places were often renamed by the latest political or military organization in command of the oft-changing landscape. As many other authors have done, I use the most familiar names for key historic figures, particularly if their names in pinyin may confuse readers unversed in the nuances of romanization. Thus *Chiang Kai-shek*, *Soong May-ling*, and *T. V. Soong* appear in this book, not *Jiang Jieshi*, *Song Meiling*, or *Song Ziwen*, as they are in pinyin. However, I defer to pinyin where the names will not confound the reader, as with *Mao Zedong* and *Zhou Enlai*.

Similarly, I rely on the present-day place-names *Guangzhou*, *Suzhou*, *Chongqing*, and *Taiwan*, rather than *Canton*, *Soochow*, *Chung-*

king, and *Formosa*. For street names, I use the name as known by the book's characters, for example, *Avenue Joffre* and *Jessfield Road*, not the current *Huaihai Lu* and *Wanhangdu Lu*. However, to make those former street names relevant to present-day Shanghai, I've placed an endnote with the current name on the first reference to each. I also refer to Chiang Kai-shek's government as *Nationalists*, which is how they were commonly known in English, rather than *Kuomintang* (in the Wade-Giles system) or *Guomindang* (in pinyin).

Finally, some words appear that are peculiar to Shanghai: Expatriates called themselves *Shanghailanders*, a term applied only to the city's foreign residents, whereas *Shanghainese* refers only to its Chinese residents—a distinction that would be well appreciated if one were transported alongside the characters of this book.

PROLOGUE

BING SAT STRAIGHT UP IN THE PEDICAB, GRIPPING THE HARD seat as the driver cursed and spat. She watched with alarm as his feet, clad in sandals cut from old tires, seemed to slow to a snail's pace just when she most needed speed. This stylish-looking young woman had imagined that her last hours in Shanghai would be spent waving farewell from a ship's deck to envious onlookers below as a river breeze gently lifted her dark hair, just as she'd seen in the movies. After all, she was about to leave China's biggest, most glamorous, and most notorious city. Shanghai had been Bing's home since she had arrived following the Japanese invasion nearly twelve years earlier, as a frightened girl of nine. But now, with the imminent threat of a violent Communist revolution, she was running away again, along with half the city's population, it seemed. And instead of standing at the rail, exchanging smiles with the ship's other passengers, she was stuck in traffic, terrified that she wouldn't reach the Shanghai Hongkou Wharf in time. That would spell disaster.

She lurched forward as the pedicab driver stood on the pedals of his three-wheeled cycle and came to a stop. Around her was a sea of other pedicabs, rickshaws, cars, buses, carts, and trucks—all screeching and honking, their drivers yelling every manner of obscenity. The cacophony reverberated against the walls of the stone-and-concrete canyon of Nanjing Road. Bing was no stranger to Shanghai's mayhem, but she had never seen anything quite like this. Of all times to be stuck in such bedlam—on the very day she had to get to the riverfront, the date set for her departure from this desperate city.

She'd sewn her floral-print *qipao* for this special occasion. Each careful stitch had captured her growing anticipation. With her oval face, big eyes, and full, red lips, all crowned by a tiara of black permanent waves, the twenty-year-old might have been mistaken for a coy Shanghai poster girl but for the panic in her eyes. Like her, everyone in Shanghai seemed to be in a frenzy to escape, to use any means to get away from the impending arrival of the Communists. But unlike those who were still clamoring for a seat to anywhere, Bing was one of the lucky ones: She possessed a precious one-way ticket out. On a ship. To America.

Finally, the driver managed to break through the crush. He harangued everyone in his path, shouting, "Move along, you worthless mule scrotum, smellier than pig farts!" She didn't blink at his choice of words, which came as naturally as breathing on Shanghai's streets. She didn't care as long as he got her to the wharf. The ship's smokestacks came into view just past the stately Astor House Hotel and the towering nineteen-story Broadway Mansions apartments, where the Suzhou Creek meets the bend in the wide Huangpu River, the last major tributary of the mighty Yangtze River before it joins the East China Sea. Massive granite buildings, all in European style, lined the signature waterfront boulevard and docks.

To the foreigners, this prime section of riverfront was known as the Bund, from a Hindustani word meaning embankment. The Chinese called it Waitan, meaning outside or foreign shore—a reference to the foreigners who had once ruled this proud imperialist showcase of Shanghai. British and American businessmen had wrested away the best sections of the port city with the full support of their governments. Land and sovereignty had been ripped from China, spoils of the Opium Wars that had forced the narcotic onto China one hundred years before. Everything about these monuments to international capitalists and pale "big noses" seemed foreign, including the British Big Ben chime of the giant clock tower over the Custom House. Soon it would be up to the Communists to decide what would happen to these grand stone edifices.

SHANGHAI WAS CHINA'S MOST modern, populous, and cosmopolitan city. One of the leading metropolises of the world, the "Paris of the Orient" was also home to tens of thousands of foreigners, who were despised as imperialists by the Communist Party and its leader, Mao Zedong. The city was the launching point for major inland routes and international traffic, whether by boat, plane, train, or wooden cart—making it the epicenter for the massive exodus of the late 1940s.

Stoked by the anticipated Communist victory over the Nationalist government headed by Chiang Kai-shek, panic and terror had first infected the wealthiest, most educated, and most privileged classes—and sent them running in what they fully expected to be a brief exile. It was assumed that the Communists would target the rich and the pampered in the same way that the Bolsheviks had gone after the czarist White Russians, many of whom had come to Shanghai as refugees from that 1917 revolution.

No one knows precisely how many people fled Shanghai during the early years of the Communist revolution. Scholars and journalists have estimated that more than a million people set off from or through that port city. Many of those who ran for the exits belonged to the city's capitalist and middle classes, who presumably had the most to lose under the Communists. These two groups comprised about 5 percent and 20 percent, respectively, of the city's 6 million residents, or about 1.5 million people. On the other hand, the remaining 4.5 million who made up Shanghai's majority saw no need to escape—they included Shanghai's industrial workers, coolies, and drivers, the destitute. But it was not only members of the upper classes who fled. They were joined by old-regime loyalists, from high Nationalist government officials to lowly foot soldiers, as well as those who simply got caught up in the frenzy or were especially fearful. Unfortunately, there are no records of the exodus since the retreating Nationalists destroyed as many documents as they could, while the incoming Communists inherited a country in such disarray that no accounting of the departures is known to have taken place.

Unlike the stories of other such mass migrations from revolutions and human crises, the exodus of Chinese from Shanghai in this era has yet to be told. There are no books or dissertations in English that track their saga through the geopolitical tectonics of modern China. In the Chinese language, only a handful of accounts have been published—in Taiwan. Even today, the People's Republic of China fails to acknowledge that any exodus took place.

This book opens a missing chapter of modern history by tracing the lives of four real people—Benny Pan, Ho Chow, Bing Woo, and Annuo (pronounced ann-wah) Liu—starting from their childhoods at the time of Japan's attack on Shanghai in 1937, the defining battle that marked the start of the Pacific War and altered the course of global politics. These four main characters and their families didn't know one another, but they were selected from more than a hundred other remarkable individuals for the combined depth and range of their collective journeys. The interwoven stories of their lives before, during, and after the Communist victory in Shanghai present a view of this historic exodus that no single family story could capture. Adding to the rich complexity and color of that era are accounts drawn from the many others interviewed who also bore witness to this time of war and revolution, sacrifice and betrayal, courage and resilience, when every move could spell doom as modern China erupted.

In today's millennium, when more-recent conflicts and disasters have forced millions of people around the globe to weigh the same desperate choices of staying or fleeing, the experiences of these Shanghai migrants offer a window into the current human condition.

WHEN BING ARRIVED AT the crowded pier, she waved away the hungry dockhands and touts, not wishing to waste her precious yuan when she could manage herself. In spite of her fashionable appearance, she was no spoiled Shanghai miss, clapping her hands to summon the servants; nor was she like the foreigners bellowing, "Boy!" at their slightest whim. Her cloth valise held only a few lightweight dresses, sweaters, and underclothes—no heavy photograph albums, gold jewelry, or mementos from family or friends. Nothing to remember her father and mother, who might have died in the war, for all she knew. No, there were no keepsakes from loved ones for her to take along.

Hundreds of people milled about, their desperation permeating the air, evident from the frenetic energy of foreigners and Chinese alike. The children, too, looked anxious under the watchful eyes of minders intent on keeping them from disappearing into the crowd. A group of nuns snaked by in single file, their pallid, ghostlike faces floating in a long curtain of black habits. News stories reported that missionaries had been asked to leave by their religious orders overseas because of the imminent Communist threat. Many had spent the greater part of their lives in China and were reluctant to abandon their flocks.

Stocky shipping agents, fat from the cumshaws that routinely greased their palms for "special consideration," barked orders to columns of sinewy men stooped over by impossibly heavy loads on their backs. Those dock coolies, clad in loose rags, managed to lug huge crates and overstuffed suitcases up the steep gangways using only their muscle and mettle. None of them seemed disturbed by the impending "liberation" of Shanghai. After all, the revolution was supposed to help them, the workers and the dispossessed—the proletarians who had nothing to lose but their chains, according to Karl Marx. In 1921, the Chinese Communists had founded their party in Shanghai, home to China's first industrial workforce, and now their propaganda leaflets flooded the city unconstrained, in spite of Nationalist prohibitions.

Bing scanned the long line of foreigners and Chinese as they waited to show their tickets, passports, exit visas, and other documents to indifferent immigration agents. At the head of the queue, Bing could see customs officials rifling through possessions, presumably searching for forbidden quantities of precious metals, jewelry, and currency. Once past this final hurdle, passengers could join the elated-looking group of those approved for departure.

Anxious to find her sister in the crowd, Bing was just about to step down to the pavement from the pedicab when a loud voice shouted, "Out of my way! Look out!" A gleaming black Buick came careening next to her pedicab. It jolted to a stop when its wheels hit the high curb, landing exactly where she had been about to alight.

The Buick's driver jumped out of the car, a clean-cut-looking fellow about her age, with slicked-back hair, a neat white shirt, and gray slacks. He was clearly a well-heeled college man. "Sorry, miss, sorry," he said in Mandarin, a more high-toned dialect than her own Shanghainese. Even as he apologized, his eyes darted anxiously. He was clearly in a hurry to get his car back on the road.

"You nearly killed me!" she exclaimed, frightened and indignant.

"Please forgive me," he blurted. "I'm Ben Char and I'm in a rush to get this car to my elder brother in Taiwan. The ship is loading today, and I have to get there. But my brakes failed, and I could only shift gears to slow the car."

Bing's pedicab driver was scouring his vehicle for any signs of damage. Finding none, he launched into a tirade: "Shit-faced rich boy, stay home with your amah before you kill somebody!"

Ignoring the insults, Char asked a passing guard about the ship headed to Taiwan, the designated island escape for retreating Nationalists. The official pointed toward another pier farther down the road, and the young man jumped back into his car. "When this madness is over, perhaps you'll let me make this up to you?" He winked, popping the clutch into first gear after some coolies pushed his car off the curb and into a roll. The engine roared, and he sped off toward the next dock, honking and lurching as people scurried out of his path.

Shaking off her close call, Bing again surveyed the crowd. Where was her sister? If Bing didn't find her, she'd be left behind, since Elder Sister had all the tickets and documents. As usual, she had taken charge of everything, because she was the clever one, a point that she was fond of making. If her sister hadn't filled the car with all her luggage, Bing could have ridden to the docks with her and her family. Now how would she find them?

Suddenly the ship blasted a piercing baritone horn, and Bing whipped her gaze in its direction. She saw the restless crowd straighten with excitement, then surge in a wave of bodies toward the ship, as if the people could will themselves aboard. At the far edge of the crowd, she spotted a shapely woman in a bright red, formfitting Western-style dress. No question, that was Elder Sister. Even from this distance, Bing could see men slowing their gaits, turning their heads to admire her. If only they knew how tough this woman could be, they would have thought twice. Bing hurried, weaving through the crush of frantic people while bracing herself for Elder Sister's wrath.

"Where have you been? What took you so long? We've been waiting for you! One more minute and we would have left without you—and in that case, we'd lose all the money we paid for your ticket!" A thunderous barrage poured out of Elder Sister's mouth with such force that Bing didn't dare answer, knowing it would be best to ride out the storm. Her sister marched Bing over to the immigration table where her sister's husband, Kristian, a tall European with slicked-back graying hair, was holding a place near the head of the line.

"Thank goodness you made it," he said with a look of relief, "or we'd have never heard the end of it."

The couple's two handsome Eurasian boys rushed over to hug Bing. She had watched over them from the day they were born. "We would never let Mother leave without you," five-year-old Peter whispered.

The immigration officer snatched the papers from Kristian's hand. After giving the biracial boys a long, hard stare, he applied red ink to his chop and stamped their passports, waving them on. He didn't try to hide his disapproval as he glared at the older white man with the young, attractive Chinese woman. Slowly, he studied each page of their documents as though looking for some discrepancy. Failing to find any, he stamped their pages and turned to Bing. His eyes shifted from her face to Elder Sister's, then back down to Bing's passport with agonizing deliberation. "You say you're sisters? You don't look alike. She's from Singapore?" he asked, jerking his head toward Bing.

Before she could open her mouth and answer, Elder Sister jumped in to interrupt, hoping to distract him from noticing that Bing possessed a black market passport that falsely listed Singapore as her birthplace. Elder Sister spoke in her sweetest, most unctuous voice. "Yes, Officer. My baby sister Bing was born in Singapore but grew up right here in Shanghai. If you doubt, sir, just listen to her Shanghai dialect. She's the governess for my sons—see how they cling to her?" She smiled warmly as she fixed her wide eyes on the gruff man.

He looked back at her and shook his head. "Here, go on then," he muttered with a snort, stamping his chop in red ink and onto Bing's passport.

Bing felt her heart lighten as she followed her sister's rapid pace toward the big ship. Each step took her farther from Shanghai, the Communists, and her life of war, turmoil, and heartache. She could hope only that this journey to a distant land would lead to something better than what she had known in China.

Just as they neared the boarding ramp, a voice rang out. "Bing! Bing!" At first she didn't even bother to look at the caller, certain the shouts were for someone else since no one there could possibly know her. Finally she turned and saw that it was Ah Mei, her one and only friend. Ah Mei, nine months pregnant, edged her way over with her husband, a dark, handsome foreigner from Iran.

"Ah Mei! You needn't have braved the crowds in your condition." Bing nodded toward Ah Mei's full belly, but Bing's pleased smile belied her words.

Ah Mei scoffed, reaching for Bing's hand. "Of course I had to see you off—my best friend is going to America! Everything will be wonderful for you there, just like in the movies." When they were younger, the two had occasionally escaped from their chores to see a show at one of Shanghai's many cinemas. Since the films had no subtitles, ushers had handed out detailed programs in Chinese while the girls had fun trying to pick up some new English words from the dialogue.

"What about you?" Bing asked. "You can't stay with the Communists."

"The Reds will surely ignore us since my husband is a Jew. We'll be leaving soon enough," she replied. "After the baby comes, we'll join the airlift to Palestine with the other Jews still here. We're going to make our home in that new country. Israel."

Their goodbyes hastily concluded, Bing and her sister's family climbed the steep gangway onto the *General Gordon,* a World War II troop transport. After the war ended, in 1945, the American President Lines chartered it for use as a passenger ship, in 1946. Though its look was still functional and military gray, the ship seemed to welcome Bing, another wartime survivor. Soon she took a spot along the deck railing to watch the Huangpu River's churning brown water, the color of milk tea, laced with the city's dark sludge.

Around her, other passengers were ebullient, glad to be on the foreign vessel, no longer on Shanghai's ground. "Goodbye and good riddance, Shanghai!" some shouted, impatient for the ship to sail away. Others were more subdued, waving mournfully to the dear ones they were leaving behind. Bing shook her head, refusing to let the regrets of others stir her own buried memories of Shanghai. She was grateful to be safely aboard, standing at the rail, just as she'd envisioned. She wanted to relish this moment, to savor her departure from her difficult past and her passage to a more hopeful future. As the granite façades of the Bund slipped from view, Bing waved farewell with all her might—to Ah Mei, to hard times, to the parents she would never find now. To everyone and to no one.

WITH A MAXIMUM LOAD of freight and a record number of passengers, the *General Gordon* sat low in the water. Columns of black smoke belched as the ship heaved down the Huangpu River toward its confluence with the great Yangtze, China's longest river, and then onward to the sea. Modern warfare had turned that fifty-mile stretch into a harrowing passage. During the war against Japan, the Chinese Nationalist army had sunk "volunteered" commercial ships in the river to blockade the enemy. When the Japanese took over China's coast during their eight-year wartime occupation, they had mined the channel. As the end of World War II approached in 1945, American air squadrons dropped hundreds of mines into the river to hinder Japan; then the Nationalists followed suit to stop the Communists. By the time Bing was scheduled to depart, the Red Army had fought its way to the north shore of the Yangtze. Once the ship entered the Yangtze, it would have to run a gauntlet of live mines and Communist shore batteries before it reached the open sea. Their safe passage was far from assured.

In case their vessel came under fire, all passengers were ordered to their cabins and away from portholes. The order was unnecessary—

everyone was all too aware of the unlucky ships that hadn't made it. Only five months earlier, in December 1948, the overloaded passenger ship *Jiangya* had exploded soon after it left Shanghai, packed with escapees bound for Taiwan. Among them had been some of Shanghai's most notable rich and famous. Every newspaper and newsreel in China had carried the shocking story: "Between two and three thousand Chinese evacuees fleeing from Shanghai were believed to have lost their lives when the overcrowded SS *Jiangya* sank outside Woosung on Friday." Journalists rank it as one of the greatest shipping disasters in world history, with fatalities far in excess of the *Titanic*'s.

Within a few weeks after the *Jiangya* sank, in January 1949, over one thousand people drowned in another maritime disaster when the *Taiping* collided with the cargo ship *Jian Yuan*. The *Taiping* was said to have been dangerously heavy with the silver reserves of the Central Bank of China—headed for Nationalist coffers in Taiwan.

Then, fourteen days before Bing's ship had been scheduled to depart, another disaster: Communist gunners attacked the British HMS *Amethyst* on April 20 as it chugged toward Nanjing to protect British subjects there. In a devastating blow to the British Empire, twenty-two of its crew were killed and thirty-one injured.

Determined to keep his old troopship from ending up like the *Amethyst*, its damaged hull and remaining crew still stuck in the river, trapped by the People's Liberation Army, the *General Gordon*'s captain gunned his engines. Along the route, distant artillery boomed, and the acrid smell of gunpowder wafted from charred battlefields where the Communist and Nationalist armies had clashed.

Bing lay on a hammock in the third-class hold, which was crowded with other women on double- and triple-decker sleeping berths supported by metal poles. She had boarded the ship too late to grab one of the stationary berths. All that remained were these hammocks that bounced and swayed with the ship's motion. Bing clutched at her stomach but found no sympathy from other passengers, all preoccupied with their own woes. As the *Gordon* threaded its way through the precarious channel, the women around her fell into a nervous quiet. Bing could hear the murmur of their prayers above the drone of the engines. She closed her eyes and tried to banish all thoughts of the unlucky ones on the sunken vessels.

In the days that followed, no other big ships dared to trail the *General Gordon*'s wake past the Communist positions between Shanghai and the sea, with some ships changing course completely to avoid Shanghai and the expected Communist onslaught. The American President Lines and other companies canceled their future Shanghai sailings in spite of sold-out bookings. Even rescue ships kept their distance from Shanghai's waterways. Elder Sister congratulated herself for not buying tickets for the Royal Dutch ocean liner *Tjibadak*, the British *Tairea*, or the HMS *Constance*—they were all still moored in the East China Sea near the Yangtze's mouth, waiting to learn if it would be safe for them to approach the port city.

Countless thousands were still trying to get out of Shanghai. They soon found that alternatives to a sea escape were no less daunting. Communist gunners narrowly missed taking down three chartered planes hired to airlift Shanghai's Portuguese residents to Macao. For weeks, China's airlines had abandoned their normal schedules and were operating continuous flights out of Shanghai. As soon as a plane arrived, it was boarded in a rush, crammed beyond full with people and cargo, to be dispatched immediately in a race against time. Big foreign carriers like Pan Am and Northwest had added flights, but as the Red Army drew closer to the city, they terminated their Shanghai service. Only Alaska Airlines soldiered on when its president, James Wooten, ordered more DC-4s to help evacuees. Railways, too, had become increasingly perilous—yet train fares continued rising into the stratosphere as the trifecta of runaway inflation, the collapse of the Nationalist currency, and the unquenchable demand sent all ticket prices soaring higher by the hour.

When the *General Gordon* finally made it past the mouth of the great river at Wusongkou, the captain announced, "All clear." Everyone broke into cheers of relief. Bing rushed onto the deck, thankful to have reached the open sea.

———

THE PEOPLE OF SHANGHAI in particular feared the Communists' wrath. The very nature of their metropolis was forged from China's century of humiliation imposed by the opium-peddling British, Americans, and other foreigners. Shanghai was a bastard city: too Western to be Chinese and too Chinese to be Western. The Bund, Shanghai's fabled waterfront, looked more like a postcard from Europe than from China. Shanghai's capitalist traditions and privileged urbanites encouraged a sensibility that welcomed modernity to this city "on the sea"—the literal meaning of the words *shang hai*.

To the Communists, *modern* was synonymous with *Western*, while *Western* was interchangeable with *foreign*. Westernized Shanghainese were nothing but *yang nu* and *zou gou*—foreign slaves and imperialist running dogs. Shanghai's wealthy and middle classes, intellectuals and Nationalist partisans were certain to become targets in the coming Communist revolution.

Yet for most, the decision to flee from home, country, and all that is familiar was heart-wrenching. The Chinese people had emerged from eight years of brutal Japanese aggression, terror, and occupation during World War II. For China, that war had begun in 1937, making it twice the length that China's allies in Europe had faced, and the country had fought with limited foreign support. When the war ended in 1945, the long-simmering civil war between the American-supported Nationalists and the Soviet-allied Communists reignited even before the ink had dried on the Japanese surrender documents. With this fratricidal blood feud raging on, the ruling Nationalists, led by Generalissimo Chiang Kai-shek since 1926, were unable to stabilize the economy, fueling a death spiral of speculation, hoarding, and hyperinflation.

By late 1947, the United States had lost confidence in Chiang and begun withdrawing troops and material support. Some farsighted capitalists began to leave Shanghai that same year, for they had the money, means, and connections to set up a life elsewhere—just in case. Then, in the autumn of 1948, the Communists crushed the Nationalists in three major battles. The outcome of the civil war was no longer in doubt as the Red Army pressed forward to capture the prize: Shanghai.

At the dawn of 1949, even Shanghai's middle classes began to flee. The trickle of exodus grew into a torrent, propelled by rumors and Nationalist propaganda that the Communists would confiscate property, collectivize land and businesses, even break up families and steal wives. Nationalist officials warned of mass arrests and mass killings, further inflaming the panic.

Any remaining faith in the old regime crumbled as the delirium of fear descended upon Shanghai's former foreign concessions, where the better-off Chinese resided. Nearly every family there was embroiled in the same fierce debate. In Bing's household, too, they asked themselves the same questions each day: Should they stay or leave? And if they left, where would they go? Communist rule couldn't possibly be worse than the Japanese occupation had been, many argued. Why should they leave? And yet, how could they stay?

Running away seemed unthinkable when everything they knew and valued was right there in Shanghai. In the calculus of possible escape, fleeing would mean splitting up families, with separation from children, elders, and other loved ones who were unable or unwilling to make the leap into the void. Running away also involved great risk: Besides the deadly toll from air and sea collisions, newspapers were filled with stories of Shanghainese who had fled to Hong Kong with their life savings, then, after losing everything to the inflated prices there, were forced to return to Shanghai as paupers. Or they were stuck in Hong Kong as impoverished refugees, reduced to menial work, begging, even prostitution.

Yet with each passing day in early 1949, newspapers headlined the departures of the well known and well-to-do. Numerous political officials suddenly decided they needed medical treatment abroad. The city's middle and wealthy classes could no longer deny the inevitable: The impending Communist revolution would invert the social pyramid that had provided their status and privilege. Some of Shanghai's wealthy industrialists managed to transfer money, machinery, and key personnel to Hong Kong, which they had always disdained as a sleepy fishing village when compared to their vibrant city. But Hong Kong was still better than Taiwan—in their view, a place fit only for country bumpkins. The burgeoning exodus included Shanghai's many foreign residents, forced to give up their pampered expatriate lifestyles before the Communists began ridding China of the "bloodsucking imperialists."

By the time the Red Army surrounded Shanghai, waves of people had bolted: the city's upper classes, the educated and resourceful, residents who had bet on the old guard—anyone who had anything to fear. Like the White Russians who had vanished from Bolshevik Moscow, the German Jews who had escaped Hitler's Berlin, Vietnamese waiting for helicopters on the roof of the U.S. embassy in Saigon, or Syrians dodging bombs and bullets to brave the Mediterranean Sea, they fled: By boats so heavily laden they could not avoid collisions at sea; by planes so overweight they could not clear obstacles ahead; by trains with so many people clinging to every surface, the cars could only creep forward. Many had to flee in a frenzied rush, taking only what they could carry. Exile from their beloved city would be tolerable only because they expected to be gone no more than six months or a year at most. That was the longest they figured the Communist peasants would last, never imagining that more than thirty years would pass before they could return and reunite with loved ones.

EVEN WITHOUT DEFINITIVE RECORDS on the numbers of those who fled Shanghai, the magnitude of the exodus can be estimated from the counts of refugees that swelled in other regions. Hong Kong's population doubled in 1949, increasing by more than a million refugees in that single year. In Taiwan, approximately 1.3 million to 2 million "mainlanders" descended on the small, largely rural island: Incoming Chinese Nationalist officials, retreating soldiers, loyalists, and their families thrust themselves onto the existing society of 9 million Taiwanese, taking total control of the island. Many thousands of other Chinese dispersed to Southeast Asia—Indonesia, the Philippines, Malaysia, Singapore, Burma, Vietnam—and as far as South America, Africa, and India. Only a trickle could enter the United States or Britain, with their long histories of restrictions against Asian immigrants, and even fewer went to Australia because of its virulent "whites only" policy.

The exodus out of Shanghai, like other human stampedes from danger, scattered its desperate migrants to any corner of the world where they might weather the storm. Seven decades later, stories of courage, strength, and resilience have emerged from the Shanghai exodus, offering a glimmer of insight, even hope, to newer waves of refugees who are struggling to stay afloat in the riptides of history.

IN THE PREDAWN HOURS of May 25, 1949, three weeks after the *General Gordon* pulled away from its Shanghai pier, the People's Liberation Army marched victorious into Shanghai. Thousands of battle-weary soldiers, many just country boys with cloth shoes on their feet, moved swiftly and quietly along the city's main avenues and the Bund to seize control of the Pearl of the Orient.

Shanghai had fallen. Shanghai had been liberated.

The *General Gordon* was still en route, cut off from any news of home.

When its 1,946 passengers finally learned the fate of their city after docking in San Francisco on May 28, they realized that they had escaped by a razor's edge on the last boat out of Shanghai.

All communications halted between China and the United States. It wasn't possible to wire family members in Shanghai the news of their safe arrival. Any relief for themselves was dwarfed by concern about the tsunami of revolution back home.

To survive, this untethered diaspora of Shanghai migrants would have to face the unknown and forget the lives they once knew in their city on the sea. That world had ceased to exist.

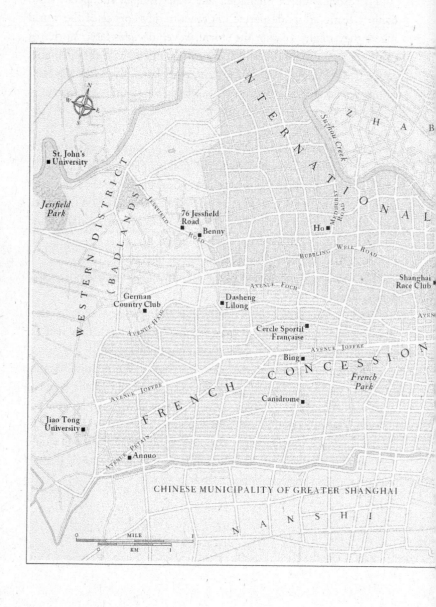

St. John's
University

Jessfield
Park

Su-chou Creek

INTERNATIONAL

ZHAB

WESTERN DISTRICT (BADLANDS)

Jessfield Road

76 Jessfield
Road
Benny

Ho

MEDHURST ROAD

BUBBLING WELL ROAD

AVENUE FOCH

German
Country Club

Dasheng
Lilong

Cercle Sportif
Française

AVENUE HAIG

AVENUE JOFFRE

Bing

Shanghai
Race Club

AVEN

FRENCH CONCESSION

French
Park

Canidrome

AVENUE JOFFRE

Jiao Tong
University

AVENUE PÉTAIN Annuo

CHINESE MUNICIPALITY OF GREATER SHANGHAI

N A N S H I

MILE
0   1

KM
0   1

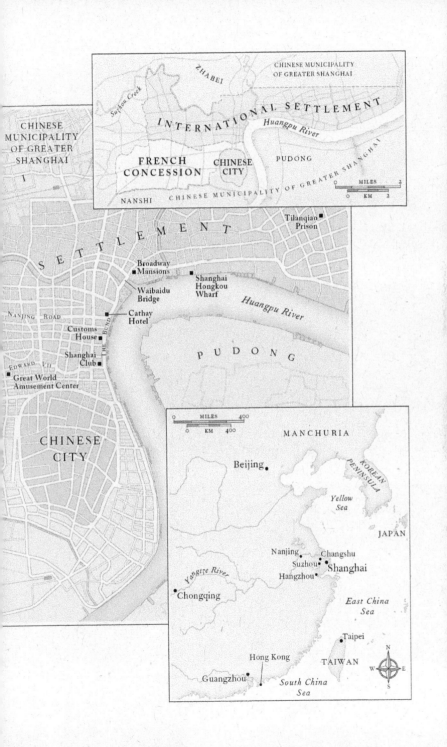

CHINESE MUNICIPALITY
OF GREATER SHANGHAI

ZHABEI

Suzhou Creek

INTERNATIONAL SETTLEMENT

Huangpu River

FRENCH CONCESSION

CHINESE CITY

PUDONG

NANSHI

CHINESE MUNICIPALITY OF GREATER SHANGHAI

MILES 2

KM 2

CHINESE
MUNICIPALITY
OF GREATER
SHANGHAI

SETTLEMENT

Tilanqiao
Prison

Broadway
Mansions

Shanghai
Hongkou
Wharf

Waibaidu
Bridge

NANJING ROAD

Cathay
Hotel

Huangpu River

Customs
House

THE BUND

PUDONG

Shanghai
Club

EDWARD VII

Great World
Amusement Center

CHINESE
CITY

MILES 400

KM 400

MANCHURIA

Beijing

KOREAN PENINSULA

Yellow
Sea

JAPAN

Nanjing

Changshu

Suzhou

Shanghai

Yangtze River

Hangzhou

Chongqing

East China
Sea

Taipei

Hong Kong

TAIWAN

Guangzhou

South China
Sea

N
W E
S

PART
ONE

THE
DRUMBEAT
OF WAR

CHAPTER
I

BENNY

Age 9

RACING NORTH ON THE TREELINED FRENCH CONCESSION SIDE of Avenue Haig, a nimble boy weaved his way around the sidewalk's throngs, dodging ahead of basket-laden shoppers and old men out for an afternoon stroll. He barely glanced at the hawkers with their motley goods spread out on the pavement or the threadbare beggars cross-legged on the hard ground, their bony hands extended to passersby for some pity and a coin.

With his unruly black hair, his knee socks bunched at the ankles, and the tail of his white shirt climbing out of his short pants, there was still no mistaking this child for a street urchin making off with something pilfered. Benny Pan was lithe and strong, his skin fair and his cheeks ruddy with a healthy glow. More telling was his open, confident manner, his eyes wide without a trace of guile. He could have been any child of the city's sizable middle class of professionals and service workers who tended to the giant metropolis. He might have even been a scion of Shanghai's bourgeoisie, the newly rich Chinese capitalists who had taken over the sectors of industry and commerce not already controlled by the foreigners. Or, most exclusive of all, his family could have been compradors, the Chinese who served as trusted go-betweens for the rich and powerful foreign taipans, the European and American empire builders whose vast wealth derived from the opium trade. In return for being their agents, the compradors were richly rewarded with the money and access to power that were held only by the foreigners in treaty port cities like Shanghai, concessions established after China failed in its effort to halt the opium traffic.

For this privileged child of Shanghai, the broad expanse of Avenue Haig was a playground. Its wide, curving lanes formed the western border of the French Concession, where he lived. He could ride his bike northward on the avenue into the British-run International Settlement to the elite American missionary institutions: McTyeire School, St. John's University, and St. Mary's Hall; his parents had attended the latter two and expected him to study at St. John's one day. A mile farther south was St. Ignatius Cathedral and its towering spires.

Benny had explored all points of interest on the east side of Avenue Haig. He was forbidden, however, to cross to the west side of that border street, an area of contested jurisdiction. Shanghai's foreign settlements stood as virtual islands inside China's sovereign territory, allowed to rule themselves with foreign laws—an arrangement forced upon China by the British and Americans after their "gunboat diplomacy" defeated the Qing dynasty emperor in the Opium Wars of the mid-1800s. Though the boundaries of the foreign-ruled enclaves were clearly delimited by treaty, over the years the British had continued to push out roads, country estates, luxurious villas, schools, country clubs, hunting grounds, and a racetrack beyond the border and into the "extra-boundary" or "extra-settlement" areas, all against China's objections. In this zone of ambiguous jurisdiction, gambling houses, opium dens, brothels, and gangsters also flourished, just out of reach of British or French police. The area was so lawless and dangerous that it was known to locals as the Badlands. Benny's father forbade the boy to cross Avenue Haig into the crime-ridden Badlands.

On rare occasions, Benny accompanied his father, an accountant and officer in the police auxiliary, into those nether reaches. At such times Benny saw for himself the stark conditions of the Chinese sections: dilapidated shacks and squalid tenements reeking of raw sewage and general decay, overcrowded with people in tattered clothing who navigated the unpaved lanes in rope sandals or bare feet. These were the city's laboring people, who toiled in the factories and carried the backbreaking loads, pulling the rickshaws, carts, and pedicabs. But at least they had roofs over their heads, his father would note, unlike the homeless beggars and refugees forced to sleep in any vacant patch they could find. Boys like Benny could be kidnapped for ransom—or worse—in those dangerous areas, his parents sternly cautioned.

They needn't have worried, for Benny was not the sort to defy his parents' wishes. He found plenty to keep himself occupied in his neighborhood on the east side of Avenue Haig, where the extremes of Shanghai society collided in curious ways. With two hospitals nearby, afflicted and frightening-looking unfortunates lingered on the sidewalks each day, hoping to be treated before they expired. None of that was shocking to Benny. After all, his amah had taught him from the moment he could walk, "If you see a dead body on the street, just go the other way." That was a simple rule of self-preservation in this unforgiving metropolis where abject misery coexisted with unabashed opulence.

On this day, Benny noticed something different in the usual assemblage of deformity and disease lined up at one of the hospitals. Several people had fresh wounds to their heads and faces or bloodied rags wrapped around twisted or missing limbs. Startled, he realized they might be casualties from the battle with Japan that had begun the day before on the north side of the city in Zhabei, a Chinese section. At any other time, his curiosity might have slowed him for a better look. But he was in too much of a rush to get home: He had to tell his mother what he had just seen in the sky.

As Benny approached a busy intersection, a tall, bearded police officer standing in a kiosk above the street raised his baton, forcing the boy and the traffic to an abrupt halt. "Phooey," he declared in the American accent that he had learned at school. The swarthy, bearded cop wore a standard-issue khaki police uniform—topped by a telltale red turban. He was a Sikh, one of a few hundred warriors that the British brought from their India colony to be cops in Shanghai. *Hong du ah sei*—red-hatted monkey—was the disparaging name that local Shanghainese gave these fierce Sikhs.

Near Benny, some pedicab drivers and their well-dressed foreign passengers pulled to a stop. The sick and infirm nearest the foreigners thrust their hands out for alms. One was a boy about his own age with no legs, only stumps, while an old woman had just one eye. Benny knew instantly that the foreigners must be longtimers in Shanghai since no one flinched or displayed even the slightest dismay at the appalling humanity beside them.

When the red-hatted traffic cop finally waved them on, Benny spied a fox pelt on the shoulders of one of the yellow-haired women. Its glass-eyed head bounced with each lurch of the pedicab before disappearing through the gates of the German country club off Avenue Haig. As the little fox head bobbled out of sight, Benny's eye caught something else: a red band adorned with a black swastika on the arm of a pale-faced foreigner in one of the pedicabs. He recognized the symbol from the flags that were cropping up with greater frequency on the German buildings in his neighborhood. To the boy, it was just another foreign curiosity in his international city.

Soon he reached the gate leading to his neighborhood, the Dasheng *lilong*, a Shanghai-style enclosed residential complex that was popular with both foreigners and well-to-do Chinese. Just outside the gate, the proprietor of his favorite bookstall called out to him: "Benny, come have a look!" The boy raised an arm in greeting without pausing for his customary scan of the latest magazines and comic books. Turning, he nearly slammed into an old man whose heavy baskets of neatly stacked bitter melons dangled from the pole that he balanced on one shoulder.

"Damn you, little devil," he snarled.

By then Benny had already mumbled, "Excuse me" as he passed by the heavy iron gate and dozing watchman into the narrow lanes of his *lilong*. He stopped only after reaching the thick green door of a three-story building attached to its neighbors on each side.

Once inside the mosaic-tiled vestibule, he shouted: "Mother! Amah! The Japanese are coming!"

"Young Master, be quiet or you'll wake Little Brother and Little Sister!" his amah scolded.

A slender woman appeared from behind a polished wood-paneled door. Her movement was so graceful that the air seemed undisturbed by her approach. As usual, she looked impeccable in a stylish *qipao* dress, with her hair knotted in a neat chignon. "Long-Long, what are you so excited about?" she asked with a puzzled look. She addressed the boy by his nickname, Little Dragon, chosen because he was born in 1928, during the Year of the Dragon, the most powerful creature of the Chinese zodiac.

"I saw them, Mother. I saw the planes! The Japanese planes are flying to the Waitan!" he shouted, referring to the famous Bund by its Chinese name.

His mother gently brushed the hair from his face with her fingers. Before she could reply, an unmistakable boom shook the quiet of the house. "See, Mother? Let's go look from the roof!" He was already dashing up the three flights of stairs, his mother not far behind. As they climbed, they could hear another loud boom in the distance. On the roof, they ducked under the drying laundry to reach the open patio where fragrant gardenias and peonies bloomed in large pots. Toward the east, plumes of black smoke rose above the cityscape near the tall Broadway Mansions, a clear landmark.

"The Japanese must be bombing Zhabei, just like on 1-2-8!" he ventured, using the colloquial shorthand for the date January 28, 1932, which was seared into the minds of schoolchildren and grown-ups alike because of the infamous Japanese attack on Shanghai that day, just five years earlier.

Throughout the country, Chinese were seething with outrage at Japan's most recent aggressions. Their island neighbor had launched numerous "incidents"—as Tokyo euphemistically called their incursions on Chinese soil—each bolder than the last. In 1931 Japan had invaded Manchuria, with its rich coal and mineral reserves, in China's northeast, locking in its control after installing a puppet government with Puyi, the deposed last emperor of China, to be the region's figurehead ruler. Such puppets would become Japan's model for occupation in China.

The Chinese Nationalist government had protested these incidents at the League of Nations to no avail. Just one month earlier, on July 7, 1937, Japan had staged another aggression—this time in Beijing at Lukouqiao, known to Westerners as the Marco Polo Bridge. Frustrated Chinese leaders had been calling on Generalissimo Chiang Kai-shek to respond decisively to Japan in a united front that included the Communists. But instead of confronting Japan, he seemed focused on eliminating the Reds. Only the year before, in 1936, one of Chiang's own generals had precipitated a national crisis by kidnapping him, to force the generalissimo to stand up to Japan. Finally, after this latest provocation in Beijing, Chiang's army was fighting back—with Shanghai as the battleground.

JUST BEYOND THE GATES of his *lilong*, Benny could hear newspaper hawkers barking out the latest headlines each day. Usually, he paid them no mind, letting their voices blend into the din. But in recent weeks, more than three hundred thousand Nationalist soldiers had been mobilized to the countryside surrounding Shanghai. Young boys like Benny who lived in the protected foreign enclaves with little fear of attack were thrilled at the prospect of soldiers, weaponry, and the coming showdown.

This new battle for Shanghai had been launched only the day before, on Friday, August 13, 1937. The sound of distant artillery reverberated through the city. Could it be that Japan was mounting an air attack on Shanghai? That would explain the low-flying aircraft.

Five years earlier, many residents in the foreign concessions had watched from their rooftops as that previous battle with Japan had raged in the nearby Chinese sections. Mesmerized, they had oohed and aahed at the glowing cannon fire and ensuing infernos as though they were spectators at the races. This time would be no different—or so everyone thought. After all, the French consul still ruled the French Concession, and the British and Americans governed the International Settlement through the Shanghai Municipal Council. In addition to the British, Americans, and French, there were tens of thousands of foreigners from nearly every European country living in these two jurisdictions, as well as thousands of Japanese civilians. No one imagined that the Tokyo government would want to fight Britain or America or that it would risk killing off its own nationals living in Shanghai. That's why Chinese from surrounding areas habitually ran to the foreign concessions in troubled times and why families like Benny's who could afford to live anywhere chose to live among Shanghai's many foreigners.

Bombers over Shanghai's commercial skyline near the Bund after "Bloody Saturday," August 14, 1937, at the start of the Pacific War.

From their rooftop, Benny's mother gazed out toward the billowing smoke and nearby landmarks. Her face turned pale. "Oh no, Long-Long! Those fires aren't in Zhabei. They're inside the International Settlement!"

Around them, other rooftop patios were filling with people, all straining for a glimpse. Someone shouted, "The Waitan has been bombed. Smoke is rising from the Cathay Hotel!" The pyramid-shaped copper roof of the ten-story hotel was the showpiece of Victor Sassoon, one of Shanghai's most prominent Jewish businessmen. A stunned murmur of disbelief arose from the observers—the presumed shield over the foreign concessions had been shattered.

As they watched intently, another small plane appeared. A man with binoculars on a nearby building suddenly shouted, "Those planes have *Chinese* insignia on their sides—the blue, red, and white of the

Republic of China! They're *our* planes, not Japan's!" The onlookers gasped as more bombs fell, their thunderous blasts reverberating in the air.

Just then the plane veered west toward Avenue Haig, and Long-Long's mother pulled him from the roof. "Hurry. It's not safe up here," she said, dragging the boy inside as he wriggled for a better view.

Back downstairs, Benny ran from window to window to see if any soldiers were coming down the streets. With his mother and amah busy gathering up his sisters and brother, he slipped out the door. Beyond the quiet lanes of Dasheng *lilong*, fire trucks and police cars sped by, sirens wailing. People buzzed about, seeking news and sharing rumors. Some said that thousands of people had been killed near the British racecourse, in the heart of the International Settlement.

Suddenly a hand clamped on to his arm. Benny jumped. It was his amah. "Young Master, you must come home now. Your mother is talking on the telephone with your father. He will be very angry if a bomb kills you!" Amah had been with the family for so long that she had been his mother's amah too. On another day, Benny might have dared her to catch him, but he sensed that this was not the time. Back inside their home, he could hear his mother talking on the phone in his father's study.

"What? In the International Settlement on Tibet Road? Thousands of people killed near the Great World?" She paused, then asked, "How is Grandfather?"

Benny straightened as his mother spoke of his beloved grandfather, whose large mansion was on Tibet Road, not far from the Great World Entertainment Center. His grandfather sometimes took him there to wander through its funhouse mirrors, roller-skating rink, and multiple stories of curiosities and attractions. His mother disapproved, wary of the drunken sailors, beckoning women, and other unsavory characters who lingered there.

If anyone would know the details about the bombings, it would be Benny's father, Pan Zhijie. On most evenings and weekends, Benny's father was on duty with the Shanghai Volunteer Corps, the uniformed auxiliary to the small, British-run Shanghai Municipal Police. Pan

Zhijie was a high-ranking officer in the Volunteers, which was established to defend against Chinese rebellions. The troopers were organized into militia companies by their nationality and nearly every group of foreigners had their own volunteer corps. But the Chinese were long forbidden to organize an armed militia in case they might start a bloody insurrection as the Boxers and Taipings had done decades earlier. In more recent years, though, the Chinese residents of the foreign concessions had forced the British to allow them to organize a Chinese "C" Company. Benny's father was a stalwart in this Chinese corps.

Standing outside his father's study as his mother spoke into the phone, Benny gleaned that his grandfather had been in his home when the bombs fell—just two blocks from his house. Had the bombs fallen a few minutes later, Grandfather would have been walking to his favorite social club, right across from the worst carnage, where a few thousand people now lay maimed or killed. Grandfather was shaken and had suffered some minor bruises from falling debris but was otherwise unharmed. Benny's father was on his way to the bomb site to assist with relief efforts.

When his mother got off the phone, she shared what she had heard with Amah, who had been minding the babies: The planes they had seen were part of China's fledgling air force. The Chinese pilots had intended to surprise the Japanese fleet moored in the Huangpu River along the Bund by bombing the *Idzumo*, the flagship of the Imperial Japanese Navy. Somehow the Chinese pilots had miscalculated terribly, missing the ships and instead dropping their bombs on the International Settlement. "How unthinkable!" his mother exclaimed. The streets had been mobbed with thousands of refugees from the previous day's battle, all seeking safety in the foreign concessions. The first two bombs blew up by Nanjing Road, between the Palace and Cathay Hotels on the Bund, where crowds of refugees had congregated and wealthy foreign shoppers scurried by. One hit the top floors of the Cathay Hotel. Another two bombs exploded over Avenue Edward VII and Tibet Road, just as a few thousand refugees were queuing up for food dispensed by a local charity. Nearly all those civilians must have perished.

Mother's voice grew more indignant as she told them what she'd learned. Not even the Japanese had dared to harm Shanghai's protected foreign concessions. And now this—from their own Chinese pilots! Mother and Amah shook their heads, sputtering their dismay and disbelief. "How can such an army overcome the Japanese?" they repeated. The Pans' superstitious cook banged the pots in disgust as she readied the evening meal, all the while clucking, "Bad omen for Chinese people. Very bad."

AFTER IT BECAME CLEAR that the bombing sortie was over, Benny quietly made his way back up to the roof. Looking over the tops of buildings in the French Concession toward the Bund, he traced the tall smoke trails down to the Great World in the vicinity of Grandfather's mansion. That was Benny's first home, where his father and mother had lived after they were married. That was where he was born and had learned to walk and talk, where he would sit on Grandfather's lap and peer out the upstairs windows to watch crowds gather for the horse races at the British-run Shanghai Race Club. He still spent his summers there. Benny wanted to rush to his grandfather's side after the news of his close call, but his mother said that it was too dangerous; they would have to wait until the wreckage was cleared.

Benny knew he was his grandfather's favorite—and with good reason. After all, he was the first male born of his generation: the first great-grandson, first grandson, and Number One Son. It was an exalted position in any extended Chinese family. Benny's formal Chinese name, Yongyi Pan, meant longevity and good fortune. It would be recorded in the Pan family's book of names, where all Pan males for more than a hundred generations were listed. His sisters wouldn't be named in the book—no females were. Benny's formal name would dominate his entire generation, because every Pan boy born after him would have to use the *"yong"* character from *his* name in *their* names. His privileged position also came with great responsibility: The Number One Son was expected to care for his ancestors and elders and to maintain the family's traditions and honor.

Just beyond the columns of smoke from the Cathay Hotel was the old Cantonese section of the city, north of the Bund in Hongkou. The original Pan family compound had been built there by Benny's great-grandfather, off Haining Road, after he grew wealthy in Shanghai's boom times in the late 1800s. Hongkou sat on the northern banks of the Suzhou Creek and Huangpu River, and many Cantonese such as his great-grandfather had settled there.

From his earliest memory, Benny had always greeted the first day of the Lunar New Year with a visit to that Pan family compound to pay his respects to his ancestors. His great-grandfather had passed away long before he was born, but Great-Grandmother was still living. She had been in her nineties when Benny was born and reigned as the Pan family matriarch. It was Great-Grandmother who had given him his dragon nickname, Long-Long. But he was hardly brave in her presence. As a toddler, he had been required to approach his wizened great-grandmother to show his respect. Dressed in ceremonial silk robes, young Benny had refused to move toward her until his father gave him a stern push. Upon reaching her throne-like chair, he had to prostrate himself on the cool parquet floor, just as his father and other elder males had, bowing three times at the small embroidered silk slippers covering her tiny bound feet. When Great-Grandmother beckoned him to come closer, he stared at her fingernails—so long that they curled into spiral claws. She'd look him over carefully and pat his head, nails dangerously near his face. When she dismissed him, after handing over a lucky red envelope containing a New Year's gift of money, Benny would run back to his father in relief.

Benny had no such fears of his adoring grandfather. They loved to stroll through Grandfather's garden together, the boy's little hands clasped behind his back just like the old man's. His grandfather would point out his favorite lotus blossoms and new buds on the magnolia trees. He taught Long-Long to recite classic Tang dynasty poems. They rode together in his old but pristine Packard with a white-gloved chauffeur behind the wheel. Sometimes they stopped at the Public Garden across from the British consulate, in the triangle bordered by the narrow and meandering Suzhou Creek and the Huangpu River. Grandfather would tell Benny about the infamous sign that was long gone but had become a legend that every Chinese knew and could not forget: "No Dogs or Chinese Allowed." Some foreigners claimed that there had never been such a sign, but they couldn't deny that Chinese had been barred from that park and many other places. It wasn't until 1929, the year after Benny was born, that the Nationalist government had succeeded in forcing the British and French to allow Chinese in the parks.

Sitting on a once-forbidden bench, Benny and his grandfather studied the junks, barges, and sampans weaving between the huge oceangoing ships. With a certain fondness, Grandfather would regularly point out the docks and godowns—warehouses—of Jardine Matheson, the generous employer of three generations of Pans—Great-Grandfather, Grandfather, and Big Uncle, Benny's father's elder brother. They often ended their excursions at the immaculate grounds of Le Cercle Sportif Français, the elegant French country club, where Grandfather would sip a cup of tea while Benny devoured a dish of Hazelwood ice cream.

When Grandfather grew tired, they'd return to the big house on Tibet Road to rest. Benny spent many contented hours lying next to his grandfather on the hard divan in his cool, darkened smoking room. The old man would suck on his opium pipe and regale his eldest grandson with family lore. By the time Benny was old enough to attend school, he'd heard the tale of his great-grandfather Pan's arrival in Shanghai so many times that he could recite his grandfather's rendition of the story by heart:

Nearly one hundred years ago, the rulers of China's great civilization were weak and corrupt. The long-nosed foreign devils came in with their gunboats and forced the emperor to allow them to conduct trade in Shanghai and other cities that had previously been closed to the foreigners. Enterprising young men from all over China came to find work in these port cities. The hardest working of all came from faraway Guangdong Province in the south, where drought and famine drove them out in search of a livelihood. My father, your great-grandfather, was one of those young Cantonese. He stowed away on a cargo ship headed to Shanghai with no more than a cloth bag and the thin rags on his back. An umbrella protected him against ruffians more than rain. It was a terrible journey of twelve hundred miles. Lesser men didn't survive, but your great-grandfather Pan was strong and smart. Cantonese like him already knew the ways of the pale-faced Anglos and could even speak some English. In Shanghai, Great-Grandfather sought out the number one English trading company: Jardine Matheson. He was hired to work as a coolie, doing backbreaking labor on their docks. But his clever mind never rested. He learned more skills and improved his English. Gradually, he rose to become one of the few Chinese that Jardine Matheson entrusted with the title of comprador— the highest position a Chinese could reach under the foreign taipans. It fell on the compradors to negotiate with Chinese government officials and manage the Chinese workers. The Chinese compradors were paid well, though they were always considered beneath the foreigners. Nevertheless, thanks to your great-grandfather Pan's intelligence, courage, and industry, the Pan family has prospered in Shanghai.

His grandfather would end his reminiscences by saying, "You must never forget our family's humble beginnings. When you drink the water, you must remember the spring."

Even after Benny's parents moved out of his grandfather's home, the boy often stayed there overnight. His visits were happy, magical times, spent in the sweet-perfumed haze of the opium pipe, enriched by Grandfather's tales. Sometimes Grandfather quizzed him on the lessons of those stories. Benny liked to please him by recounting his lessons smartly: honor his ancestors; bring respect to the Pan family name; strive to improve himself. Most of all, remember the sacrifices of Great-Grandfather, the stowaway who brought good luck and prosperity to subsequent generations of Pans.

Young Benny didn't always understand his grandfather's languid ruminations. Sometimes after a few opium pipes, Grandfather murmured his disappointment in his second son, Benny's father. Although Pan Zhijie hadn't followed the family trajectory to become a compra-

*A confident six-year-old Benny Pan (center) poses
with sisters (left to right) Annie, Doreen, and Cecilia.*

dor, he had started out on a business track by studying accounting at
St. John's University, an American missionary school that taught
classes in English and imbued its Chinese students with the ways of
the Western elite. Benny was also expected to go there one day. But in
1925, his father's last year of college, he had veered off course by taking part in national uprisings known as the May Thirtieth Movement,
named for the date that student demonstrators were shot and killed by
the British-run police force in the International Settlement. Inflamed
with patriotic fervor, students all over China had risen up against foreigners, the "imperialists" who stole the wealth of China while crushing the Chinese people. Tensions were so high that missionaries and
other foreigners feared for their lives in a possible reprise of earlier
violent rebellions.

As student protestors at St. John's University, Benny's father and
others demanded that the Chinese flag be raised alongside the Stars
and Stripes as a show of equal respect. And it was Benny's father, the
Boy Scout vice-master in charge of raising the American flag over the

campus, who presented the demand to the university president. Benny's grandfather always winced at this recollection. When the Episcopal missionary refused the students' demands, hundreds at St. John's rebelled and boycotted classes, Pan Zhijie among them, almost shuttering the school permanently. The university survived, but Benny's father was changed. After he left St. John's, he refused to work for the foreign company where his grandfather, father, and elder brother had become compradors. Instead, he set up his own accounting practice with an office in Grandfather's big house. Benny and his elder sister, Annie, were born there.

In his opium haze, Grandfather would bridle at the choices made by his second son. "Your father never complained about the prosperity our Pan family achieved from the foreign imperialists," he'd say to Benny. "If he so disliked the foreign taipans, why does he now work with the British police? To make the police more Chinese? Or to become more like the foreigners?" Benny would wait silently for the answers that never came to his grandfather's rhetorical questions. The old man's eyelids would inevitably flicker from such weighty thoughts as he nodded off to sleep. But not before he advised his grandson: "Do not follow your father's path. Police and politics will only lead to trouble."

Benny would listen patiently to the mumbled words that were warmed by his grandfather's affection for him. He paid no mind to the opium-laced criticisms of his father, for Benny was most proud of his father's service in the Shanghai Volunteer Corps. His father had risen to a position of leadership of the all-Chinese "C" Company of the Volunteers, which, along with more than a dozen foreign companies, provided critical backup to the British police. From the time he was a small boy, Benny watched, mesmerized, as his father transformed from an accountant in a Western business suit into a Shanghai Volunteer corpsman, with shiny brass buttons on his uniform and spit-polished leather boots. His father's broad shoulders and muscular arms, developed from his years as a wushu-style martial arts champion, bulged through his uniform. Most impressive to Benny was the police-issue Colt .45 cradled in a fine-grained leather holster on his father's belt.

Each day after work and every weekend, his father left their house in his starched uniform, looking to Benny like a hero. Other boys might have fathers who were rich industrialists or compradors like his grandfather, great-grandfather, and uncle, but *his* father protected the International Settlement. On occasion, Benny accompanied him on his evening rounds. Shop owners in western suits, mobsters in long silk gowns, street vendors, and labor-gang bosses all greeted his father with respect. Even the British officers of the Shanghai Municipal Police exchanged pleasantries with his father, who could converse with the foreign bobbies in the perfect English he'd honed at St. John's.

Once, on his father's rounds, a merchant placed a fat envelope on his shop's counter. Benny saw his father pick it up and casually tuck it into his uniform jacket without looking inside. "A small appreciation in return for a favor," his father told him. "The merchant will lose face if I don't accept. It's the Shanghai way."

Benny thought nothing of it, especially when his father's colleagues patted him on the head and crooned, "Listen to your old man. If you're lucky, you'll be a big shot like him one day."

THAT NIGHT, SATURDAY, AUGUST 14, Pan Zhijie returned home much later than usual, missing dinner. Bounding down the stairs, Benny came to a sudden halt at the sight of his father: His impeccable uniform was streaked with dark bloodstains, from his khaki epaulets to his fine leather boots. His eyes were cold and hard, a look Benny hadn't known before. A servant helped him out of his stiff, reeking clothes and into a robe. As a hot bath was prepared for him, his father told Benny's mother of the horror on Avenue Edward VII near the racecourse. "The center of Shanghai is a sea of human blood, overflowing the gutters."

Benny's father had spent hours sifting through the rubble for survivors. The rumors that thousands of people had been killed or injured near the racetrack were all too true. The first bomb had blown open a huge crater, followed by another that had exploded in the air just above ground level. Limbs, heads, and other body parts had flown in all directions. The chauffeur-driven cars of foreigners had exploded, incinerating their passengers. On Nanjing Road by the Bund, in an intersection packed with wealthy hotel guests as well as refugees from the fighting, the blast was so strong that the body of a boy no older than Benny was flattened high against the building's side, a ghastly sight.

To Benny's ear, his father's voice seemed flat, without emotion, as he recounted the details of the bombings. Two of the inexperienced Chinese pilots, just out of American Claire Chennault's Central Aviation School, had been hit by Japanese antiaircraft fire and tried to drop their payloads on the racetrack, while the other fliers attempted to bomb the *Idzumo*. They had all failed, with terrible results. The clock at the Cathay Hotel had stopped at 4:27 P.M., the time the first bombs struck.

"The war has begun," Benny's father said. "If this is the best our Chinese forces can do, we are surely lost."

His mother conveyed what she had heard from her friends. "Some people say that Chiang Kai-shek and the Nationalist government are planning to leave Nanjing, Shanghai, and the coastal provinces for the interior of China. Should we think about moving inland too?" she asked.

"Japan's fight is with China, not Europe or America," his father replied. "Better to take our chances here and stay in the concessions with the foreigners."

"What if your company in the Shanghai Volunteer Corps is ordered to fight against the Japanese? You're too old to be a soldier," his mother fretted.

"Japanese bombs or Chinese bombs, best to get out of the way. I will not become cannon fodder for a losing cause."

His father glanced in Benny's direction and suddenly seemed to notice him. "This is grown-up talk, Son. Go to bed. Everything will be back to normal soon."

Benny climbed back up to the third floor where all the children stayed. He quickly fell asleep, comforted by his father's words.

———

ALMOST AS QUICKLY AS the bombs had rained on Bloody Saturday, as that tragic day became known, the blackened hulks of cars and other debris were swept away by an army of laborers. Repairs began on the Cathay Hotel's roof and top-floor ballroom. Just as his father predicted, the shops and offices around Avenue Edward VII soon reopened. Unidentified human remains were dispatched for dumping at the city's outskirts. But the acrid smell of charred flesh and the heavy, cloying stench of human blood lingered in the air. Stains from human projectiles high on building walls had to wait for heavy rains to wash them away. Everything else would be covered by a new layer of grime from the ash and gunpowder of the battles that continued to rage beyond the foreign concessions.

In September, a few weeks after Bloody Saturday, the new school year began, and Benny returned to his primary school. The teachers and students carried on as best they could, ignoring the near-constant explosions coming from Shanghai's defenseless Chinese sections. Still, the sheltered schoolchildren of the foreign concessions couldn't stop buzzing about what they had witnessed on Bloody Saturday. Benny described his father's bloodstained uniform with enthusiasm. But no one came close to the tale of Benny's schoolmate Tingchang "T.C." Yao, whose family had lived for four hundred years in Shanghai's old Chinese walled city, near the nine-turn bridge.

As a Chinese jurisdiction, the old walled city was a prime target for Japanese attack, so T.C.'s father had packed his eldest son and eleven other members of the large Yao family into a LaSalle sedan. They had driven only blocks away into the International Settlement, to stay at the luxury Opera Apartments, where his father's friend kept a place for trysts with his girlfriends. By crossing into the foreign concession, T.C.'s family expected to be protected from the war. Young T.C. was out on the balcony watching the crush of refugees in the street when the low-flying Chinese planes passed overhead. He dove back into the apartment as the bombs whistled through the air. The impact shook the building. Unhurt, the boy peeked outside. The sight of human remains hurled into piles like snowdrifts so shocked him that he stood, staring and paralyzed, until his father yanked him inside. As soon as the streets reopened, his father ordered everyone back into the LaSalle, which their chauffeur had luckily parked away from the site of the blasts. This time they drove east to Hongkou to stay near Shanghai's sizable Japanese civilian population, confident that the enemy wouldn't bomb its own people. Their new place was next to the city's huge hog abattoir. The loud squeals of pigs being butchered were periodically drowned out by the roar of bombs and cannon fire slaughtering people in nearby Zhabei.

Thousands of refugees from the prior day's battle had gathered to receive food relief from charities on August 14, 1937, only to become part of the terrible casualty toll in one of the busiest parts of the foreign concessions.

T.C.'s account was so graphic that the schoolboys gasped and groaned, begging him to retell it.

NEW WARTIME RESTRICTIONS, like the war itself, didn't put a noticeable dent in Benny's comfortable life. He still spent his school days enjoying himself with his friends, collecting and trading stamps, and coming up with war-inspired games, identifying fighter planes and battleships by their shapes. He took up badminton, a sport that suited him better than the demanding wushu regimen preferred by his father.

Instead of playing on Avenue Haig, Benny now spent more time riding his bike, perusing the bakeries, confectionaries, and cafés on busy Avenue Joffre, the stylish commercial boulevard that ran through the French Concession. Benny always had enough pocket money for hot chocolate and cheesecake at DD's, a coffee shop run by White Russians. He'd sit near the window with his friends and watch the antics of other boys. Charlie and John Sie, who lived nearby, would ride their bikes up to the back of a moving trolley car and hold on, staying out of the conductor's mirror. Then they'd coast all the way to the Bund. While Benny admired their daring, he knew to stop short of anything that might draw the anger of his father. Should Benny cause any trouble, everyone in the neighborhood knew how to reach the Shanghai Volunteer Corps officer. Also, Benny's sophisticated mother rewarded his good behavior with special excursions, allowing him to see the latest Hollywood movies at the Cathay, the Grand, or one of Shanghai's other gleaming movie palaces. He also liked to accompany her to the rooftop terrace of Sun Sun Department Store to ride the escalator, China's first. When he was small, he could spend hours going up and down that escalator, his amah trailing behind, fussing and scolding.

FOR FAMILIES LIKE BENNY'S—FROM the wealthy and middle classes of the foreign concessions—the war was more an inconvenience than a danger. The biggest disruption came from the endless wave of refugees, who seemed to multiply a hundred times over, crowding the already numerous beggars. On the heels of Bloody Saturday, 1.5 million terrified refugees had swarmed into the nine square miles of the concessions, less than half the area of America's Manhattan. By then, the British and French authorities had put up barbed-wire barricades and gates at major intersections—to keep out refugees more than Japanese soldiers. Desperate, frightened people now occupied every square inch of sidewalk and alleyway. With each cold spell, lifeless bundles appeared along the roads and sidewalks. Sheltered in his privileged routine, Benny didn't even notice such unpleasantries.

By December 1937, after three terrible months of heavy shelling and ground skirmishes in the Chinese sections beyond the foreign concessions, the Battle of Shanghai was finally over. Just as Benny's father anticipated, the Japanese prevailed, and the Nationalists fell back. Still, they had fought courageously and far longer than anyone had imagined. The Imperial Japanese Command had planned for Shanghai to fall in three days. They had expected China to surrender in three months. Though Japan was vastly wrong on both counts, it had won the first major conflict of the Pacific War in what would become the Pacific theater of World War II. Shanghai and the surrounding areas fell under Japanese occupation and martial law—except for the International Settlement and the French Concession. Cut off from the rest of the city's suffering, these foreign jurisdictions came to be called Gudao by the Chinese—the Solitary Island.

Having secured control of Shanghai, the Japanese commander in chief General Iwane Matsui ordered the victorious Japanese troops on a hundred-fifty-mile quick-time march to take the Nationalist capital of Nanjing. As incentive, the soldiers were permitted to rape, loot, and kill without restraint. Their gruesome massacre in Nanjing took place under the watch of Prince Yasuhiko Asaka, Emperor Hirohito's uncle and emissary. Asaka ordered his men to "kill all captives." When the Imperial Japanese troops reached the capital, they embarked on a horrific six-week orgy of mass killing and rape, torture and disembowelment, that left an estimated 200,000 to 300,000 men, women, and children dead. Most were civilians. Japanese officers posed for cameras as they competed in a contest to see who was fastest at killing 100 people with their swords. When they lost count, they held a rematch to see who would first behead 150 prisoners. Other Japanese soldiers formed killing teams, with some assigned to toss heads and corpses into piles as if they were firewood. Tens of thousands of Chinese women were mass-raped, dismembered, slaughtered. For entertainment, Japanese soldiers ordered Chinese men to commit necrophilia, incest, and other abhorrent acts. When they refused, they too were tortured and killed. John Rabe, a German Nazi who witnessed the carnage, wrote in his diary of his shock at the extreme inhumanity. Initially, the news of Japan's barbarism was suppressed in occupied China, but reports of the atrocities began to filter out. *The New York Times* reported on "ghastly events" so egregious that "atrocities of all kinds reached an unprintable crescendo." As news of the Rape of Nanjing spread, the people of China wept—and resolved to defeat the despicable enemy.

IN THIS UNSETTLING TIME, Benny's father decided to make a major switch in his life: He shut down his accounting practice and ended his leadership of the Chinese unit of the Shanghai Volunteer Corps. Instead, Pan Zhijie signed on with the British-controlled Shanghai Municipal Police as a full-fledged inspector. Only a few years earlier, such high-ranking positions had been reserved for the British police, who reviled the Chinese whose streets they ruled. "This bunch of worthless, treacherous, yellow-skinned reptiles," wrote one officer to his aunt in England. But Inspector Pan stood out with his fluency in English and Chinese, his years with the SVC, his St. John's education, and his prominent family background. The pay was modest for a man from a comprador family, but the perks of such a position of influence would more than compensate, especially when everyone was desperate for protection from war's misery.

Benny couldn't have been prouder of his inspector father—he looked even grander in his new blue serge uniform. But the boy was too young to know that there could be a price to pay for his father's choice at this ominous moment in history.

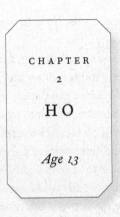

SHANGHAI, 1937

A LANKY TEENAGED BOY, BEDRAGGLED AND BEWILDERED, nervously stepped up from the rocking fishing boat into the noisy chaos of a city quai along Shanghai's Bund. Water spurted from his black cloth shoes as he stumbled along the wharf toward solid ground, his dark Chinese gown clinging to him, soaking wet. Stinking, fishy water had sloshed around the boat's hold, where he had spent a sleepless night packed in with dozens of other frightened refugees, anxious to escape the coming war with the Japanese. They were desperately hoping that the big city, with its many foreigners, would protect them.

His mouth agape, Ho Chow lifted his close-shaved head to stare at the monumental granite buildings towering before him. Such a strange sight, lined up alongside the Huangpu River, the last leg of the frightening trip from his town of Changshu, sixty miles to the northwest in the Yangtze River Delta of neighboring Jiangsu Province.

The Chow family had lived there as landowning gentry for generations. In the past few weeks, tens of thousands of soldiers had been assembling near their home. Nobody doubted that the coming conflagration would be enormous. It seemed that everyone who could was rushing to escape the bloodletting. It had been Ho's grandmother's decision that their family had to leave. Their boat was just one of thousands of floating vessels of every kind tying up at a Shanghai dock to unload their human cargo.

From the very start, Ho's trip had been a nightmare. Only the day before, he'd said goodbye to his mother and fifteen-year-old brother back in Changshu. He'd never been apart from his mother, and he, too, felt like crying when he saw tears well up in her eyes. Some townspeople advocated splitting up families to ensure that someone would survive, so his mother and elder brother were headed west to a remote village further inland, near the ancient canalled city of Suzhou, while he and his sister, Wanyu, were to take a boat to Shanghai with Grandmother. But the country roads to the boat dock had been clogged beyond belief: armies of people tugging at pull carts stacked with household goods with the young and elderly seated on top and seemingly endless streams of women and men lugging bundles on their backs or balancing bamboo poles on their shoulders. Ho had clung tightly to his sister and grandmother as the human tide swept them along. Thanks to Grandmother's strongest servants, who cleared their path, they managed to reach the dock where the boat she had paid for their passage was waiting.

At the pier, there was more pushing and shoving as people tried to buy or force their way onto any departing vessel. The gangplank onto the boat was so narrow that people could go only one at a time. First Grandmother, then Wanyu gingerly climbed aboard. Just as Ho was about to step onto the plank, the crowd surged, and the boy felt himself pushed aside, back to the dock's edge. As the restless crowd rushed forward, the crew swiftly pulled up the gangplank, and the heavy boat slowly began to pull away—with Ho still ashore.

The unruly mob swelled, and Ho teetered as he looked down into the dark water. Just as he was about to fall in, some strong arms reached over and grabbed him, yanking him onto the ship. Ho collapsed onto the smelly deck and looked up. It was his sister, Wanyu. She had spotted him and, with the help of other passengers, managed to grab him at the last possible moment. At first Ho was too stunned to speak; then finally he cried out, "Big Sister, you saved me!"

The boat slowly chugged to Shanghai. With such a heavy load of people aboard, the captain didn't dare push ahead too quickly—the boat was too low in the water and could capsize. Ho spent the uncomfortable ride in shock. The terrifying scene repeated in his mind: Had he fallen into the water, he'd have been crushed to death between the boat and the pier, or he could have drowned in the deep, murky blackness. This was not a propitious start to his refuge in Shanghai.

YOUNG HO HAD ALWAYS felt secure at his home in Changshu. There, he had never had to worry about getting flattened by a boat, car, or double-decker tram. In Changshu, the Chows' status as part of the gentry class that dominated China's vast rural countryside was secure. Ho had been born in his large family home located near the center of town and was surrounded by the web of canals and waterways that crisscrossed and irrigated the lush farmland of the Yangtze Delta. Their home was typical of a prosperous landed family: Three long buildings sat parallel to one another, their two-story rectangular shapes separated by two courtyards. A moatlike canal spanned by a small wooden bridge surrounded the Chow home, adding to the sense of safety. Chinese families were deemed blessed with longevity and fertility when they had four generations living together. Three generations of Chows lived there when Ho was born, with plenty of room for a fourth.

More than thirty people lived at the Chow family compound: In addition to the extended family, there was a retinue of servants and employees—cooks, maids, amahs, tailors, drivers, accountants, managers, and advisers. A few had their own families living with them as well. On the Chow lands beyond the compound were the hundreds of peasant farmers who worked the rich alluvial soil brought by the mighty Yangtze River from the Himalayas and across China to coastal Jiangsu. The very name of Changshu means "ever fertile." For generations, the Chow family had lived off the rent from their tenant farmers, whose rice and cotton were destined for Shanghai's huge population and busy textile mills.

Life on the compound centered on the middle building, where Ho's grandmother, as Chow family elder, lived on the first floor facing the favored southern exposure. Her three sons and their families each had their residences in other parts of the complex, and the entire family took meals together in the main hall off one of the courtyards. The adults sat at one table while Ho, his siblings, and many cousins sat together at the other, under the watchful eyes of their amahs. As a big landlord family in one of China's most productive regions, the Chows ate well; their rice bowls were always full, with a variety of dishes at every dinner. There was no lack of vegetables and legumes, eggs and tofu, fish and even meat on the Chows' tables. In November during crab season, they feasted on their area's famous delicacy from nearby Yangcheng Lake: fresh hairy crab, known for its succulent meat and roe.

Ho's father was the eldest of the three Chow sons. When his father died, he became the family's head, inheriting the responsibility for the Chows' lands, tenant farmers, and businesses. But Ho's father fell ill and died at just thirty-eight, when Ho was only two. Ho's mother was left in the tenuous position of being a widowed daughter-in-law with three young children. Ho was the youngest. His sister, Wanyu, was seven at the time, and his brother, Hosun, four.

At their family home in Changshu, thirteen-year-old Ho Chow (third from left) stands between his elder sister, Wanyu, and their widowed mother. Elder brother Hosun is on the far right. Two young cousins join them.

Although Ho could not remember his father, the boy knew well the strain that had befallen his mother after his father's death. Chinese lore is filled with stories of the mistreatment of daughters-in-law and widows left at the mercy of unkind in-laws. But Ho's paternal grandmother was a fair and generous woman who didn't threaten to cast her son's family out of the compound. Instead, she enlisted the help of her son's young widow to manage the Chow family's enterprises. The two women proved to be capable and sharp in business. They supervised the accounts, oversaw the land, and collected the rent from the farmers, while Ho's two uncles ran the family's bank and shops that kept the money in the family's network. By their own accounts, the Chow family was respected for their fair treatment of their tenant farmers. That view reflected the Confucian ideal of the benevolent ruler as opposed to the Communist condemnation of landlords as an evil, exploiting class—a view that was gaining ground among China's vast population of peasant farmers.

Even without Ho's father, the Chow home in Changshu was an idyllic cocoon. Ho's boyhood was spent playing games and pranks with his cousins and the servants' children without the slightest concern for harm or danger. His only fears sprang from what he and the other children conjured to terrorize one another. They'd hide in the large ancestral hall in the first building of the compound, with its dark urns and offerings of incense to statues of patron gods and long-dead ancestors. The servants would warn them to stay away from the ancestral shrines. "If you disturb the hungry demons and ghosts," they'd scold, "they'll pull you to the spirit world and you'll never return." When Ho was younger, he believed their superstitious talk, but once he was old enough to go to school, he laughed at their warnings about evil demons, scoffing to his cousins that they were silly to be afraid of such stories.

Going to and from school in Changshu was a carefree walk through the city park. After crossing the family's moat, he'd traverse the city's central gardens toward the Fangta Pagoda, dedicated to Changshu's patron deity Kwan Yin, goddess of compassion and mercy. His school was located next to the pagoda and surrounded by ancient ginkgo trees. If he didn't dawdle, his journey took him only about ten minutes. But the curious boy liked to stop on the way, visiting the vendors along his path to school. He enjoyed teasing the tailors who sewed his family's clothes and jabbing at the bookkeepers who sat huddled over the accounts in the courtyard. They pretended to try to grab him, calling him "*jo guei*"—naughty little devil.

Ho's school in Changshu was so small that there was only one teacher much of the time, so Ho and his elder brother and sister were often in the same class. That one teacher covered all the traditional primary-school subjects, including the Chinese classics and language, basic mathematics, and the multiplication tables. It didn't matter to Ho if the lessons were aimed at the older children; he absorbed them all. From an early age, he demonstrated a gift for numbers. He was less enamored by the language and literature classes, but he did well enough to rise to the top of the small school.

Even so, Ho didn't take his education for granted—not after the time he brought home some upsetting news:

"Mother, tomorrow there is no more school. The teacher is leaving."

Ho's mother put down her embroidery. "What do you mean?"

"He said there is no more money to pay him, so he must leave."

Ho's mother sprang into action. She went to a locked box in her bedroom and took out a small piece of her wedding jewelry. Ho accompanied her to a pawnshop in town, where she traded her jewelry for cash. Next, she visited the teacher and persuaded him to stay by paying the rest of his salary.

As Ho grew older, he watched his mother dip into her shrinking stash of wedding jewelry again to hire a tutor to teach her children basic English and calligraphy after school. His mother didn't know a word of English herself, nor could she write, but she wanted her sons and daughter to be equipped for the modern world.

Seeing his mother pawn her jewelry for his education sobered Ho's outlook on school. He resolved early on to be a good student, to make her proud.

IT WAS HO'S EDUCATION, not the threat of war, that had started him on this trek to Shanghai. By early 1937, he had completed his primary schooling. In small towns and cities like his, that signaled the end of studies for most children—if they had been fortunate enough to go to school at all. Since Changshu didn't have a secondary school, it was unlikely that Ho would be able to continue with his education.

After his classes ended that spring, his teacher took the unusual step of visiting the Chow family. Ho was playing in the courtyard when he saw his teacher crossing the bridge over the canal. He ran to greet him.

"Hello, *Lao Shi,* how may I help you?" Ho asked, bowing his head in respect.

"Good day, Young Master Chow," he replied. "Can you please see if your mother might allow me to speak with her?"

Ho brought his teacher to the courtyard where his mother was going over dinner preparations with the cook. Ho stood quietly outside the open door, straining to listen as his teacher spoke.

"Chow *Tai-tai,* please forgive me for disturbing you," he began. "I beg to inform you that your second son, Ho, has a gift for mathematics and science. With further study, he could go far. These are troubled times for China, as we all know. Nevertheless, I hope you will consider sending him to study further in Shanghai, where there are many fine schools."

Ho felt his pulse quicken. He was secretly longing to continue his schooling somehow, but he knew from the adults' talk about Japan during dinner each night that they had many urgent questions on their minds. He listened closely for his mother's response. There was only silence. His heart sank as he imagined his mother's expression, her creased brow and pursed lips. He knew that she had already taken exceptional measures by educating all her children through primary school. Many Chinese families poured their limited resources solely into their Number One Son.

Finally he heard his mother speak.

"Thank you, *Lao Shi,* for bringing me such good news about my second son. He has been fortunate to have you as his teacher. I am grateful that you have made this special trip to speak so highly of him." After another pause, she began again. "As you mention, there are difficult times ahead. Like many other families, our Chow clan is unsure where we will be in the coming year. With so much uncertainty, I don't know if I can send my youngest child away to such a big city," she said. "He's still just a boy. Who would take care of him? But I will think about your words."

After his teacher left, Ho's mother said nothing about the visit. Nor did he dare broach the subject when he, too, had mixed feelings. He was elated by his teacher's high praise and the thought of continuing with school, but he could not imagine living apart from his mother and family.

In the weeks after his teacher's visit, the adults became singularly preoccupied with the growing threat of war in the Yangtze Delta area. Signs of an approaching clash were everywhere. Nationalist soldiers set up encampments in the areas outside of Shanghai as the army built up its troop strength. Changshu's proximity to the Yangtze River and the East China Sea made it a prime staging area for both friend and foe. Its location near Shanghai, Suzhou, and Nanjing, China's capital, put their town directly in the line of march. If a war came, any battle would roll over Changshu. Ho's grandmother, mother, and uncles all agreed that they should follow the time-honored practice when catastrophe loomed: They would need to *tao nan*, to flee. But to where? What about the land, the rent, their businesses, and the compound that supported so many people?

The ultimate decision fell to Ho's grandmother. It was customary for ownership of a family's property to be held only by male heirs, but an elder dowager could maintain control. Grandmother ran the family and its holdings, taking responsibility not only for the Chow fortune but also, most important, for keeping the Chow family's heirs and lineage safe.

Weighing their options from fragments of available information, Grandmother reminded her family of the stampede of refugees to Shanghai in 1932, the first time that the Japanese attacked the city. No one could forget how the foreign concessions had been unharmed amid the carnage in that terrible year. There had been other panicked swarms into Shanghai, such as during the violent Taiping and Boxer Rebellions in the 1800s, when the foreign presence had also offered Chinese some protection against the chaos.

"If war comes to Jiangsu Province, who knows what will happen to Changshu and our Chow family home?" Grandmother warned. "But everyone will rush to Shanghai for safety, as they have for almost a hundred years. Of that there is no doubt. We must plan for that day as well."

Grandmother made her decision: The family had to leave their beloved home and find safety elsewhere. She and Ho's mother would prepare the family and the household's servants for their departure. They made arrangements for the collection of rents from the tenant farmers in the Chows' absence. In the meantime, Grandmother dispatched her second son, Ho's Second Uncle, to Shanghai with instructions to find the family a suitable house in the city's foreign concessions.

ONCE IT WAS CLEAR that they would all leave, Ho's mother had her own difficult decisions to make. Shanghai was not a good place for Ho's elder brother, Hosun, who was recovering from early-stage tuberculosis. His mother didn't dare expose his lungs to the city's damp, sooty air. Before the visit of Ho's teacher, she wouldn't have considered splitting up her family. But now there was the teacher's prediction that Ho could do well if he continued with school.

Then came the news that Second Uncle had purchased a *lilong*-style house in the British and American section of Shanghai. Though the price had been high, he'd been lucky to find anything. The house was considerably smaller than their compound, but there would be room enough.

With the knowledge that Ho could stay with his grandmother in Shanghai, Ho's mother decided to find a middle school for him there. She'd send her daughter to Shanghai too. Wanyu would attend nursing school—a practical profession for a daughter. The two could stay together at the family house that Second Uncle had found while Mother would take Hosun to a safe and healthier place near Suzhou. She was mindful, too, that separating her children could improve their chances that some would survive the war.

Ho's mother turned her energies to assisting Grandmother in shuttering the compound. Only one trusted servant would stay on the property as a caretaker. Most of the others had already left for their own home villages.

Ho didn't know which school he would attend, and he didn't care. He was excited to be able to study again and that his sister would be there too. With his elder brother ill, young Ho knew that his family might have to depend on him one day. He vowed that he would try his best to show his mother that he was worth the expense of an education.

AFTER ALL THE PLANNING and preparation, they had finally reached Shanghai. Ho's grandmother didn't hesitate to remind him of his close call. "The water ghosts almost pulled you into the sea; you're lucky that your sister snatched you from their hungry mouths! You must be more careful here in Shanghai. There are many wicked demons looking for you in this dangerous city."

Head down, Ho replied, "Grandmother, I won't cause you any worry." Well aware of his sheltered, small-town background, the boy didn't need to be reminded that death had brushed his sleeve. He would have to be more careful.

The towering stone buildings seemed to mock his discomfort. His hometown had just one tall building, the Fangta Pagoda. At nine stories high, it was the landmark for miles around. None of these Shanghai buildings remotely resembled the Chinese style he knew. A riverfront clock tower with Western numerals suddenly rang out an odd and unfamiliar tune. Was he now in the land of foreigners?

Soon Second Uncle arrived to take them to the house. With so many people on the crowded street, Ho stuck close to his big sister. He and Wanyu climbed into a rickshaw, and Second Uncle and Grandmother each took their own. The coolies proceeded to pull them through the busy streets along the length of Nanjing Road. Ho had never seen such crowds, all walking much faster than anyone did in Changshu. And the foreigners! Some wore dapper white suits; others were red-turbaned Sikh police in Western-style uniforms, directing traffic from tall raised booths. There were Annamese gendarmes in conical hats, Japanese women on high wooden sandals, pale Europeans with long noses and straw-colored hair. He craned his neck to peer at the tops of the multistory department stores, their colorful neon signs brightening the streets with their names: "Wing On," "Sincere," "Sun Sun," and "The Sun." And there were fancy-looking Chinese people dressed in foreign-style clothing—men in pants and jackets and women with short curly hair, showing their legs and high, spindly shoes. Shanghai was simply overwhelming.

But what impressed Ho even more than the tall buildings and the exotic people were the shiny automobiles. He had seen a Model T in Changshu and observed how it worked, but these looked so sleek and fast, he imagined that they could fly. Back home, wooden carts powered by water buffalo or by humans were the everyday vehicles, and Ho could always outpace them. His eyes widened at the sight of the polished, chauffeur-driven Packards and zippy red MG convertibles. He twisted and turned to stare as they sped by.

Before long, their rickshaws stopped at a large complex of attached homes on Medhurst Road connected by a web of lanes. Second Uncle called them *lilong* houses—a distinctive Shanghai style of identical row homes. Each was three stories high, with three to four rooms to a floor and a kitchen toward the back where a few servants could live. Grandmother would stay on the first floor, the two uncles and their families on the next, and Ho and Big Sister in the attic. The building was compact and modern compared to the sprawling old compound in Changshu. Most curious to Ho was the running water in the kitchen and bathrooms—and the flush toilets. Ho pulled the chain on one of them several times, intrigued by the swirling water. In Changshu, they had dumped all waste into the canals, but Ho saw no waterway by the house. Where did it all go? he wondered.

Their house on Medhurst Road was located almost directly behind the Lido Ballroom, one of the busiest dance halls and cabarets in Shanghai. On the night that Ho arrived, he could hear the music and gaiety drift up to the dormer window of his third-floor room. Before he could think of stepping outside for a closer look, his uncle warned that the Lido nightclub was frequented by members of the powerful Green Gang, the underworld organization that served as a shadow government in some parts of Shanghai. This information prompted his sister and grandmother to launch into a new round of stern warnings about the big city and its fast-talking slickers, enemy soldiers with rifles and bayonets, and fellow Chinese who might be thieves, gangsters, prostitutes—or Communist bandits. A naïve country boy like Ho, unfamiliar with the dangers all around him, should focus on his schooling and stay clear of trouble in this city ruled by mayhem, they repeated at every opportunity.

HO WAS JUST SETTLING into his new home when Japan's conquest of China began. With Medhurst Road two miles from the Huangpu River, where the Japanese flagship *Idzumo* and two dozen other enemy warships were moored, Ho learned about the Bloody Saturday bombings only from his uncles' dinnertime accounts of the day's news. But the fighting that continued for the next three months took place barely a half mile away in Zhabei. Ho tried to block out the whines and booms and the shaking of his house from the continual air and naval bombardment in the Chinese neighborhoods just beyond the International Settlement and French Concession. At night, Ho could hear the rat-tat-tat of machine-gun fire from the urban trench warfare only a few blocks north of his open attic windows.

It was hard to sleep when Ho felt the city tremble with each explosion. These were the moments when the boy missed his mother the most. She hadn't gone to school herself and hadn't known how to go about finding one in Shanghai for Ho. From a distant relative, she had learned of a vocational school in the French Concession, not far from Medhurst Road. She hastily arranged to pay the tuition, enrolling Ho there while frantically making the preparations to flee. Ho wished he could show his mother how grateful he was, that he was diligent in minding his grandmother and sister, that he wouldn't let her down. He hoped that she and his elder brother were safe and away from the bullets and bombs. He was convinced that they would all be together again one day. Then he would prove that he was deserving of her trust.

THE ZHONGHUA VOCATIONAL SCHOOL became the center of Ho's universe. He started each day with a quick breakfast of rice porridge and pickled vegetables, prepared for him by the cook Grandmother had hired. Then he set out on his march to school.

Wanyu, just four years older, had mapped his route to avoid fast-moving autos, electric trams, and possible disturbance or danger, such as Japanese sentries and roadblocks, choosing smaller streets that weren't packed with refugees. His grandmother gave him the same advice every morning as he set off: "Don't pause to behold the temptations of this sinful city. Don't slow down. If you go quickly and avert your eyes, the ghosts and demons will leave you alone." Though the science-minded student had long rejected such superstitions, he would never challenge his wise grandmother. It was his filial duty as a son and grandson to obey his elders.

Cutting through the maze of *lilong* complexes like his own, he crossed narrow lanes full of people heading to the hot-water "tiger stove" shops with large thermos bottles in hand or standing in their nightclothes, waiting to buy fried *youtiao* and plump steamed *baozi* from the street stalls that inhabited many doorways. He gave wide berth to the pungent *ma tong*, chamber pots, set outside to be emptied by the night-soil collector. It took all of his willpower to ignore the vendors with bright displays of candies and snacks.

By following his sister's carefully drawn route, Ho could reach his school while bypassing the worst traffic of Bubbling Well Road, one of the International Settlement's main thoroughfares leading away from the Huangpu River and the Bund. As Ho walked to the French Concession, he had to be most careful crossing Avenue Foch, the border between the International Settlement and the French Concession. The traffic on that busy route was only part of his concern. At such jurisdictional boundaries between the British-, French-, and Chinese-governed areas, petty thieves, gangsters, and assassins could evade police simply by crossing the street from one jurisdiction to the next. Shootouts between police and thugs occurred often enough at such boundaries, so he had to stay alert, as his sister and grandmother often reminded him.

Luckily, school wasn't far, just about a mile away from home. At his brisk pace, he took only fifteen to twenty minutes to reach its central location near Avenue Joffre, the commercial heart of the French Concession. Attractions along the route included the popular Lyceum and the Cathay theaters, with colorful posters for the latest movies produced by Shanghai and Hollywood studios. Though Ho did his best to ignore them, sometimes he'd steal a glimpse through the fences of Le Cercle Sportif Français and the British country club, with their elegant private grounds for foreigners and the wealthiest of Chinese.

When he returned to the house from school, all eleven family members would eat dinner together, just as they used to, except without his mother and brother. Even the cook was from Changshu, so Ho continued to enjoy his favorite hometown dishes, with finely chopped vegetables and steamed fish seasoned with light vinegar, sugar, and soy sauces. Meat was harder to come by after the war began. Ho took care not to fill his bowl when there wasn't enough for everyone.

As Ho's education progressed, he became aware of the limitations of his school. A vocational school, he found, was intended to teach him a trade, not to prepare him for college. Neither he, nor his mother, nor the relative who had advised her to send him there had understood that. Ho thirsted for more scientific studies, but he continued without complaint, for he knew his mother had already paid dearly for his tuition. He was determined to learn everything the school could teach him about applied math and sciences, machine tooling, and mechanical devices.

During his first year at the school, Ho tried to focus on his studies. His mother was only sixty miles away, but with the occupation of Shanghai and the horror of Nanjing, marauding Japanese troops were everywhere. Ho and his mother didn't dare travel to see each other.

Ho had promised to mind Big Sister Wanyu, and he did so without reservation, for she watched over and protected him. She warned him about many things, telling him to stay away from the bad boys who hopped onto the trolleys and buses, evading the fare to go to unfamiliar and possibly dangerous parts of Shanghai. To keep his promise, Ho resisted the urge to climb onto the double-decker buses that had been outfitted with coal-burning engines at their back ends—since the Japanese occupiers had taken the available gasoline for their soldiers. The buses filled the air with black smoke as they lurched forward. Ho hadn't gone back to see the Bund since the day his boat had landed in Shanghai. Whenever he was tempted by a diversion, he forced himself to remember his singular purpose for being in the city. In short order, Ho rose to the head of his class, just as he had in Changshu.

As the Japanese occupation of Shanghai dragged on, the enemy soldiers grew bolder and more aggressive toward the foreign concessions. Their special extraterritorial status turned the safe havens into magnets for agents, spies, and assassins of every nationality and political ideology. Japanese secret police, German Nazi agents, British Secret Intelligence Service/MI6, American military intelligence, and others kept tabs on one another while waging their own clandestine intrigues. The streets of Shanghai turned into arenas of terrorist violence between pro-Nationalist loyalists versus the Japanese invaders and their collaborators. Communists, who were hunted by all, stayed in the deep underground.

In the early weeks of 1940, during Ho's third year of secondary school, a local newspaper editor was decapitated, and his head was stuck on a lamppost in the French Concession. The victim had worked for *Shen Bao,* the most prominent Chinese-language newspaper in Shanghai, well known for its anti-Japanese stance. Wanyu told Ho to stay away from that part of the French Concession. When it was rumored that agents from Shanghai's secret police were collaborating with the Japanese and based at 76 Jessfield Road, that area became off-limits as well. So did the border with the Chinese section a few blocks to the north that was barricaded with barbed wire and sandbags, patrolled by Japanese sentries armed with rifles and bayonets.

Sequestered though he was, it was still hard for Ho to ignore the growing tensions all around him. Japanese soldiers couldn't directly impose their military presence on the International Settlement since Japan wasn't at war with Britain or the United States. But they had other ways of applying pressure. Chinese, rich or poor, had to bow down like slaves to the enemy whenever they crossed the soldiers' paths—or face savage beatings. Food and fuel were increasingly hard to come by, especially with the Japanese military seizing crops and matériel to use in its war against China. The Japanese commanded Chinese to scavenge for scrap metal, from the smallest screws to the radiators and pipes of fine mansions, to be turned over to the occupiers. The scrap would be smelted into bombs and bullets to kill Chinese. The British, American, and French authorities, no match for the Japanese military that surrounded them, agreed to aid Japan by apprehending and handing over Chinese resisters.

Ho did his best to block out the terror around him. He believed that he could contribute something despite the war and destruction. Maybe he'd be able to attend college one day. After dinner each evening, he went to his attic room and studied at a small table under the dim lightbulb suspended from the ceiling. Chiang, Hirohito, Mao—none of the armies or generals mattered to him. His only wish was to get through these harsh times with as little harm to his family as possible.

Yet for all of his care to keep a wide berth from anything remotely dangerous, the devastation and turmoil were in the very air he breathed, ready to envelop him, his family, and all of China.

OUTSIDE SUZHOU, LATE 1937

A T THE ROUGH WOODEN DOOR OF A ONE-ROOM FARMER'S cottage, a woman was speaking to an unexpected visitor. Hiding behind the woman, clinging to her long skirt, a small girl named Bing tried, unsuccessfully, to mute her squeal of surprise and delight. The visitor, a young man dressed in Western-style shirt and pants, had come to the small village outside of Suzhou to get her, to take her to Shanghai. Madame Hsu had sent for her!

Bing hadn't known happiness for so long that she had forgotten how buoyant she could feel. Her joy was mixed with relief: When the Japanese army seemed certain to turn their home in Suzhou into another battlefield, Mama Hsu, whom Bing called "Mama" even though she was not her mother, had sent her from the city with the Hsus' maid to stay in this farming village, the servant's hometown. Mama had said that Bing would be safer there and she'd send for her when the danger subsided. But these few months in the village had been interminable. It already seemed ages ago that everyone in Suzhou had turned frantic overnight as it became clear that the Japanese soldiers would head toward the capital of Nanjing—with their city directly in the army's path. Bing had fretted constantly that Mama wouldn't send for her. What if Mama had already been caught by the Japanese? What if Mama couldn't reach her?

Now she could forget her worries. The young man, a relative of Mama's, was going to college in Shanghai, where Mama had found a place to take refuge among the foreigners. The college student said it was safer there now that the worst of the fighting was over. Bing was overjoyed that she hadn't been left behind—again.

THE HOURS-LONG TRAIN RIDE brought Bing to the big city of Shanghai for the first time, but all she could see from her seat was miles of scorched earth and piles of smoking rubble. The farm people were nowhere to be seen, though the young man assured her that the fighting was over. The small towns and hamlets the girl observed from her window were ruined and empty. Fierce-looking Japanese soldiers were everywhere, gruffly patrolling the railway cars and stations, poking and prodding anyone who didn't move fast enough to obey their shouted commands.

When they reached Shanghai North railway station, Bing stood close to the college boy, afraid that the fast-walking big-city people might mow her down. They took a pedicab past the tallest buildings she had ever seen, through a busy shopping area with foreign-looking three- and four-story residences that the student said was in the English section of the city. What a thrill to see Mama waiting for her in front of one of those big houses, smiling warmly at her. But in the formal way of Chinese families, Mama didn't reach out to hug Bing in greeting. She simply took Bing's hand and led her up two flights of stairs and into the room she had managed to rent with two women friends from Suzhou.

Inside, Mama's friends greeted Bing. Happily, she recognized them both. Auntie Fong was a doctor, and Auntie Rose had attended nursing school with Mama. Auntie Fong always dressed in a Western man's suit with matching slacks and jacket, white shirt, and tie, while Auntie Rose wore a *qipao,* like Mama. To Bing, there was nothing remarkable about this threesome of modern, educated young women in their mid-twenties—independent, westernized, and comfortable in the huge metropolis. The little girl was simply glad to be reunited with Mama and her welcoming friends.

The large, sparsely furnished room contained a small table, some wood chairs, and two narrow beds. Bing and Mama slept together. Bing noticed that Auntie Fong and Auntie Rose seemed especially devoted to each other and they didn't mind crowding into the other small bed. The shared kitchen was downstairs. There was no bathroom— they would bathe in a washbasin and use a *ma tong* or "horse bucket" for their toilet, just as they had in Suzhou. Each morning, the night-soil collector pushed his foul-smelling cart through the neighborhood and dumped each pot's contents into his stinking vat, to be used as fertilizer on the fields.

Mama said they would be safe in the apartment, that the Japanese soldiers wouldn't come to this "Englishtown" settlement. Though their new place felt comfortable, even pleasant, when Bing lay down that night, she couldn't sleep. An overwhelming sadness washed over her. She was thankful it was dark and hoped that Mama wouldn't see the tears streaming down her face as she remembered the first time she had been left behind.

BEFORE BING WENT TO live with Mama Hsu, her home had been a two-room cottage with dirt floors, the house where she had been born. There, she was known only as Little Sister—not as *Bing* or some nickname. The outer room was dominated by a large earthen wood-burning stove, leaving just enough space for a table and some hard chairs. The stove heated the kang, a big hard bed fashioned from mud that filled the other room. Little Sister had her own small stool, which she dragged with her everywhere, inside and out. Little Sister was the second child, a girl sandwiched between two boys, and it was her job to look after her brothers when her mother was busy working. Their village, surrounded by wide green fields of rice and cotton, was located in the prefecture-level city of Changzhou, 120 miles northwest of Shanghai. In the distance, Little Sister occasionally spied the tall triangular sails of junks gliding through the rich network of waterways in the Yangtze River Delta, cutting through the flat plain like serrated blades against the sky. At night, the parents and three children slept together on the kang. If one person turned, everyone did.

Bing's childhood routine was broken up by her father's periodic visits. He wasn't home most days since he worked several miles away on a landowner's large compound. Bing missed his playful teasing and cheerful attention because her mother was too busy with her brothers to notice her. Whenever she saw her father approaching on foot in the distance, she'd squeal and run toward him shouting, "Baba! Baba!" as he held his arms out for her. He would hoist her onto his back, and she'd laugh with glee as she rode her *baba* like a water buffalo all the way back to the house.

If she was very lucky, her father would slip her a piece of sesame candy bought from the peddler who went from village to village, clacking his wooden blocks to announce his arrival. Baba would whisper, "Don't tell Ma," and she'd nod, knowing that Ma would scold him for such extravagance.

Treats of candy, like meat on the table, were infrequent luxuries. The adults often complained that their lives had grown harsher and scarce goods scarcer after the Japanese attacked Shanghai the first time on January 28, 1932. The "1-2-8 invasion" was a painful reminder of what a war could do to towns like Little Sister's. Any place spared from the devastation of battle faced the chaos of their own Chinese armies in retreat. No one could forget how soldiers seized crops and women for themselves and men as conscripts for labor or armies, driving the lives of the poor farm families deeper into crisis. By 1935, when Little Sister was six, China was gearing up for war again. The demands of the Nationalist armies left the countryside with so little that many families were forced to make impossible choices, deciding who would eat. And who would starve.

One night during those especially lean times, Little Sister lay on the kang, trying to go to sleep. She heard her mother and father talking. In her dreamy fog, she thought her mother said something about giving her away.

Startled, she cried out, "Ma, Ba—don't give me away!"

"Hush, Little Sister," Baba answered. "You're just having a bad dream." His words quieted her, and she soon fell into a sound sleep.

Not long after that nightmare, Baba announced that he would take her on a train ride to Suzhou, sixty miles away toward Shanghai. She remembered every moment of that journey, for she had been giddy that Baba had chosen her, not one of her brothers. She sat on her father's lap, her eyes glued to the window, mesmerized by the neat rice fields and towns just like hers sweeping by in a blur. When they arrived in Suzhou, she was surprised at how much bigger and busier it was than quiet Changzhou. Men and women dressed in fine silk fabrics and even foreign outfits, unlike her mother and father, who wore roughly woven traditional dress. Big posters showed pretty ladies with curly black hair wearing tight *qipao*s, promoting cigarettes, mosquito coils, and rat poison.

When they left the train station, Baba flagged down the driver of a wooden moon-wheeled cart. She clung to her father's arm while perched on the roughhewn plank alongside the wooden wheel. The gnarly driver weaved his way through the mazelike streets and lanes. After a twisting, bumpy ride over arched stone bridges and canals lined by weeping willows, they finally came to a stop at a small store. Inside, her father spoke to the shopkeepers in a low voice while she stood waiting by the door, looking out at the parade of vendors and hawkers on the street. There was so much more to see here than in her town.

Soon Baba called for her and told her to stand still beside him. The shopkeepers looked into her mouth and squeezed her thin arms. When they were finished poking and prodding her, one of them took her hand and led her toward another room. As she turned to look for her father, she saw his back as he headed out the door.

"Baba! Baba!" she had shouted after him. He didn't turn around. "Baba, come back!" she cried. How could he leave without her? The stranger gently pushed her into a small, dank storeroom and locked the door. Alone and terrified of what might lurk in the darkness, at first she could only whimper. Then she steeled herself and called for her father as hard as she could until she grew hoarse and couldn't shout anymore. Exhausted, she sobbed herself to sleep. When the little girl awakened on the musty dirt floor, she thought she had had a terrible nightmare. But when she tried to open the door, it wouldn't budge. She could see the glare of daylight around the cracks. Once again, she screamed for her father. Baba never came.

———

IT SEEMED FOREVER BEFORE she was let out of the storeroom. Blinking from the sudden brightness of daylight, she twisted around, looking for her father as the shopkeeper gripped her arm. But instead of finding Baba this time, she saw a beautiful lady standing nearby, watching and staring intently, as if to study her.

Frightened, Little Sister looked toward the door. Maybe Baba was outside, waiting. But the shopkeeper tightened his hold, keeping her in front of the lady.

"She's a pretty one, but so small and thin," the woman had murmured, her voice not unkind. "Are you sure she's six?"

The shopkeeper nodded, uttering some reassuring words. Apprehensive, Little Sister watched in silence. This woman was nothing like her mother or the other women in her village in Changzhou. This woman seemed soft and delicate, yet she was in charge, letting the shopkeeper know what she wanted. Her smooth, clear skin was not toughened by the sun, like Ma's, and her pretty flowered *qipao*—so different from the dark loose clothing that Ma wore—showed off her figure.

Seemingly satisfied, the lady told Little Sister to come along with her into a pedicab. The girl followed as if in a trance. They stopped at a building that was damp and steamy inside, with rooms that contained big wooden tubs. An attendant removed Little Sister's thin clothes and prepared to immerse her in a tub filled with hot water. At first, Little Sister recoiled in fear. Were they going to cook her?

"This is a bathhouse," said the lady. Little Sister couldn't remember ever having a bath in a big tub before. Then the attendant began scrubbing her from her head to her toes with a soap that smelled like the incense her family lit for Buddha at the start of the New Year. After her bath, the attendant combed her wet hair and dressed her in clothes that the beautiful woman had brought. They were softer and finer than anything Little Sister had ever worn. Her old clothes had disappeared.

The beautiful lady examined her closely. "Good," she said, sounding pleased.

"My name is Madame Hsu," the woman told her. "From now on you may call me Mama."

As they left the bathhouse and climbed into a pedicab, Little Sister saw a shadowy figure of a man not far away. "Baba!" she called out in a panic. Had he come to take her home? Tears filled her eyes.

Madame Hsu quieted her. "Your new home is with me. I am now your mother, and my husband will be your *baba*. You will have a new name too. I will call you Bing."

She explained that the new name was from a famous saying, "*ping shui xiang feng*"—"leaves on water graze" and two strangers meet by chance.

"Do you understand, Bing?" she asked.

"Bing" had no words. She could only nod in assent.

But she didn't understand. What was happening? Where was Baba? How would she find her family now? Where was this pretty lady taking her? So many impossible questions swirled around, each sending shock waves through her body. This must be how the chickens feel when farmers clip their wings and take them to market, she thought. She had seen chickens flap and squawk, desperately trying to escape before their necks were broken. And even after their heads hung limp, they continued to flail in protest. Perhaps she should follow their example and scream out in desperation. She tried, but she couldn't even squawk like a chicken. She was too stunned to cry.

MAMA HSU WAS THE young wife of a government official. To Bing, she looked just like the pretty women on the billboards and posters for the latest movies. Mama Hsu had gone to school to become a nurse and said she would send Bing to school too. She assisted occasionally at the local clinics because she wanted to, she said, not because she had to.

She brought Bing home to a large walled house along one of Suzhou's canals. It looked grander than anything she'd seen in Changzhou. Overnight, Bing found herself in a different world, cared for as though she were a child of money and privilege.

A servant bathed and dressed her, even putting Bing's shoes on for her. This alone took getting used to since she had never worn shoes before. The house was so grand that even the floors were of smooth, lacquered wood—not the dirt or rough, hand-hewn wood she was accustomed to. A cook prepared meals with vegetables, fish, meat, and fine, aromatic rice—delicacies that she had rarely known in Changzhou. Her thin frame grew stronger.

True to her word, Mama Hsu sent Bing to school. Bing had never imagined that she, a girl, would be educated. In her part of Changzhou, only rich families could afford to send children to school, and that expense was almost always reserved for their sons. Her mother in Changzhou had said many times that it was pointless to pay good money to educate a daughter, who would eventually move to a husband's family, just as it was a waste to spend a single fen on candy for a girl.

But Mama Hsu *wanted* Bing to get an education and enrolled her in the nearby primary school. At first, Bing was afraid, worried that a girl like her didn't deserve to be there, that the teachers would tell her to leave because she had been abandoned. But to her delight, she soon discovered that she, too, could learn to read and write. She enjoyed arithmetic and couldn't wait to go to school each day. She did so well that she imagined her *baba* and ma would be glad to take her back once they saw how useful she, a daughter, had become.

In spite of the comforts of her new life in Suzhou, Bing would have traded it all to be back in Changzhou with her *baba*. She awoke feeling sad every day, under a cloud of gloom that followed her everywhere. She looked for Baba whenever she left the house. Sometimes she thought she saw him, only to find a stranger. And for all of Mama Hsu's kindnesses, Bing didn't truly feel accepted as her child. Mama Hsu didn't introduce her as "my daughter" to other people. She had Bing sleep by the kitchen, near the servants. Worst of all, Mama Hsu didn't tell her husband that she'd adopted Bing. Since he was often away, working in Nanjing or elsewhere, he never seemed to notice her when he came home.

Bing might have been able to ignore those slights had Mama Hsu's servants not taken every opportunity to stab at her pain, needling Bing whenever Mama's back was turned. "You think you're better than us?" they sneered. "Madame hasn't told her husband about you because the master doesn't like children—he will never accept you." Or they said, "You'll never find a husband; no one wants a wife from an unknown seed, with no ancestors to give her good luck." They told Bing that Mama Hsu had taken her in only because adopting a young girl was supposed to bring fertility to a childless woman.

Not long after Bing arrived, the servant who was assigned to be her amah played a cruel joke. She informed Bing that Mama Hsu was pregnant and expecting a baby boy. "Do you think she'll want you when she has her own son? They'll put you out to live as a beggar," the amah said. At school, Bing told her teacher that Mama was pregnant. The teacher, in turn, congratulated Mama Hsu. Perplexed, Mama and the teacher asked Bing how she could say such things.

The unkindest cuts came from the children of the servants, who, taking their cues from their parents, were relentless in their torment. "Nobody wants you! Your family gave you away!" they taunted. They ridiculed her new name, a homonym of the Chinese word for bottle."You're a *bing*, an empty bottle. A nothing, a nobody." They took every opportunity to pick at her. Bing wanted to run and hide whenever she saw them, but there was no escape. She grew to hate her name and its constant reminder of her shame.

As time passed, Bing despaired that she could no longer remember the surname of her Changzhou family. It was getting harder to recall details of her father and mother, her two brothers. In her dreams, she imagined she could still trace the curve of her mother's face, the strong muscles in her father's arms, the rough contours of the earthen floor, and the joy she felt whenever her *baba* returned home. But it was also true that her parents had given her away because she was a girl. They would never have given those precious sons away, she knew. And now she was a *bing*, a "nothing." If only she could find her parents and show them all she had learned.

Even those gossamers of hope seemed to slip away as the threat of war with Japan sent Bing's new life with Mama Hsu spinning. Although Bing was happy when she was reunited with Mama and living with her two friends, the news about the assault on Nanjing—China's capital before Shanghai's fall—reached them soon after her arrival, casting a pall of gloom that only grew over their rented room in the new year of 1938. Mama's husband had already fled inland with the Nationalist government for the new wartime capital of Chongqing, but Japanese soldiers ruthlessly killed many thousands of civilians— old people, women, children, even babies. Like Suzhou, Changzhou

Thousands of refugees flee from the devastating Chinese jurisdictions on the north side of the Suzhou Creek, streaming into the International Settlement and its famous Bund via the Waibaidu (Garden) Bridge.

was in the path from Shanghai to Nanjing. What if Bing's parents' home had been flattened like the ones she had seen as her train passed near the Chinese section of Shanghai?

Bing overheard Mama talking with her friends in hushed tones of the Japanese soldiers who raped, killed, and mutilated girls and women in Nanjing, slicing women's breasts off to keep as trophies and ripping babies from their mothers, tossing them in the air to be caught on bay-onet points. When Bing cried out in horror, Mama warned her to stay far away from the Japanese soldiers who patrolled Shanghai, for they, too, might grab a young girl like her and do horrible things.

During the day, while the adults were at work, Bing played in the neighborhood streets and alleys with a girl from the next-door apart-ment. Since Mama didn't know how long they'd be in Shanghai, she didn't enroll Bing in school. Mama added to the list of shady charac-ters for the girl to avoid: beggars, spies, gangsters, puppet police. But Bing was already wary of *all* the strange people she saw: big-nosed foreigners accompanied by Chinese servants in starched white uni-forms; brown-skinned Indian police with thick black beards, curled moustaches, and red turbans; Japanese women in kimonos and high wooden sandals; raggedy beggars huddled in doorways.

With her new playmate, Bing learned to speak the Shanghai dia-lect, which was similar to her Suzhou dialect. Bing found Shanghai pronunciation to be harsh-sounding compared to the soft lilt of Suzhou speech. According to Auntie Fong, the doctor, the Suzhou dialect was so mellifluous that women from that canalled city were considered to be the loveliest in all of China.

Other friends of Mama's, also nurses, sometimes stayed overnight in their one-room home. It was too dangerous for women to travel home alone, especially when nightfall approached. Anyone lucky enough to have a place to stay, no matter how temporary or crowded, made room for friends and relatives in need. Sometimes the women slept in shifts, occupying all available space night and day. At those times, Bing slept on the floor. She didn't mind. The women were all kind to her, as if she were really Mama's daughter, never ridiculing her the way the servants had. On occasion, Mama or the aunties took her around Shanghai by rickshaw, pedicab, or tram to visit the big department stores on Nanjing Road, the beautiful parks in the treelined French Concession, and the ancient City God Temple, set amid the narrow, winding lanes of the Chinese walled city.

After she had spent a few months in Shanghai with Mama and the aunties, removed from the taunts of the servants, the protective shell that contained Bing's sadness seemed to crack ever so slightly. There were brief flashes when she let herself imagine that she could possibly continue to live as Mama Hsu's daughter in this strange and exciting city. When Bing had first arrived in Shanghai, she had often been both startled and thrilled to see men who resembled her *baba*. Then she'd sink into the disappointment of her mistake. But after nearly a year in Shanghai, she understood how difficult it would be to spot her father on the city's crowded streets. In her darkest moments, she wondered if the Japanese had attacked Changzhou and if her *baba* and family were still alive. There was no one she could ask.

As the Japanese occupation dragged on into a second year and the enemy soldiers grew more arrogant and aggressive, Bing overheard Mama and the aunties talk about leaving Shanghai to join the Nationalist government in the deep interior of "Free China," so named because it was not under Japanese occupation. One day in December 1938, Mama received a message via an undercover Nationalist agent who worked with her husband in Chongqing, the distant wartime capital. The plainclothes messenger spoke in a whisper, making hardly a rustle as he came and went. Mama warned Bing not to tell anyone that such a man had stopped by. His message was simple: Mama Hsu's husband wanted her to join him in Chongqing. The man told Mama that the trip would be very difficult, a journey of more than a thousand miles through enemy territory and across battle lines. Traveling on any route was dangerous: The Japanese were bombing the free, unoccupied regions while the retreating Chinese Nationalists were blowing up bridges and rails to prevent them from falling under Japanese control. The plan was for Mama Hsu to accompany the undercover agent when he traveled back to Chongqing.

Bing noticed a change in Mama. Instead of being cheery and bright, she seemed worried and distant. Soon enough, Bing learned the reason. Three years had gone by since Mama Hsu had adopted Bing, but she still had not told her husband about the girl who called her Mama. How then could she take Bing to live with them in Chongqing?

The nine-year-old had assumed that she would be going to Chongqing. But Mama presented her with a terrible choice: Bing could come along with Mama Hsu on the dangerous journey, which would be many times more arduous for a child, Mama told her. Or Bing could stay in Shanghai, and Mama Hsu would find her a new family to live with. "It's *your* choice. Which do *you* prefer?" she asked.

The old hole in Bing's heart ripped open again. Her sadness and shame at being an unwanted girl had never truly left her, and now it came flooding back. She could no longer remember where she had lived in Changzhou. She didn't know her own birth date. The names and faces of her first family—even her *baba*'s—had gradually sifted from her memory. But she was certain of one thing: If Mama really wanted her, she would never have posed such a question. A real mother would take her real daughter with her—that much Bing knew.

It took only a few seconds for Bing to answer. She shrugged her small shoulders and stiffened the shell around her heart. Then she gave the answer she thought Mama wanted to hear: "I guess I'll stay in Shanghai."

When Mama didn't try to dissuade her, the heartbroken girl knew she had been right.

THE NEXT FEW DAYS were a blur as Mama prepared to leave for Chongqing while looking for a new home for Bing. One of the aunties spotted an ad in a newspaper: "Shanghai family wishes to adopt a girl." Mama called the number, and soon a smartly dressed woman named Huiling Woo appeared at their door. Mama and Miss Woo sat at the table. So did Auntie Fong and Auntie Rose. Bing stood nearby, watching and listening intently. While the women sipped tea in the small room, Bing tried to appear casual as she scanned the visitor. To her eyes, Miss Woo was as poised and as beautiful as Mama Hsu, but there was something different about her. She was more like the pale-skinned foreign ladies Bing sometimes saw ordering store clerks and servants around. Unlike Mama, Miss Woo wore a *qipao* that seemed like a second skin around her body, and her face was carefully painted, with rouged lips and cheeks, blue shadows on her eyelids, black eyebrows drawn in perfect arches.

Miss Woo said that she lived with her mother but was going to be married soon. She was looking for a girl to adopt, not a *xiao yatou* housemaid. The girl would be a daughter to her mother and a younger sister to her. Bing could tell that although Miss Woo was a bit younger than Mama and the aunties, she seemed mature and worldly. She spoke loudly and was more direct in her manner compared to their gentler Suzhou ways. She had a Shanghai style and attitude that gave her a confidence that verged on *haipai*, the Shanghai arrogance that Mama Hsu and the aunties sometimes joked about. But *haipai* was a good trait for a woman trying to survive in Shanghai, they all had to admit.

"Bing is a bright child and has attended school for three years. Her education has been interrupted by the war. It's very important that she resume," Mama Hsu said to Miss Woo. "Will you promise to send her to school?"

Miss Woo said that she herself had completed middle school and attended college for a year, until the Japanese war. She promised to continue Bing's education. With that vow, Mama was convinced that Bing would be in good hands. It was decided. Bing would go to live with Miss Woo.

Bing waited expressionless, not happy or sad. Numb. This was how she had felt when the mean servants maligned her, when other children ridiculed her, when she gave up looking for her *baba*. She had no expectations, no wishes, no fears. Miss Woo seemed as good as anyone she might be sent to live with. Going with Miss Woo was better than going to live in the village with a servant. Better than landing on the street as a beggar. At least she would be able to go to school again.

That night, Mama packed a small bundle of clothing for Bing and took her to the apartment where Miss Woo lived with her mother. It was a short distance away, in the French Concession. They climbed the stairs to the second-floor apartment in a large house near French Park. Huiling Woo's mother was a small, hunched-over woman who said little as she looked Bing over. Her hair was pulled tightly back, and she wore a traditional matron's *qipao* that made her look as severe as Huiling was modern.

Since the Woo family appeared to have a decent home for Bing, Mama Hsu was satisfied to leave her. The family even had a telephone—a sign of well-being in such a volatile time. Before Mama said goodbye, she took Bing aside and held her hands. "I'm sorry that I can't bring you along with me, but it is good luck for you to be joining the Woo family before the start of the New Year. Miss Woo promised that she will take good care of you and send you to school. Just in case, I've asked Auntie Fong and Auntie Rose to check up on you. If you ever need to find me, you can go to my uncle's big house in Suzhou; he'll know how to reach me."

Bing nodded. Mama Hsu gave her the address to memorize, and Bing repeated it back.

"Be a good girl, and do as Miss Woo asks," Mama Hsu said. Then she walked out the door. Gone. Just like Bing's father. She didn't cry this time. She was older, and she knew better than to expect anything for herself. She locked the sadness and hurt into a dark place. That would make the pain go away.

Miss Woo put Bing's things in a cabinet and showed her where she would sleep: on a bedroll on the floor next to her mother's bed. "Bing, now you are part of the Woo family. You can call me Elder Sister, and you will call my mother Ma. She is your mother now."

AT TWENTY, HUILING WOO was eleven years older than Bing and the kind of Shanghai woman who bowled people over with her strong personality and big-talking ways. In addition to the Shanghai dialect, she spoke enough English, Japanese, and French in her throaty, cigarette-smoke voice to command attention in any crowded room. Elder Sister seemed to love the good times, nightlife, and opportunities that Shanghai had to offer. She went out almost every night, leaving Bing to stay with Ma.

Soon after Bing moved in, Elder Sister threw a welcome party in the apartment, inviting her close friends and family members to meet her adopted sister. She hired a cook to prepare all of the delicacies that Shanghai was known for: succulent lion's head meatballs, chewy *nian gao* rice cake, tender five-layered pork belly, and steaming hot *xiao*

long bao, the special Shanghai soup dumplings. Ma's sisters came—
Big Abu and Small Abu, along with Auntie Li, Ma's eldest daughter,
and her children. There were also several of Elder Sister's girlfriends,
dressed in the latest Shanghai fashions. They were all there to meet
Bing and welcome her into their family.

"This is a happy day for the Woo family; we have a new daughter
and a new sister. Welcome to Bing!" Elder Sister announced, her voice
booming over the din. "I hope you will all show her every kindness
and treat her as your own kin, for she has joined our Woo family."

Bing was so surprised she could hardly eat the fancy food. She
could never have imagined a party just for her. And unlike the situation in her last mother's household, with the Woos at least there would
be no ambiguity. Everyone knew she was the adopted daughter and
sister. Bing was both embarrassed and relieved to have it out in the
open. Still, the party couldn't fill the empty place that her *baba* used to
inhabit. She felt a pang, too, for Mama Hsu and the Suzhou aunties.
And no party could erase the shame she felt in being abandoned. Not
once but twice.

One day, Auntie Fong, Bing's Suzhou mother's friend, stopped by
the Woos' flat. As usual, she was dressed in a man's Western-style suit,
with a gray fedora on her head.

"I've come to see how you're doing. Are you going to school?" she
asked. Bing answered yes. Elder Sister had enrolled her in Nan Guang
primary school in the French Concession. It was so close by that Bing
could see the children playing in the schoolyard from the apartment window.

But Bing didn't tell Auntie Fong about the other changes in her life.
In Suzhou, servants had taken care of her every need. At the Woo apartment, it was different. Not only did she have to quickly learn how to
wash, dress, and feed herself, but she also had to attend to Ma. Bing had
never known anyone so demanding. Whenever Ma shouted, "Bing!"
the nine-year-old was expected to bring her hot tea, pound on her back,
straighten up the apartment—whatever Ma wanted.

Bing was stunned by this sudden reversal. She tried to please Ma, to
do whatever she asked, even though Bing had never done such things
before. Setting up the opium pipe and lamp was especially challeng-

ing. Ma needed Bing's help with her paraphernalia, but she didn't trust Bing to handle the expensive "black gold" that she bought from the itinerant peddler.

When Ma's sisters or friends stopped by, Bing was to bring out the opium pipe and accessories. Ma and her visitors would lie down in her bedroom as the sweet, unmistakable fragrance filled the air. Once when Bing was cleaning up, Ma accused her of throwing out some tiny scraps of the drug. Ma flew into a rage, berating Bing for hours. "Stupid girl, you are no better than a mule's penis!" When Ma was cross, she lashed out at Bing with her endless nagging in the most florid language. That was yet another part of Bing's new life.

She had to fight back her tears the first several times that Ma scolded her. Then she realized that Ma cursed Elder Sister just as often. When Elder Sister took Bing out to see a movie or to shop with her at the big department store with the moving stairs, Ma would direct a torrent of angry words at Elder Sister as soon as they walked through the door: "If you spend money like a whore, then go out and get money like a whore! Even a beggar on the street is smarter than you!" No matter what Ma said, Elder Sister never talked back, never seemed bothered by the harshness, never said a sharp word in reply. Bing tried hard to do the same.

School offered Bing a welcome relief from Ma's volatile temperament. Walking the few blocks to get there, when she looked south from the French Concession toward the Chinese jurisdiction, she could see only charred rubble before her, the devastated remains from the intensive Japanese bombing raids. She imagined that Mama Hsu was headed to a war zone like that. She wants me to be safe in Shanghai, to spare me from the bombs, Bing told herself.

Elder Sister's busy social life kept Ma's critical eye distracted from Bing. Elder Sister and her girlfriends often went out dancing. They were mindful to stay in the foreign concessions and to avoid the Badlands where gangsters and the puppet police ran wild. But Ma harangued Elder Sister anyway, warning her that women out at night had to be on alert for rapacious soldiers, sailors, crooked police, gangsters, and assorted other Shanghai ne'er-do-wells.

Bing learned to recognize the other tenants, including the famous

Shanghai movie director Bu Wancang and his girlfriend, but she soon realized that she had to be very cautious in her own building. A new tenant, a single man named Mr. Lo, had moved into the room on the floor below. He was a pleasant man. Whenever he saw Bing, he made a point of asking, "How's the young miss today?" He whistled a cheerful but unrecognizable tune the way her father used to. Ma was suspicious of him. He never had visitors, but he occasionally knocked on Ma's door, asking to use the telephone. Ma would pretend to be busy while she listened in on his conversations—almost always about arranging meetings at different hotels in Shanghai. One day, a dozen or so police officers came bounding up the stairs looking for Mr. Lo. They forced his door open and searched his room.

As Bing peeked over the stairwell, Ma whispered, "These are not ordinary police; they are from 76," referring to the deadly police headquarters at 76 Jessfield Road. The police found a gun and concluded that Mr. Lo must have been an underground agent for the Nationalists, tasked to kill Japanese and traitors. Ma murmered, "When they find him and take him to 76, he'll wish he were dead." After the police from 76 left the building, Ma got on the phone and called her sisters and friends, describing her brush with 76 and the would-be Nationalist assassin downstairs. When she finished her calls, she wagged her finger at Bing. "Remember, you must never trust any strangers, not even if they smile at you. They might have guns and kill you!"

BY THEN BING HAD learned to nod in silent agreement at whatever Ma said, no matter how outrageous. As Ma frequently pointed out, the streets of Shanghai were full of children abandoned or orphaned by war. The girls were likely to end up as virtual slaves in households, sweatshops, or brothels if they didn't die first from hunger. Bing was lucky to have been adopted, Ma would insist. Occasionally, Bing allowed herself to think about her gentle Suzhou mother and her kindly ways. She wondered where Mama Hsu was now. Maybe the Year of the Rabbit, 1939, would be a luckier year for Bing. But she knew better than to count on it.

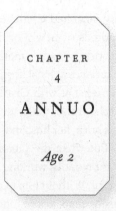

CHAPTER
4

ANNUO

Age 2

SHANGHAI, 1937

THE TINY GIRL COWERED IN FRIGHT FROM THE LOUD BLASTS and the shrill whistle of the missiles that streaked toward their targets on August 13, 1937, that terrible day when the war with Japan came to Shanghai. The walls of her family's small flat in the French Concession seemed to recoil from the rain of bombs on the Chinese jurisdiction just a few blocks south of them. Little Annuo Liu crouched in a corner. Her five-year-old brother, Charley, tried to reassure her. "Don't be afraid; I'll protect you," he promised as the windows rattled. He told her the stories he heard in school, about patriotic Boy Scouts and Girl Guides only a little older than they who were delivering messages and ammunition across enemy lines to aid China's cause.

After days, then weeks, of the unending cacophony of war, the little girl no longer ran for cover with each explosion, but her eyes still widened with alarm when the floor shook beneath her feet and the acrid smell of charred wood and burning diesel filled her home. The Imperial Japanese Command had introduced a new military tactic in the course of their attack on Shanghai: the relentless aerial bombing of civilian areas, designed to terrorize and annihilate the population. The Nazi Luftwaffe would later employ the same type of blitz attacks over Europe.

Countless civilians were killed or maimed in the massive destruction of Shanghai's densely inhabited Chinese neighborhoods. People rushed to the aid of hundreds of newly orphaned babies, donating money, food, beds, and diapers. Annuo's mother, Shangying, jumped at the chance to offer her services at local hospitals. She was trained as a physician but had been pregnant with Charley when she graduated at the top of her medical school class and hadn't yet gone into medical practice. After her son was born, her husband, Yongchio, had discouraged her from working. But when the Japanese attacked Shanghai, Yongchio had been away for months, working for the Nationalist government in a distant province. Without him to dissuade her, she rushed to the makeshift hospitals to tend to the injured and sick, exposing herself each day to the risk of enemy fire. Annuo anxiously followed her mother to the door when she left each morning.

The young girl would wait by the window for Muma, as she called her mother, in the Shanghai dialect. When Muma came home, disturbing smells would waft in with her: disinfectant, rubbing alcohol, gunpowder, vomit, blood. After her mother changed clothes and washed away the frightening odors, Annuo would feel more at ease. Muma said the Chinese army was bravely continuing to fight the Japanese in Shanghai in order to give the government time to retreat. People and equipment were moving far inland, nearer to where Annuo's father had been working to establish the Republic of China's fledgling Nationalist administration in spite of the growing influence of the Communists among China's peasant farmers.

After nearly three months, the saturation bombing finally stopped. By the end of October 1937, the Chinese army was in full retreat. Japanese martial law was imposed on the Chinese sections of Shanghai. "The enemy is in control now," Muma warned Annuo and Charley. "You mustn't tell anyone about your father's work."

The two children were never put to the test, for word of the Chinese defeat and the Japanese occupation of Shanghai soon reached Annuo's father, Yongchio Liu, stationed in the southwestern province of Guizhou, more than eleven hundred miles away. Millions of retreating soldiers and residents of China's east coast migrated toward that inland region. With more of China falling under Japanese military rule, her father worried about his family's safety. He dispatched a courier to Shanghai with an urgent message for his wife: Leave the enemy-occupied city at once, and join him in Free China.

MUMA HAD TO PLAN a circuitous trip around the war zones: First she booked their passage to Indochina on the *Empress of Japan*. It galled her to take the enemy's ship, but there was no other choice when Emperor Hirohito's navy controlled the harbor. At least they wouldn't bomb their own vessels, she reasoned. Once in Indochina, they would have to cross mountainous jungles on dirt roads and remote waterways to journey back into China from the south until they reached Guizhou.

Charley was terribly seasick most of the way. But not Annuo. The cheery girl was friendly and playful, glad to make so many new friends on the trip. She sang and danced at every opportunity, happily entertaining her captive audience. But long and difficult trips to escape danger were nothing new for Annuo. From the time she was born in 1935, she'd been moved from one place to another in search of a safe haven.

In 1935, Yongchio Liu had decided that he and Shangying Dai would stop living the pampered party life of Shanghai socialites. They had come of age when Shanghai was at the peak of its bright and hopeful decade that began in 1927, after Generalissimo Chiang Kai-shek united various regional warlords under his leadership while crippling his Communist rivals. Annuo's parents and their generation of forward-looking Chinese intellectuals had reveled in the possibilities of a brave new Republic of China. During those ten years of Nationalist rule before Japan's invasion, the Chinese republic envisioned by its founder, Sun Yat-sen, had finally seemed within reach.

Yongchio and Shangying were students in Shanghai then. Both born into wealthy, landowning merchant families, they had been pulled toward the dynamic, magnetic city from the neighboring provinces of Anhui and Jiangsu. They met by chance at the home of a mutual friend—she an aspiring doctor at Dongnan Medical School, he a charming, ambitious student at Dongwu Law School.

Annuo's parents epitomized the Chinese republic's brief golden age. They were eager to break from the old ways of the feudal dynasties. Shangying had been a girl who was determined to get an education. After convincing her father to halt the agonizing foot-binding process that had begun to mutilate her feet, she had then persuaded him to send her to school. Yongchio had had his own childhood challenges, becoming the head of his family at the age of eight. Dressed in fine robes and carried to meetings with advisers in a sedan chair like a child emperor, he had been tasked to make the important decisions about the family's welfare and business enterprises. When Shangying and Yongchio first met, they had long been betrothed to others through marriage contracts that would benefit their families. But in Shanghai, where audiences flocked to movie palaces to watch films of romance and adventure, a new generation of Chinese wanted marriages based on love. To the dismay of their families, Shangying and Yongchio broke their respective engagement contracts and took their vows in a newfangled love marriage.

As an educated young couple in Shanghai's boom years of the late twenties and early thirties, Annuo's mother and father enjoyed the thrills that the big city could offer its privileged elites. A newly minted lawyer, Annuo's father entered a law practice that defended petty criminals. Some may well have been linked to the Green Gang, the city's largest criminal syndicate. Regardless of that, he was paid handsomely at a time when businesses soared in the years after Chiang Kaishek and the Green Gang worked together to kill off labor leaders and suspected Communists. Construction projects boomed, with each new building more extravagant than the last. China's upper crust—the bourgeoisie of wealthy businesspeople and the big landholders from rural areas—flocked to the international city. So too did profiteers and adventurers from around the world. A flourishing middle class of professionals, intellectuals, and shopkeepers emerged to meet the city's growing needs. Publishing houses, modern schools, hospitals, and universities blossomed in those gilded years.

On Yongchio's extravagant salary, Annuo's parents embraced Shanghai's glamour: its skyscrapers, elevators, automobiles, electric lights, telephones, indoor plumbing—all the conveniences of a new era. They danced at glitzy nightclubs with big bands, dined at foreign restaurants that served *ching lung*—Western-style cuisine made palatable to Chinese tastes. They rented apartments in the brand-new buildings that sprang up like bamboo in the foreign concessions, with more modern conveniences than were widely available in New York or London. The international set and foreign intelligentsia—from Charlie Chaplin, Albert Einstein, and Bertrand Russell to George Bernard Shaw, Eugene O'Neill, Emily Hahn, Noël Coward, and W. H. Auden—visited the blossoming Chinese city.

Shangying and Yongchio were part of a generation looking toward China's rebirth in a bright and modern future. In 1932, a year after their marriage, their son, Charley, was born. Annuo came along three years later.

But Shanghai's golden decade had come at a steep cost. Following the birth of the Chinese republic in 1912, the conservative wing of the Nationalist Party, with which Chiang Kai-shek was associated, was challenged by several competing warlords, parties, and factions, including the Communists. To consolidate his power as he unified China militarily, in 1927, Chiang embarked on eliminating his Communist rivals in Shanghai and other industrial cities. In the words of the consul general of the French Concession, Chiang made a "pact with the devil" by joining forces with Shanghai's powerful and notorious Green Gang. The gang's leader was Du Yuesheng, known as "Big-Ear Du" for his prominent earlobes. Du claimed to command one hundred thousand armed thugs—more foot soldiers than in all the foreign garrisons combined—and could mobilize them at a moment's notice.

With the aid of British, French, and American authorities, the unholy alliance of Nationalists and Green Gang mounted a bloody massacre of labor activists, leftists, and Communists on the streets of Shanghai. The "White Terror" extermination campaign began on April 12, 1927, and continued for several weeks. Chiang's henchmen executed suspected leftists and labor activists on the spot. Women sporting bobbed hair were meted out special punishment for their modern hairdos: After torture and execution, their decapitated heads were placed on men's headless bodies to mock the women's "radical" behavior. The violent purge spread to other cities, until the leftists and Communists were driven deep underground and into the hinterlands, where Chairman Mao would greatly strengthen his base among the struggling farmers of rural China.

Shanghai's capitalists and industrialists flourished in the golden decade of the bourgeoisie, with labor demands and disruptions quelled in China's most industrialized city. But not everyone reveled in Shanghai's burgeoning wealth. The vast majority of the city's population lived in poverty and squalor just beyond the fashionable foreign concessions. Yongchio's elder brother, a renowned Paris-educated bacteriologist, scorned what he saw as his brother's self-absorbed pursuit of Shanghai's good times. He dismissed Yongchio as a playboy, a label that many Chinese applied to wealthy young men who spent dissolute days and nights partaking of Shanghai's temptations.

By the time Annuo was born, her father was ready to quit his party life. Perhaps the growing patriotic fervor against Japan's aggressions prompted his change of heart. He, too, came to believe that his extravagant life, funded by his defense of criminals, was decadent. When his close friend, photographer Wu Yinxian, decided to join the Communists to fight the Japanese, Yongchio intended to accompany him. At the last minute, he came down with a fever and couldn't go, while his friend became Mao's personal photographer. Yongchio soon found another calling when the new Nationalist governor of Guizhou offered him a job as an administrator helping to bring that distant province under the seven-year-old government's authority. Like many Chinese who were moved by patriotism more than by ideology, Annuo's father didn't draw a big distinction between the parties. He accepted the challenge to help strengthen China.

Annuo's father had departed for remote Guizhou just days after she was born. Thinking that his wife and children would be safer living in his mother's household, he dispatched them to his hometown of Yangzhou, about 170 miles to the northwest of Shanghai. That was the beginning of newborn Annuo's life as *taonan* running to escape from the dangers of war. But Yongchio's mother resented the educated woman who had broken up her son's arranged betrothal, and she made Shangying's life miserable. After two years trying to please an intractable mother-in-law, Annuo's mother packed up the children and returned to Shanghai, having decided that she'd be better off alone as a single mother in the city than spending another moment with inhospitable in-laws. For a brief time, she put her hard-won medical education to use, helping to treat the overwhelming number of casualties in the weeks following Bloody Saturday—until her husband sent for her and the children.

As Japan's invasion and occupation engulf Shanghai in 1937, Annuo's physician-trained mother, Shangying Dai, must soon flee with the two-year-old and her five-year-old brother, Charley.

NOW TWO-YEAR-OLD ANNUO WAS a *taonan* again, this time running from occupied Shanghai to join her Nationalist father in Guizhou. He had left so soon after her birth that he was a stranger to her. After singing and dancing her way across Indochina and the southernmost Chinese border, Annuo finally came face-to-face with him. The toddler stared at the handsome man who was tall and commanding in his khaki Nationalist uniform. She watched as he laughed and joked with the people around him, all of them deferring to his every word. Muma had told her and Charley that their father was an important man who ruled over the entire county for the Nationalist government.

The towering man in the uniform finally spotted her as she tried to hide behind her mother's skirt. He bellowed to her, "Come here!" Annuo jumped and shrank back even farther. She peeked out and saw him studying her, his face registering disapproval. Then he turned to her mother and asked, "Is there something wrong with her? She looks like my worthless ninth sister." Young Annuo sensed that she should stay out of her father's way.

To Annuo's relief, her father was too busy to pay attention to her. He was the chief magistrate for the region surrounding the town of Pingba in Guizhou, in charge of consolidating the control of the young Nationalist government and enforcing its laws. Annuo learned from the servants that people respected her father for his fairness. He hadn't forced the local people to burn their opium fields, their only source of income, as his superiors had commanded. Instead, he found more gradual ways to bring people to his administration's side of the law.

When Annuo was almost four, her brother, Charley, learned that an execution was to take place the next morning—their father had ordered the beheading of some criminals. Charley persuaded Annuo to go watch with him. The two got up early but arrived too late. By the time they reached the square, the severed heads of the condemned men were already stuck atop poles, on display. Annuo closed her eyes, but Charley described the scene to her in graphic detail anyway. When her father found out they had gone to the execution grounds, he shouted at them in fury. Annuo ran to hide, afraid of how he might punish her.

Growing numbers of Chinese were fleeing the Japanese occupation in coastal cities like Shanghai and migrating to the inland zones of Free China, to the wartime capital, Chongqing, and such areas as Guizhou. Important-looking people in uniforms often visited to pay their respects to the magistrate.

Annuo's mother was busy being hostess to all the visitors. Even though there was a great need for doctors, her husband insisted that she no longer practice medicine. The man she had wed in a Western-style love marriage had changed, despite his assurances to her father that she could put her education to use. His reputation now meant more than his promise or her wishes—he could not tolerate losing face by having a working wife. Even with her modern education, Annuo's mother couldn't buck the weight of tradition that dictated she acquiesce to her husband.

Two years in Guizhou passed quickly through the scorching hot summers of the region known as "the furnace of China." Annuo was soon speaking the local country dialect like a native. She played games in the courtyard of their government housing compound, running around with big brother Charley and other officials' children. But in Free China, she also learned to run for cover when the air-raid siren sounded. The children played "war," fighting against a pretend enemy, while on alert for real Japanese planes that flew bombing raids over the region every day. Charley wore a pint-sized Nationalist uniform, and for a long time, he refused to wear anything else. He'd stand tall in the khaki jacket and pants, his hair slicked back and chest puffed out, trying to mimic their powerful father. Toward the end of those two years, Annuo's sister, Li-Ning, was born—a happy event in their rural outpost.

BY LATE 1939, JAPAN'S modern air armada had stepped up attacks on the interior. The Nationalists had no antiaircraft weapons to defend against the onslaught. More than thirty million Chinese had migrated inland with Chiang's Nationalist government, bringing with them the machines of a thousand factories in order to maintain the war effort. These newcomers carried libraries, schools, laboratories, hospitals for more than a thousand miles—often on foot—carving out caves in mountainsides to protect their new locations. The Nationalist capital of Chongqing was subjected to daily saturation bombings as part of Japan's scorched-earth approach of "Kill all, loot all, burn all." The invader's planes flew close to the ground with so little opposition that survivors reported seeing the faces of the pilots and gunners as they mowed down civilians. Thousands of men, women, and children were killed, many while seeking safety in air-raid shelters that were specifically targeted by Japanese bombers.

Because Guizhou was two hundred miles away from Chongqing, it didn't suffer the same intensity of air attacks as the capital. But a nearby southern supply route to the Nationalists through Burma had been carved out of rugged mountain terrain by two hundred thousand laborers, with the help of U.S. General Joseph Stilwell's troops. To disrupt the Burma Road, a furious Japan increased its bombing attacks. Annuo's father decided it was time to move his family again. This time he concluded that Shanghai's foreign settlements would be safer for his family, even if the Japanese occupiers surrounded the solitary island of the concessions.

The journey back to Shanghai would be far more dangerous than their difficult trip two years earlier at the start of the war. It would take four months of circuitous travel through the even more remote provinces of Yunnan and Guangxi, then to Hong Kong via Indochina to avoid the Japanese. Along any part of the route, they could encounter the enemy—certain death for a Nationalist family. By then, Annuo was a veteran at running for cover as soon as she heard the sound of airplanes, knowing her small legs would have to outrun the bombs and machine guns.

But the girl's strongest impression during the long trip came when she saw her mother take a bad fall as they tried to skirt the war zone. When the bus that was to take them across Southeast Asia finally arrived and was ready for boarding, Annuo and Charley scrambled aboard to grab seats on the crowded vehicle. Their mother followed slowly, cradling their infant sister. But this time, their mother's feet, forever crippled from the binding initiated in her childhood, gave way as she climbed into the bus.

Annuo watched in horror as her mother went crashing down to the pavement, headfirst. "Muma!" Annuo screamed as she saw her mother twist her body and bend forward to protect baby Li-Ning. Muma landed on her head. Li-Ning was unhurt, but her mother lay on the ground, her head cut and bleeding. Afraid that her mother was dead, Annuo couldn't stop crying—first out of fear, then in relief when she saw her mother try to sit up.

After her head was bandaged, Shangying wobbled up the steep

steps again. Annuo's father commented: "Good job, you saved the baby."

Two years earlier, Annuo had been the belle of the journey. On this trip, however, she was fearful and jittery. Somehow her mother managed to persevere through the long bus ride, her head swathed in a bloody bandage. Annuo clung to Muma, needing to feel her mother's warmth, to know that she was there. Her mother had always been the strong and stoic one, the lioness guarding her cubs. Under her mother's watchful eye, Annuo had always felt safe. Now she was less sure.

WHEN THE FAMILY FINALLY reached Shanghai in the late fall of 1939, they returned to their familiar neighborhood in the French Concession. They rented the same small apartment at 474 Rue Lafayette where Annuo's father had lived as a law student. It was nothing like the fine residences her parents had had when they were living the high life, before Annuo was born. But the enemy-occupied Shanghai of 1939 was very different from the city in its gilded age of the late twenties and early thirties. With the foreign concessions surrounded by the Japanese occupation force, Nationalist loyalists and sympathizers were targets for assassination. The foreign concessions were the epicenter of intrigue and violence in the city. Annuo's father, the Nationalist and former magistrate, would be a prime target.

One afternoon that autumn, not long after they had moved into the apartment on Rue Lafayette, Annuo was playing in the main room when her father entered with his coat on, a small travel bag in hand. Her mother sat nearby, holding Annuo's baby sister.

"My commanding officer, General Han Deqin, has been appointed governor of the Nationalist resistance forces in Jiangsu Province," he said to Muma. "He has asked me to be his aide."

Annuo saw her mother's eyebrows arch in surprise over the top of her round wire-rimmed eyeglasses.

"I'm going to join him, to fight behind enemy lines." It was the same firm tone he had used when issuing commands in Guizhou.

For a few moments, her mother was silent.

"What about your family, your children, the baby?" she finally asked.

"China must come first. If we lose to Japan, my children won't have a future worth living," he replied.

The worried look on her mother's face alarmed Annuo.

Then her father asked, "How much money do we have?" Without waiting for her mother's response, he added, "Give it all to me."

In silence, Annuo's mother rose with Li-Ning in her arms. She reached into a drawer and pulled out a small purse. As she emptied it, handing him every yuan inside, she asked, bewildered, "How will I feed our children?"

He shrugged. "Ask Shu-shu for money." Uncle Shu-shu, Annuo's father's best friend from law school, had married Muma's younger sister.

Annuo's father turned to leave. As his hand reached for the doorknob, her mother asked in a clear voice, "Don't you want to say goodbye to the children?" She held out the baby to him.

For a split second, Annuo thought her father hesitated. Or maybe she imagined it, for he walked out the door and pulled it shut. Not even a goodbye to her and Charley.

Annuo ran to the window overlooking Rue Lafayette. Pressing her palms and forehead against the glass, she watched as her father stepped out into the cold afternoon, the sky graying as the sun dipped below the trees and nearby buildings. His back was straight and his stride long. In Guizhou, her father had worn a Nationalist uniform, but in Shanghai, it was too dangerous. He dressed in plain Western-style clothes—both he and Charley had been forced to leave their uniforms behind.

Her breath fogged the glass, and she turned to peek at her mother. The baby was still asleep, and her mother's expression was blank. She clutched Li-Ning to her bosom. Annuo felt a twinge of envy. At five, she was too big for that kind of attention but she wanted Muma to hold her. Instead, she searched her mother's face for reassurance. None came. Annuo's father had been their protector, the imposing man whom everyone in Guizhou admired and obeyed. Who would protect them now?

AFTER HER FATHER LEFT for the Jiangsu front, Muma followed his instructions, including his wish that she not look for work. She went to Uncle Shu-shu and asked him for money. He earned a good salary as a lawyer for an American company. After a few visits, Uncle Shu-shu handed her some bills and looked down at the parquet floor. "This is all we can spare," he said. "Now we are digging into our children's *hong bao*"—their New Year's savings.

His message was clear: She was now taking money from his children. She couldn't go back for any more.

Annuo's mother held out for as long as she could, cutting back on every conceivable expense. Though the Japanese military didn't enter the foreign concessions, it was restricting the flow of food and other essentials into the city. The cost of rice was so high that Muma could afford only plain corn mush for the family. She served it for days on end. It tasted so bad that Annuo could barely swallow it, no matter how hungry she was. Finally, her mother knew she had no choice but to find a job, in spite of her husband's opposition.

It wouldn't be an easy search with her husband a known Nationalist. Applying for work would be tricky and dangerous. The Chinese officials who ran the government under the Japanese occupation were all puppets of the enemy—collaborators, traitors to the Chinese people. Anyone who checked her medical credentials might find her husband's identity. If they did, she could be hauled off to the puppets' police headquarters at 76 Jessfield Road, where she'd be questioned, tortured, or killed. Nobody left 76 alive, it was said. Then what would become of the children?

Through sheer serendipity, Annuo's mother saw a job posting while looking for a primary school near their apartment for eight-year-old Charley. A sign posted on its bulletin board read: "School Doctor or Nurse Needed—Apply Within." She got the job by producing her diploma from Dongnan Medical School; no other background check was required. The job was perfect, for she was unlikely to run into former associates who might know her. Because she worked for the school, Charley could enroll for a reduced fee. An added bonus was that Annuo could enter kindergarten, even though she was younger than the other students.

At first, school was a nightmare for Annuo. She had lived in Guizhou from the ages of two to four and had learned the local dialect. When she opened her mouth, the strong country accent tumbled out, completely unintelligible in Shanghai. Nor could she understand the Shanghai dialect. Other children teased her, calling her "stupid" and "country bumpkin." That much she understood. She hated the bullies and was afraid to be around them. After a few intolerable months of ridicule, she was speaking Shanghainese as if she had never been gone, her embarrassing Guizhou dialect banished forever. She found other children to befriend—ones who didn't call her names. School became her stable refuge from all the running, moving, and talk of war.

As the last day of the school year approached, Muma bought Annuo a beautiful rose-colored organza dress. A celebration was planned for the graduating children, and the dress would be perfect. Annuo waited expectantly as the teachers called each child by name, handing out a certificate to mark his or her successful completion of kindergarten. Each child also received a special gift—a fancy pencil box full of erasers, rulers, and other treasures. Annuo couldn't wait to get hers. Before long, all the children in the class were standing at the front of the room, holding their trophies—except for Annuo. When she was the only one left seated, a teacher handed her a notice and informed her of its message written in red ink: "Repeat kindergarten."

The mean children who had teased her before now snickered and pointed at her. She struggled to keep the tears from flowing. The paper burned in her hand while she counted the minutes until she could leave. Finally the school bell rang. Annuo ran all the way home. By the time she'd reached her building, she was sobbing. Once inside the vestibule, she wrapped her arms around the cool lacquered baluster of the staircase, as though it could comfort her.

When her mother found Annuo at the bottom of the stairs, Muma gently pried her away. Glancing at the teacher's note, her mother said, "I asked the school to hold you back a year. You're so much younger than the other children. With your difficulties learning the Shanghai dialect, this will be best for you."

Her own mother held her back? Annuo's heart couldn't have sunk any lower. Especially when Muma often told her and Charley the proud stories of her own childhood achievements. Eventually Annuo followed her mother upstairs. She was glad that her father wasn't there to see her shame. Her rosy dress, limp and wrinkled, had turned ugly.

THERE WAS ONE PERSON in the building at 474 Rue Lafayette whom Annuo looked up to: Zhonghe Yu, the teenaged second daughter of their landlord. Zhonghe lived downstairs and had long, flowing black hair that she clasped in a tortoiseshell barrette. In spite of their age difference, Zhonghe always greeted her little neighbor with a radiant smile, asking her about school or her day. The kindly teenager never failed to lift Annuo's spirits, assuring her that all would be well. Whenever she could, Annuo lingered by the front of the building, waiting to see her idol.

One day in the fall of 1940, as the war against Japan entered its fourth year, Zhonghe's mother ran out of their apartment building in tears, a crumpled note crushed in her hands. Zhonghe had run away with some friends to fight the Japanese enemy. She and her idealistic schoolmates wanted to do their part to liberate China. "Has anyone seen Zhonghe?" her mother cried out. "Does anyone know where she went?"

Within a few days, she had her answer. Zhonghe and her girlfriends had encountered some Japanese troops at a river crossing. Their bodies were found by the river: raped, bayoneted, and discarded.

A pall fell over 474 Rue Lafayette. Annuo no longer lingered at the front door. Instead, she ran quickly to her apartment, not wanting to face Zhonghe's family, not knowing what to say. Annuo had never known this word *bayonet* before, though she was too familiar with the word *war*. Suddenly its horror was clear and stark. What kind of cruel people could hurt someone as kind and gentle as Zhonghe? she wondered. It was Annuo's first lesson on the tragedy of war. It would not be her last.

CHILDHOOD UNDER SIEGE

SHANGHAI, 1939

TWO YEARS AFTER THE BOMBS HAD FALLEN NEAR HIS GRAND-father's home, Benny Pan and his schoolmates continued to speak of Bloody Saturday, the terrible juncture of their time. It was the moment when their safe, protected lives in the foreign concessions became vulnerable to the enemy threat that now violated their formerly untouchable sanctum.

Yet in spite of that shocking event, the daily routines of middle- and upper-class children hadn't changed significantly. With the passing months, the battlefront had moved farther away. Meanwhile, everyday life in polyglot Shanghai simply carried on. The British asserted, "Keep a stiff upper lip." *C'est la guerre,* shrugged the Franco-phones in their concession. "When the eaves are low, you must bow your head," the Chinese repeated to one another. Police, bankers, tex-tile workers, business managers, and coolies went to work each day. Journalists filled the multitude of newspapers and magazines under the watchful eyes of pro-Japan censors. Buses, trams, automobiles, and streetcars plied the streets crowded with rickshaws, pedicabs, and hand-pulled carts. Peddlers and hawkers called out in English, French, Shanghainese, Cantonese—every conceivable dialect and language. The sweet seduction of brothels and opium dens still beckoned while the gambling halls throbbed with the whir of roulette wheels and constant click-click of mah-jongg tiles.

Well-to-do Shanghai schoolboys had no fears of conscription at a time when country boys their age, lacking strings to pull or money to hire surrogates, were dying at a shocking rate, with hundreds of thousands sometimes killed in a single battle. "Don't use good iron to make bullets," was the saying among the privileged. In the rarefied world of Shanghai's foreign concessions, Benny and his friends could attend to the more refined interests of school and sports, cars and comics, dances and girls.

Benny's daily life couldn't have been more different from life in the battle-scarred Chinese jurisdictions. Each morning, his amah roused him from sleep, helped him wash and dress for school, and pushed him to eat his breakfast of *qifan*, rice porridge, with eggs and pickled vegetables. "Hurry, Young Master. If you're late, it will greatly displease your mother and father," she urged when he dawdled. She prodded and pecked like a hen, hustling Benny and his school-aged siblings together for inspection by their mother, if she was up, or their father, if he had not yet left for the police station. While Benny fidgeted, waiting in line with his three sisters to greet their parents, his amah tied his shoelaces and smoothed his hair.

If his mother wasn't too tired after a long night of mah-jongg with her friends, she would come to the door to give them a quick glance and a nod. Her days as a society matron were filled with the details of running the household and the demands of entertaining for her husband, who was becoming prominent in certain circles. Benny looked forward to his mother's gentle reminder, "Be a good boy, and mind your manners."

His father's appearances were becoming less frequent and therefore even more special. The proud Number One Son would stand as tall as he could, his starched white shirt tucked into his gray schoolboy slacks. His father would furrow his brow as if reviewing his former Shanghai Volunteer Corps "C" Company before a dress parade. Under his glare, Benny tried to look straight ahead, but he couldn't resist an admiring look back at his father, so magnificent in his impeccable Shanghai Municipal Police inspector's uniform. Sometimes, if Benny was lucky, his father would pat him on the head and say, "Make me proud today, Long-Long."

"Yes, sir," Benny would reply with a snap. To his mind, there was no better way for a boy to start his day.

Then the eleven-year-old was off to St. John's Junior Middle School, part of the preparatory pipeline that would lead to St. John's University, his father's college. When Benny was younger, he had taken a pedicab to school each day, as his sisters still did. But now that he was almost a teenager, he rode his bicycle whenever the weather allowed. Along the way he'd meet up with his chums, and they'd ride the mile to school together. From their bikes, the boys would peruse their favorite confectionary shops, scouting for new goodies that they could stop and taste on their way home.

When classes ended, the boys would hop onto their bikes with a whoop. They'd head back to the shops that they had noted on their way to school that morning, ready to pick out some treats. Together, they studied movie posters outside the Cathay Theatre and thumbed comic books at the bookstalls. Among Benny's favorite after-school stops were DD's on Bubbling Well Road for a sandwich or hot chocolate and the popular French bakery for its famous chestnut cake.

The schoolboys paid no mind to the various political parties and factions around them, which were heatedly debating the future of China, some resorting to terror and assassination on the very streets where the boys biked. Pro-Nationalists argued that the war could end if only the Brits and Yanks would help China halt Japan's onslaught. They denounced their opponents as enemy collaborators and traitors. On the other extreme were those calling for cooperation with the Japanese to end the hostilities and to rid China of the Euro-American imperialists. Such arguments meant little to schoolboys like Benny when the foreign concessions acted as their protective bubble.

Beyond Shanghai, the Nationalists had lost vast swaths of territory to Japan. Only the sheer grit and determination of China's fighting forces had kept the enemy from advancing farther inland. Tokyo had expected to conquer China within three months. Two years of grinding war had gone by with no end in sight. What the Chinese forces lacked in matériel and skill, they made up for with courage and numbers in an uneasy united front of Chiang's Nationalist forces, Mao's Communist guerrillas, and various regional warlord armies. Their tenacious resistance came at a high price for civilians. Chinese troops slowed the Imperial Army by destroying China's bridges and rail lines, sinking their own commercial ships in waterways, and giving up human casualties and territory in a cruel bargain for more time. In one instance, as many as eight hundred thousand civilians drowned after the Nationalist army blew up dams holding back the Yellow River, the second longest in China, to impede the Japanese advance.

By early 1939, Japan controlled the Chinese coastline from Manchuria in the north to Hainan Island at the southernmost point. The Nationalist government had been able to move military and industrial resources inland, but Chiang Kai-shek desperately needed international support. In spite of urgent appeals from the generalissimo and his eloquent American-educated wife, Soong May-ling, the British and American governments were hesitant to offer assistance. China continued to fight the war alone.

After the bombing of the Shanghai South railway station in August 1937, this photo of a burned baby brought worldwide attention to Japan's military strategy in China: to terrorize the civilian population with saturation bombings and a scorched-earth campaign of total destruction.

To the comfortable schoolboys who had grown up with so many beggars around them, the swarms of newly impoverished refugees from the flattened battlegrounds seemed to blend into the scenery. More than a million people made homeless by war had packed into the International Settlement and French Concession. They followed the well-fed boys with their hungry eyes, ready to grab a carelessly held package or treat. Beggars huddled in alleys and unattended spaces between buildings, just beyond the reach of shopkeepers' broomsticks.

Blinded by their own good fortune and privilege, the children of Shanghai's elite didn't notice when their own neighbors couldn't afford to buy food. Essentials such as rice, cooking oil, medicines, and fuel became scarce at any price. The Japanese military that surrounded Shanghai controlled the flow of goods, seizing whatever it wanted for its war effort or for its comfort. Scarcity drove prices into a dizzying inflationary spiral as hoarders and speculators gorged themselves on the desperation of others—those who couldn't afford to pay black market prices starved. Without kerosene or coal, the poorest had frozen in the two harsh winters that had come and gone since the start of the war. Bodies of the poor and homeless lay as rotting detritus on the streets and alleys of Shanghai until corpse-removal trucks eventually took them away.

Benny didn't have to think about the present when his future seemed predetermined and rosy, war or no war. Since he had passed the difficult entrance exam for admission to St. John's Junior Middle School, his path all the way to its eponymous university was automatic as long as he continued to pass his courses. His parents had no worries for their son when everyone knew that doors opened for St. John's graduates. They stood out in every crowd, speaking fluent English and carrying themselves as though they were proper English gentlemen and ladies. At both St. John's and its sister institution, St. Mary's Hall, classes were taught in English. Thanks to his alumni parents, Benny could already speak English well and would fit right in. So many of China's most powerful political, business, and intellectual leaders had studied at its schools: T. V. Soong, former finance minister and governor of the Central Bank of China; Wellington Koo, representative to the League of Nations and ambassador to France; Lin Yu-tang, influential writer and philosopher; and a long list of others. The well-connected were well served. That was the Chinese way.

With his pedigree and school ties, Benny was set. Still, the boy harbored a secret wish for himself. He wanted to chart his own course, the way his father must have when he left accounting to join the police ranks. Benny hoped to pursue medicine when he reached college, for St. John's had a medical school that was affiliated with the University of Pennsylvania in America.

But there were plenty of pitfalls in the sin city for boys like him. Shanghai was notorious for its spoiled firstborn sons who had nothing better to do than become playboys, squandering their families' wealth on opium, women, and gambling, bringing shame to their families. Benny's mother and her friends gossiped about the latest scandals about young men from reputable families during their all-night mah-jongg games. "Pay attention in school, and stay away from those bad boys," she'd admonish her son afterward.

"Yes, Mother," he'd reply obediently. Benny had already resolved to stay away from opium. He'd known what the narcotic had done to his grandfather.

Benny could easily have pursued a life of pleasure, as other Shanghai scions did. His family appeared to have unlimited resources. His father was thriving in spite of the war. Or as others might say, because of it.

Just as Benny didn't see the beggars all around him, he had never thought about the ample food and luxurious goods that his police inspector father managed to bring home at a time when rice riots were breaking out in the city. Benny didn't wonder how his mother could continue her shopping habits that allowed her to dress in the latest foreign fashions, adorned with ever-fancier jewelry. It was unthinkable for proper Chinese children to question their parents. Even when Benny noticed that some of his father's associates looked rather tough and unsavory, like the kind of men that his mother warned him to avoid when he rode his bicycle, he would have never thought to ask about them. They were just people that a police inspector needed to know, like the assortment of British, Americans, Russians, Japanese, and other foreigners with whom his father dealt.

———

BENNY'S DAILY LIFE WAS so far removed from the war, he didn't imagine that his own father was at the very center of it. In 1939, Pan Zhijie—or C. C. Pan, as Benny's father was also known in English— was promoted to be departmental chief of police of Shanghai's Western District, or Hu Xi in Chinese. The Badlands in any language. It was the same area Benny's father had long ago declared off-limits to his son. The majority of the crime, terrorist bombings, kidnappings, and assassination attempts in the foreign concessions were thought to originate from illicit dens in the Badlands.

Within the space of a few years, more than 150 political assassinations of suspected Chinese collaborators, enemy sympathizers, and Japanese soldiers had taken place in Shanghai, many on public streets and in public establishments—credited to the Nationalist underground resistance headed by General Dai Li. He was Chiang Kaishek's top spy, referred to by some as "China's Himmler," an allusion to Hitler's ruthless chief of the Nazi SS. One particularly brazen execution engineered by Dai Li's men took place on the pleasant treelined street of Yu Yuan Road, not far from Benny's home. Spacious mansions and villas, as well as attractive brick *lilong* row homes, occupied this part of the International Settlement, including the heavily guarded home of the Chinese foreign minister—a puppet and traitor, according to the Nationalists. Minister Chen Lu and his wife were hosting a dinner party and had just ushered the guests into their living room. Dai Li's assassins managed to tiptoe through the house and burst into the room while Chen's bodyguards stood by in surprise. After shooting Chen point-blank before his cowering dinner guests, the Nationalist killers unfurled a scroll over the body that read DEATH TO THE COLLABORATORS! LONG LIVE GENERALISSIMO CHIANG KAI-SHEK!

It was the responsibility of the new police chief C. C. Pan to quell the crime wave. Benny couldn't have been prouder of his father's new charge.

———

AS IT HAPPENED, C. C. Pan was perfectly situated at the unseemly intersection of the British-run Shanghai Municipal Police and the city's extensive criminal underbelly. A charismatic and smart businessman, Benny's father had for some time been making good use of his elite St. John's education, his fluent English, and his Shanghai pedigree to move up the police ranks. It hadn't escaped Inspector Pan's notice that clever officials in Shanghai at every level got ahead by leveraging their influence in the city's complex web of police jurisdictions, where vice and crime were rampant and the mob ruled the streets. Even Generalissimo Chiang Kai-shek himself, it was whispered, was a sworn member of the powerful underworld Green Gang syndicate. Chiang had rewarded its leader, Du Yuesheng, for his instrumental role in helping the Nationalists exterminate the Communists in 1927, naming him to such government positions as overseeing banking and opium suppression. Having gained respectability and political power while continuing his opium rackets, Du reciprocated, giving his sworn brother Chiang a percentage of his lucrative underworld profits to help fund the Nationalist government. Such mutually beneficial arrangements were commonplace in Shanghai, where it was said that money could buy anything.

With China's top leader cozy with the gangs, Benny's father, too, became a sworn member of the Green Gang, his police uniform notwithstanding. By the time C. C. Pan was named chief of the Western District, he had created his own extensive network of influence, with four hundred constables and sixty detectives on his unlawful tab. At a time of war and scarcity, he and his men extracted personal favors and payoffs from businesses and the wealthy in the International Settlement. They also protected the shady enterprises of the Green Gang.

C. C. Pan even offered his minions job protection: If any cop was fired for corruption, the chief would continue to pay his salary. In his perfect English, Benny's father could ensure secure livelihoods for his British bobbies at a time when most foreigners in Shanghai worried about their jobs if the Japanese took over. As Shanghai's wartime inflation shrank people's buying power, Chief Pan doled out generous monthly retainers to his personal network. His familiarity with Western culture made it easier for him to identify vulnerable officers. Pan made offers they couldn't refuse, and they did his bidding.

Benny's father was becoming a powerful and well-known man in both the policing and criminal worlds of Shanghai. His rise in status earned him a new nickname: Pan Da, meaning Big Pan. When Benny was out with his father, businessmen and fellow officers greeted Pan Da and then turned to Benny. "Hey, Xiao Pan"—Little Pan—"would you like to grow up to be like your father one day?" they'd ask.

Without hesitation, Benny would nod his head vigorously. Of course one day he'd like to be respected the way his strong and distinguished father was.

"Good lad," they'd chuckle. "You'll do well if you're like your old man."

PAN DA'S JURISDICTION COVERED the extraterritorial Western District, where the British had been encroaching on the Chinese section for years. Wealthy foreigners and Chinese alike had built enormous estates in the area. Some of the most prominent missionary schools were located in the district as well, including St. John's, St. Mary's, the McTyeire School for Girls, Jiao Tong University, and the Fudan Middle School. But the Western District was also home to the notorious Badlands, the most crime-ridden and politically contested area in Shanghai. Pan Da's new office was located at 76 Jessfield Road. Shockingly, "76," this place that should have been the headquarters for maintaining law and order, was in fact the epicenter of violence.

This was where suspected Nationalist agents were taken to be interrogated and tortured. It was where journalists and officials were "persuaded" to cooperate with the Japanese. Businessmen were kidnapped and held there for ransom. If their families couldn't or wouldn't pay up, they might never be seen again. The place became known as "the Black Hellhole" of Shanghai, from which few emerged alive. If they did, they were shadows of their former selves. And Benny's father was chief at 76.

For Benny, 76 was a private park. Chief Pan Da allowed his son to ride his bike on the spacious paths around the buildings. It was thrilling for the boy to enter the highly secured location. He broke into a grin each time he passed the gruff sentries who guarded the three levels of gates before he entered the grounds. None of his school chums were permitted to ride with him there. Benny felt like the luckiest boy in Shanghai, thanks to his father. And then another boy was allowed to ride around the secretive grounds—the son of Li Shiqun, reputed to be the principal torturer at 76, who ran the puppet Secret Service at the will of the Japanese command. Benny knew nothing of the other boy's father and didn't mind sharing the honor of admittance, for now he had a playmate to pal around with.

The two raced each other from one end of the manicured estate to the other. The scent of fragrant peonies and roses in bloom surrounded them as they rode circles around the buildings. The largest, a big brick-and-stone mansion, was off-limits and blocked by fierce-looking armed men. Benny never suspected that prisoners were held in the mysterious building. He heard no frightening sounds, no screams or moans from the torture pits that he learned of much later. To Benny, it was just where his father worked, but it was also the exciting, secret domain that only he and Li's son were privy to.

Benny's parents preferred that their son ride his bike there rather than in the streets. With so much factional violence throughout Shanghai, they felt 76 was a safer place for him to play. As Chief C. C. Pan's power continued to grow, they worried that their adventurous son could be a kidnapping target.

Around this time, Benny's mother decided that her eleven-year-old boy should live as a boarder on the St. John's campus, to protect him from the crime and violence that his father encountered each day. Many other students became boarders at Shanghai's exclusive missionary schools for the same reasons. An older St. John's student, Tao-Fu Ying, actually had a bodyguard following him on campus. The big White Russian sat by Tao-Fu in class, in the lunchroom, even accompanying him to the movies when he went on a date. The other boys laughed and poked fun at Tao-Fu and his huge White Russian shadow. There was nothing Tao-Fu could do but grit his teeth and bear it, for he, like Benny, was the Number One Son of a wealthy comprador family, and its patriarch insisted that his grandson and heir be protected at all times.

For the most part, the serene missionary school campus insulated Benny from the waves of terrorism and crime that swept Shanghai, including its foreign concessions. The Japanese military occupation force violently quashed resistance by arresting, torturing, and assassinating its critics. Journalists, officials, and bankers were particular targets: Banks deemed to be China partisans had bombs tossed into their lobbies, while judges were routinely shot to death as they headed to their courthouses. In 1938, six journalists were decapitated, and their heads were put on display at busy locations in the French Concession. Reporters like William Yukon Chang, a Hawaii-born Chinese whose parents sent him to study at St. John's University, never knew when he might receive packages containing dismembered body parts or bullets as warnings. On July 16, 1940, Samuel Chang, a high-ranking editor and America-trained graduate of Haverford College, was gunned down as he ate lunch at a German restaurant on Nanjing Road. No voice of resistance was safe.

At the same time, the Japanese occupiers sought local Chinese leaders to be their surrogates and do their bidding. The Chinese people derisively called such officials *hanjian*—traitors, puppets, collaborators. Meanwhile, Nationalist underground agents countered with their own assassinations of *hanjian* and Japanese alike. Terror reigned on Shanghai's streets to intimidate the populace into submission. Amid such turmoil, ordinary crime burgeoned as criminals with no political agendas staged their own gunfights in the streets, disappearing into the maelstrom.

Part of the problem lay in the disorder and chaos created by the occupation itself. Nearly three years after taking Shanghai, Tokyo had not yet found anyone to run the city as its mayor. Japan's top choice had been Green Gang boss Du Yuesheng. But Du was loyal to Chiang Kai-shek and declared that he would never work for the "bandy-legged dwarves," referring to the gaiter-wrapped calves of the short-statured Japanese soldiers. Du declined the job and fled to Hong Kong, fearing retaliation. The Japanese finally persuaded Fu Xiaoan, a respected elder Buddhist leader and a vocal critic of Chiang, to become

Shanghai's collaborationist mayor. Almost immediately, Nationalist secret agents made assassination attempts against Fu. In 1940, the Nationalists managed to enlist the aid of Fu's longtime cook, who was so trusted that he slipped past bodyguards into the mayor's bedroom on the night of October 11, 1940, and hacked him to death with a meat cleaver.

But it would take another event, in 1940, to make a significant impact on Benny's world. Japan's machinations finally bore fruit to find a suitable "puppet" to act as president over all of Japanese-occupied China: Wang Jingwei, the charismatic leader of the Nationalist Party's left wing and Generalissimo Chiang's main internal party rival. Wang Jingwei had once been hit by an assassin's bullet supposedly intended for Chiang, though Wang's wife always believed Chiang had ordered her husband killed.

Wang advocated making peace with Japan. He asserted that it made economic sense and would save countless Chinese lives if China joined Japan's much-vaunted Greater East Asia Co-Prosperity Sphere in opposition to Western imperialism. He didn't believe China could win the war and felt that Japan would help them get rid of the "white devils"—the Americans and Europeans who had bullied the country for a century with their gunboats, opium, and colonial arrogance.

Instantly reviled by both Nationalists and Communists as a Benedict Arnold and, later, the Vidkun Quisling of China, Wang Jingwei quickly appointed a new mayor to replace Fu—someone who would have tremendous influence as the head of the biggest and most important city in occupied China. He chose his fellow left-wing Nationalist Chen Gongbo, who, in turn, needed someone to contain Shanghai's vice and violence while squeezing revenue out of the lucrative gambling halls, opium dens, and brothels. That revenue was needed to finance Wang Jingwei's puppet government, in the same way the Green Gang had supported Chiang Kai-shek's.

For this important job, the new puppet mayor chose Police Chief Pan Da. Benny's father was promoted once again, this time catapulted to the newly created position of police commissioner of the Western District of Shanghai. In his elevated role, he would keep 76 Jessfield

Road as his headquarters. China's darkest hour became Pan Da's greatest opportunity.

THE POSITION OF POLICE commissioner in charge of the Badlands raised the Pan family's position in status-conscious Shanghai by several notches, bringing a whole new level of perks: new cars, a new home, bodyguards, chauffeurs, unlimited goods of every kind.

Commissioner Pan assigned some of his Special Police officers to locate a house suitable for a man of his rank. His special agents knew of an unoccupied estate at 40 Jessfield Road, only a block south of 76, just beyond the International Settlement. The elegant English-style mansion had belonged to Zhang Yuanji, one of the founders of Shanghai's Commercial Press, well known to 76 for its anti-Japanese publications. After Shanghai fell to Japan, the owners had fled. To the victors and their collaborators at 76, such properties were fair game. Commissioner Pan Da sent a half dozen of his officers to seize the estate. When the plainclothes agents from 76 arrived, they ejected the absentee owner's staff. One worker promptly went to the Shanghai Municipal Police, where the British inspector scrawled a handwritten message on the typed crime report: "Sir, these men are from 76." The case went no further. Without delay, Benny's family moved into the mansion at 40 Jessfield Road, so conveniently close to Pan Da's station house and torture chambers.

Benny learned of his father's big promotion when the family's chauffeur came to pick him up at boarding school in a shiny 1940 Buick sedan. Benny let out a loud "Jiminy crickets!" and rushed over to examine the luxurious new car, running his fingers over the smooth black finish. The chauffeur followed Benny around the vehicle with a clean handkerchief, wiping away the boy's prints before holding the door open. Hopping in, Benny admired the leather upholstery and quizzed the longtime family servant. "Where did this super car come from?"

"Young Master, your father is now the number one boss at 76. A big man must have a big car and a big house," he said.

When the car turned off Jessfield Road, past a gated fence and onto a private drive, Benny's jaw dropped in surprise. Set back against a large grassy lawn was an enormous three-story house with a separate wing for the servants and a carriage house that could hold three cars. Sure enough, there were two other cars inside: a Ford Willys GP "jeep" for the bodyguards now assigned to his family and his father's old black sedan, now for his mother's use. Benny jumped out of the car and bounded up the terra-cotta steps to the grand terrace flanked by tall Greek columns. Pushing open the massive carved wood doors, he stepped into a high-ceilinged foyer with gleaming wood floors. On either side was a large parlor lined by dark-stained bookshelves and wood paneling. Benny ran through the house, marveling at each room. He'd never seen such a cavernous dining room. A den and study were on the other side of the house, along with a billiard room and a covered porch overlooking the flower garden that extended nearly an acre, complete with a pond occupied by giant orange carp, he would soon discover.

As he rounded the wide, curving staircase, he almost ran into his mother outside one of the large bedrooms. "Mother, do we really live here?" he asked, breathless.

His mother smiled broadly. "Yes, Long-Long. It's still a bit dreary with all the dusty scrolls and antique statues. I'm getting rid of all that and planning to make the place much brighter. You'll see." Benny and his siblings, she said, would sleep on the third floor, just as they had at the Dasheng *lilong*.

That weekend, C. C. Pan was too busy organizing his newly created Western Shanghai Area Special Police Force to come home to the mansion. Benny was disappointed but not surprised, since his father's important work increasingly kept him away from home.

Benny watched his mother with admiration as she stepped into her demanding new role. He had always known that his gracious mother was smart and capable. Now she managed an enormous house and grounds with many employees. She was redecorating the mansion with enthusiasm, consulting with famous designers and taking full advantage of her husband's access to warehouses of loot "requisitioned" from those in disfavor with the political order. Most important, she wanted to make Police Commissioner Pan Da's presence known in

Shanghai society. She took charge of his social calendar and public face, organizing fancy dinners and inviting the influential people she felt her husband needed to know.

To kick off their entrée into Shanghai's social elite, Benny's mother planned a lavish party to celebrate her husband's fortieth birthday, choosing to hold the special banquet at one of the best Cantonese restaurants in the International Settlement. Pan Da and his wife invited officials from the top echelons of the puppet elite to his birthday bash. Benny, who would be thirteen at the start of 1941, had never seen such an array of bejeweled socialites and cigar-puffing captains of industry and commerce. He watched the festivities from a table near the kitchen, seated with his siblings, Annie, Cecilia, Doreen, Edward, and Frances, in alphabetical order. All were on their best behavior. Benny beamed with pride as his father held court in full dress uniform, brass buttons and belt buckle shining, a glass of brandy in one hand and his silver cigarette holder in the other. Benny's elegant mother, as beautiful as a movie star, exuded the charm and social graces she had learned at St. Mary's Hall, easing the way for the family's social ascent. When the Chinese band began playing the latest popular dance tunes, it was time for Benny and his siblings to go home with the chauffeur.

THE PARTIES CONTINUED AT their mansion every Sunday, when Benny and his school-aged sisters came home from their boarding schools for the weekend. The newly inaugurated Sunday dinners brought Shanghai's prominent and powerful to the Pan front parlor and dining room. With Pan Da's bottomless purse, Benny's mother spared no expense, serving Russian caviar and French foie gras, sparkling champagne and well-aged Scotch. She managed to procure the finest porcelain dishes, elaborate silver, and delicate etched glasses, all glimmering under the bright crystal chandeliers.

It was a great show, and Benny enjoyed being part of it. Wearing a proper suit and tie, he looked every bit the schoolboy of Eton, Exeter, or St. John's, great-grandson of a Shanghai comprador, and eldest son of the police commissioner. Benny and his five siblings would troop down the wide, curving staircase to greet the guests before heading to the children's table. As the Number One Son, he felt it was his responsibility to keep the others on point, at least until they were out of the guests' sight. His mother, the perfect hostess, would flash him her biggest smile when they finished their bows and curtsies. How Benny loved seeing her eyes twinkle at him and her face light up.

Benny's third sister, Doreen, had passed the difficult admissions exam for St. Mary's. Of all his siblings, Benny felt closest to her, even though she was three years younger. Doreen, like Benny, enjoyed book learning while the two sisters closest to his age were more interested in shopping and parties. On Sundays, he and Doreen sat together, quietly practicing their English as they closely observed the dinner guests. Brother and sister played a game of guessing whether people were British or American, French or German or Jewish, just by looking at their pale faces. Benny swore he could tell them apart, but to Doreen they all looked alike.

Then there were the Japanese guests—not only the military officers with ominous-looking samurai swords, but civilians as well. The growing number of Japanese noncombatants far exceeded that of all the other foreigners in Shanghai combined. Initially Benny was perplexed by their presence. Here they were, welcome guests in his house, the military in dress uniforms, with everyone cheerfully eating and drinking. Benny would never have questioned his parents, but he had also heard the many anti-Japanese comments and ditties in his schoolyard, even though the American campus banned any activities involving China's political situation. Benny couldn't understand why his parents welcomed these Japanese into their home.

His father must have noticed Benny's confusion. One Sunday, before the guests arrived, his father called him to his study. He glanced up from his work and began speaking as soon as the boy stepped into the dark-paneled room.

"Son, every man deserves to be judged on his own merits. Not all Japanese are bad; not every Chinese is good. These Japanese officials can make life easier for the Chinese in Shanghai. I hope to encourage them. Do you understand?"

"Yes, sir." Benny nodded, grateful that his father seemed to have noticed his uncertainty.

"Good. Now go and get dressed for dinner," his father replied, his head already turned back to his work.

The exchange helped Benny feel more relaxed through the dinners. He tried to see the Japanese he met as individuals. At that night's dinner, he observed how the Japanese officers were respectful of his father, how they toasted him when they drank, how attentive and polite they were to his mother. At the end of each dinner, the guests adjourned to the big parlor to take seats at the card tables that servants had set up. Commissioner Pan Da offered the men Cuban cigars. They puffed away and drank imported whiskey as they played poker and the women sat down to mah-jongg. The next morning, the children headed back to school. Benny rode in the car with Doreen since St. Mary's was near St. John's, while Annie and Cecilia went to Aurora Middle School of the Sacred Heart in the French Concession.

The glamour and sparkle of the Sunday banquets, the beautiful people with their finery and smart conversations, felt to Benny like a vision from a movie. Except that this movie was real. It was his family and his home. How lucky they were for all the good fortune that kept coming to them. Sure, there was a war going on somewhere away from them. But for Benny, it was the best of times.

SHANGHAI, LATE 1939

THE TEACHER STOOD AT THE FRONT OF THE CLASS AND WROTE "三民主義"—*San Min Zhu Yi*—on the blackboard: Three Principles of the People, the guiding ideology of the Nationalist Party, outlined by Dr. Sun Yat-sen, the founding father of the Republic of China. After putting down the chalk, she picked up a long wooden ruler and began pacing the room, slowly scanning the students through her thick round spectacles. Suddenly she stopped and slammed her stick hard on a table. The students flinched, startled. Pointing her stick across the room, she demanded, "You. Bing. What are the Three Principles of the People?"

The girl rose slowly, smoothing out her uniform, a dark blue *qipao* that hung loosely over her small frame. Standing erect with her eyes straight ahead, she cleared her throat and started to answer, speaking softly.

"Stop mumbling! Speak up so that everyone can hear you," barked her teacher. A girl nearby snickered.

"Yes, Teacher," Bing replied, energetically. "The Three Principles are people's self-determination, people's democracy, and people's livelihood."

"That is correct. Very good, Bing. You may be seated."

Buoyed by the praise, Bing sat down with a smile—after sending a hard look at the girl who had mocked her. She'd entered the class nearly a year before, after Mama Hsu, her second mother, had gone to Chongqing, the capital of Free China. Bing's new "elder sister," Hui-ling Woo, had sent Bing back to school, as promised, to her great relief. But the other children all seemed to know one another. Some liked to pick on her, perhaps because her Suzhou accent marked her as an outsider, or because she struggled at times to keep up after having missed so much school, or because she was smaller than they were. Whatever the reason, Bing was determined not to let them distract her, for she didn't take her schooling for granted.

Every day, she carefully practiced writing the assigned Chinese characters onto the square exercise grid, marking each stroke in the prescribed order to ensure a proper and balanced appearance. Sometimes her strict teacher complimented her penmanship. In occupied Shanghai, Bing was also required to study the Japanese language and the idea of the "Greater East Asian Co-Prosperity Sphere"—Japan's ideological justification for war. But she didn't object; she was happy to be back in school.

Being at home with Elder Sister's mother, however, was a different story. Bing might have been content were it not for Ma's quick temper and harsh tongue. Ma gave Bing a few chores to do before school—putting away the bedding, sweeping the dark wood floors, helping with breakfast. Ma wasn't always cross. Sometimes she told Bing stories about ancient China, hardships under the reign of the last emperor, her own challenges in coming to live in Shanghai. Bing coveted those peaceful moments between Ma's volatile flare-ups. She tried to make herself as quiet and unnoticed as possible, hoping not to provoke Ma by making a mistake.

Because to Ma, any mistake was unforgivable. And once she was angry, she carried on for hours, sometimes for days. No matter how hard Bing tried, the furies were never far away. Bing was unaccustomed to household chores, and now she had many. But her fingers weren't clever, and the more Ma demanded of her, the more nervous Bing became. If she spilled some food or dropped something, Ma's eyes instantly narrowed, and she fixed a terrifying glare on Bing, lashing out with a torrent of angry words:

"You stupid girl, what sewer did you crawl out of? You aren't even worth a piece of shit—at least farmers can use shit in the fields."

By watching Elder Sister, Bing had learned to say nothing and show no reaction. The slightest expression of unhappiness would set Ma off on a new tirade: "You don't like it here? The Huangpu River doesn't have a lid on it; you can jump in anytime." Once Ma worked herself into a froth, she'd continue late into the night, raging from her bed. She'd pause only to light a cigarette, chain-smoking while chain-cursing. On her bedroll, Bing would try to block out Ma. At times, she could almost hear the Huangpu River calling to her.

Before going to school, Bing would help Ma prepare breakfast. It was simple fare: *pao fan,* leftover rice from the previous night warmed with boiling water, along with some small Shanghai-style pickled vegetables and a bit of brined duck egg if they could find any. One morning, Ma instructed Bing to bring the pot of steaming *pao fan* from the fire. The pot was too heavy for the slight girl. As Bing strained to lift it, the pot tipped over, and the bubbling-hot rice landed on the girl's bare ankle and foot, instantly scalding her. Bing screamed from the searing pain.

This time there was no cursing from Ma. She scooped Bing up and carried the wailing child down the stairs. Ma had been crippled by foot-binding, having missed being spared by the new Chinese republic's ban against the practice in 1912, but somehow she managed to carry Bing to a nearby doctor. The burns on Bing's foot were so bad that she couldn't walk. Going to school was out of the question. Ma changed the dressings on Bing's blistered skin to keep the wound clean. She fixed meals for Bing without nagging. Ma didn't seem to mind that Bing could no longer help with the housework. Sometimes Ma even told Bing stories as she busied herself in the small apartment, describing how she had come to Shanghai years before from Changzhou with her two daughters, Elder Sister and Auntie Li, after her husband had died. Bing's ears perked up at hearing *Changzhou*—the very city where she had been born, before her *baba* gave her away.

As weeks went by, Bing's skin healed slowly, with a thick scab on the top of her foot. She began to feel that maybe Ma cared for her, at least a little. Bing was unable to go out, so her only entertainment revolved around Elder Sister, whose life was a busy social whirlwind. Each morning Bing waited for Elder Sister, a late riser, to awake so that Bing could sit on her bed and watch her spend hours fixing her makeup, hair, and clothing. When she had finished, she'd achieved a look that attracted admiring stares wherever she went. By evening, Elder Sister would be ready to head to the city's famous nightclubs with her girlfriends—and a long list of gentlemen suitors.

Bing most enjoyed the nights when Elder Sister's girlfriends gathered at their apartment before heading out to their favorite dance spots. It was almost like being with Shanghai movie stars. Ma never failed to offer her usual admonitions: Stay in the foreign concessions and away from the Badlands where gangsters and the puppet police run amok. Avoid marauding soldiers, crooked police, gangsters, and other assorted troublemakers. And "Remember, men in Shanghai are interested in only one thing!" Elder Sister and her friends insisted that they just wanted to enjoy themselves and forget about the seemingly endless war. Ma would snort and reply, "If you dress like bitches in heat, you'll attract men who are no better than horny dogs."

But even at the dance halls, political intrigue and wartime terrorism were unavoidable. In the spring of 1938, a group calling itself the "Blood and Soul Traitors Elimination Corps" set off bombs outside Ciro's, one of the most popular night spots in the International Settlement, as well as several other dance halls that Elder Sister and her friends frequented.

The self-proclaimed patriots left flyers at clubs with a message titled "A Warning to Our Dancing Friends":

Dancing friends: Some of you can dance the foxtrot, others the waltz. Why don't you go up to the front to kill? Some of you spend lavishly on brandy and whiskey. Why don't you give the money to our troops so that they can buy more munitions to kill the enemy?

Dancing friends: Why spend your money for cosmetics when your bodies smell [of] the odor of a conquered peo-

ple? The only way to remove that smell is to give our warm
blood to the nation. . . . Our meager gift tonight—bombs—
will help to give you added pleasure.

Because of the curfew, Elder Sister's girlfriends often stayed over at
the Woo apartment after their late-night escapades, taking up the floor
space. Bing would sit among them, soaking up the stories about their
glamorous adventures. The women would gossip and laugh late into
the night about foreign men—stuffy British, loud Americans, stiff-
limbed Germans, smooth-talking French, emotional Italians, cold
Japanese, and the hulking White Russians who grew weepy when
drunk, crying about their wonderful lives before the Bolshevik Revolution. Elder Sister drew the line at Chinese men, refusing their ad-
vances. She complained that they expected to have more than one wife
and when that happened, the first wife suffered. "Who needs love? A
wife needs money for her children. Her life is cursed if the money
goes to other wives!" The women laughed about the Western missionaries who had been duped by Chinese men claiming to accept Christian monogamy while they kept their concubines. A concubine was
still a wife, and her offspring were legitimate heirs. It was the men's
mistresses and prostitutes who had no legal status.

There was no shortage of foreign men to amuse women like Elder
Sister. *Yang gueizi*—foreign devils—carried on with their plush expatriate lives in the midst of the war and occupation. The "Shanghailanders," as the foreign residents called themselves, still attended their
churches and synagogues, racetracks and restaurants, dance halls and
theaters, bars and casinos. They sent their children to the guarded enclaves of private schools. There were the multitude of exclusive clubs,
the foreigners' oases of national pride, each more opulent than the
last. The Shanghai Club of the British was on the Bund, its 110-foot
mahogany bar reputed to be the longest in the world. Reflecting the
club's rigid hierarchy was the tradition that every member had an assigned seat at the bar, with seat number one being the most prestigious.

The Shanghailanders weren't entirely oblivious to the tensions of
war. They were subject to inspections by Japanese soldiers posted at

the wood-and-barbed-wire blockades that funneled and controlled all movement at major streets entering the foreign concessions. War refugees huddled in every doorway and vacant spot. The demographic mix of the foreigners was changing too, with the fifty thousand Japanese civilians becoming more numerous than all the Europeans and Americans combined. So many of them lived in the Hongkou section of the International Settlement that it was dubbed Little Tokyo.

Initially, Bing found it shocking that Elder Sister and her friends seemed to prefer foreign men. In Suzhou and Changzhou, Bing had been afraid of foreigners, whom everyone referred to as devils, ghosts, and demons. Before the Woos had adopted Bing, Elder Sister had said that she was getting married soon, but Bing had never suspected that Elder Sister's intended was a *foreigner*.

When the tall Shanghailander Elder Sister was planning to marry first came to their apartment, Bing ran to the next room and peered through a crack in the doorway. He looked so much older than Elder Sister, who insisted that Bing come out to meet him. The foreigner flashed her a smile. His name was Kristian Kronberg Jarldane. He'd worked in Shanghai for almost thirty years as an engineer with the Shanghai Water Conservancy, charged with keeping the navigation lanes of the Huangpu River dredged and open for big ships. Bing had never met a foreign devil before. Ma didn't seem to mind that Elder Sister often spent the night at his place. That was all right with Bing too, for when Elder Sister wasn't home, Bing could sleep in her bed.

TOWARD THE END OF 1939, Bing's foot had healed enough for her to wear shoes again, but she'd missed too much school to jump back in. Ma said that she'd have to wait until the next year to repeat her grade. But now Ma actually needed Bing at home for another reason: While Bing had been recuperating, Elder Sister had given birth to a baby boy. She and the balding foreigner weren't yet married, but they gave their baby a Danish name: Ole Egner Jarldane.

The foreigner said it would be two years after he had filed for a divorce from his first wife, a Russian woman, before he could marry again. When he stopped coming by soon after Ole was born, Elder

Sister explained that her fiancé had to return to Denmark to complete the divorce. Ma grumbled that they might never see him again, that dirty old man. As usual, Elder Sister paid her no mind, confident he'd return.

In the meantime, Ma oversaw the care of her new grandson while Elder Sister sprang back into her busy social life. Right after her son's birth, she was out shopping, playing mah-jongg, and visiting with her friends again. She even treated herself to a trip to Hong Kong after the unpleasantries of pregnancy and childbirth. She hired a wet nurse to suckle the baby and left him with Ma and Bing.

Six months later, the foreigner returned. One afternoon in early 1940 when Bing was almost eleven, he and Elder Sister went to the Danish consulate to be married. They didn't bother with a reception, a decision that pleased Ma. "What's the point of having a party when there's already a baby?" she asked. Ma was surprised that the foreigner had returned. Her face even stretched into a rare smile.

After their marriage, Elder Sister and her husband moved to a building on Avenue Joffre, the French Concession's main boulevard. Their modern apartment had all the latest Western-style conveniences: electric stove and refrigerator, a gleaming bathroom with a flush toilet, and telephone service. Elder Sister was the only Chinese person living in the building—all the other tenants were foreigners.

Ma and Bing moved into a smaller one-room flat on a side street closer to Elder Sister. After the morning chores, they would walk there, Ma shuffling so slowly on her painful bound feet that Bing had ample time to study the fancy shops along the way: the photography studio with portraits of beautiful people displayed in its window; a restaurant opened by two Japanese sisters who smiled and bowed as Bing and Ma walked by; the Jewish grocery in the eight-story, flatiron-shaped Normandie Apartments, with exotic-smelling salamis, cheeses, and braided breads on display.

After lunch each day, Elder Sister left to socialize while Bing and Ma looked after Ole. When Elder Sister and her husband returned at the end of the day, they all sat down together for a dinner prepared by the couple's cook. Bing still felt awkward around the Danish gentleman. Elder Sister conversed in English with him since, like most foreigners, he knew only a few words of pidgin Chinese: *chow, chop-chop, savvy, no can do, catchee me rickshaw.*

Even more awkward for Bing was the question of what to call him. Was he her brother-in-law or "Uncle"? Elder Sister used his name, Kristian, but Ma referred to him as "Lao Touzi"—old man. So Bing started calling him Lao Touzi as well. It seemed fitting since he was a good thirty years older than twenty-one-year-old Elder Sister. He wasn't interested in what they said in Chinese anyway. Bing learned to ignore the disapproving clucks from Chinese and foreigners alike who stared at the interracial couple and their Eurasian child. Elder Sister never seemed to mind—not when Kristian's expatriate salary, paid in foreign currency, supported them all so handsomely.

With Elder Sister and Ma depending on Bing's help to watch the baby, the eleven-year-old knew there would be no more school for her. Whenever she saw other children with their books, she wistfully imagined herself in the schoolyard, skipping rope and chasing friends. But then she'd hold the helpless little baby and wouldn't mind as much. She thought the half-Chinese, half-Danish child was beautiful. And he needed her. When he laughed, so did she, with a lightness she hadn't known in a long time.

Besides, going out every day on errands with Ma was an education too. They'd get boiling hot water at the "tiger stove" shop on the corner and wait in line with the ration coupons when the subsidy vendors had some salt, rice, or oil to sell. Each errand was a chance to explore the neighborhood. Bing wasn't afraid of crowds. Small and agile, she was able to wriggle through to get closer to the front—a skill that Ma appreciated.

The markets became Bing's school, with lessons in math, social studies, and economics. She listened as the adult shoppers complained bitterly about the wartime price inflation from illegal manipulation of supply and demand. The enemy Japanese, they said, weren't the only ones to blame for shortages of goods. Rich and well-connected Chinese were hoarding every kind of consumable, diverting international charity relief supplies from the starving poor and selling them as prices soared. Everyone blamed the cronies and relatives of Generalissimo Chiang Kai-shek, especially Madame H. H. Kung, the sister of the generalissimo's powerful wife, Soong May-ling, whose wealthy family was notorious for its godowns filled with basic necessities. The family extracted vastly inflated profits from its desperate fellow Chinese, getting still richer from the resulting windfalls. Whenever Bing went to the market, she heard angry denunciations of the greedy speculators—usually followed by an emphatic spit in disgust.

Sometimes Bing accompanied Ma to the street corners where black markets popped up. All kinds of goods were for sale, including food, gasoline, and other items, with vendors blatantly displaying their wares on the ground, in baskets, or simply in hand. Fascinated, Bing could weave her way to the front of crowds that gathered to watch as people haggled over otherwise unavailable goods for astonishing amounts of money in silver, gold, U.S. dollars, or barter—but never in Chinese currency, which was deemed worthless. To Bing it was street theater, a drama performed by sellers and buyers until the climactic exchange that allowed both sides to claim victory.

The most despised vendors were the shopkeepers who deliberately sold adulterated foods, such as the "red rice" that still had husks and was often mixed with gravel, birdseed, and dirt to cheat people out of receiving their full rations. At least half of each measure was inedible. Ma would rant and rave, cursing these vendors as *mi ze zung*—rice worms. It was Bing's job to handpick each precious grain from the dross. She dreaded the tedious chore and silently agreed with Ma that such vendors were parasites, worse than worms and smellier than dog farts.

Sometimes, Bing would spot a man whose clothing, or walk, or way of tilting his head reminded her of her father. Her heart would pound as she stole a glance, but it was never her *baba*. Nearly six years had gone by since she had last seen him. She was almost twelve and worried that he wouldn't recognize her anymore—nor she him.

Bing kept such thoughts to herself, never mentioning her waning hopes. It had been a long time since she had cried herself to sleep over her family in Changzhou. Sometimes she found herself thinking more about Mama Hsu than Baba. The dull ache was still present but had dimmed enough that she could focus on the everyday: watching baby Ole, assisting Ma, and doing nothing to provoke her.

Ma made a point of teaching Bing what she thought a girl should know. She warned that Bing must always be alert for sharp-eyed street touts who might grab a girl like her, as well as "third-handed" pickpockets who lurked in crowded places. Though beggars seemed to be idly picking lice off one another while sitting on the sidewalk, they were ready to spring after anyone so careless as to drop a few grains of rice and to snatch anything not safely tucked away. Soldiers of any type should be considered potential rapists.

When Bing seemed unhappy, Ma would ask, "If you don't like it here, how long can you survive out *there*?" Then she'd point out the many young girls on the streets who were alone, orphaned or abandoned, forced to fend for themselves. Some, not much older than Bing, lingered on certain street corners to sell themselves to strange men. Ma called them *hei su mei*—the saltwater girls, frequented by the multitudes of sailors prowling the streets of the port city. Bing couldn't keep from staring at their rouged cheeks and bright ruby lips, made up to look thicker and wider. Ma said their red painted faces looked like a monkey's ass.

Bing found a reflection of her own sadness in some of these girls. In her French Concession neighborhood, there were plenty of girls like herself, not street girls but others who had been abandoned and adopted. Many toiled unhappily as virtual slaves. Girls like these were so common that they had their own name, "*xiao yatou*"—little servant girls. Some had to face the beggars and thieves by themselves each morning, something Ma wouldn't let Bing do, saying she was too young to go out alone. But when she was out with Ma, Bing often saw other girls who were younger and smaller than herself alone on errands. In the nearby lane, a girl of seven or eight named Marlene Yang had to fetch hot water and breakfast every morning for her sick mother. Each day, before the sun was up, Marlene headed to the tiger stove shops by herself, lugging a hot water thermos in each hand. The thermoses were heavy when full and unwieldy for a girl trying to evade the beggars around her. Then there were the small bundles on the street that had to be passed by with care—crudely wrapped corpses of babies who hadn't survived the night. Once Marlene saw a stray dog chewing on the limb of a dead infant. She screamed and ran home,

In the harsh war years, children's corpses could be found on the streets each morning. Several bodies are stuffed into one coffin, awaiting collection.

the sight so grisly that she could never rid her mind of the terrible memory.

If Bing expressed her sympathy for Marlene or any of the other unfortunate people she saw, Ma dispensed some curt advice: "Save your pity. It is their fate to be born into unlucky and miserable lives because of their bad deeds in a past life. Maybe they will have better luck in the next life." Bing hoped *she* would have a better fate in her next life. Yet she had to agree with Ma that her life with the Woo family was better than those of the beggars, thieves, and saltwater girls whose numbers seemed to multiply each day while the rice grew scarcer. She would always be grateful to Elder Sister and Ma for that.

EVERY SCHOOL DAY AT EIGHT, ANNUO MARCHED TO THE HEAD of the class and commanded the other children in her loudest voice, "All rise" and "Bow" as the teacher entered the room. More than a year had gone by since that humiliating day when everyone had proudly graduated to the first grade except her. In her year of repeating kindergarten, Annuo had blossomed into an outgoing, confident child who looked forward to each day of school and her new classmates. She had a quick mind and especially loved hearing stories from the Chinese classics that her teacher read to the class. Annuo was so popular that her classmates had selected her to be the classroom monitor, a role she took seriously. At the end of the school day, she happily stood up front again, belting out commands as students bowed goodbye to their departing teacher. Annuo loved her school routine.

In their small apartment on Rue Lafayette, Annuo's family life had settled down following her father's departure more than a year before to join the Nationalist effort against the Japanese invasion. He was somewhere with General Han Deqin's forces in the enemy-occupied province of Jiangsu, bordering Shanghai on the northeast. There was no information available about the Nationalist resistance because pro-Japan censors closely monitored the few newspapers that they had not already shut down.

Her father's absence didn't bother her. He hadn't been around for most of her six years. Though Muma's salary as the school medical officer was modest, she earned enough to hire an amah to cook meals and keep an eye on the children while she was at work. In the old days, when money flowed like water from their father's lucrative law practice, Annuo's parents had had plenty of servants to cook and clean for them. Now having just one amah was a luxury that allowed her mother to go to work without worrying that her children might be harmed by Japanese soldiers, desperate beggars, or puppet police.

Annuo had never heard her mother complain about the lack of money, but she noticed a difference in Muma now that she was working. Her face seemed softer, less tense, her jaw less tight. Annuo didn't feel the need to tiptoe around her anymore. The amah also brought a noticeable improvement to their meals, especially since she could queue up in the long lines for food rations, something Annuo's mother didn't have time to do.

Triggered by the severe food shortages, a major riot had taken place during a soccer game at the Canidrome entertainment complex, with its sports arena, dog racetrack, and giant ballroom, only a few blocks away from their apartment. On March 15, 1941, a Chinese team had been pitted against the mostly European players of the Shanghai Municipal Police. More than twenty thousand Chinese spectators stormed the field and surrounding streets in protest. Annuo's parents used to watch greyhound races at the Canidrome and dance in its beautiful ballroom in the days when Chinese had finally been allowed to patronize the once foreigners-only facility. But now Muma said to avoid the area, in case there was more unrest.

The food riot, however, brought no relief. The Japanese navy had set up a blockade around Shanghai, preventing the city from receiving shipments of rice and other supplies. Meanwhile, the occupation force continued to siphon away Chinese crops to feed its own invading troops. At markets in Shanghai, people often stood waiting with their ration coupons long before dawn, only to find out that rice and other staples were unavailable. Even for those who could pay the exorbitant prices of the black market, food was hard to come by—a single egg could cost more than the monthly income of most families in Shanghai. On lean days, Amah could cook up only some plain millet pan-cakes for each meal. To Annuo, that was still better than mush.

With Annuo's father away in the Nationalist resistance, her mother took painstaking care not to reveal anything that might expose her family. She sternly instructed Annuo and Charley never to speak of their father beyond the walls of their home. Snitches and collaborators were everywhere, and even a casual comment to another child could bring disaster.

For Annuo, such fears became the background noise of war. Yet compared to her years of moving from one province to the next, ready to dodge some new danger, her life in Shanghai took on a reassuring stability. For the first four years of the war, after the Battle of Shanghai in 1937, the Japanese occupation army largely avoided the British- and American-run International Settlement. They kept a low profile in the French Concession as well, even after France fell to Hitler in 1940, so she rarely encountered a Japanese soldier on her walk between home and school. Indeed, the Japanese had little need to enter Frenchtown when the pro-Axis Vichy consul general cooperated fully with Japan as well as with Shanghai's Nazis.

Aside from her mother's occasional worried conversation with the amah about food, Annuo's life in Shanghai had become so steady that she finally had a chance to blossom. On some days she skipped all the way to school. Yet there was one thing the child had already learned: In war, nothing is safe. In a moment, everything can change.

ON DECEMBER 7, 1941, Japan bombed the American fleet at Pearl Harbor in the U.S. territory of the Hawaiian Islands just before 8:00 A.M. local time. In Shanghai, across the International Date Line, it was almost 2:00 A.M. on December 8. In the early-morning hours, Japan's military coordinated devastating attacks on several other strategic sites across the Pacific: Hong Kong, Singapore, the Philippines, Wake Island, Guam, Malaya, Thailand, Midway—and Shanghai.

At 4:20 A.M. in Shanghai, two hours after radio monitors first learned of the Pearl Harbor attack, Japanese marines on the Huangpu

River seized the American gunboat USS *Wake* and sank the British warship HMS *Peterel*, both moored off the Bund. Survivors were taken as prisoners of war.

With the United States and Britain declaring war on Japan, the International Settlement instantly lost its protected status. The Gudao, Solitary Island, was no more. Japanese soldiers could make their presence known in every part of Shanghai. Soon the occupation force began making unannounced door-to-door searches in the French Concession and the International Settlement at any hour of the night, demanding to see identification papers of all residents.

This was a terrifying new development for Annuo's family. Muma was always on guard—as the wife of a high-ranking Nationalist resistance official, she would certainly be arrested. She could be subjected to torture from the Chinese puppet police at 76 Jessfield to extract what knowledge she might have of her husband's whereabouts and activities. Or she could be taken to the equally hideous Bridge House on Sichuan Road, just across the Suzhou Creek in Hongkou. It was just a matter of time before trouble would reach their door.

Late one night, not long after the Japanese attacks throughout the Pacific, someone came running up the stairs to their floor and applied a light but insistent tapping on their door. Muma cautiously checked: It was a woman, a messenger from the underground Nationalist resistance.

"The Japanese are coming for you! You must leave now! Be quick!" she said. Japanese secret police had obtained the names of Nationalists in the foreign settlements, and they were rounding them up for arrest and possible execution. Yongchio Liu, Annuo's father, was on the list, but because her mother used her maiden name, they had a little time to leave before the Japanese could locate them.

Muma and Amah roused the sleeping children. Amah pulled some clothes over Annuo's head, her hands trembling as she buttoned the winter quilt jacket. Muma hurriedly carried two-year-old Li-Ning down the steps. Annuo, Charley, Amah, and the messenger were right behind, each holding a few possessions. They had managed to run a couple of blocks away when Annuo heard the sound of heavy leather

Japanese soldiers in Shanghai demonstrate their bayoneting and beheading prowess to foreign journalists in 1937, using live Chinese prisoners.

boots stomping in the direction they had just come from. A harsh voice barked commands in Japanese. When she turned back to see, the soldiers were entering their apartment building.

Terrified, Annuo could feel her heart pounding. They had barely escaped the Japanese Special Agents who had come looking for their father. Since it was no longer safe to return to their apartment, the four went to stay with Muma's sister and brother-in-law, Aunt Yiniang and Uncle Shu-shu, who also lived in the French Concession. Annuo and her family didn't dare go out for several days. There was no school for Annuo and Charley and no work for Muma. When Annuo mustered the courage to ask when she could see her beloved teacher and schoolmates, her mother's reply was terse: "Never. We can never go back there. The Japanese will be looking for us."

Annuo's heart sank. How could she disappear without saying goodbye to her friends, who had entrusted her as their class monitor?

But she dared not complain when it was clear that they had narrowly averted disaster. At her aunt and uncle's apartment, the anxiety was stifling as her mother fretted over what to do. Without an income, she had to let their amah go. In worried, hushed tones, Muma spoke with her sister about having to find other means to earn money.

What now? They couldn't stay indefinitely with Aunt Yiniang and Uncle Shu-shu when their sudden presence could attract unwanted attention. With Annuo's father fighting with the Nationalist underground somewhere in Jiangsu Province, Muma certainly couldn't seek help from him either.

Muma weighed the risks of going back to her old job against the dangers of seeking a new one. But it was clear that she couldn't start again with three small children in tow. Muma concluded her only option was to find other, temporary homes for Charley and Annuo until she could work things out. A close family friend offered to put up nine-year-old Charley. Muma and Li-Ning would stay with their aunt and uncle. But where would Annuo go?

Muma found a family that would take in the six-year-old girl for a price. When her mother brought Annuo to the small flat, the frightened girl wrapped her arms around her mother's legs.

"No, Muma, please don't leave me here," she cried.

Her mother replied without emotion. "We have no choice. You must mind these people. Don't make any trouble. I'll come back for you as soon as I can."

She pried off the weeping child and left her with strangers.

ANNUO'S DAYS PASSED IN a blur. She hadn't seen her family in months. No school, no friendly faces. The bright little girl withdrew, hibernating inside herself, waiting for her mother to rescue her. When her mother had sent her away, the chill of winter had already set in. The next time Annuo saw her, Shanghai's warm, sticky summer was in full bloom. By then it was 1942, and Annuo had turned seven.

"You're coming home, everything's better, and we have a new place to live," Muma assured her, taking Annuo to an awaiting pedicab. They rode past the grand shops and stately homes of the French

Concession. Sunlight streamed through the broad green leaves of the plane trees that France had planted along the boulevards long ago. Sitting at her mother's side, Annuo felt a calm she hadn't known in months.

Soon they arrived at the second-floor apartment of a three-story building on Avenue Pétain, a wide and busy street in a newer section of the French Concession. The building was owned by White Russians who lived on the first floor. The third floor was occupied by another tenant—also European. It was better to live among foreigners, her mother said, because they couldn't understand Chinese and wouldn't be as inquisitive.

Inside the apartment, baby sister Li-Ning was now walking and talking. The toddler didn't even recognize Annuo and cried for their cousins instead. At last Annuo saw Charley. She brightened as she observed that, at ten years old, he looked taller and more handsome than ever. "Big Brother!" she exclaimed, delighted to see him. He straightened and saluted her, grinning widely. "You're just the same!" she chided.

But Annuo didn't realize how much *she* had changed. Before she was sent away, she had been a confident, outgoing child, unafraid to shout out commands to her class or to sing and dance for strangers. Now she was hesitant and quiet. Where she had been healthy and active, she now appeared fragile. She wouldn't speak of the time she was separated from her family and seemed not to remember the strangers who had minded her. That period became a blank slate, wiped clean by sudden amnesia. To the little girl, it was as though it had never happened.

If her reunited family noticed the change in Annuo, they said nothing. There were more pressing concerns. Muma gathered the children around the table.

"Listen carefully; I have some important news," she said quietly. Her voice dropped to a near whisper. Annuo strained to hear.

"These past months, I've been working to find a way for us to be together in Shanghai. Because the Japanese are looking for your father, we will all have to take on new names. You must forget that your family name is Liu. From now on, your family name is Chang. No matter who asks for your name, you must think of your new name as if it has always been your own. If you slip up even once, we will all be in peril."

Muma had other instructions. "Don't be too friendly to the neighbors," she warned. She also told them Japanese troops were using the campus of Jiao Tong University, only a few blocks away on Avenue Haig, as their garrison. The Japanese military police headquarters was even closer. "Just stay calm if any soldiers are near. They'll be less suspicious if we are living under their noses."

Annuo's new name would be Chang Tsen. She repeated it over and over, trying to memorize the words. There were other names to remember. Her mother would go by Chao Keping, taking a new maiden name. Charley, who had always been called by his English name, became Chang Ping. Their younger sister didn't have to change her first name. Muma had obtained forged identification papers for all of them with their new names.

"You must never, never tell anyone your real name." Speaking in her sternest voice, her mother looked directly at Annuo, then Charley. "Not your teachers, not your friends. Otherwise, the Japanese and their Chinese puppets will take us away." Her mother didn't need to repeat her warning. "Tsen" never wanted to get sent away again.

ANNUO'S MOTHER HAD FOUND a different job. She was now a sales representative with the CBC Pharmaceutical Company, calling on physicians to sell the company's antibiotics. She was good at it and had saved enough to pay the exorbitant "key money," commission, rent, and deposit for their new apartment at 275C Avenue Pétain—a building nice enough for foreigners. She even hired a new amah to cook and care for the children. Zhongying, the amah, had two young daughters who moved into the apartment with her. Zhongying was from outside of Shanghai and spoke a dialect that was different from the local Shanghainese, making it harder for her to gossip with the other amahs. Everything was calculated to reduce the chances of exposing their new identities, Muma said.

In 1942, after missing more than half of the prior school year,

Annuo was back in class only a few blocks away from their new home. But she could never go back to her former school, lest someone recognize her. Instead, she entered the second grade at the Pétain Primary School as Chang Tsen.

Annuo no longer raised her hand to answer a teacher's questions. Nor did she volunteer for special assignments. She never wanted to be a classroom monitor again and shrank away from extracurricular activities, afraid to draw attention to herself. Her underground life constrained her every move.

Annuo's mother had to be especially careful. Her new job with the pharmaceutical company paid her more than her previous job, but it was also more dangerous, requiring her to make sales visits throughout Shanghai. According to Charley, that meant Muma would have to pass Japanese checkpoints frequently. Although she managed to carefully plot her sales routes to bypass most Japanese sentry posts, she could not always avoid crossing the Waibaidu (Garden) Bridge, where the occupiers had built a narrow gated checkpoint out of wood, barbed wire, and sandbags. The belligerent and cruel sentries not only demanded to see identification papers but also required all Chinese to bow to them. It didn't matter if a Chinese was rich or poor, old or young, male or female: All had to stop and bow deeply to the Japanese—or face their wrath. One evening, the soldiers stopped an old man carrying such a heavy load on his back, he was bent like a beast of burden. The old man displeased the guards by failing to prostrate himself quickly enough. One of the guards loudly cursed the old man, whipping him with his rifle butt, then stabbing him through the heart with his bayonet and hurling his lifeless body off the steel bridge and into the fetid Suzhou Creek. None of the other guards even blinked while the horrified bystanders waited their turns in silence, each of them afraid of becoming the next victim.

At home in the evenings, Annuo and Charley would listen as Muma and Amah discussed the latest dangers in the foreign concessions. Even the tellers of the Bank of China, the financial arm of the Nationalists, had come under attack from the Chinese puppet police at 76 Jessfield. In the middle of the night, 128 bank employees had been arrested at 96 Jessfield, their residential compound, and interrogated for several days. Three of the accountants were shot to death in the drive-way of the compound while their families and coworkers looked on. Immediately after the shooting, all of the employees and their families packed up and headed far inland to Chongqing. Their vacant residences were swiftly taken over by the employees of the Japan-friendly Central Reserve Bank.

Sitting at the kitchen table, Annuo couldn't help but absorb the adults' talk as she did her schoolwork. It frightened her to think of the horrid enemy stopping her mother. Even second-grade girls her age knew that the enemy wouldn't hesitate to snatch them off the street. On her way to school, she always kept a watchful eye out for possible danger. Other girls she passed by in her neighborhood did the same. On nearby Rue Boissezon, a girl named Rosalyn Koo cut her hair short and wore boys' clothes over her lime-green *qipao* uniform and removing them when she arrived at McTyeire School, while the mother of Theresa Chen-Louie, another nearby McTyeire student, bound her daughters' breasts to hide their female shapes. Some girls and women rubbed dirt on their faces to make themselves unappealing. The precautions were terrible reminders for Annuo of her beloved young neighbor Zhonghe's gruesome bayonet death.

From the apartment window, Annuo could see Japanese troops marching in lockstep to their garrison. She would freeze in terror, afraid that they might come to her building and find her family. Annuo sometimes believed she could hear their heavy boots, the thought of each harsh thud sending a chill through her body. To her, it was the sound of evil approaching. If she wasn't careful, the boots would find her.

ONE NIGHT, ANNUO WAS jolted awake by those dreaded footsteps on their quiet boulevard. Not even the leafy trees could muffle the unmistakable sound of the soldiers terrorizing the neighborhood with their random searches. Annuo's worst nightmare was coming true: The Japanese soldiers were making their way up her building. On the first landing, they banged on the door, waking the White Russians and demanding to see their identification papers. Soon an angry fist banged on the door of Annuo's family's home. "Open up! Open up, and show your identity papers!" a gruff voice shouted.

Muma sent Amah Zhongying to the door, asking her to stall the soldiers so she could get dressed. Awake, Annuo and Charley huddled together and peeked into the main room. Their mother emerged looking neat and calm, as if she were going on a sales call with doctors, not to meet the angry soldiers.

"We have nothing of interest to you," she said to the officer in an even, unflinching voice.

As the brown-suited officer stormed into the small apartment, he drew his sword and raised the gleaming blade toward Annuo's mother.

"Show me your ID!" he barked.

She calmly gave them her documents. "No need to get excited, please. You'll frighten the children."

He looked over the papers as the other soldiers glanced around. "Where is your husband? What is his name?"

Muma gave them the phony name and the answer she had rehearsed. "He's not here. He's with his mistress tonight," she said.

The officer snorted. As he moved closer to Annuo's beautiful mother, she stepped back and said firmly, "That will be all then." Another soldier pointed his bayonet at her, but the officer only grunted and signaled to his men to leave. They stormed out and stomped up the stairs to the next door.

Zhongying quickly shut and locked the door, while their mother put Annuo and Charley back to bed. "It's all right. They're gone," she said softly.

Annuo squeezed her mother so tight that Muma smiled and said, "Don't be afraid. These Japanese invaders have no right to be in China. Your father and his brave soldiers will drive them out. Then he'll come home, and we'll be together again."

NOT LONG AFTER, ANNUO'S father did reappear. Three years had gone by since Yongchio's family had last seen him. That had been in 1939, when he had left without saying goodbye to his children. Now it was 1942, and he showed up at the Avenue Pétain apartment one night, surprising them all. At first, Annuo didn't recognize him. With only the ragged clothes on his back, he looked as disheveled as the beggars who lined the streets. The clothes weren't even his. He'd had to ditch his Nationalist uniform to get past the enemy. His commanding officer had promoted him to be legal director of the Nationalist resistance in Jiangsu Province, which, like Shanghai and the entire Chinese coast, was under enemy occupation. His unit had come under attack, forcing him and other survivors to disperse like leaves in the wind. Somehow the Nationalist underground had led him to his family. He had no choice but to hide out with them in Shanghai until he could regroup with his unit in Jiangsu.

For days, Annuo's garrulous father filled their apartment with stories of his dramatic escape from the enemy. The children were spellbound. After his Nationalist command center in Jiangsu was attacked, he and other Chinese had been captured. The Japanese soldiers had intended to execute their prisoners alongside a ditch. To save bullets, instead of shooting them, they lunged at and twisted their bayonets into the Chinese soldiers, one by one, kicking the twitching bodies into the ditch. When her father was next in line to be killed, his would-be executioner noticed the gleaming watch on his wrist, a memento of his more prosperous years as a Shanghai lawyer. The Japanese soldier dropped his rifle to grab the watch. Annuo's quick-thinking father was ready: He tossed the watch past the guard and escaped as his captor scrambled for the booty.

To reach Shanghai, her father had to evade both enemy patrols and Chinese informants. He shunned the cities, towns, and major roads, but also had to be wary of possible Communists. Though the Nationalists and Communists were supposed to be fighting the Japanese enemy together, neither faction trusted the other, and the two often clashed. He told the family how he'd waded through muddy rice paddies, hiding among the water buffalo, hitching a ride in the bottom of a sampan along a route on the Grand Canal that coursed from Beijing to Hangzhou, and somehow managing to sneak past Japanese outposts. It was impossible for the Imperial Japanese Army to watch over every village, field, and waterway of the vast territory they occupied. People in some remote villages were unaware that China was at war.

Her father had to barter his way along, offering up his Parker fountain pen, his leather shoes, his reading glasses. By the time he reached Shanghai, he had nothing left but the threadbare clothes he was wearing.

Her father sat in Muma's chair as he captivated the three children with his thrilling tales. Annuo sat cross-legged on the floor, her head propped up on her hands. While her father spoke, little sister Li-Ning climbed onto his lap, beaming. Annuo felt envious as her father squeezed Li-Ning with a warm smile. He's never looked at me like that, she thought, but then she could never cozy up to him either. Charley seemed eager for their father's attention too, rushing to bring him a cup of tea before being asked. Annuo just couldn't do this sort of thing. What was wrong with her? she fretted.

Luckily Annuo didn't have much time to brood, for her father was staying only long enough to get outfitted. Then he planned to leave and rejoin the resistance fighters. To avoid suspicion, Annuo's mother continued her usual routine. On her way home from work, Muma shopped for the clothes, eyeglasses, shoes, and other provisions that Annuo's father needed. Annuo noticed that her father seemed less than pleased with her mother's employment and her independence. He frowned when her job was mentioned but said nothing, for he depended on his wife's financial support as much as their children did.

In spite of the dangers, her father couldn't resist going out on the streets of Shanghai—the underground resistance fighter in the midst of enemy secret agents and Chinese traitors. He was always at risk of being recognized by an old friend from his days as a bon vivant in Shanghai's clubs. Though the city's population was by then more than five million, with an ever-growing number of refugees, the area of the foreign concessions was compact, not even ten square miles. As a disguise, her father donned a long Chinese men's gown instead of the Western-style suits that he preferred. He pulled a fedora down past his eyes, wearing the common mix of foreign and Chinese styles. Once, he took Li-Ning out with him, holding the toddler in front of his face as a shield. Muma chastised him for drawing more attention to himself that way.

One day, he said, China would be rid of the Japanese enemy and all foreign control. China would eliminate the Communist menace too, to keep the Red Bandits from wrecking China the way the Soviets had destroyed Russia. As he spoke, he lowered his voice so that no one, not even their amah, would overhear. But Zhongying was no threat—she was a loyal servant who had sized up their situation long ago.

After a few weeks, Annuo's father disappeared into the night once more. His family didn't know when—or if—he would return. Annuo didn't mind. To her, it was as though he had never been back.

SHANGHAI, AUTUMN 1942

THE LEAVES OF THE PLANE TREES LINING HIS ROUTE TO SCHOOL had begun to fall as Benny started the first of his three years at St. John's Middle School. But he could hardly sit still as his teacher droned on about the similarities between Chinese characters and the Japanese kanji. Nobody was paying attention. Students across Shanghai refused to study Japanese, to protest the occupation's order that they all learn the language. Benny didn't share their anger since he had met decent Japanese people through his father. But the teacher, a Chinese who had been ordered to teach the enemy's language under the occasional supervision of a Japanese proctor, seemed as unenthusiastic as his students. Everyone was eager for the class to end.

Benny's eyes were glued to the large athletic field beyond his classroom window. He thought he spotted some of his teammates from the school track team readying to compete against another Shanghai private school. Though he enjoyed the camaraderie of the team, he had joined only to please his father, who wished him to be more athletic. Benny could run a decent sprint, but he knew he'd never be the champion athlete his father had been. Benny preferred badminton to martial arts, his father's favorite sport. His father spurned the Englishman's game, but its popularity had swept Shanghai, and Benny hoped to join the school's team.

Just beyond the playing fields was the busy Suzhou Creek. Hundreds of sampans and barges chugged by each day on their way to the Huangpu River. As Benny and his classmates looked on, a barge came around the bend in the creek, its coolies straining to push the heavily laden boat with their long poles. When the barge drew near, its contents became obvious: looted goods—a piano, carpets, furniture, and other valuables, even metal radiators to be melted into bullets, all stripped from the homes of the well-to-do, perhaps from relatives of St. John's students. Much of the booty would be diverted to the Shanghai residences of the Japanese occupiers and their puppets.

Someone sitting behind Benny muttered "thieves" and "vultures." Benny didn't turn around.

The barbs weren't aimed at Benny, but his face reddened anyway. His father's name was often in the news as the police commissioner under the Japanese-approved Wang Jingwei government. Sometimes Benny heard angry whispers from other students, but no one said anything to his face. That would be unseemly at a school like St. John's, where the official policy was to stay neutral on political matters. The two dozen or so private schools in the city were supposed to shelter children from politics and war, emulating the civility and decorum that presumably existed at English and American boarding schools.

Benny's mother had enrolled him as a boarding student when he was eleven, to stay at St. John's Junior Middle School, believing the fenced and gated St. John's University campus, shared with the middle and junior middle schools, would be safe, away from the hostilities. A guardhouse with watchmen monitored the school's main gate across from Jessfield Park. Students who rode their bicycles to the campus had to leave them at the park entrance and pay a small fee to walk through to the St. John's gate. But not even the well-trimmed park was safe: One of Benny's schoolmates, Frank Kwok, was attacked there by a vicious Japanese military dog that was trained to kill. Enemy patrols now roamed freely throughout Shanghai, and no one was immune from their arbitrary violence. Though he had dog bites on his arms and legs, Frank's backside was spared by the wallet in his pants pocket. St. John's guards had to rush him to the hospital for treatment and the painful regimen against rabies.

Benny never encountered the military dogs because he returned to school in a chauffeured car on Sunday evenings. In that haven of dignified gray brick buildings, mature trees, green campus fields, and fences topped with barbed wire, for the most part, Benny could be just another student. Except for the occasional whispers, no one made a fuss if a boy's parents were Nationalists or Communists, gangsters or collaborators. Many but not all families of St. John's students were rich. Others came from middle-class families; some received scholarships, while children of the school's teachers attended tuition-free. Overseas Chinese who had migrated to such distant places as Hawaii, Southeast Asia, and the Americas also sent their children to boarding school in Shanghai. There were even a small number of Europeans attending, including Jewish refugees. Whatever their backgrounds, at school the students considered themselves to be "Johanneans" first.

From Monday through Friday, Benny stayed in a plain dormitory, leading a life of puritan simplicity. At 6:45 A.M., he awoke to campus bells, followed by a bugler calling the students to morning exercise on the broad lawns. Morning service at the chapel for Christian students, optional for non-Christians, was followed by breakfast in the dining hall. Bells chimed again at eight for the start of school. Classes ended by four, giving students time for the many clubs and sports programs at St. John's gymnasium and pool, inside the first modern college athletic center in China. Dinner in the dining hall was followed by evening prayers and study in the dim light of their dormitory rooms or at the library. Dorm lights were out by ten, with roll call taken each night.

Benny thrived there and eagerly returned to school after each weekend. His favorite times were spent outdoors on the protected campus, climbing the hundred-year-old camphor tree or crossing the Suzhou Creek on the school's wooden bridge. Benny didn't miss living at home, which, as for most other boarders, was only minutes away. He was glad to be free of the constant monitoring by his amah, the bodyguards, other servants, and his parents' sharp eyes.

Moreover, his good friends were at school, including his closest pals, Dennis Yu and George Cheng. The three boys organized their own school club: the BDG Club—for Benny, Dennis, and George.

They studied and played sports together and rode their bikes in and around the campus. When they tired of the dining hall, they went together for hawker fare at the portable food stalls that congregated just outside the school gates. The BDG Club always had ready cash for off-campus treats—Hazelwood ice cream, Bakerite biscuits, or Tip Top toffee. Even better, Dennis and George had motorcycles, so the boys could ride through the streets of Shanghai, stopping for a sandwich at Bianca's or at Kiesling's for chestnut cream cake. On Shanghai's hot, humid days, they made their way to the fancy Sun Ya Cantonese Restaurant, which featured the miracle of air conditioning.

The boys had much in common. Dennis's and George's parents were wealthy industrialists who had managed to forge an advantageous coexistence with the Japanese and their collaborators. The fathers of the two boys weren't as connected to the Japanese or the puppet government as Benny's, but their businesses were booming under the occupation. The fact that their families were able to keep their cars running with gasoline—and not the coal-burning contraptions that some inventive people rigged to their vehicles—was a clear measure of their wealth and special status.

Benny did his best to be the model of Western civility that St. John's expected of its students. Proper etiquette was a priority at the school, its handbook advising: "Good manners mark the conduct of a gentleman," and "Politeness is the oil that lubricates the wheels of social intercourse." In comportment class, students learned which utensils to use at a Western-style meal. They took dance lessons to learn the fox-trot and waltz, which they happily practiced at parties with girls from St. Mary's, McTyeire, and other private girls' schools.

In spite of the careful grooming, Benny occasionally fell short of the behavior expected of him as the son of the police commissioner. Some St. John's students had their own cars. Benny didn't—but he had access to a few. When Benny was fifteen, he took his father's black Buick and drove it to school—and promptly crashed into some bushes. The damage was negligible, but his father was so furious that his neck bulged out of his police collar like an overstuffed sausage.

"I'm sorry, Father," Benny mumbled, looking down. "I won't do it again."

"I will make sure that you never do it again," his father declared in his most fearsome tone. "I forbid you to drive the cars." But later that day, Big Pan bragged to his cohorts that his son had his spunk. "That's my boy, just like his old man!" Not long after, Pan Da brought home a German-made police motorcycle, ostensibly for use by his bodyguards. It wasn't a forbidden *car*, and soon Benny was zooming around with his pals, three privileged boys on motorcycles with the enemy-occupied city as their playground.

FOR ALL OF ST. JOHN'S campus egalitarianism, at the end of each week, when most students went home, their dissimilarity became abundantly clear. Some students headed to cars driven by chauffeurs in white livery who opened the doors of gleaming limousines. Faculty children, attending on reduced tuition, walked to their nearby university housing, while others on scholarship or of lesser means hopped on bicycles or walked to the public tram.

When it came time for Benny to head home, he looked for the Ford Willys GP with the canvas top and his father's husky bodyguard, standing at attention with his revolver strapped to his side. Then it was back to the English Tudor–style estate at 40 Jessfield Road, where life seemed even more dazzling than the weekend before. His mother had redecorated the big house with new artwork, carpets, chandeliers, English dinner settings, and other items "requisitioned" from Nationalist homes. Whatever she tired of, she replaced with another extravagance.

There had never been a reason for Benny to question his family's continued good fortune. So many of his wealthy classmates also seemed to live in luxury despite the war. And after all, his father was the admired and feared police commissioner Pan Da. In his refined enclave, Benny remained blissfully unaware of the growing criticisms of his father for failing to curb the rampant vice in the Badlands throughout his time as police commissioner. The gambling, prostitution, and other debauchery in the Western District were so out of control that even Japanese politicians in the National Diet in Tokyo were appalled. Wang Jingwei's presidency was dubbed the "Monte Carlo government" because of its flagrant dependence on kickbacks and bribery. Wang actually owned a casino in the French Concession. But Pan Da couldn't reduce the ubiquitous vice of the Badlands. Not when he was busy extracting revenues for himself as well.

Benny had been unaware that, in late 1941, his father had been demoted to another position at 76 and given the reduced title of "major general of the Special Police." After almost two years as police commissioner, Pan Da could no longer outmaneuver the many rivals for his lucrative position. C. C. Pan was replaced by another member of the Chinese puppet police force. However, because of his vast network of friends in high places, he wasn't banished to another city as some of his colleagues had been. And there was no discernible impact on the Pan family's lifestyle. The Sunday dinners, chauffeured cars, armed bodyguards, and extravagant habits of Benny's mother all continued without pause, as did Benny's excursions with the BDG Club, the parties, and after-school visits to eateries. The Pans' good times continued to roll.

YET BENNY COULD NOT have failed to notice how Shanghai had changed after December 8, 1941. Overnight, the once-protected foreign concessions had become fair game to the Japanese occupiers who had been tyrannizing the Chinese jurisdictions of Shanghai for the past four years.

On Benny's American missionary campus, the numbers of American teachers had dropped sharply as several headed back to the States, if they were lucky enough to find passage. Any teachers who were Allied nationals choosing to stay in Shanghai were required to wear red armbands marked with the letter *A, B, D,* or *X* for American, British, Dutch, or other. Unsurprisingly, few foreign teachers remained, although some had chosen to stay and tough it out.

To replace St. John's president F. L. Hawks Pott after the seventy-seven-year-old American had been among those evacuated, the university appointed its first Chinese to head the school: Dean William

Zu Liang Sung, a leading advocate of sports and physical education in China. President Sung's first priority was to keep the American school open and to prevent the Japanese from taking over the campus. The Japanese military had already seized other schools, such as Jiao Tong University on Avenue Haig. With St. John's strategic location on the Suzhou Creek near the Shanghai West Railway Station, Generalissimo Chiang Kai-shek himself was said to have asked Sung to keep the school open and out of the hands of the Japanese. President Sung called Benny's father for advice on how to deal with the occupation officials. "Do as they request; don't provoke them," Pan Da recommended. In addition to the mandatory language classes, there were Japanese observers stationed around the campus to monitor the school. Sung also added some noted Japanese Christians to the faculty. His actions alarmed some at the campus, but the school remained open.

As Japan's strength grew, the Allied positions in Shanghai became more tenuous by the day. At the very start of 1943, the United States and Britain signed treaties with the Nationalist government to restore China's sovereignty in Shanghai: The century of those countries' extraterritorial privileges that had so humiliated and angered China was over. The United Kingdom and United States needed to keep China in the Allied fold by countering the pro-Japan propaganda of puppet president Wang Jingwei and his denunciations of Western imperialism. However, these moves provoked great consternation among the foreign Shanghailanders, whose privileged status depended on their exemption from China's legal authority.

Not to be outdone, Vichy France, a partner in the Hitler-Hirohito-Mussolini Axis, soon followed with a similar recognition of Chinese sovereignty. The century-old treaty-port era of the International Settlement and French Concession had ended. With the waning of Anglo-American influence, Japan-friendly officials like Major General Pan Da seemed more deeply entrenched than ever.

By the summer of 1943, all the American and British teachers and their families had vanished from St. John's. Many had been rounded up and imprisoned in internment camps around Shanghai. The only foreign teachers remaining were from Vichy France or Axis or nonaligned countries, stateless Jewish teachers who'd escaped from the Nazis. At St. Mary's, one of the music instructors was a Jewish opera singer from Munich. But Chinese nationals were now in leadership positions at St. John's and other foreign schools for the first time since the missionaries had come to China in the mid-1800s. President Sung and other staff paid regular visits to their interned colleagues, as did students, passing some of their own limited food and clothing through the prison fences to the internees.

Benny hadn't joined any of those visits. He was too busy taking the daily boxing lessons that his father had arranged, insisting that the teenager build up his physique. When school ended each day, his father's White Russian bodyguard picked him up and chauffeured him to the boxing gym on Bubbling Well Road by the Lido Theater, where Benny pounded a punching bag, dancing and dodging with his trainer. His father was pleased when he began to change from a gangly teenager to a muscle-bound youth.

Benny proudly shows off the muscles he developed in the
course of his daily boxing regimen insisted on by his father.

Occasionally, Major General Pan Da asked his son to accompany him to official ceremonies, and sometimes Benny went alone to represent his father. He'd stand in his neatly pressed suit and tie with his chin up and back straight, trying to look older than fifteen or sixteen. Though his father never told him so, Benny sensed that he was being groomed in Pan Da's image. It was a role that he cherished.

O NCE BRITAIN AND THE UNITED STATES DECLARED WAR AGAINST Japan, life for Shanghailanders—the foreigners—swiftly changed. Immediately after December 8, 1941, all Allied nationals aged fourteen and above had to report to the Hamilton House near the Bund to register with Japanese gendarmes and receive ID numbers, as well as the red armbands they would have to wear at all times when in public.

Worse yet, Japan froze all bank accounts belonging to its enemy nationals. They were allowed to withdraw only two thousand yuan each month—a paltry amount for foreigners accustomed to pampered Shanghai lifestyles, effectively reducing them to the same income level as their Chinese servants. Each day, the Japanese military issued new edicts that further restricted where foreign Allied nationals could go, what they were allowed to do, how they conducted their lives.

Faced with bitter austerity, the Allied nationals were in a bind. Many expatriates worked for American telephone, gas, and electric utilities or the British waterworks, police, port, and customs. Now these entities were controlled by Japan, aiding its war effort. If Allied Shanghailanders quit their enemy-supervised jobs, they'd be stuck in China, destitute. Plenty of British bobbies, former coworkers of Pan Da, stayed on as members of the Shanghai Municipal Police—enforcing the will of Japan to crush all resistance. When their fellow

Americans and Britons back home learned of their work for the enemy, they angrily denounced them, accusing them of collaboration, even treason.

The glamorous Elder Sister, here with her husband, Kristian, is completely at ease in the company of Shanghailanders—the city's many foreign residents.

At the start of the war in Europe in 1939, after Germany's invasion of Czechoslovakia and Poland, Denmark had been a neutral country. As a Dane in Shanghai, Kristian Jarldane had expected his Danish passport to shield his family from trouble. Before Pearl Harbor, his household in the French Concession had carried on as if things were normal, in spite of the war outside their home. Bing and Ma watched baby Ole while Elder Sister socialized. Kristian still had his engineering job with the Shanghai Water Conservancy, which paid him in foreign currency—better than gold in the inflationary wartime economy. He joined other Shanghailanders in maintaining the three-hour lunchtime "tiffins," as well as afternoon high tea. Kristian would return to the apartment promptly at four o'clock for some strong English tea and thick slabs of dark bread from his favorite Russian-Jewish *boulangerie,* to be served with eel, fish, or some other meat fried in pork fat and onions.

But the expanding world war began to disrupt everything. The first shock hit Elder Sister and her husband on April 9, 1940, when Germany invaded Denmark. The Copenhagen government immediately surrendered to the Third Reich, becoming part of the Axis with Germany, Japan, and Italy. The couple wondered if that would be a plus in Japanese-occupied Shanghai.

As a Dane, Kristian wasn't required to wear an armband, nor was he subject to the mortifying financial restrictions confronting other Shanghailanders. He had plenty of company, for the nationals of other Axis-occupied countries were also exempt, as were the stateless White Russians, Ashkenazi Jews, and Indian Sikhs. But then, one week after all Allied nationals had to register, Kristian received orders from the Danish consular staff. He was required to provide them with the names and contact information of all Danish members of his household. Everyone in occupied Shanghai was to be accounted for.

Elder Sister's usual optimism was wearing thin. "What's next? The Jews coming from Europe say this was their port of last resort," she said. "If Shanghai is the last port, where can we go?" Her husband would shrug in reply. He and Elder Sister were friendly with some Jews living nearby who had fled the Nazis and been turned away from the United States, Canada, Britain, and other countries. Altogether about twenty thousand Ashkenazi Jews had arrived in Shanghai, the only major port in the world willing to accept them. Bing had learned of their ordeal on her daily walks with Ma, who pointed out the foreign men with long beards, some wearing yarmulkes.

To keep up with the rapidly changing situation, Kristian and Elder

Sister pored over newspapers and magazines each day, some of them borrowed and traded among his friends. He would try to sift news about the war from propaganda in *The Shanghai Times,* one of the few English-language papers permitted to continue publication—under Japanese supervision. Elder Sister would sit opposite him, reading the *Shen Bao,* one of the major Chinese dailies. Or she would thumb through copies of *Life* magazine and Shanghai tabloids. As they discussed the news in English, Bing would listen with interest, trying hard to understand and pick up new words.

Ma would scan the *Shen Bao* headlines after Elder Sister finished reading, later discussing it all with her friends. Thirteen-year-old Bing would perk up when they dissected the latest gossip about the movie stars featured in the Chinese newspapers. Her favorite magazine was *Life.* While she couldn't read most of it, the photographs introduced her to people around the world. Bing's vocabulary in both Chinese and English was growing. Though her formal schooling had stopped, she was determined to keep learning.

"The Germans are bombing the civilians in London day and night, the same bombing strategy the Japanese have used here," Kristian announced one day, looking up from his paper. "The casualties will be worse than in the Great War."

In early 1943, the Japanese issued the order that Shanghailanders had dreaded: All citizens of Allied countries were to be imprisoned. Kristian and Elder Sister watched helplessly as friends and neighbors were loaded onto trucks and shipped to one of the eight crowded and squalid internment camps on the outskirts of the city. Most of them were British and American men, women, and children. Some were forced to walk for miles and carry their own baggage, like coolies. Because the prominent Sassoons, Hardoons, and Kadoories—wealthy Baghdadi Jewish families who had lived in Shanghai for many years— were British citizens, they, too, were subject to internment. About seventy-six hundred Americans, British, Dutch, and other civilians were imprisoned between January and July 1943 to "prevent fifth-column activities and guarantee stabilized livelihood for the enemy nationals," according to the pro-Japan *Shanghai Times.* Ironically, this same rationale was being used by the U.S. government to incarcerate 120,000 Americans of Japanese descent in 1942—and duly noted by Japanese propagandists to label critics as hypocrites.

Bing had never seen the supremely confident Elder Sister so worried. She was unnerved at the prospect that men like her Danish husband might be sent away too. Though he wasn't interned, he had recently been fired from his job. The Japanese occupation authorities intended to replace foreign employees with Japanese civilians or pro-Japan Chinese. Now the family had no income—and Elder Sister was pregnant with their second child. Another boy, Peter, was born before the year was out.

At first, Kristian stayed home, smoking his pipe and reading the paper all day while Bing watched over the two boys. He soon tired of spending the day in the apartment and instead visited his Danish and other non-Allied friends. They passed the time at nearby parks or at Viennese cafés opened by Jewish refugees, sipping one cup of tea for hours. The cafés were full of aimless and apprehensive foreigners, since jobs for those who remained in Japanese-occupied Shanghai were now scarce.

With their money running low and no prospects of the war ending, Elder Sister sprang into action. Her workable English and smattering of other languages landed her a job as a typist in a trading company. She worked there for a few months—just long enough to observe how commodities were bought and sold. Then she struck out on her own.

First, she chose an English name. She liked the actress Betty Grable and took on her first name, becoming Betty Jarldane. Then she reached out to all the men she knew: anyone she might have danced or flirted with, especially any Japanese. Elder Sister knew her assets—her looks, her smarts, and her ability to talk a man into anything. And men, after all, had the money. Did they need any goods? Did they know of anyone looking for an apartment or a godown? One of her former Japanese acquaintances had a shipment of khaki cloth to sell—Elder Sister offered to find buyers. She was out on the pavement, talking to wholesalers and retailers, finding out what they needed and what they wanted to unload. With every deal, she earned a commission.

Elder Sister's unselfconscious ease with foreigners and their languages gave her an advantage in brokering apartments vacated by internees and others who had left the city. With each rental, she claimed the key money, a special Shanghai fee that was far more than the commission, which of course she claimed as well.

Bing watched with awe as Elder Sister transformed herself, wheeling and dealing with strangers to support the entire household. She also instigated drastic measures to cut their expenses. She convinced Kristian to rent out one of the two bedrooms in their apartment, reorganizing the space so that their household occupied two rooms instead of three. With Bing moving in to help with the boys, there would be five crowded into the smaller space—Elder Sister, Kristian, the two boys, and Bing. Ma stayed in a small inexpensive apartment two blocks away.

A renter was quickly found. He was a Chinese businessman from Fujian Province who had graduated from Keio University, one of Japan's leading schools, and now worked for a Japanese company in Shanghai. His girlfriend moved in too. Neither Elder Sister nor Kristian seemed to mind that he worked for the Japanese—it was becoming harder to find work in occupied Shanghai that did not have some association with their occupiers. To Bing, the tenants seemed nice enough, and they kept to themselves. Now that seven people lived in the apartment, Bing did her best to stay out of everyone's way.

IN 1943, THERE WAS an additional twist in Bing's life: Elder Sister brought another adopted girl into the crowded household. Ah Mei was thirteen, just like Bing, and had also been abandoned. Bing had never known a girl like herself before, though abandoned girls were everywhere in China. Ah Mei wasn't embarrassed at all to share that her parents had given her away when she was too young to remember. All she knew was that she had been born in Shanghai. A relative of Ma's had adopted her but had fallen on hard times. Ma had suggested that Ah Mei move in with Elder Sister, who could use more help.

Once again, Elder Sister rearranged the apartment. In wartime every household made room for extra people. Ah Mei and Bing were to sleep on the floor of a small area off the kitchen, and once that was settled, no one gave the new girl another thought. Except Bing. She was thrilled.

From their first meeting, the two girls hit it off. Ah Mei was taller and rounder in places, whereas Bing still looked like a child. She was outgoing and confident, while Bing was quiet and shy, imprinted with the soft manners of Suzhou. Ah Mei would say things that Bing wouldn't dare, freely expressing her likes and dislikes. She sometimes mimicked Ma's rants behind her back, forcing Bing to choke back her laughter or risk Ma's wrath.

Bing had never had a friend before. Now she had someone to confide in, to whisper about silly things and giggle into the night with. Bing shared her frustrations about Ma and school, her shame and sadness at being abandoned twice, her dream of finding her beloved father one day. She felt lighter after telling Ah Mei the painful secrets she had held in for so long. Even Ma's scoldings felt less oppressive now.

And finally Bing had someone to pal around with. When Ma took her afternoon nap with the boys, Bing and Ah Mei walked arm in arm along busy Avenue Joffre to see posters of the latest movies playing at the Cathay and Paris movie theaters and to admire the goods in the windows of fancy stores, chocolate shops, and the Russian cafés selling pastries and bright red borscht.

One Sunday in the fall of 1943, when the steam heat of Shanghai's summer was turning cool and dry, Elder Sister and Kristian borrowed a car for an excursion to Hangzhou for the day with their sons. Bing and Ah Mei decided to go on a trip of their own. With a few yuan that Elder Sister had slipped them, they rode a tram all the way to the Bund. The two girls gaped at the massive stone buildings and, for good luck, rubbed the heads of the bronze lions in front of the imposing Hongkong and Shanghai Bank. They shivered at the sight of dozens of Japanese warships, their flags proudly displaying the rising sun against the white background. When they reached the big four department stores, they rode up and down the moving stairs at the Sun Sun.

By the time they reached the British racecourse, at Tibet Road, it was late afternoon. The extensive grounds were being used by the

Japanese to garrison their soldiers and store their booty, looted from the homes of Chinese and now from the interned foreigners as well. The nearby Great World Amusement Center had been rebuilt after the Bloody Saturday bombing. Bing laughed at the clever puppet shows and her distorted reflections in the Hall of Mirrors. As suppertime approached, the girls spent the last of their coins at the hawker stands, choosing from foods grilled on sticks, slices of melon, pork buns and curried pastries, candied lotus roots, and sweets of every kind. There wasn't a single sign reminder of the thousands killed in the bombings only six years before.

With no money left for a tram, the two walked the mile or so back home. When they arrived at the apartment on Avenue Joffre, Bing was exhausted—and happy. It was the first time in her life she'd had a day of pure fun.

"WHAT MAKES YOU THINK you can sit around like some no-good lazy dog who eats, sleeps, and shits all day while I bend my old back for you? You're wasting time looking at those pictures. No one in America wants a worthless girl like you."

Ma was just getting started, Bing knew. She reluctantly put aside the copy of *Life* magazine. She'd had a busy morning, pounding bedding to shake out the bedbugs, doing her best to chase after and stomp them as they scurried away. She had taken four-year-old Ole on a long walk, playing with him until he fell asleep, while Ma and the wet nurse minded infant Peter. Bing had hoped to enjoy a few moments with her favorite foreign magazine before Ah Mei returned from the marketplace with the day's slim rations for lunch. The photographs of smiling people living in spacious American homes were so unlike their lives in war-torn China.

Once Ma latched on to a nit to pick, she never let go. There would be no end to her litany of complaints, curses, and vituperations. Bing picked up a broom and tried to look busy until Ah Mei returned. At least Bing could commiserate with her friend. Ma's fuse had grown shorter and her temper flared hotter ever since Kristian had lost his job earlier in the year. Anything could set her off—the paltry food ration coupons, a change in the weather, Ole's naughty behavior. And just about everything that Bing or Ah Mei did.

Only two things prevented Ma from exploding. The first was the simple presence of Elder Sister's husband. Although he couldn't understand everything Ma said, Kristian had lived in Shanghai long enough to recognize her choice curses. She moderated herself when he was present.

The second was opium. A few puffs from her long opium pipe relaxed Ma. She said it took all her aches, pains, and worries away. But the price of everything was so inflated in those days that Ma's "medicine" was harder to come by. And that made her more peevish than ever.

Without those small breaks from Ma's temper, Bing didn't think she could stand it anymore. To be fair, everyone, including Ma, had good reason to be on edge after six years of unrelenting wartime hardship. Elder Sister often came home without finding a single customer for her trading and barter activities. As talented and clever as she had proven to be, even she was having trouble keeping up with inflation, and the scarcity and high cost of food.

Elder Sister and her foreign husband were better off than many, but their circumstances were worsening. Ma had started doing the cooking because there was no money for servants. This, too, added to her irritability. Parsing out the rations each night, she saved the best for the man of the family—though even he was lucky to get a single egg or slice of meat. Food was served first to Kristian, then to Ole, Elder Sister, and Ma—in that order. Luckily Peter needed only milk, which they made from Klim powder. Bing and Ah Mei got what was left. When there was nothing left, the girls had to eat plain corn or barley mush.

Bing wasn't sure which was worse—Ma's temper or the inedible mush. At night, in their bedrolls, the girls whispered their frustrations and, when they dared, their dreams.

"I took some mush to the alley for the dogs to eat, but not one mangy cur took a bite!" exclaimed Ah Mei. "It's not fit for a dog."

Bing smiled grimly. "Even if I'm aching from hunger, I can't swallow any more of that mush."

Then she hesitantly told Ah Mei about her recurring nightmare. In it, her *baba* was waving and calling to her, smiling. She'd run to him, but just when she was close enough to grab his hand, he vanished. In his place, Mama Hsu appeared, looking elegant in her plain *qipao* and beckoning for Bing to follow. Just as Bing was about to reach her, she disappeared too.

"I don't know how to find my *baba*, but I still know the address that Mama Hsu gave me. Before she left me with Ma and Elder Sister, she told me to memorize it in case I wanted to reach her. Do you think she's calling for me through my dreams?"

Excited, Ah Mei answered in the affirmative. "She must be sending you a message, just as when Ma says the ghosts of her dead ancestors are trying to contact her."

"Could Mama Hsu have returned to Suzhou from Chongqing? I'm sure she would treat us better," Bing ventured.

"Let's go and find out!" Ah Mei shot back.

Startled, Bing paused. "You mean, run away?"

Ah Mei nodded. "Why not?"

THE TWO TEENAGERS STARTED planning. It was already November. With winter approaching, they had to move quickly. Between them they had a few yuan, saved from their New Year's *hong bao* and the occasional change Elder Sister used to give them when times were better. But then Bing had second thoughts about running away, especially when four-year-old Ole clung to her. He'd cry for her, she knew. She would miss him and the new baby. Elder Sister needed her and had always treated her well.

Just when Bing was about to change her mind, Ma blew up over something she'd done.

"Go ahead and jump in the Huangpu River; see if I care! You won't even know how to drown yourself!" Ma barked at Bing, complaining into the night and chain-smoking until she finally fell asleep.

"Let's do it," Bing told Ah Mei.

It had been four years since Bing had last seen Mama Hsu, and she longed to know what had happened to her. Had she made it to Chongqing? Had she survived the heavy bombings that the Japanese bragged about in their propaganda? If Mama was alive, would she take Bing back? Even if she didn't, maybe she would know how to find Baba. Bing still held on to that hope.

Planning their move carefully, the girls decided to leave early in the morning, while everyone was still asleep and before the gatekeeper opened the bamboo fence of their building's courtyard. Each carrying a small cloth bag containing her worldly possessions, the two girls climbed over the fence to Avenue Joffre and jumped onto the back of a tram headed to the Shanghai North railway station. From there, they planned to catch a train to Suzhou.

But the frequent bombings of the railway were causing long delays, clogging the station with people. By nightfall, there was still no train. With nowhere to go, Bing and Ah Mei squeezed onto a bench in the station and waited. Bing didn't mind—she was determined to get away. She kept reciting the location she had memorized, desperate not to forget any part of it. It was the location of Mama Hsu's uncle. After their long day, the girls huddled together and fell asleep on the cold bench.

The next morning, they spent a few fen on some plain steamed bread and pieces of dried ginger to help stanch their hunger. Finally the train to Suzhou arrived, and the crowd surged forward in one terrifying wave. Swept up and pushed forward, Bing and Ah Mei somehow scrambled on board. When they arrived at the Suzhou train station, they had no money left for a pedicab to take them to the uncle's address.

Ah Mei, the more streetwise of the two, had anticipated that they'd need more money. When they left the apartment, she had stuffed Kristian's leather house slippers into her sack. The European slippers still looked new. The girls went from shop to shop at the train station, trying to sell the slippers. Sure enough, one of the shopkeepers bought them. With the money, the girls hopped into a pedicab and soon arrived at the doorstep of Mama Hsu's uncle.

Bing swallowed hard, and Ah Mei gave her a nudge. Bing raised her fist to the heavy wooden door and gave a firm knock.

An elderly man with the wispy beard and long gray gown of a scholar opened the door. Bing instantly recognized him.

"Uncle, I've come to look for Mama," Bing told him. "Before she left for Chongqing, she instructed me to come to you if I needed to reach her. She said that you would know where to find her. Is Mama back in Suzhou?"

The old man stroked his beard. "Bing, it's been five years since I last saw you. You were just a little girl. Now you've grown into a fine young lady," he said gently. "But I don't know where my niece is. The Japanese are in control here, and we can't get letters from the interior. The last time I heard from her was two years ago. She was in Chongqing then. I pray to Buddha each day to look after her."

Bing looked down to hide her disappointment. She had dared to imagine a happy reunion with her kindly Mama Hsu. Ah Mei touched Bing's arm to comfort her. After all their planning, they'd hit a dead end.

The old uncle looked closely at Bing, then Ah Mei.

"You girls can stay here for a few days," he said. "I'm sorry I cannot offer more than that. Life here has been difficult under the Japanese. If you wish to remain in Suzhou, I'll help you find a place to stay and work, but that's the best I can do."

Bing nodded slowly. She would take her chances in Suzhou.

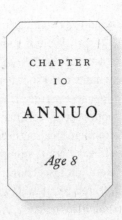

CHAPTER
10

ANNUO

Age 8

"TWINKLE, TWINKLE, LITTLE STAR. HOW I WONDER WHAT you are . . ."

Annuo hesitated for a split second. Then she plowed on. Reciting her poem in English, she raised her voice so it would reach the far corners of the room full of students and teachers. As she spoke, she lifted her arms toward the sky, making the most of her moment to shine.

In Shanghai, many schools had traditionally begun teaching English in the third grade. Pétain Primary School, Annuo's school for the past two years, was holding its last English contest before the school would have to switch to Japanese, under fiat of the occupation authorities. Annuo had a knack for English, with its strange conjugations and peculiar "he-she-it" constructions so foreign to Chinese. The quiet girl with the nom de guerre of "Chang Tsen" overcame her shyness to win the competition and a beautiful certificate that read CHANG TSEN: FIRST PLACE.

Eager to show Muma her award, Annuo ran home to 275C Avenue Pétain. With Muma still at work in her pharmaceutical sales job, Annuo proudly showed it off to her eleven-year-old brother, Charley. He looked up from the book he had borrowed from the corner stall and exclaimed, "Gee, that Chang Tsen is really something!" then went back to reading.

Annuo waited at the window, watching for her mother. The same nagging fears tugged at the girl: What if some cruel Japanese sentry detected Muma's false identity papers? What if she didn't come home?

Muma had drilled them many times to stay alert on their way to and from school and to avoid Japanese patrols. If Annuo was ever stopped, she was to bow and be cooperative—as Chang Tsen. Nor could they feel secure at home, where their location near the Japanese garrison and the frequent sound of heavy boots stomping by triggered a panicked reminder of their late-night inspections.

Finally her mother appeared in the walkway below. Annuo could hear her slow footsteps coming up the stairs. After Muma got comfortable in her big chair, Annuo pulled out the certificate from behind her back.

"What's this? First place? Very good!" Muma looked up and gave Annuo a smile of approval. "Can you show us your first-place performance?" Muma called over Charley, Li-Ning, and their amah, Zhongying, to watch the show. But first, she glanced out the window to see if anyone was listening.

Annuo held her head high and began, pointing upward. At the end, her family applauded, and Annuo swelled with pride. For a moment, all thoughts of war had vanished.

ONE AFTERNOON IN THE EARLY months of 1944, when Annuo was already home from her fourth-grade class and the sky had turned to winter's dusk, she heard a light knock on the door. She called over to Zhongying. Peeking at the unexpected caller, the amah let the strange man enter. His hair was unkempt and his clothes bedraggled. At first, Annuo just stared, thinking a beggar had come into their home. Suddenly, she wondered, Could this be my father?

At that same moment, the man growled, "Is this how you greet your *baba*?"

Annuo's face burned. She had seen him only once, more than two years earlier, since he had left to join the resistance in Jiangsu in 1939. This time he had arrived just as he had the last time, with nothing but his ragged clothes.

Before Annuo could reply, five-year-old Li-Ning came bounding over, shouting in her high-pitched baby voice, "Baba, Baba, you're home at last!"

Her father scooped up Li-Ning and held her tight. "Shhh, not so loud, my *nai baozi*, my cutie pie! We can't let the neighbors hear." Annuo slowly inched her way out of the room. Baba didn't even notice that she had gone.

When Muma arrived home that evening, she was just as surprised to find her husband there as Annuo had been. She immediately warned them all to keep their voices low and act as though nothing had changed, especially near the landlord and neighbors.

"You'd better stay indoors and away from the windows," she said, looking at her husband. "In these two years, life has become much more harsh. The Japanese have tightened their controls. Spies are everywhere—the Japanese and their puppets have created a list of every household. They've organized a neighborhood network of *bao-*

Japanese sentries check identity papers at major intersections and bridges, while creating a network of spies and watchdogs to monitor everyone in occupied Shanghai.

jia snitches to spy on everyone. Even the foreigners have *baojia* captains. It's more dangerous than ever."

Under this *baojia* identification system, a number and card had been issued to every person in Shanghai. This ID card had to be carried at all times and produced on demand for any Japanese authority—on the streets, in restaurants, and in other public places. Ration coupons for rice, cooking oil, and other essentials were handed out only to those who registered, making it impossible to escape the *baojia*. Every neighborhood had its watchdog who reported to the puppets and their Japanese masters. Waiters and servants were ordered to spy on people in their establishments and households. Everyone, even foreigners, had to register births, deaths, overnight guests, and family members who were away. It was increasingly difficult to hide from the watchful eyes of the enemy.

By 1944, in Shanghai and elsewhere in occupied China, the enemy's depleted war machine was bearing down on civilians more severely than ever to squeeze out critical resources. The Americans were making headway against Japan in the Pacific, but Chinese resistance efforts in Jiangsu Province, where Annuo's father was based, had suffered serious losses to the enemy. To evade capture by Japanese soldiers and Chinese Communists, her father had once again had to weave his way through rice fields and small villages, looking like any other refugee. In Shanghai, he could get reoutfitted. Once again, Annuo's mother had to shop discreetly during her work rounds for the items he needed: clothes, eyeglasses, Parker pen, watch—Rolex preferred. This time it was much riskier, and goods were harder to come by.

With all the excitement surrounding her father's homecoming, at first Annuo paid no attention to her scratchy throat. She had once been a healthy child, but during her months of living with strangers, she had become more fragile. When Annuo finally realized she felt sick, she said nothing, not wanting to disturb her father. No one noticed that she barely touched her food. Within the week, Annuo had a raging fever.

By then her mother knew that Annuo was quite ill, unable to swallow even a spoonful of broth. But Muma still kept her home, afraid that their identities would be compromised if she took her to a hospital. That could bring certain disaster from the Japanese Kempeitai—their fearsome military and secret police—and the puppet police at 76, all constantly on the hunt for Nationalists like her father. A trained physician, Annuo's mother tried to treat her daughter while continuing to go to work to keep up appearances, leaving the girl in the care of her amah and father during the day.

But Annuo's condition deteriorated. Her neck was swollen and painful, and she was struggling to breathe. Worried, her mother stopped at home in the middle of her workday to see how Annuo was doing.

Annuo's father reported, "She's good—she hasn't made any noise all day."

"What?" her mother asked in alarm. "It's a bad sign if she's that quiet!" She could no longer avoid taking Annuo to the hospital.

It was too dangerous for her parents to go. After bundling the sick girl for the cold ride in a pedicab, Muma took her to one of her husband's sisters who lived in Shanghai and asked her to rush Annuo to St. Luke's Hospital. She couldn't even let the sister know where the family lived—better not to give the *baojia* snitches any information for 76.

At the hospital, the doctor took one look at Annuo and instantly diagnosed her condition: an advanced case of diphtheria. He chastised her aunt. "Why did you wait so long? In another hour, she'd be gone." Annuo was so ill that she looked like a ghost. In her delirium, she thought she had become one. The doctors insisted that "Chang Tsen" stay quarantined in the children's ward until her condition stabilized. She was too weak and her diphtheria too contagious for them to release her. Doctors worried that the crowded and unhealthy living conditions in Shanghai could lead to an uncontrollable outbreak. Japan had already attacked the Chinese with special bombs containing fleas infected with bubonic plague, cholera, anthrax, and other deadly germs. Any infectious disease could turn into an epidemic, further devastating the war-weakened populace.

Several days passed before Annuo's fever broke—or had it been weeks? Her mind cleared enough for her to know that she was in a hospital room, plain, antiseptic, white. No one from her family was there. Where was her mother? The hospital was unfamiliar and scary, with air that stank of rubbing alcohol, disinfectant, and other unsettling odors. Perpendicular to where she lay, a boy of about six was in another hospital bed. He too was feverish. Family members surrounded him all day long, his doting grandmother always by his side. She stayed until she was forced to leave at night. Annuo heard someone say "typhoid" and figured that it must have been as bad as her diphtheria. The boy's many visitors deepened her own loneliness. No one came to see her. Annuo thought she caught looks of pity from some of the boy's family members.

Finally, her mother stopped by to check on her but could spare only a few minutes from her work. No one else came, and days went by before Annuo saw her mother again. Each visit was brief. Sometimes her mother didn't even sit down.

Annuo couldn't help thinking how lucky that boy was to have so many people lavishing attention on him. She knew that her family had to stay hidden, but she still envied the loving care he received. Whenever he groaned or whimpered, his grandmother sprang up to apply a cool compress to his forehead, plump his pillows, or tell him a story. She'd made it clear that she didn't approve of the Western medicine or the foreign-trained doctors. Whenever they left the room, she'd chant to one god or another to ward off evil spirits, and pray for her beloved grandson's good health. Annuo found some comfort in her rhythmic chanting, a small consolation for the long days without a single visitor.

One day, against strict doctor's orders, the grandmother brought some homemade porridge for her grandson. Because the typhoid was in his intestines, he had been allowed very little to eat and kept moaning that he was hungry. When the boy started to gobble up the delicious-smelling porridge, Annuo could almost taste the food. Wishing that she could have some, she turned away and closed her eyes. Soon she dozed off.

Suddenly Annuo awoke to the grandmother's scream. The boy was convulsing. All at once he stopped, then stiffened as a hideous gurgle came from his throat. Annuo couldn't bear to keep watching. Soon there was silence. In a moment, a high-pitched wail rose out of his grandmother. Nurses rushed into the room. Annuo peeked from behind her covers and saw the boy's white face, his eyes staring ahead. His little body seemed to be shriveling as she watched. Was he hovering somewhere in the room? He'd been alive when she fell asleep. Now he was a ghost.

His bed was so close that she could have touched it. So close that his ghost body could have touched her. Terrified, Annuo curled up in the corner of her bed, her heart pounding. She turned her back to the corpse and the chilling scene around her. The boy's body remained for hours as distraught relatives poured in, each shrieking and sobbing louder than the one before. Annuo tried to block out the wailing and the horror of what she had seen. When someone finally came to take the boy's body away, she shut her eyes tight. But she could not shut out that look of anguish on his face after he'd turned into a ghost.

Would this happen to her? she wondered. After all, the doctor said she'd been close to dying too. She was terrified and full of questions, but there was no one for her to ask. And no one to comfort her.

Alone in her room, Annuo's only companion was fear. A few days later, her mother stopped by, but Annuo couldn't talk about the ghost boy or ask her anxious questions. Her mother's visits were too short, and children were not supposed to bother their parents. But at night, Annuo had trouble sleeping. When she did sleep, she was haunted by the ghost boy. Nightmares forced her awake. On better days, she dreamed that Muma had brought her some special treats: Shanghai *xiao long bao* soup dumplings, petits fours from the Russian bakery, and—her favorite—roasted chestnuts. She imagined her mother sitting by her bed, peeling the chestnuts, and feeding her pieces of the precious nutmeat. Just pretending made Annuo feel a little better.

Weeks passed before the doctor would allow Annuo to go home. In anticipation of her release, her mother brought her some small cans of food—bamboo shoots and wheat gluten. It was the first regular food she had eaten in a long time, and it was the best she'd ever tasted. The black-market delicacies must have cost her mother dearly. Annuo brightened. Her dream was coming true.

Finally Annuo could leave. She couldn't wait to return to the apartment on Avenue Pétain, to her brother and sister, and to Zhongying. Her father had left while she was in the hospital, to return to the enemy-occupied war zone in Jiangsu, she was relieved to hear.

Annuo desperately wanted to get back to school, to catch up on what she had missed of fourth grade. Her mother had bad news for her.

"You're not better yet. The hospital released you because you're no longer in danger. But you're still contagious, and you must stay in until you're well."

Annuo became a prisoner in the apartment, quarantined from everyone, even from her younger sister. Her mother relegated Annuo to one room, explaining that even the air she breathed could make others ill. Her mother also instituted some new sanitary practices at home. She lectured her children on the health hazards of using one's own chopsticks to jab at the food in communal serving dishes. She introduced two different colors of chopsticks: red for serving food from the common dishes, black for personal use and not to be shared. No one was to touch Annuo's utensils or food. She was a pariah at home, retreating into her room and further within herself. There were no more thoughts of returning to school. Instead, Annuo took up her perch by the window. From there, she could watch as Shanghai passed her by.

ANNUO'S BIG BROTHER, CHARLEY, became her eyes and ears to the world. When he got home from school, she would ask him to make sense of what she had observed from her window: Why were there so few cars on the streets? Where had all the foreigners gone?

While trying to keep a safe distance, twelve-year-old Charley patiently shared what he knew: No one could use cars anymore because there was no gas. The Japanese and the traitors took it all. Some people fixed their cars to run on coal, but the Japanese took the coal too, just as they'd taken the rice and the good food. They'd taken most of the cars too, so the people who still had cars must have been enemy Japanese or Chinese traitors. The foreigners from countries at war with Japan and Germany—like America, Britain, and Canada—had been sent to special prison camps on the city outskirts. But plenty of foreigners remained in the city—Germans, Japanese, and their French, Danish, Portuguese, and White Russian allies. The Jews hadn't been sent to prison camps, but the Japanese had ordered them to move to Hongkou. Everything was changing, only the red-hatted Sikh police remained the same, directing traffic and hitting Chinese with their police sticks.

Charley ended his descriptions with some brotherly advice: "When you get better, you'll have to be very careful because the Japanese soldiers are everywhere."

BEFORE CHARLEY CAME HOME from school, he'd stop at sidewalk bookstalls where vendors displayed their wares, allowing passersby to browse and borrow books for a few fen. Charley loved to thumb through comics and magazines with photographs. He often brought books home, and Annuo devoured them. Kung fu novels, translations of *The Three Musketeers* and other foreign books, *Dream of the Red Chamber* and other Chinese classics—Annuo read them all. Books were her one true escape from war and illness during her months of quarantine.

Though Annuo's condition improved, for a long time she wasn't strong enough to go out. She could often sit unnoticed as her mother and Zhongying discussed the latest problems. She listened to them talk about the black market, where white rice was nearly impossible to buy for any amount. They speculated about the neighborhood snitches and mapped out the best routes for avoiding encounters with Japanese patrols. Annuo learned basic arithmetic and economics from their observations about prices that increased wildly each day. She listened to them compute the relative value of the different currencies being used in Shanghai: the Nationalist yuan and the Wang Jingwei puppet-government yuan, the U.S. dollar, small gold bars, and Mexican silver dollars. The complexities of daily living in occupied Shanghai provided alternative schooling to Annuo.

Still, no matter how Zhongying tried to make their rations palatable, the coarse red rice, the limited cooking oil and other foodstuffs offered scant nutrition for Annuo's weakened body. Diphtheria had left her so emaciated that she barely had the energy to walk around the small apartment.

Beyond the walls of her home on Avenue Pétain, the seven-year war with Japan was beginning to shift. Though Japanese censors and propagandists touted their nation's strength to cover up its string of battlefront defeats, they couldn't hide what everyone in Shanghai could see: On June 9, 1944, the Americans conducted their first air raid on Shanghai. The United States was soon sending B-29 bombers over the city-on-the-sea with regularity, pounding Japanese military installations. Charley showed Annuo pictures of the planes, pointing out the differences between Chinese Curtiss Hawks and Flying Tiger Warhawks; American Mustangs, B-24 Liberators, and B-29 Superfortresses; Japanese Mitsubishi "Zeros" and Kawasaki fighters. She patiently kept watch for air strikes from her window. When night approached, she helped Zhongying close the blackout drapes ordered by the occupation and puppet authorities.

Japan was so weakened by early 1945 that the drone of American B-24 and B-29 bombers flying overhead had become a daily noontime event. To protect its munitions depots and garrisons, the Japanese military took over more homes, schools, and office buildings to camouflage their soldiers and supplies. Munitions were moved into the first floor of the Embankment Building, a luxury apartment complex and the largest residential building in Asia, built by Victor Sassoon. Insinuating themselves into the core of the city, the Japanese planned to hold the civilian population hostage against Allied attack.

NEWS OF THE AMERICAN air raids over Shanghai reached Annuo's father in his distant Nationalist base in Jiangxi Province, thanks to the Nationalist army's intelligence network. He feared that Shanghai was no longer safe for his family and sent a message to his wife via courier: She must leave her job and apartment immediately and move with the children to a distant post in Jiangxi Province, part of Free China, nearly five hundred miles southwest of Shanghai. He would meet them there.

In early 1945, Annuo was just turning ten. She could see that her mother was disturbed by the message. The journey to Jiangxi would be far more difficult than their last trip six years earlier. It was winter. They would have to circumvent enemy lines, cross rivers, and navigate snow-filled mountain passes. Wouldn't it be safer to remain in the former French Concession than to cross a war zone with three children? In addition, the money Annuo's mother had saved from her work was tied up in the apartment, from the key money and deposits she'd paid to move in to the small stash of medicines and samples she had accumulated to sell or barter. But Annuo's father wouldn't have any of it. He sent another message, instructing his wife to abandon everything. To ensure her compliance, he arranged for a squad of Nationalist troops in Pudong, across the Huangpu River, to escort his family.

It was disconcerting for Annuo to see her smart, competent, and beautiful mother struggle with this new directive from her husband. After all, Annuo's mother had ensured their survival all these years while their father had been absent. Yet her modern education, style, and sensibility were no match for the weight of Chinese tradition that compelled her to obey her husband's command.

There was at least one exciting prospect ahead for Annuo: She would be freed from her quarantine. She hadn't ventured outside in several months, and her leg muscles had atrophied. Muma warned that it would be a long, hard journey. Annuo didn't care; she couldn't wait to get out.

Annuo's mother gave her weakest child a long look as she described the trip. "Annuo, it won't be easy, but you'll have to try your best." Annuo, not knowing the hardships ahead, nodded vigorously. She was elated to be freed from her cage at last! Besides, Zhongying was coming along too. Everything would be all right.

OUTSIDE, ANNUO SWAYED LIKE a toddler learning to walk. Zhongying helped her along at first, but soon she could stand on her own, a bit wobbly but exuberant. The five of them—the four "Changs" and Zhongying—left on an early February morning in 1945 for a remote part of Pudong, where they met their Nationalist escorts—

underground soldiers of the resistance. If the Japanese discovered any of them, they would be summarily executed.

The soldiers walked while the women and children rode on moon carts—single wooden wheels with planks on either side to sit on. Scrawny laborers pushed them along over the bumpy country roads. Annuo clung tight to Charley, afraid that she might fall off and get crushed by the heavy wheel. When they reached the shore along the East China Sea, the soldiers carried the women and children on their shoulders and waded through the water to a small fishing boat. Annuo's family and the soldiers lay at the bottom of the boat's stinking cargo hold, packed in like sardines. Gunshots whizzed by the vessel as it ventured past the Japanese patrol lines. Once at sea, the rickety boat tossed and rocked like a toy.

The next day, they reached shore in southern Zhejiang Province. It too was in enemy-held territory. A soldier plucked Annuo out of the boat as if she were a mere chicken feather and loaded her onto a three-wheeled wagon. She thought her bones might shatter from the herky-jerky ride across the rough country trails they took to avoid Japanese soldiers. As the pathways narrowed, they switched to sedan chairs, hoisted on the shoulders of coolies. Where the sedan chairs couldn't be used, they walked—southward through Zhejiang Province, westward across Fujian, then northeast to Jiangxi Province, the whole journey encompassing more than four hundred miles.

At night they slept in farmhouses, shacks, and small family tombs used as ancestral shrines that were scattered about the countryside. Crowding into dirty rooms, they slept on cold, damp floors, remaining fully clothed in case they had to make a quick getaway. The soldiers slept in other shelters. When they were lucky, they bought food from local farmers. For much of the trip, they subsisted on hard-boiled eggs.

The shy, delicate city girl pushed herself along, timidly crossing rugged terrain and rocky streams as they slowly made their way to Jiangxi Province. In the last, most difficult stage, the family had to walk single file on steep mountain paths too narrow for Annuo to hold on to anyone. On one side was a sheer mountain wall. On the other, a precipice of jagged rock falling a thousand feet below. Sometimes rain turned the path into slippery mud.

At one point, Annuo knew she was in trouble when her legs began to wobble. Beyond her feet was a dizzying drop. One slip and she would be swallowed up by what appeared to be a bottomless chasm. Unable to move for fear of slipping over the edge, she squatted in her tracks, terrified.

"Annuo, we can't stop here; you must get up!" Muma implored. Annuo moved her foot and watched a rock tumble down the side of the cliff. "Don't look down," her mother said calmly. "Just put one foot in front of the other. You can do it." Annuo willed herself to get up. That night, they found a small ancestral shrine belonging to a nearby household. Inside, they each ate a boiled egg and tried to sleep amid some family's gods and ghosts. Sleep brought Annuo little peace; she couldn't forget that she would have to brave the mountain again with the morning's light.

THE FOUR-MONTH TREK WAS more difficult than anything Annuo could possibly have imagined. Somehow she just kept going. When they finally reached Jiangxi in June, it felt like a miracle.

On the cool, cloudy day that they reached the Nationalist government outpost, her father wasn't there. Exhausted, the family moved into a dorm-like rooming house. Eventually her father returned from the battle zone, and they were reunited, laughing and crying together. He moved them into a large ancestral shrine that was almost as big as a small house, but then he mostly stayed away, busy with his official responsibilities. Annuo saw little of him.

During their long march through remote areas, the small band of travelers had had no news of the war. They didn't know that Germany had surrendered until they reached Jiangxi and even then didn't realize that Japan was close to defeat. Just two months after they arrived in Jiangxi, Annuo's father came rushing to their quarters, shouting, "The war is over! At last the war is over—Japan has surrendered!" He and Annuo's mother jumped up and down, hugging each other and laughing. Annuo, too, shouted in both joy and amazement. She had never seen her parents so happy—or in an embrace.

But then, everyone was hugging and cheering. A joyous celebration erupted all around them. People streamed out to the road and alleys all at once, shouting, jumping, laughing, crying. Temple gongs rang out as firecrackers and gunshots exploded. The terrible eight-year war was over! War had darkened ten-year-old Annuo's young life for as long as she could remember. Even her mother and father could barely remember a time of peace without the fear of imminent war.

Overnight, experienced Nationalist administrators were urgently needed to rebuild the government and country. Annuo's father was dispatched to Shanghai by airplane. With millions of relocated people living in the interior, Annuo and the rest of her family would have to wait to return by boat. They joined others on crowded barges pulled along the Yangtze. Annuo passed the weeks-long return sharing war stories with other children, like Nellie Sung Tao, who had witnessed many bombings in Chongqing and told how she'd watched scavengers sift through body parts for rings and other valuables in the aftermath. The river voyage was a less arduous and more direct route than the family's long trek.

Before Annuo's father left with the other Nationalist officials, he had informed his wife that she would be moving with the children to Hangzhou, not Shanghai. He believed that there would be chaos in postwar Shanghai: Soldiers of many armies were converging there, and arrests and executions of collaborators were likely, as was the possibility of street violence. His pronouncements had stunned Annuo's mother—all the money she had saved as "Mrs. Chang" was still in Shanghai. It didn't matter, he had declared. "There's a simple solution—we'll give it all away."

There was no further discussion. He had already arranged everything with General Han Deqin, who was in the process of sending his own family to Hangzhou. Thanks to her father's high rank, Annuo's family would be moving into one of the mansions that the Nationalists were taking back from Japanese officials and their Chinese puppets. Annuo's mother would have to follow his wishes without question, and Annuo would start a new life in Hangzhou.

CHAPTER
11

BENNY

Age 16

SHANGHAI, 1944

OXING LESSONS HAD TURNED BENNY—NOW IN HIS THIRD
and last year at St. John's Middle School—into a strapping young
man. His tailored suits accentuated his athletic physique, and Major
General C. C. Pan beamed with pride when he introduced his son to
the rich and influential of Shanghai at his extravagant Sunday dinner
parties.

Except for those special moments with his father, Benny rarely saw
him on his weekends home from school. In recent years, Pan Da had
made it a habit to depart soon after the Sunday dinners. Benny assumed that the demands of his father's position called him away—and
in fact, he was glad for the reprieve from his father's critical eye.

Benny's mother also seemed busy and content, visiting her wide
network of society matrons, making obligatory social appearances
with the major general, or playing mah-jongg late into the night.

Debonair and charming men were always showering his elegant
mother with attention and lavish gifts. She was courteous and gracious
to all her guests, whether high-ranking Japanese officers in their flawless dress uniforms, rich playboys from Shanghai's social set, or artists
from nearby Suzhou and Hangzhou. A Japanese businessman presented Benny's mother with the gift of a dog—a prized Japanese Spitz,
highly valued for intelligence and loyalty. The friendly white dog was

always by his mother's side, bringing a cheerful domesticity to the cavernous mansion.

His parents' divergent lives weren't unusual in Shanghai's sophisticated society. Married men of even modest means spent their time with concubines, mistresses, dancers, singsong girls, and prostitutes. Their wives found distractions as well. Modern Shanghai women who could not accept their husbands' dalliances increasingly turned to divorce. But not Benny's mother. Though she was a modern woman of her time, traditions and appearances had to be observed. If she was unhappy, she never let on.

As far as Benny and his siblings knew, all was well at 40 Jessfield Road—and in Shanghai, for that matter. Because of martial law and stringent Japanese censorship, few people in occupied China had heard of Japan's string of military defeats that had begun with the Battle of Midway in 1942 and continued across the Pacific, at Guadalcanal in the Solomon Islands, the Marshall Islands, and by 1944, the Marianas and on to the Philippines. Radios were forbidden contraband, but even in Shanghai there were signs of Japan's weakening. The Imperial Army had lost so many soldiers that boys much younger than Benny were being conscripted from the city's Japanese civilian population.

None of that interfered with Benny's contented life. Instead, in 1944 the Pan family was focused on preparations for his elder sister Annie's wedding. His mother was intent on making her firstborn's wedding one of the city's most glorious social events. She had arranged the ceremony and reception at the Paramount—the grandest of Shanghai's grand ballrooms. His sister was stunning in her French silk wedding gown. His father was at his finest, elegant in his British morning coat and tails, puffing away on his diamond-studded cigarette holder. But to Benny, his mother was the star, more beautiful than ever, outshining even the bride.

Benny felt very grown up in his first tuxedo, complete with a cummerbund and Windsor-knotted tie. He blushed when Doreen said that he looked like Errol Flynn. Swaying to the strains of the Paramount's famed Filipino orchestra, Benny imagined that he was floating on the glass dance floor, its lights glowing from below. On that magical day, Benny's family was together and joyful, resplendent in their finery.

His sister Annie's wedding, in late 1944, at the Paramount Ballroom, with one of its dance floors lit in colored lights from below, was the pinnacle of good times for Benny and his family.

The excitement of his sister's wedding was soon followed by Benny's middle school graduation. He was filled with anticipation that he would finally be entering St. John's University, just as his father and uncle had. Benny still dreamed of becoming a physician, a healer of people. He looked up to the medical students who walked about the campus in their white lab coats, commanding the respect of all. The six-year medical program at St. John's ran from college through medical school, with a joint medical degree from the University of Pennsylvania. Benny was determined to get into the program in the fall, certain that his parents would approve. He had much to look forward to.

——

IN EARLY SUMMER 1945, Shanghai's civilians were still unaware that U.S. troops had taken over the Japanese islands of Iwo Jima and Okinawa. The latter had been turned into an American base capable of sending B-29s with greater frequency to bomb Japan—and its strongholds in Shanghai. Sometimes the bombs missed their targets—one American bomb accidentally struck the Jewish ghetto in Hongkou, killing and wounding hundreds of civilians.

With their schools located in the Western District, students at St. John's and St. Mary's began to worry about errant bombs, especially when more than two hundred American planes bombarded the city on one afternoon. To protect themselves from a likely bombing raid on the nearby train station, St. Mary's students painted a huge Stars and Stripes on the tennis courts. This, they hoped, would alert the Yanks to their Allied sympathies. By then, it was clear to everyone that the Empire of Japan was in trouble.

Finally the long-awaited news came: On August 15, 1945, Japanese military officers assembled at the British racetrack grounds to listen to Emperor Hirohito's metallic voice over the loudspeakers. He announced that "a new and most cruel bomb" had destroyed Hiroshima and Nagasaki. Japan was surrendering. Two weeks later on September 2, the formal surrender took place aboard the USS *Missouri*. In Shanghai, people spilled out of their homes, filling the streets in joyous celebration. The eight-year Japanese war and occupation had ended— China's five hundred million people could rejoice at last!

But not everyone was cheering. Officials like Benny's father were caught by surprise. They'd hitched a ride to power on Japan, and it would now be their turn to pay. Chen Gongbo, the Shanghai puppet mayor who had appointed Pan Da police commissioner, had become president of the collaborationist government in late 1944, after Wang Jingwei died unexpectedly in surgery. Following Japan's defeat, Chen fled to Tokyo, but the American occupation forces there extradited him back to China. He was arrested and imprisoned in Suzhou to await trial for treason. Chen claimed that he had been a voice for peace, a buffer to reduce the harm done by the Japanese invaders to the Chinese people. His remonstrations were to no avail, and he was executed. His wife and a mistress were also tried as traitors.

Benny's father hunkered down with his Special Police colleagues, calculating how much time they might have to work out a plan before the regime change. The Nationalist government was still far off in the interior hinterlands of China, a journey that could take weeks by land. Many collaborators expected to have several days at least to plan their exits. After all, the Japanese military was still patrolling in Shanghai and elsewhere because Chiang Kai-shek and the American forces preferred to have the defeated Japanese maintain order, rather than give the Communists a possible opening. The generalissimo even ordered the Japanese to keep fighting in the rural northern provinces—against the Chinese Communists. Collaborationist officials were unaware that the Americans, preferring Chiang's Nationalists to Mao's Communists, had ordered the U.S. air fleet to fly hundreds of thousands of Nationalist officials and soldiers back to liberated Nanjing, Shanghai, and other coastal areas.

Benny was at home on the morning of September 27, 1945, when military trucks barged through the gates at 40 Jessfield Road. After running up the terra-cotta steps, armed troops pounded on the ornate carved door to the mansion. His father was in his study.

When Benny heard the commotion below from his third-floor bedroom, he ran to the hall and leaned over the polished mahogany bannister to look down at the foyer. He was stunned to see uniformed Nationalist soldiers storming their house to arrest C. C. Pan, the major general of the Western Shanghai Area Special Police at 76 Jessfield Road. His father, immaculate in a tailored suit, made no protest and allowed them to bind his hands. Looking straight ahead, he accompanied them as Benny and his siblings stared, aghast. His mother stood near the front door, speechless, as they loaded Pan Da onto the back of a truck with other prisoners. Benny ran down the stairs and out to the driveway just before the tailgate was slammed shut. He thought he recognized some of the other prisoners from their Sunday dinners. Armed guards with tommy guns stood at the ready as the truck drove off.

A few Nationalist soldiers stayed behind. The commander started barking orders: "All property of puppets and collaborators is stolen property! Everyone is to leave the premises immediately. Do not take anything with you!"

Benny hadn't had a moment to recover from the shock of his father's arrest. Now the soldiers were hustling everyone in the house out the door—eight-year-old Frances and ten-year-old Edward; Benny's two younger teenaged sisters, Cecilia and Doreen. Annie was married and living with her husband. Benny muttered to himself that she was so lucky to miss this dreadful spectacle. When one of the soldiers grabbed his mother's arm, she yanked it back and walked out calmly, her head held high. Once they were all outside, the Nationalists slammed the door shut. Someone quickly plastered a sign across the door: "Confiscated from Puppets of the Enemy. Property of the Chinese War Authority."

The commander turned to the family again. "Get out now. Onto the street, where you belong."

"But where will we go?" asked Benny's sixteen-year-old sister Cecilia, her voice trembling.

The officer spat on the ground by their feet. "Did you wonder where the loyal Chinese went when they were taken to your father's torture chamber? The street is too good for you enemy puppets. Get out!"

As they stood outside the gate to their former mansion, young Frances began to whimper. Benny's mother pulled her two youngest close to her and said, "I know where we can go." Benny was surprised to learn that his father kept another house several blocks away in the former French Concession. It was his private hideaway, in case there was trouble and he needed a safe house. It was also where he spent time with his mistresses. "We'll have to walk there," Benny's mother said.

From behind, a familiar voice said, "No, Madame. I'll get some pedicabs. I managed to hide some money."

It was his father's manservant, his number one boy. With him was Benny's amah—she would stay with them too. "I was your amah when you were a girl and the amah to your firstborn children," she said to his mother. "I won't leave you now. But I'm sorry you must go to *that* place."

The house was much smaller than the mansion but large enough for all of them. Everything about the house was a reflection of his father: his medals, sashes, and sword from his years as a commander of "C" Company with the Shanghai Volunteer Corps; his inspector's hat from the Shanghai Municipal Police; his special gun collection; even his Boy Scout vice-master badges and insignia. While his mother agonized over how she would ever show her face in her city again, Benny felt strange to be in his father's secret lair. Did Benny know this man, his father? Was he really a terrible man who should be locked up?

And then there was school. Benny would miss part of his first term of college, his one dream. But how could he worry about that when everything he knew was disintegrating? The big mansion, the fancy parties with high-toned people, the retinue of servants—all were gone, even the little white dog. Gone were the cars, the motorcycle, the fine furnishings and fur coats, the grand piano, and the Victrola. Now they were being reclaimed as stolen property belonging to the Chinese people, not to traitors like his family, not to *hanjian*, the Nationalists had said.

Benny, his mother, and his younger siblings had only the clothes on their backs and the shelter of his father's getaway house. At least they had somewhere to stay. But within a few days, another group of Nationalist soldiers came pounding on the door. Their heavy knocking reverberated through the building.

"Out, out! Do you *hanjian* think you can hide yourselves? This house belongs to the loyal Chinese people. Get out, and see what it feels like to be one of the poor people you stole from!"

Once again, the family was herded outside. Benny was the last to leave. Out of the corner of his eye, he saw a longtime servant in the next room, helping himself to Pan Da's prized handguns, including his father's favorite German Mauser. Benny was stunned. As he left the house, he saw one of the Nationalist officers thank the thieving servant.

"He's the scoundrel who tipped them off!" Benny whispered to his mother.

Now they were truly homeless, only a rainstorm away from joining the bedraggled refugees who crowded in doorways. When he turned to ask his mother what they should do, he saw the dazed look in her eyes. Her hands were shaking.

Benny hesitated before speaking. "Mother, we have to find a place to stay. Who can we ask for help?"

In a small voice, his mother shook her head and whispered, "I can't."

Benny had never seen his smart and capable mother like this. Alarmed, he squared his shoulders. "All right, I'll go and ask our relatives. You take everyone to the French Park and wait for me."

Benny's panic seemed to electrify his body. He took off in a sprint. When he reached the nearby home of an uncle, no one would open the door. Benny raised his voice to speak loud enough for the relatives inside to hear.

"Uncle, please let me in. It's Benny, Pan Da's son."

"Sorry, we can't help you. Please leave. We don't want to be labeled *hanjian*," his uncle replied from behind the closed door.

"But my younger sisters and brother need your help. They're just children and have nowhere to go."

"I'm sorry. Don't come back."

One by one, Benny ran to the homes of every relative he could think of. Some slammed their doors in his face. Others didn't bother to answer. These were the same family members who had begged to be invited to his parents' Sunday parties, he remembered. They had enjoyed the fine food, the champagne, the expensive cigars. When Benny was a little boy, these same relatives had smiled at and flattered him. Now they wouldn't even lend a hand to the children. It was a bitter lesson.

Still, he couldn't blame them. He knew they were afraid of being thrown into prison like his father. The Japanese were defeated, the Nationalists were back, and who knew what was in store for the accused *hanjian*? Rumors were flying that some presumed traitors were being beaten to death in towns outside of the city. Everyone was fearful of what this round of regime change would bring.

As he ran to the next house and the next, Benny kept wishing for his grandfather, who had died a few years earlier. How Benny missed him. And now he really needed him. Grandfather would have let them in, no question. But then, he was glad that Grandfather had not lived to see this shameful day.

Finally Benny made his way to the home of his father's elder brother, across the Suzhou Creek in Hongkou. His uncle lived on a small parcel of Great-Grandfather's original compound, where Benny used to bow down before Great-Grandmother's menacing curled nails. In response to Benny's pleading, Big Uncle agreed to take them into his house.

Rushing back to French Park with the news, Benny found another surprise waiting. One of his father's bodyguards was standing close to his mother. His mother stared into the distance as she spoke to Benny.

"I can't live like a refugee, the shamed wife of a traitor," she said, her voice flat.

Her words poured out in a torrent: She couldn't stay in Shanghai to face the bragging circle of her mah-jongg friends, the shop clerks who once fawned over her, the women who had fought for invitations to her parties. They would lift their noses and look away when she crossed their paths. That would be unbearable. She was leaving—to stay in Suzhou with the bodyguard. She was relieved, she said, that Benny had found a place for all the children to stay.

But what would you have done if I hadn't? Benny felt like shouting. He stayed silent.

Before she left, his mother spoke to his younger siblings as if she were sending them off to school: "Be good children, and mind your big brother."

Benny was speechless as he watched his mother leave with his father's servant. At seventeen, Benny had never been responsible for anything, not even for himself. Servants had bathed, clothed, and fed him until he left for boarding school. Even there, almost all decisions had been made for him. Now this lightning bolt.

His mother was running off with another man and leaving him with four younger siblings. His father was locked up somewhere; Benny had no idea how to find him. His dreams of college and becoming a doctor had imploded. Heaven and hell had traded places.

SHANGHAI, 1945

ARTIME SHANGHAI HAD CHANGED HO CHOW. HIS YEARS
as a teenager had been spent in utilitarian vocational school classrooms and an unfinished attic room that was so hot in summer that his
perspiration left unsightly streaks on his books and assignments and so
cold in winter that water froze overnight in his drinking glass. Even
the room's single five-watt bulb flickered unreliably, thanks to the enemy's relentless austerity. The playful second son of the landowning
Changshu family had transformed into a no-nonsense student and serious young man. From the moment of his arrival after his near disaster with the boat bringing him to Shanghai, Ho had associated the
teeming city with war and danger, separation and loss. For him,
Shanghai was the place to work hard and study, not to play, especially
with his mother sacrificing a small fortune on him.

Ho had breezed through his four years at Zhonghua Vocational,
learning all he could about the practical applications of science at his
nonacademic school. The lad from Changshu kept his promise to stay
focused and to steer clear of trouble, even when he saw other boys
having fun at the Great World Amusement Center, sneaking a peek
into the Lido dance club next door to his Shanghai home, or watching
the latest films in one of the popular movie palaces. He had too much
at stake to get sidetracked.

In 1942, Ho's mother and elder brother, Hosun, had managed to rejoin the rest of the family after making their way through Japanese-occupied areas to Medhurst Road. Ho had been sad to see that his mother's hair had turned almost completely white, the harsh years etched in the lines on her face. She soon added her voice to the cautious admonitions of his grandmother and sister, Wanyu, to stay on the straight and narrow path. Other boys his age were earning money to help their families, but Ho's mother still encouraged his studies. Struggling Chinese families sometimes pooled the money of many relatives to support the education of a promising son, even sending him to graduate school overseas with the hope that their investment would pay off one day. Ho was grateful for his family's belief in his ability to accomplish something worthwhile. His thoughts before he went to sleep each night were always the same: Mother, I will do my best to be a good son. I promise to make you proud.

There was just one thing that could turn Ho's head: a shiny, sleek automobile. He was fascinated by them, all of them. DeSotos, Fords, Bentleys, Renaults, LaSalles, Buicks, Citroëns—he admired their beauty, their utility, and the science that created them. China needed to produce its own cars, trucks, and planes to free itself from dependence on foreign imports, he believed. One day he would produce a homegrown car for his country. He was certain it could be done, and he was just the one to do it. That was his dream.

Later that year, Ho graduated at the top of his vocational school class. Teachers there recognized his talents and encouraged him to apply to Jiao Tong University in Shanghai, the "MIT of China." One of the nation's most respected universities, the school had been established by the emperor himself in 1896. Many of its graduates successfully pursued advanced degrees abroad and were responsible for building China's bridges, dams, and power plants. The more that Ho learned about Jiao Da, as the school was also known, the more he was certain that he needed to study there.

But that would prolong the financial strain on his family. Ho reluctantly asked his mother about applying to the school, knowing that the cost of food and other necessities was skyrocketing. To his surprise, she didn't balk. With his elder sister and brother both working, his mother was confident they'd manage. She added, "I still have a few pieces of wedding jewelry to sell, if needed. When the war is over, we'll be able to collect rent from our land once again. It is my wish that you apply to the university."

Jiao Da's entrance exam was more difficult than any test Ho had ever taken. He was competing with several hundred other middle-school graduates for only thirty seats in the mechanical engineering program. Many had gone to better schools like Fudan or the missionary schools. He knew that his preparation at the vocational school had not been as rigorous as theirs. But on the day the test results were posted, it didn't take long to find his score: He ranked number twenty-seven for the class of thirty. He had made the cut.

Ho's first year at Jiao Da, starting in the fall of 1943, challenged his self-confidence. Classroom seating was determined by test-score rank. His was seat number twenty-seven at the back of the class. For the boy who had always been first, it was embarrassing to take an unfamiliar spot in the last row. He also discovered that he was nearsighted when he couldn't see the blackboard from his seat. Ho started wearing thick eyeglasses rimmed with wire. To reduce time wasted on matters he deemed trivial, Ho clipped his hair short, almost to his scalp, not caring that other boys were styling their pomaded hair into a Clark Gable look. With his thick glasses, high forehead, and close-cropped hair, Ho looked more bookish than ever.

Once he was able to see the classroom clearly, he had a better sense of his competition. To improve his class standing, he tried to study harder than before. He bought a secondhand bicycle, which saved him time and made it easier to circumvent military patrols. One student missed almost a full day of classes because a Japanese soldier decided to march back and forth across Nanjing Road, one of the busiest thoroughfares in Shanghai. The lone soldier, with his bayonet-topped rifle in hand, brought traffic to a standstill for hours. Chauffeured businessmen, socialites in pedicabs, rickshaw coolies, and cart pullers—no one dared to cross the path of the mad soldier.

In 1944, when Ho was twenty and in his second year at Jiao Da, he moved from his grandmother's attic into one of the crowded dormitories. Living as frugally as possible and studying constantly, Ho steadily advanced, step by step, to the number one seat in the class. His Jiao Da professors were encouraging him to consider graduate school in the United States. But during the war years, the Nationalist government had ceased offering the competitive national exam that granted top scorers the permissions and visas needed for overseas studies. Only the very wealthy and well connected were able to circumvent travel restrictions to send their children out of China. Students like Ho had to wait until the visa program resumed. His professors urged him to pounce if the chance arose. An engineering degree from America would top off his honors from Jiao Tong University, they said, and his family's investment in him would pay off a hundredfold.

When Ho shared his professors' advice with his family, once again his mother was enthusiastic. To have a son with an advanced degree from the United States would bring great honor to their family. She promised her support, no matter what the sacrifice.

Ho's dream was coming into focus. He wanted to study with the world's best engineers and scientists in America so that he could one day build his cars in China. Not even the lilting voices of the singsong girls around his campus could distract him. Other, less motivated schoolmates fell prey to the cabarets, gambling joints, brothels, and opium dens that proliferated in the former foreign concessions and the Badlands. But not Ho.

Still, there were other, less decadent pursuits in Shanghai that could have derailed him. Protests and upheavals were common occurrences at Jiao Da, which was also known for its fervent activism. Underground Communists, Nationalists, and other Chinese political parties always wanted to recruit Jiao Da students. Many of his classmates aspired to use scientific methods to modernize China. Ho wanted that too, but he had been warned many times by his family to shun politics. Everyone knew stories about idealistic students who disappeared, most likely meeting a tragic end. Ho had ideals—but he was also pragmatic. He believed he could best help China by keeping his head down, focusing on his dream. As the number one student in his department, he'd have a good shot at graduate study in America. Then he'd build a car factory in China and bring good fortune to his family.

HO WAS IN HIS last year at Jiao Da when some astonishing news came over a forbidden radio that students had secretly rigged up. On August 6, 1945, the United States had dropped a deadly new "atom bomb" over Hiroshima, Japan. The blast was so strong that it had flattened the city, destroying everything in its vast range. Three days later, another A-bomb devastated Nagasaki. Thousands of Japanese civilians were reported incinerated to death or critically burned from the blasts. The Jiao Da scientists and engineers buzzed, speculating about the powerful energy this weapon had unleashed and wondering if it would be enough to halt the eight-year war.

On August 15, they had their answer from the Japanese emperor himself. The enemy was surrendering!

Ho rushed into the streets with his fellow students shouting, "It's over; it's over! Japan is defeated; China has won!" Exuberant, Ho joined in the dancing with complete strangers. Then he jumped on his bicycle and pedaled as quickly as he could to Medhurst Road, yelling as he pushed open the door.

"Mother! Elder Sister! Brother! Have you heard? The war is over!"

His mother reached her arms around her children as they jumped for joy together. "Finally, we can go home to Changshu," she laughed, tears streaming down her face.

Yet at Ho's campus, anger soon followed the announcement when the same Japanese soldiers who had cruelly occupied the city for eight long years continued to patrol its streets. Indignant students gathered to read news posted on bulletin boards that reported on Japanese troops still fighting against Chinese—the Communists—in the country's northeast after the surrender, logging more than one hundred clashes in September, on direct orders from the Nationalists and Americans. In Shanghai alone, one hundred thousand armed and uniformed Japanese soldiers were still in control after the formal surrender on the deck of the USS *Missouri* on September 2, 1945. Many students believed that the decision to use "the Japanese to hold off the Communists" had been made at the highest levels in Washington, D.C.

Shanghai's residents could only fume as their despised enemy continued to hold them at bay. Once again, Ho's cautious family warned him to avoid trouble. But the delay gave Japanese and German officials plenty of time to pack up their war booty. Kempeitai torturers at Bridge House burned records of their war crimes, while many enemy soldiers simply discarded their uniforms and blended into the Japanese civilian section of Hongkou. The uncertainty stymied the sixty-six hundred interned Shanghailanders, who were reluctant to leave their decrepit camps without knowing where they might go.

It came as a relief, then, when American GIs began arriving to disarm and demobilize the Japanese—and to bring back Chiang's Nationalists from the inland provinces before the Communists could step in. After the surrender, crews from the U.S. Tenth Air Force began flying continuous missions on their Dakota transport planes to ferry 110,000 Nationalist officials and crack troops to Shanghai and other key cities.

Jubilant, cheering crowds lined both banks of the Huangpu River on September 19, 1945, to welcome the USS *Rocky Mount*, flagship of the Allied fleet, as it entered the port of Shanghai, offering indisputable evidence that the devastating war was over. Ho's family stayed home to celebrate their survival through the war years, his grandmother and the cook arranging a special meal with dishes that Ho hadn't tasted since he'd left Changshu.

Three entire U.S. fleets soon followed—the Fourth, Sixth, and Seventh—with a British naval task force not far behind. Shanghai's new pecking order was clear when the *Rocky Mount* berthed in the number one spot, which had been the privileged reserve of the British for nearly a hundred years until the Japanese *Idzumo* had taken it over during Japan's occupation. Before long, more than one hundred thousand American sailors, soldiers, and fly-boys—farm boys who had been fighting on remote islands and jungles in the Pacific, now waiting to be demobilized—were let loose among the people and temptations of notorious Shanghai.

Ho and his fellow students watched in amazement as nearly every other storefront in Shanghai was converted into a bar overnight to accommodate the soldiers hungry for R and R. Prostitution became more blatant than ever. The U.S. military command declared several brothel districts off-limits until venereal disease could be contained. The unenforceable order brought hoots of derision on the Jiao Tong campus, its location in the Badlands giving students a clear view of the vice dens and their eager customers.

The Americans began to reshape Shanghai. Even the simple act of crossing the street required greater care. For a hundred years, Shanghai had observed the British left-sided traffic flow. Now American GIs were powering through Shanghai streets in their fast jeeps and trucks—on the wrong side of the road. Newspapers, freed from Japan's censorship, earnestly reported the details of accidents and deaths caused by American soldiers, to the great consternation of Shanghai's locals. But the Americans won the right-of-way. On January 1, 1946, all traffic in the city was ordered to switch to the right-hand side of the road—a change that many predicted would shut down the city. The process intrigued Ho, especially when Shanghai adjusted without a hitch. The British Empire's influence on the city was waning fast.

THEN CAME THE MASSIVE transition of power and property from vanquished to victor. At first, everyone cheered at the arrests of traitors, collaborators, and puppets of the Japanese enemy who had benefited from the suffering of their fellow Chinese. But the demand to punish war criminals exploded into sweeping recriminations. Anyone with a grudge and a modicum of authority could point a finger and shout, "*Hanjian!*" The initial optimism for peace was soon dampened as accusations of collaboration spread like a poisonous cloud through the former occupied areas. Colleagues and neighbors, teachers and university presidents, were arrested while well-known traitors—even Nazis and other Axis officials—avoided prosecution and landed positions in the returned Nationalist regime.

The toxic claims began to infect students at Jiao Tong University, and other schools as well. Ho and his classmates who had stayed in Shanghai during the war found themselves publicly accused for attending the *wei* Jiao Da—"fake" Jiao Da. Some returning Nationalist officials insisted that the true patriots and "real" Jiao Tong students had gone inland after 1937, answering Generalissimo Chiang's call to establish the wartime capital in Chongqing. Indeed, the faculties and students of many universities, including some from Jiao Tong, had made the thousand-mile trek inland from Shanghai on foot, with great numbers falling ill and dying along the way. Those who made it to Chongqing established makeshift universities without the benefit of textbooks, laboratories, or chalkboards. At war's end, two parallel Jiao Tong universities emerged: the returned students from the make-shift Jiao Da in Free China and Ho's campus in Shanghai.

Over the weeks and months after the surrender, the split grew wider on every campus. Instead of having a joyful reunion, the students who had lived under enemy occupation were now stung by accusations. Ho and the other "fake" students were being called out as puppets and collaborators. Some accusers were embittered returnees seeking targets to blame for their years of misery, while others saw an opportunity to get revenge or to climb over the disgraced.

Ho's discomfort turned to alarm and dismay as his own academic record was challenged. Living under the Japanese occupation hadn't been easy. His family, too, had suffered the privations of war. Now, after all his hard work and his family's sacrifice, everything he had accomplished was diminished, and his loyalty to China was in question. To make matters worse, the students who stayed in Shanghai were academically much stronger than the students from the interior, who had lacked essential tools for a solid education—and it showed.

In 1946, the returned Nationalist authorities imposed a "reconversion" training program on the teachers and students who had remained in Shanghai. They declared that "fake students" like Ho were "corrupted," just like the collaborators and traitors. They even called Ho and his cohorts "puppet students" who lacked the political understanding of the "real" Jiao Da students. The new Ministry of Education questioned the validity of the academic records of graduates from colleges and middle schools in occupied Shanghai. It created a special program in Nationalist ideology, requiring all such students to take the course. Students and graduates who failed the exam would be considered corrupted, their reputations tarnished and their diplomas and academic credits rendered worthless. Teachers were also to be tested for their loyalty to and knowledge of Nationalist principles.

Ho was horrified—and indignant. Why should he be stigmatized solely because his family hadn't joined the difficult exodus to the interior? He had been only thirteen in 1937. Neither his elderly grandmother nor his sick brother could have endured the journey. Everyone had personal reasons for the choices they had to make during the long war. How could all of the thousands of students in Shanghai during the eight years of enemy occupation be corrupt puppets? With such accusations of ideological inferiority, Ho worried that his dream was slipping away, falling like a stone into the filthy Huangpu River.

Just as Ho was beginning to lose hope, he saw that some of his fellow students were fighting against the gross unfairness. Campus activists stood on the steps of buildings, arguing that they should not be treated as though they had supported the Japanese enemy. Ho stopped to listen. They hadn't joined the Wang Jingwei puppets in Nanjing or aided Pan Da's puppet police at 76, the students asserted. Didn't the accusers know that many students and teachers in Shanghai had been arrested and executed for their anti-Japanese resistance? Or that students across Shanghai had refused to study the Japanese language?

The protests against the Nationalist sanctions spread like wildfire. Shanghai's workers, too, called for relief from the years of hardship and repression. The students and workers combined forces in massive citywide demonstrations that seemed to explode with greater ferocity each day as the postwar unrest spread.

Ho found himself pulled into the groundswell. He agreed with the protest organizers. After all, they had been children during the war. It was unfair and outrageous to condemn them as traitors and ruin their lives. It made sense to Ho that he should stand up for his own future and not depend on others to do that for him. When students in his dormitory asked if he would support them, Ho surprised himself by joining the protests in spite of rumors that some of the students were secret Communists. Ho didn't care. He had to show everyone that he was a student, not a traitor.

A massive mobilization called on all students to gather at the Shanghai North railway station, the major rail terminus in the former International Settlement. Ho fell in step with throngs of Jiao Tong schoolmates as they marched the five-mile distance. He, too, shouted, "Fair treatment for all students and teachers!" and "Punish the real traitors, not the ordinary people!" Along the way, the ranks swelled with men and women from other campuses: Shanghai University, Tongji, St. John's, Fudan, Aurora, and the many other schools that were an important part of Shanghai's intellectual life.

As China's postwar conditions continued to spin out of control, in 1946, Shanghai's universities exploded in protests over multiple issues, including some of the protestors' own legitimacy as students.

Ho felt energized by the passion of the thousands of other students around him. Wide-eyed, he watched as articulate student leaders urged the others not to fight only for themselves but to rise up for fair treatment of all. Some called for the various political parties in China to end their antagonisms and to work together to rebuild China. Others denounced the returning Nationalist Party as corrupt. Some, angered by rumors that an American marine had raped a Beijing University student, demanded, "Foreign devils out of China!" and "Yankee, go home!"

When the huge demonstration reached the North station, student protestors swarmed onto the tracks and blocked all trains from coming or going for hours. Hundreds of students took over an empty train, announcing their intent to commandeer the locomotive and drive it to the reestablished capital in Nanjing. But the students faltered when no one knew how to operate the engine.

A group of Jiao Da engineering students came to the rescue, climbing aboard and taking control of the locomotive. One of the Jiao Tong students, whose father worked for the railroad, got the massive engine started. The train was on its way to Nanjing, with Jiao Da students at the helm. Ho didn't go to Nanjing. The day had been full enough, and he returned to campus, proud of what his Jiao Da contingent had done. The day was also a first: Ho felt he had accomplished something significant, something larger than himself.

When he told his family what he had done, they reacted as he had expected—with consternation. His mother worried that the Nationalist secret police might come to arrest him. His sister, Wanyu, said that he could be blacklisted as a troublemaker. His brother, Hosun, advised him to drop to the ground if he should hear gunshots.

It came as a great relief to Ho when he was able to prove to his family that the students' actions were a success: The Nationalist Ministry of Education decided that the "fake" students would receive full academic credit for their college records, provided that the students attended and passed the political ideology class. That was a condition Ho was willing to accept. The "fake students" had won a big victory, and Ho still might get to study abroad after all.

NOT LONG AFTER HO graduated at the top of his department in the spring of 1946, he heard the news he had been waiting for: The Ministry of Education announced it would conduct national examinations and grant visas for study abroad to those with the best scores.

Given that no visa exams had been administered during the war, the competition would be fierce, with potentially every college graduate from the last eight years eligible to take the new examination. In addition, the government now further required that high-scoring students be accepted by a foreign university before they could get a visa.

Students who received visas would also be permitted to convert Chinese yuan into foreign currency for their tuition and expenses— but doing so would not be easy in the volatile economy. Foreign currency exchange was otherwise prohibited for Chinese like Ho, who had no connections. During the Japanese occupation, it had been impossible for ordinary people to get authorization to exchange Chinese money for foreign currency. Now in control, the Nationalist government created tight restrictions in an effort to stabilize the terrible inflationary pressure on Chinese currency. In 1940, a hundred yuan could buy a pig; in 1943, a chicken; in 1945, a fish, while in 1946, it would buy only an egg. By 1947, it couldn't even fetch a pack of matches.

Ho would need U.S. dollars to pay the tuition and fees, but he was discouraged to learn that the U.S. government also required foreign students to have money available to them in the United States for at least a year's worth of expenses, including tuition. Ho needed a thousand dollars for the current year and another thousand to show he could cover the next year. That was a small fortune for Americans in 1947 and an astronomical amount for Chinese. Not only would Ho need a huge sum from his family, he would need it in U.S. dollars.

To make sure there would be enough money, Ho's mother had to collect rent from her tenant farmers in Changshu again. She'd waited months for safer travel routes to her Changshu home after the two million Japanese soldiers in China were disarmed and repatriated, along with another two million Japanese civilians who had worked in China. When Ho's mother and sister, Wanyu, made their first visit back to Changshu, they found bullet holes and bomb craters pockmarking their walls and grounds. Fortunately, it was all reparable. Their longtime servants began returning, and their home soon became habitable again. However, with the Nationalist government still in transition to establish control, thieves roamed the area, and lawlessness posed a grave danger. Occasional skirmishes were also breaking out between Nationalists and Communists—with the latter agitating to uproot landlord families like the Chows.

Ho worried for his mother's and sister's safety. He'd wanted to accompany them, but his mother felt it was more dangerous for a young man like Ho to travel when some army or gang was always on the prowl for conscripts or targets. Frustrated, the young engineer designed a simple mechanical alarm for his mother and sister to set up in their rooms as they slept. If an intruder entered, the device would set off a loud noise in a different part of the room. According to Ho, the noise would distract the intruder, allowing his sister and mother to escape. Luckily, Ho's invention was never put to the test, but everyone rested easier.

After his graduation, Ho went to work as an automotive lab researcher in the university's engineering department. This allowed him to eat at the school canteen and sleep in the lab for free. He found another job with Shanghai Public Utilities Commission studying the flow of the Huangpu River. With two jobs, Ho could save money for graduate school, but he had precious little time to prepare for the national examination.

Like generations of Chinese who had taken the imperial civil service exams for more than a thousand years, Ho began a rigorous review schedule to spend every available moment preparing for the big test. He simply *had* to do well.

A few days after the test, the results were published in the newspapers on full-page broadsheets listing each student's name and numerical rank on the test. Ho scanned for his name. He was not among the very top students who would receive full scholarships from the government. Ho wasn't surprised, for his English and Chinese language skills weren't strong enough to place him at the top. Finally, he found his name—with a score that would qualify him for a visa and foreign exchange so he could study in America.

Jubilant, Ho celebrated the good news with his family. A degree from America would bring honor, status, and rewards to the family. On December 4, 1946, Ho, by then twenty-two, received his official notification letter from the Ministry of Education in Nanjing:

To Whom It May Concern:

This is to certify that Mr. Chow Ho [*sic*] has passed
the government examination for students going
abroad at their own expense and is qualified to enter
the graduate school of a university in any foreign
country.

As he read the letter, Ho's face broke into a rare grin. Soon he'd be
on his way. He just knew it.

SUZHOU, 1945

DEEPLY DISAPPOINTED THAT SHE HAD FAILED TO FIND ANY sign of Mama Hsu after running away to Suzhou, Bing had figured that there was no point in returning to Shanghai. The food crisis there wouldn't have improved, and Ma was certain to be even more unhappy and irritable with them, the two adopted girls both agreed. They decided to accept the offer from Mama Hsu's uncle to help them find work and a place to live in Suzhou.

Uncle, in turn, enlisted his daughter to check around for possible jobs at the big Suzhou Customs Office where she worked. The Japanese occupation had taken over the office at the start of the war, and Uncle's daughter learned of a Japanese coworker who was looking for a maid. The coworker hired Ah Mei. Then a Chinese couple at the customs bureau wanted someone to care for their three small children while they were at work. They offered Bing room and board—there'd be no pay but no dreaded corn mush either. Bing agreed. At least she'd have Ah Mei nearby.

By mid-1945, the girls had been in Suzhou for about a year. The days had passed quickly, each much like the one before. Bing didn't care; she was biding her time, waiting for Mama Hsu to return. Even at age sixteen, Bing believed that the kind Suzhou woman would want her back. If for some reason that wasn't to be, then perhaps her return would lead to Baba and her birth family. Maybe they would want her. Bing didn't expect much for herself, but still she couldn't extinguish the small pilot light in her heart. For now, she had a place to stay, and she loved taking care of small children—she showered them with the affection she had never received, and they gave it right back. That was enough.

In August, when the steam of summer heat could be seen rising from the city's canals, news of the coming Japanese surrender erupted. People burst out of their curfew-shuttered homes, rejoicing in the narrow lanes. Bing could hardly believe it. Yet it had to be true when everyone working at the Japanese-run customs office, including the couple she lived with, was abuzz over rumors that they would all be fired or even arrested for working with the Japanese.

Ah Mei's Japanese employers flew into a panic, prompting her to consider returning to Shanghai. She asked Bing if she'd join her. But with the war over, Bing felt that her Suzhou mother would surely return and she'd finally get answers to her gnawing questions. Though Bing was sorry to see her friend leave, she decided to stay put in Suzhou. And wait.

IN EARLY 1946, a few months after the Japanese surrender, Bing answered a knock on the door of the apartment where she was living. She was shocked to see Ah Mei—with Elder Sister and her building's gatekeeper. They had taken the train from Shanghai that morning.

"Bing! I've been looking all over for you," Elder Sister said, her deep voice reverberating. Bing had forgotten how loud Elder Sister could be. In rapid-fire Shanghai dialect, she told Bing that she had been searching for the two girls ever since they ran away nearly two years before. She had enlisted the building's gatekeeper and others to help her find the girls but had had no luck. Then, after the Japanese surrender, the gatekeeper spotted Ah Mei on the street. Elder Sister found where she was staying and asked her to come back.

After Ah Mei's return, Elder Sister asked about Bing. At first, Ah Mei professed ignorance, knowing that Bing wished to stay in Suzhou. But Elder Sister persisted and gradually convinced Ah Mei that she was sincere in her concern for Bing. Once the railway line to Suzhou was safe to travel, Elder Sister asked Ah Mei to take her to Bing, bringing the gatekeeper along in case they ran into trouble with maverick soldiers or other ruffians.

"Bing, please come back to Shanghai with us," Elder Sister entreated. "We all miss you. Ole misses you. He calls out your name. Ma misses you. Kristian too. We all want you to come back."

Bing was too surprised to speak. She stared at Elder Sister, as dazzling as ever with her red lipstick and Western hairdo. Although the women of Suzhou were renowned for their beauty, they were more modest in appearance. Elder Sister was the epitome of her city: stylish, outspoken, and brash as only a Shanghai woman could be.

Bing quizzed Ah Mei. "Ma isn't mad? She really misses me?"

"It's true, Bing. Things are better now," Ah Mei offered. "Kristian has a good job—there's real food again. Ma is calmer. Ole is going to school, and Peter can walk and talk now!"

Bing stared down at the floor, thinking hard. She'd been in Suzhou for nearly two years. In that time, she had kept checking with the elderly uncle for any contact from Mama Hsu. Not one word had come through. Could Mama Hsu be dead, one of the many thousands killed in the Japanese bombings of Chongqing? If Mama Hsu never returned to Suzhou, what then? On the other hand, Elder Sister really seemed to *want* her to come back. Unaccustomed to feeling wanted, Bing hesitated. Then she squared her shoulders and said, "Yes. I'll go back with you."

ON THE TRAIN BACK to Shanghai, Bing watched villages and farms whiz by vast spaces of blackened rubble and stark wasteland. The last time she had traveled this route with Ah Mei, they'd been fourteen-year-old runaways. How naïve Bing had been to think she would knock on Uncle's door and find Mama Hsu waiting to welcome her and resume her schooling. Now she might never see Mama Hsu again. And she'd lose her only link to her father. But even if she found them, maybe they would reject her—again. And what about Ma in Shanghai? Bing dreaded the tongue-lashing that Ma would surely mete out.

Tears of uncertainty, sadness, and regret began to run down her cheeks.

To comfort Bing, Elder Sister spoke in her most soothing voice: She hadn't been able to search for Bing in Suzhou sooner because hundreds of American bombers had been flying over Shanghai, destroying roads, bridges, and rails, until the Japanese surrender. Life in Shanghai had improved: Curfews and barricades were gone, and American soldiers were now keeping the peace. American GIs were everywhere, with lots of greenbacks to spend. "And so you must be careful," Elder Sister advised. "You've grown into a pretty girl, and soldiers want only one thing, no matter what uniform they wear." Bing recognized the same warnings that Ma used to give Elder Sister and her girlfriends so many years before.

Ah Mei told Bing how the American, British, and other European civilians had been released from the internment camps scattered around the Shanghai area.

"They came back looking so thin and hollow, with tattered rags loose on their bones. Can you imagine foreigners looking like beggars? Many have no homes because the Japanese and their puppets took everything. The Nationalists are back, and everything's getting shaken up again like a fortune teller's sticks." Ah Mei described how all Japanese civilians were being deported to Japan, even decent ones like the two ladies who ran the restaurant next door on Avenue Joffre. "Now it's the puppets' turn to go to prison, especially the murderous thugs at 76. They deserve the firing squad!"

Elder Sister added some good news: Her husband had a big job at Texaco, an American oil company—and got paid in U.S. dollars.

When they reached the familiar apartment on Avenue Joffre, Bing glanced around cautiously, absorbing the changes. The building's simple lines and gray brick seemed brighter than before, without the wartime soot and grime that had coated everything. The marble lobby glistened, though the walls still had gaping holes once occupied by heating pipes and radiators, before the Japanese had scavenged them. But the bronze trim in the elevator had regained the sheen lost to the grim war years.

Bing instantly noticed that the apartment seemed roomier. The tenant from Fujian and his girlfriend were moving out, furniture had been pushed back to make more open space, and the blackout curtains were gone. Before Bing could look further, six-year-old Ole ran over to embrace her. How he'd grown while she was in Suzhou! Meanwhile, Peter stood by his father, watching shyly.

Kristian smiled broadly. "Welcome home, Bing. Son, say hello to Bing."

Without taking his eyes off her, the little boy squeaked, "*Ni hao?*" Bing laughed in delight to hear the Eurasian child speak Chinese in his baby voice. Seeing his older brother, Ole, wrapping his arms around Bing's waist, Peter rushed over and hugged her leg. Bing glowed from their affection. Then she looked up and saw Ma. Bing braced herself.

To Bing's relief, Ma was subdued. The corners of her mouth appeared to curl up a bit. Bing suppressed a nervous giggle—was that a smile? "I was very worried about you, Bing. I'm glad you came back," Ma offered.

Surprised, Bing stole a glance at Ah Mei, who smiled and nodded. Maybe they really want me, she ventured to herself. Under the new arrangement, Bing was to stay at the apartment with Elder Sister, Kristian, and little Peter, while Ah Mei would take Ole to stay with Ma. Each morning they'd all have breakfast at Elder Sister's apartment and spend the day together until the dinner dishes were put away and it was time to go to bed. It felt so familiar to Bing. Better, she hoped. Like being home.

THERE WERE OTHER SURPRISES in postoccupation Shanghai, with signs of the new regime everywhere. In place of the rising sun and swastika were the white sun and blue sky of the Nationalist flag and the American Stars and Stripes. Giant portraits of Chiang Kai-shek hung on Nanjing Road and at other strategic points around the city. The foreign concessions had been eliminated in 1943 and were now referred to as "the former International Settlement" and the "former French Concession," though everyone preferred the simpler "Frenchtown" and "Englishtown" that they were used to. Street names were changed to honor Nationalist heroes, with Avenue Joffre becoming

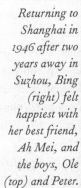

Returning to Shanghai in 1946 after two years away in Suzhou, Bing (right) felt happiest with her best friend, Ah Mei, and the boys, Ole (top) and Peter.

Lin Sen Road, named after a prominent Nationalist. Most people ignored the newly minted labels and stuck with the more familiar Shanghainese versions. Business establishments simply ran ads with both old and new names.

The most dramatic change came with the overnight omnipresence of American troops and aid, in spite of the official U.S. policy of "noninvolvement" in the tensions between Nationalists and Communists. Nine hundred million dollars in U.S. war surplus equipment arrived for Chiang's army as tens of thousands of Yanks airlifted about five hundred thousand Nationalists to north China, Manchuria, and elsewhere to block the Communists. Some fifty-three thousand U.S. Marines were occupying Beijing until the Nationalists could replace them. Other American GIs were busy rounding up the Japanese soldiers and civilians still in China to return them to Japan, now under U.S. occupation. General George Marshall himself arrived in Shanghai on December 23, 1945, to serve as President Truman's special envoy to China. On Nanjing Road, Avenue Joffre, and other commercial streets, Bing was surprised to see newly arrived American soldiers grabbing the arm shafts of rickshaws and taking their drivers for rides yelling, "Yahoo!" Ah Mei reported with a chuckle that this strange ritual was repeated with nearly every fresh batch of Yankees, who paid rickshaw drivers unheard-of sums for the privilege of pulling them. Shanghai's local riders, fearing drastic increases in fares, demanded regulatory action to limit the price paid for such tomfoolery.

The Shanghailanders like Kristian welcomed the Americans, hoping that their efforts would bring stability to the war-torn country. Local newspapers featured the efforts of General Marshall and his successor, General Albert Wedemeyer, the American military chiefs tasked with brokering a truce in the deepening civil war between the Communists and the Nationalists. Bing listened with interest as Kristian and Elder Sister discussed Chiang Kai-shek's refusal to negotiate with the Communists to end the hostilities. They and many of their friends believed Chiang's officials were too busy lining their own pockets with the spoils of war to work on a peaceful new order. About $500 million in emergency relief goods from America and the United Nations poured in—and almost immediately appeared for sale on store shelves and the black market. Chocolate, Spam, military meals, American cigarettes, chewing gum, and other emergency-aid supplies mysteriously made their way into the hands of profiteers.

Most irritating to Elder Sister was the steady stream of carpetbaggers arriving in Shanghai from Chongqing and other interior Nationalist strongholds to help themselves to the reappropriated property taken from Japanese officials and their Chinese puppets. Complaints from the original prewar owners abounded. Everyone had stories of some petty government officials they had seen flaunting their windfalls. Around the mah-jongg table, Elder Sister's friends groused about the gold bars that the Japanese had extracted from Chinese people during the occupation—and speculated about where that gold might have gone. Elder Sister's husband wryly observed that the game hadn't changed; just the flags had.

Others in Shanghai were plotting to get away, knowing that their prospects had become precarious under Nationalist rule. Elder Sister's tenant, the young Chinese from Fujian who had gone to college in Tokyo, claimed to have no interest in any political ideology, saying that he had worked for a Japanese company in order to survive the war years. That job history was now a major liability.

"I'm moving north to work with the Communists. I've heard they'll take anyone with skills," he explained. He had learned from friends that the Communists were growing in strength, steadily building an economic and political base in the mountainous hinterlands of Yan'an. The Red Army's crack guerrilla soldiers were fighting both the defeated Japanese and the Nationalists and had captured huge caches of their armaments. "The Communists will take the people shunned by the Nationalists. I'm joining the Communists."

Elder Sister was appalled by his plans. "The Nationalists may be crooks, but the Communists are crazy," she declared. Bing tried to imagine the urbane young man and his stylish girlfriend in a mountain cave with the Red Bandits. She was glad they were leaving, though, because there'd be room for a cot for her to sleep on instead of the floor.

With Kristian back at work as an engineer for Texaco, Elder Sister was in high spirits. She no longer had to work, though the war years had taught her to be prepared for anything. American businesses were back in full force, protected by the U.S. military, whose fleets lined the riverfront. Best of all, the U.S. greenbacks that Texaco paid their employees were as good as gold in postwar China. More money at home meant that Ma didn't stress as much over the continuing inflation or nag when Elder Sister replaced the dark curfew curtains with cheerful floral prints. Elder Sister returned to spending her evenings at parties and dinners with friends, both female and male, while her husband preferred to stay home sipping sherry and playing solitaire as he puffed on his cigar. Bing and Ah Mei now received allowances to spend in shops that again had plenty of stock to sell. There was even an effort to reduce the number of homeless refugees, with the new mayor of Shanghai, Princeton-educated K. C. Wu, moving thousands into some of the former military encampments, providing food and shelter to reduce the number of corpses after a cold night. Life in Shanghai had improved.

When Bing asked herself if she had made the right decision by returning, she had to allow that she was treated more as a sister and daughter than anything else. She was never treated as a servant or a *xiao yatou*—the young servant girls who were hardly more than slaves. Shanghai was filled with discarded, displaced girls, and Bing knew that she could have ended up like them. Ma, superstitious as ever, told her that she had had dreams while Bing was away about the reincarnation of her infant daughter who had died shortly after birth—in Changzhou of all places, where Bing was from. "You must be my lost daughter," Ma had declared not long after Bing returned. If such a thing could possibly be true, Bing mused, then fate had brought her to the Woo family.

AFTER BING TURNED SEVENTEEN in the spring of 1946, Elder Sister took her to get her hair permed at a nearby beauty salon. Then she took Bing shopping and bought her a couple of fashionable dresses. "You're reaching the age where men will chase after you. If you want to catch a classy guy, you've got to be a classy act," Elder Sister advised. "You have a lot to learn." Elder Sister started sharing her womanly secrets with Bing. She brought Bing along to her favorite nightclubs to join her friends as they sipped tea and Coca-Cola, and she taught Bing some simple dance steps. While puffing on cigarettes and flashing her painted nails, Elder Sister would check out the prospects and dispense advice to Bing.

"You can take a cigarette from a guy if he offers, but wait for him to light it. Then puff, but don't inhale or you'll choke," Elder Sister admonished. "If a boy asks you to dance, why not? Have some fun. But if he wants to get more serious, first find out if he can provide you with the essentials."

Without pause, Elder Sister and her friends enumerated the Essential Four Things a suitor needed to offer a girl: gold jewelry, a diamond ring, a fur coat, and a place to live. "If he can't give you these," they said, "don't waste your time."

Soon Bing had a chance to put her lessons to the test. She'd caught the eye of a handsome young reporter who had returned to Shanghai after spending the war in Chongqing. He asked Bing for a date, and they went to a movie. When he brought her home, Elder Sister appraised him.

"He has no money," Elder Sister sniffed. "Forget him."

The next time he contacted Bing, Elder Sister instructed her to meet him at Ma's apartment. Her place had no indoor plumbing, and he stopped to use the *ma tong,* chamber pot. After he left, Ma inspected the pot and rendered her verdict. "His urine is strange; maybe he has syphilis."

It fell on Bing to ask the fellow to stop calling on her. Embarrassed, she stammered an explanation. "My elder sister says I can't see you unless you can provide the Essential Four Things."

"What?" he shot back after hearing what the four things were. "The war just ended, and I'm lucky I got out of Chongqing with my life! Who has that kind of money? Your sister must be a gold digger!" After he left, Bing asked Ah Mei what he had meant by "gold digger."

"It's a woman who only wants a man for his money," she answered knowingly. "Lots of money."

Bing was indignant. How could he have said something so rude about Elder Sister? "Good riddance!" she exclaimed.

Ah Mei laughed. "Don't be so naïve, Bing. Men want women for their own pleasure. If a woman can get what she wants, what's wrong with that? Look at Elder Sister's husband. He's so old! They both got something they wanted, and they seem content."

Bing frowned. She had never thought about Elder Sister and Kristian that way. They treated her well, and she loved their two boys. That was enough for her.

Her brief first romance extinguished, Bing was reluctant to encourage other possible suitors. She hadn't dated the reporter long enough to feel anything toward him but embarrassment, and she didn't relish the prospect of another inspection process. Moreover, soon the family would be moving again. This time to a hotel.

One of Kristian's Chinese friends owned a construction company and hoped to curry favor with him, since the Dane was in charge of Texaco's construction projects in Shanghai. Expanding its China operations, Texaco was planning to build several Western-style villas in the exclusive Hongqiao area for its foreign managers. The friend offered to let Kristian and his family live rent-free in the large hotel room the friend had once kept for a mistress. By moving into the nearby building, they'd save lots of money. They'd get their deposit back from their current landlord, and they could sell their excess furniture. Kristian, Elder Sister, Peter, and Bing would move into the hotel room, while Ah Mei and Ole would continue to stay with Ma only a few blocks away. In 1947, the four moved into the Weida Hotel on the corner of Avenue Joffre and Avenue du Roi Albert. It thrilled Bing to stand at the window and see the Cathay Theatre lit up in neon at night across the street.

Big, bright, and modern, the hotel had a shiny elevator with mirrors and elegant brass trim. Their room was only on the second floor, but Bing could keep three-year-old Peter entertained for hours by riding the elevator with him. The huge bathroom had white marble on the floors, walls, and sink counter. Elder Sister arranged the furniture to create sleeping and living areas. They brought a table and chairs from the old apartment and fashioned a small cooking area with a kerosene-burner hotplate. Elder Sister and Kristian slept in the big bed with Peter on a child's bed next to theirs. There was no room for Bing's cot.

Bing didn't mind going back to the bedroll on the floor. She liked the hotel. From their balcony, Bing could watch the bustling street scene below. In the evening, shiny cars driven by chauffeurs in white uniforms pulled up to the entrance. Bellboys with pillbox caps and white gloves rushed to open the car doors. It was fun to watch a silk-stockinged leg appear as a bejeweled woman emerged in a fitted, embroidered *qipao* or a flowing French gown. Dapper men with slicked-back hair offered their arms to the ladies before disappearing into the hotel.

Sometimes Bing joined Elder Sister and her friends at the hotel's dance club. Its sparkling lights and music performed by a Filipino band mesmerized. On special occasions, American Negro musicians were the headliners, drawing in the crowds as dancers floated across the smooth parquet floor. It was a magical sight, straight out of a Hollywood movie. Except the magic was right in front of her. So close, she could almost grab it.

IN THE FIRST WEEKS OF MAY 1947, AMERICAN UNIVERSITIES mailed their admissions notices to prospective students for the fall. On May 22, Ho received letters of acceptance from both MIT and the University of Michigan for their doctoral mechanical engineering programs. He was ecstatic to be accepted by his top choices, especially knowing that every engineering graduate in China would have applied to both schools.

Ho couldn't decide which school to choose. The University of Michigan would be the less expensive alternative for his family, but MIT had the big name and reputation. As he prepared the documents to apply for his visa, he suddenly noticed that the letter from MIT had no signature. Ho went to the visa authorities to see if the unsigned letter would be accepted. Their answer was an unequivocal no. The hard decision was made for him—he would go to Michigan, home of the American automobile.

Forging ahead to make arrangements, Ho had no time to waste, for the conflict between the Nationalists and Communists was spiraling downward. At the start of the year in 1947, the American general George Marshall had made it clear that he had given up on his attempt to bring Chiang Kai-shek to the table with the Communists. Mao Zedong and Zhou Enlai had agreed to talks, but Chiang had refused. General Marshall announced that he was leaving China and pulling out most of the U.S. troops. The world war had ended two years before—now hundreds of thousands of American GIs across the globe, including those stationed in Shanghai, were mounting protests, demanding to be demobilized and sent home. Once the Americans pulled out of China, Chiang's Nationalists would be on their own against the Communists. There was no telling how the government might change its rules if the civil war exploded. Already, economic conditions had grown even more volatile.

After weeks of waiting, Ho received his passport and exit visa on July 19. With his doctoral program beginning in less than two months, he bought a one-way ticket for third-class passage on the American President Lines, the only company carrying passengers across the Pacific to the United States. The cost was 171 U.S. dollars, a large expense already but only a fraction of what his family would have to spend.

Those first postwar passenger crossings from Shanghai to San Francisco were made by two converted World War II troop transport ships, among the thousands built by Rosie the Riveters after Pearl Harbor: the USS *General M. C. Meigs* and USS *General Gordon*. Ho would sail on the *General Gordon*, departing August 24. After the sixteen-day voyage, he planned to take a train to Ann Arbor. He'd make it just in time for the start of school on September 13.

But Ho wouldn't let down his guard until he was on his way. Other students ran into problems that stopped them from leaving. Living just a few blocks from Ho, a McTyeire graduate named Lo-Lo Zhang Pan had cleared all the same hurdles as Ho: She had passed the national visa exam; been accepted for graduate studies at the University of Illinois College of Education; obtained her passport, visa, and ship's passage. Her suitcases were packed—but at the last minute, her father, a poor scholar, was unable to pull together the required amount of foreign exchange. Lo-Lo didn't make it onto the ship. Instead she wept with her parents over her lost opportunity to get an American graduate education—and to get away.

ON THE MORNING OF his departure, Ho went by taxi with his mother, brother, and uncles to the Shanghai Hongkou Wharf on Broadway. Ho

Ho, the number one graduate of his 1946 Jiao Tong University
mechanical engineering class, commands front and center in the class photo.

was so excited that he had barely slept in days. The dock was already crowded when they arrived. After going through customs and leaving his bag on his bunk among the three hundred beds in his third-class deck, he returned to the dock and his family. By then, several of his classmates had arrived to see him off, joking and teasing, "Don't forget your old friends when you're the number one PhD in America!"

His family showered him with gifts: shirts, food for the trip, and five hundred thousand yuan—worth about thirteen U.S. dollars. When it was time to say goodbye, his mother clutched his arm and began to weep. Ho's brother gently pried his mother away. As they headed to the street, she kept looking back and calling out, "Ho, my son! Ho!"

Ho fought back his tears. "Mother called after me again and again, it made my heart break," he wrote in the brand-new journal that his sister had given him. "Yet I can't feel sad, because I'm in command of my future. My ten thousand–*li* journey has begun."

THE AMERICAN SHIP OFFERED Ho a first glimpse into his upcoming life in America. To cool off from the heat of the sticky August day, he took a shower—his first experience with such a contraption. Nearby was the water fountain—another first. After a few cautious sips, he quenched his thirst from this amazing device that dispensed a continuous stream of clean water—no boiling necessary. In the third-class dining room, he waited in a long but orderly line for servings of sausages, potatoes, carrots, rice, bread, fruits, tea—and sugar, a precious commodity in Shanghai. The unlimited quantities stunned him, especially the sugar. That night he jotted down a new American phrase: "All you can eat."

With Ho, more than three hundred of China's brightest young minds were heading to the United States to continue their educations. Like him, fifty-two were Jiao Tong University graduates, and thirty-three were headed to the University of Michigan. The students held meetings onboard to prepare for life in America, with topics ranging from transportation to their schools to dealing with American culture and cold Michigan winters. Ho attended all the meetings and volunteered to compile a list of everyone's names to help them stay in touch once they scattered to their respective destinations.

The ocean voyage exposed Ho to another new concept: leisure. He'd brought along some books to study but barely opened them. Instead, he played bridge, watched movies, and spent time with new acquaintances. Most of the students were male, but several were female—including a lady professor. Ho had never gone to school with girls or women—and he was surprised to learn that they had big dreams for their educations too. At some point, Ho realized that he wasn't practicing much English, in spite of the many American passengers and crew. "I could pass the entire voyage to America speaking only Chinese!" he wrote, resolving to start using more English. It was for this reason that the father of another Shanghai student, Ming Cho Lee, insisted that his son enroll at Occidental College in California— he feared that if his son went to school in the northeastern United States, he would spend his time mostly with other Chinese.

Ho, ever the engineer, eagerly explored the bowels of the ship to understand its mechanics. He admired the genius of a vessel that could cut through the powerful waves as though gliding on ice. The vast beauty of the ocean, with its different hues of blue, gray, and black, mesmerized him.

When they reached the open sea, sick passengers began skipping meals. Ho, too, grew queasy, but he had paid for the meals and was determined to eat them all. He took careful notes on the Americans' habits. He wondered why people would want to eat bread at every meal but then realized that the rice was just for the many Chinese passengers— it was the only item familiar to most of them. By week's end, the students grew bored with the bland American food. One of Ho's cabin-mates groaned, "I miss Chinese food more than I miss my wife."

One thing disturbed Ho: the vast quantities of wasted food. He thought of the starving beggars in Shanghai. "One would exclaim in astonishment at the amount of leftover food at every meal," Ho wrote in his journal. "The leftovers are all dumped into the ocean, along with countless boxes and bottles."

On day eleven, the ship docked in Honolulu. Ho couldn't wait to step on land again. Before disembarking, all third-class passengers were assembled to play "Search for the Yellow Fish"—a hunt for stowaways—with no instructions on what to do if they found any. At the harbor, a huge crowd welcomed them, including representatives from the Consulate of China. After he'd posted his letters to his family, Ho and his friends took a tour of Honolulu. Most impressive to him was the courteous traffic on the smooth wide roads painted with lines. Motorists stopped briefly at intersections without a traffic cop, while pedestrians crossed the roads at spots designated by white lines. He questioned whether Shanghai's teeming millions could ever be so orderly.

The California coastline came into view toward evening on day fifteen. After saying goodbyes and settling accounts with the purser, Ho joined the cheering crowd on deck as they passed under the dramatic arc of the Golden Gate Bridge. He thought that with all these talented students going to study in America, they should be able to build such bridges in China one day.

Ho entered San Francisco in the early morning of September 8,

1947. He was brimming with enthusiasm: "From this day forward, everything will be new: I will see what I have never seen and hear what I have never heard before," he wrote in his journal that night. "By learning from my new experiences, I will be able to accomplish much with my life."

IN SAN FRANCISCO, the shipmates went their separate ways. Back home, the civil war between the Nationalists and the Communists was heating up. The stability that had allowed the students to exit Shanghai and to change their yuan to dollars peaceably had been a fleeting moment in time. Now the storm that had raged throughout Ho's youth threatened to explode with renewed fury. Ho and his fellow travelers were far away and unaware that they were at the front of a mass exodus soon to follow.

EXODUS

SHANGHAI, LATE 1948

AT THE SOFT EDGE OF DAWN, BENNY LAY UNDER THE COVERS staring at the ceiling of his St. John's University dormitory room, watching as the darkness faded into the first rays of the morning light. He treasured the quiet stillness, a momentary reprieve from the daily anxiety he'd endured over the past three years, ever since his father's arrest for being a *hanjian*, a traitor to the Chinese people. Ever since his family's free fall into calamity. Especially on days like this, when he planned to visit his father in prison, where he still awaited trial.

Just thinking about the prison never failed to dredge up painful memories in vivid detail. How difficult it had been to find himself responsible for his four younger siblings—without money or relatives to help. Another seventeen-year-old might have sized up the situation and run away, just as his mother had. Benny couldn't do that. Because he was the eldest son, it fell on his shoulders to care for his family and honor his parents. But in his darker moments, he had to admit that he deeply resented the father who had put his family in such jeopardy and the mother who had left them to fend for themselves.

Desperation had driven him to a resourcefulness he had never known he had, forcing him to put away the pride he could no longer afford. Soon after the five Pan siblings packed themselves into one room at his uncle's home, sixteen-year-old Cecilia had decided she'd had enough. She ran off and married an airman—a cockpit radio operator—and moved with him to Hong Kong. Unlike Benny's sister Annie, with her storybook wedding at the Paramount, Cecilia had no fancy nuptials. Benny could only wish her a better life. One bit of good news: St. Mary's Hall would allow fourteen-year-old Doreen to return as a boarding student, giving the family time to sort out the payments later.

With only the two youngest siblings left to worry about, Benny began to think about getting himself back to school. He had missed the first semester of his freshman year at the university. To go back, he'd needed to find help with the two children as well as money for his tuition. Benny made the rounds again, this time calling on his father's former associates. He reached out to the ones who had patted him on the head and praised him as Xiao Pan. Most shook their heads, clucking, or simply refused to talk with him. But two of his father's pals were willing to listen. Benny tried to disregard their cold demeanor, cunning eyes, and hulking size, as well as the likelihood that they were part of his father's Green Gang brotherhood. He needed their help.

"Honorable Uncles, my father's misfortune has caused our family many hardships. I was supposed to enter St. John's University to become a doctor, but I have no money for school. My father always told me that if I ever needed help, I could turn to you. I humbly ask if you could find me worthy of your supporting the cost of six years for college and medical school. When—if—my father is released, he will repay you, or I promise to do so once I am a doctor." As Benny spoke, he kept his head down out of respect—and to avoid looking into their hard faces.

They balked. "Six years? Who knows what could happen in six years!" Then they turned their backs on him and conferred.

Soon the man with the pockmarked face replied. "Xiao Pan, we have worked with your father for many years and have watched you grow up. Your father has always stood by us, and we know that he would want us to help you. We will arrange to pay your school fees as a favor to your father—but only four years, no more."

Benny gulped. He had always intended to enter the six-year medical school program. If he accepted their money, he would have to abandon his dream. But he was in no position to refuse. "Thank you, Honorable Uncles. I am most grateful and forever in your debt."

"Don't thank us. We will ask you to return the favor someday."

Benny bowed as they left, somewhat dismayed by the thought of the favor they might ask of him. But at least he was going to college with a chance to make something of himself, to claim a piece of his future back.

THERE REMAINED A FINAL hurdle before he could start at St. John's: He couldn't leave eleven-year-old Edward and nine-year-old Frances alone at his uncle's while he was in class. Nor would he be able to study with the children in his care. No relatives would take them in. There was only one possible solution—he would have to ask his mother for help.

Benny hadn't seen her since the day she had deserted them. She hadn't even bothered to inquire if they were alive. He knew that she was living in nearby Suzhou with his father's former bodyguard. If there'd been another option, Benny might have bypassed his mother to avoid seeing the added shame of her new living arrangements. Because he thought she might try to spurn him, Benny decided to surprise her. He and the children would take the train to Suzhou and catch her off guard. Once they were at her door, she'd have to look him in the eye to deny him.

When they reached his mother's address, Benny was in for another surprise. As he faced his mother after so many months, Benny was stunned to see her swollen belly. How could he have imagined she would be pregnant! He couldn't let it throw him. He averted his eyes to speak to her. "Mother, you must help us," he implored. "I found a way to attend St. John's, as you always wanted me to. But I can't go to college and mind the young ones too. Edward and Frances will be all alone with no chance to grow up properly. Please help them, Mother. Please help me!"

His mother paused for a long moment—so long that Benny considered turning around and leaving. Then she broke the silence, calling him by his childhood nickname. "Long-Long, don't think too harshly of me." In an instant, the softness of her voice warmed him to the mother he had adored and who had doted on him, her eldest son and favored child. "You've always been a good son. Go to St. John's." Taking Edward and Frances by their hands, she stepped back into the house.

Unnerved, Benny felt no joy. Another baby—with his father's bodyguard? He left quickly, almost running. After he rounded a corner, he staggered toward a lamppost, doubled over, and vomited.

BENNY HAD TO WAIT until the spring semester in 1946 to start at his beloved university. He would soon be eighteen. Because he had missed a full semester, he wouldn't graduate with his classmates. But that mattered little when he almost hadn't made it to college at all.

Getting back to the tranquil campus was a homecoming. Benny had lived there as a boarder since he was eleven, spending more time at school than at the big mansion. Those were his happiest years, before his family's disaster. It calmed him to sit with his books in the

The main college-level classroom buildings of St. John's University,
founded by American Episcopal missionaries in 1877, circa 1946.

shade of the expansive hundred-year-old camphor tree. He was finally able to walk into the stately gray-and-red brick university halls. As a boy, he had looked up to the college men. Now he was one of them.

His BDG Club buddies, Dennis and George, had remained his loyal and true friends. The trio still ran around together as if nothing had changed, even though Benny no longer had money to spare. Now he had to earn every yuan by tutoring and doing odd jobs on the campus. On weekends his pals invited him to their homes for dinners and parties. They welcomed him to spend the night, for they knew he had nowhere else to go, and no food was served at the campus on weekends.

But everything had changed for Benny. His shame was never far away. Not when the people of Shanghai were transfixed by the constant news of the Japanese war criminals and the Chinese traitors, collaborators, and puppets like his father. Wild accusations also flew against the innocent, including the former president of St. John's William Z. L. Sung, whose apparent crime was to have kept the school open during the enemy occupation, relying in part on the advice of Pan Da at the time. Now Sung was locked up at Tilanqiao Prison, the same jail where Benny's father was.

"*Hanjian, hanjian!* Read all about today's trial in the Shanghai High Court!" news hawkers shouted at the top of their lungs, selling their papers just outside the campus gates. *Hanjian*—that label had sent Benny's life into a tailspin. Whenever a student bought a newspaper, others flocked around as well. Everyone knew about "C. C. Pan, the traitor and collaborator"—and that the *hanjian*'s son, their once free-spending schoolmate, was Benny.

No one at the genteel school ever mentioned his father, at least not to his face. But Benny could feel the unspoken disdain of some. He did his best to avoid any awkward unpleasantries. Since he couldn't study medicine, Benny chose the major that required the fewest credits so that he could get his degree as quickly as possible. Ironically, it was politics, the one topic he most wished to avoid. Luckily, at St. John's he could concentrate on *American* politics, a subject that had nothing to do with Chinese collaborators.

Try as he might, however, Benny could not sequester himself from

news about the despicable traitors. The prosecution of local collaborators was a hot topic, just as the Nuremberg and Tokyo war crimes
tribunals were on the global stage. Benny was finally learning why his
fellow Shanghainese despised "No. 76"—his father's headquarters,
where Benny used to ride his bike—referring to it as the most dreaded
level of hell.

News accounts contained grisly details of water torture, cutting
and burning, starvation, sadistic beatings, electric shocks, and other
atrocities. His father must have known. How could he not have? Perhaps he'd participated in the torture himself. Constant insecurities
gnawed at Benny as he imagined that his schoolmates hated him, son
of a *hanjian* monster.

Even with the friendship of his two buddies, Benny felt alone. He
no longer cared to join the badminton and track teams or the other
activities that he had once enjoyed. Instead, he sought calm in the
stone Pro-Cathedral at the edge of the green, the large cross atop its
tall steeple.

Until the previous year, Benny had never given much thought to
religion. Church services were compulsory in middle school. Though
he attended the Episcopal services, the sermons had meant little to
him, no different from boring but required lectures. In that way, he
was the typical student described in his school newspaper, the *Dial:*
"By a general observation, you will find that St. John's students are
rather indifferent to religion. . . . Most students in this institution are
not believing in any kind of religion. Their attendance at the College
chapel is often looked at as a form of tradition that may be dispensed
with."

That was before Benny's inner turmoil led him to the church. At
first he'd sit quietly on the smooth lacquered pews in the back. One
day the choir director, Grace Brady, noticed him. She was an American missionary teacher from San Diego who had been at St. John's for
several years. Benny had taken her classes in English and music when
he was in middle school, and he'd always warmed to her kindness.

"Hello, Benny! Why aren't you outside on the sports field with the
other boys?" she asked cheerily.

"I don't know, Miss Brady," he replied in a near whisper, looking down at his shoes.

"That doesn't sound like the boy I remember, Benny. Tell me, what's on your mind?"

Soon, Benny spilled out the fears he had been holding in. He told her that his father had done terrible things and his mother had abandoned him, that he felt guilty for his family's wrongs, and that everyone must hate him. He worried that his fate was as doomed as his parents' and there was nothing he could do about it.

Miss Brady had been sitting beside Benny, studying his face as he spoke. When he came to a tearful stop, she took his hands and looked into his eyes. "Benny, God is merciful and will not punish you for the misdeeds of others. You are not to blame for the sins of your father. If you let God into your heart, he will help you to find the goodness in yourself and show you how to be better and more compassionate than your father."

As they sat in the cool quiet of the chapel, Benny was grateful to learn that the Christian God was forgiving. That he wasn't condemned to his father's fate. Benny found great comfort in Miss Brady's counsel.

"Don't just take my word, Benny. Come to a fellowship meeting, and read the Bible yourself. You'll enjoy the choir. As I recall, you have a nice singing voice."

With Miss Brady's encouragement, Benny joined the school choir, adding to the harmony of uplifting songs. On Sundays, he attended services without fail, returning to school in time for the sermon even when he stayed overnight with George or Dennis. He began to make sense of the sermons he used to ignore, opening his mind to a world beyond himself. In time, Benny found his way to the evening fellowship and Bible classes. He made himself useful by doing chores, sweeping and cleaning the chapel and sanctuary. Before long, he was leading the fellowship worship.

At times when Benny sat in quiet meditation, he reflected on his life before his father's fall. He could have become bitter against the world and Japan for the war that had compromised his father. He'd been angry at his father for aiding the enemy and sacrificing his fellow Chinese, bringing peril and unspeakable shame onto his family. He was angry at himself for being so ignorant, enjoying every luxury while oblivious to his father's collaboration with the enemy and the source of his unlimited funds. With God's help, Benny began to see it all in a new light. "Dear Lord," he prayed, "please forgive me for the easy life I partook in when my father was a *hanjian* at 76. Please, Lord, forgive my family for living off of other people's suffering."

As Benny progressed through college, Grace Brady continued to guide him and cheer him on. On weekends, she often invited groups of students to her campus cottage for a simple supper. Benny was always welcome there. When the damp cold of the Shanghai winter approached, she found extra blankets and sundries for Benny, knowing that he had no family to help him. She urged him to keep going when he became discouraged. Through Miss Brady and the chapel, Benny had found a spiritual family and home. In 1947, Benny decided to be baptized as a Christian. He was learning to forgive himself. He could finally hold his head up again.

EVEN BOLSTERED BY HIS new faith, Benny could not ignore his family's harsh reality. As the eldest son, he was expected to visit his father at the prison and watch out for his sister Doreen at St. Mary's. In the early days following his father's arrest in September 1945, Benny had visited his father quite often, since no one knew when it might be his turn to face the firing squad. About eight months after he was jailed, the puppet president Chen Gongbo, who as Shanghai's mayor had appointed C. C. Pan police commissioner, was tried for war crimes and executed.

By now, three years after the war's end, Benny's attitude had changed. Before heading from his campus to the Tilanqiao Prison, Benny would stop first at his aunt's flat in the Dasheng *lilong* on Avenue Haig. It was the same *lilong* complex he had lived in so happily before his father's meteoric rise. This aunt was one of the only relatives who had stayed in touch with Benny, inviting him over for home-cooked meals. She always prepared some tins of food and articles of clothing for Benny to take to his father. From there, Benny would ride the trolley through the former French Concession, past the Bund into Hongkou to the north and the Tilanqiao neighborhood further east. After traveling nearly three miles to the edge of the former International Settlement, he would reach the largest prison in all of Asia, its massive gates and towering concrete walls taking up more than 750,000 square feet on seventeen acres—more than an entire city block.

The infamous Ward Road Jail, as it was known in English, or Tilanqiao Prison, as it was known to the Chinese, had been built in stages beginning in 1901 when the British ran the International Settlement. The colossal stone dungeon, made up of eleven cellblocks, each four stories high, was a fearsome place, with thousands of inmates packed into some three thousand prison cells patrolled by armed Sikh guards. During the war, Police Commissioner Pan Da had sent countless unfortunates there—if they had managed to survive the interrogations at 76. How strange that Benny's father was jailed in Tilanqiao alongside the Japanese war criminals he was supposed to have collaborated with, all of them awaiting trial together.

Somehow Benny's father had staved off the executioner. In the three years he had spent in prison, he had not only survived but didn't appear to be suffering. He never looked haggard or unkempt like other prisoners. Benny didn't dare ask his father how he managed to maintain himself in the cellblock, but he could guess. His father had a huge network of influential friends. Many were high in the Nationalist government and the Green Gang, the police and prison systems. Benny sometimes imagined his father would one day get out of prison unscathed. In fact, that wouldn't have surprised Benny at all.

Perhaps because his father seemed to be doing all right, Benny let more time slip by between visits, which consisted of little more than a few awkward moments together under the watchful eye of surly prison guards. He dared not ask the questions that gnawed at him: Had his father tortured and killed Chinese patriots and resisters to aid the Japanese enemy? Had he enriched himself during the war at the expense of his fellow Chinese? How could he have collaborated with the enemy against his own people? Against his own family?

BENNY'S AUNT ON AVENUE Haig suggested that on this visit to the prison he pay close attention to the mood of the prison guards. With the instability of the Nationalist government and fears of its imminent collapse, she said there was no telling what changes were occurring at the prison. The Nationalists were making mass arrests of workers at the Shanghai Power Company and other workplaces, suspecting them of being underground Communists. Many, like the popular labor leader Wang Xiaohe, were also being jailed at Tilanqiao.

"Your father is lucky that the Nationalists are too busy searching for Communists to think about him," Benny's aunt surmised. "With so many Nationalist officials packing up to leave Shanghai, maybe they'll be releasing some prisoners too."

By the time Benny reached the Tilanqiao area, it was midmorning. He walked past a few blocks of squalid three- and four-story tenements known as Little Vienna, where the Japanese had ordered the thousands of Jewish refugees from eastern Europe to be confined in 1943, at the behest of the local Nazi authorities. Many had feared a Kristallnacht-style pogrom would follow, but it was said that the Japanese rejected Hitler's "Final Solution" for Jews and darker races— like themselves. The Ashkenazi Jews in Tilanqiao were poor, unlike Shanghai's wealthy and long-established Sephardic Jewish elite whose influential families had built some of Shanghai's most famous institutions. Pan Da had known them all.

Visiting his father, Benny had walked through Little Vienna and its busy sidewalk cafés many times, observing the similarities between these Jewish refugees and the White Russians of an earlier time; both had been displaced persons who had arrived with nothing in a strange land. If he fled to Hong Kong as many of his classmates were doing, Benny wondered if perhaps he'd be like these Jews, trying to re-create the life they once knew. Some had been hired as teachers at St. John's, especially after the internment of many of the school's foreign faculty. There were fewer Jews in Little Vienna now, with international relief efforts sending many of the stateless refugees to America, Australia,

Brazil, and the brand-new state of Israel. As Benny walked by the Ohel Moshe Synagogue, he saw a wedding in progress there. Celebration and renewal taking place across from the fortress of death and doom—one of life's ironies, Benny observed.

At the towering front gate of the prison with its massive wooden doors, Benny addressed a uniformed guard through a small window in the stone wall. "I'm here to see Prisoner Pan Zhijie," Benny said, using his father's formal name. The guard grunted and waved him in toward a crowd of others waiting to be inspected by the next batch of gatekeepers. They recorded visitors' names and checked their small packages—assortments of food and cigarettes, warm clothes and blankets, writing paper. Advancing to the next levels of security screening, he moved deeper into the bowels of the stone citadel. It seemed forever before he reached the austere visiting room of long bare tables and hard benches. Remembering his aunt's advice, he looked for clues of impending change from the guards, but they seemed as stone-faced as always.

With a sudden flurry, several prisoners were marched into the room. There was his father, straight-backed and proud, his face clean-shaven, hair clipped short the way he'd preferred when he was with the Shanghai Municipal Police. Even in the drab prison, he looked sharp and tough.

"Hello, Father," Benny said brightly from the visitors' side of the wide table, in the same "snap-to-it" voice he'd used when he was a boy lining up for morning inspection by his uniformed father.

No physical contact was permitted during the visit, but even if it had been allowed, Benny and his father had a formal and traditional relationship that did not include public displays of affection. Anything else would have felt odd to Benny.

"Father, you look well. I brought you some dishes that Fifth Aunt prepared for you."

"Do thank her for me. How is school? It is good that your studies focus on America."

Nodding, Benny wasn't surprised that his father still knew about his activities from his network outside the prison. His years as an inmate hadn't broken him. If the war had ended differently, Benny imagined he could be having this same conversation poolside at Le Cercle Sportif Français, a favorite club of both his father and grandfather. He could picture his father in one of his elegant silk suits, or his blue serge police uniform, with a cigar in one hand and a glass of Scotch in the other.

Benny struggled for what to say when everything of importance had to remain unsaid. Instead, they spoke of mundane matters—the winter chill, sports at St. John's, the unappetizing food at the campus canteen, same as when his father was a student. Benny was glad that his father never asked him about his mother. He would not have lied if his father had asked, but how could he have reported that his mother was living with his father's former servant, bearing that man's children? On the other hand, since his father asked nothing at all, Benny was sure that he already knew.

As if sensing Benny's unspoken concerns, his father looked at the ceiling and seemed to ponder out loud. "In times of war, there are no good choices. Sometimes one can only choose what is less bad."

Then he faced Benny. "You're a man now, and you too will have difficult choices to make. Only you can know which choice is right for you."

For a moment, Benny imagined that his father knew about his schoolmates steadily disappearing to Hong Kong, Taiwan, and elsewhere in the face of the big Communist victories. Benny's friends and even his sister Cecilia in Hong Kong were all pressuring him to join the exodus before Shanghai collapsed to the Communists. Benny hadn't mentioned any of that. As his father said, he would have to choose his path for himself.

It was almost a relief when the dog-faced guard blew a whistle to mark the end of the visitation period. Benny handed over his package of food and clothing and said, "Goodbye, Father."

Standing to leave, his father said, "I know these are troubled times for Shanghai, and if you cannot visit, don't worry. I still have my connections." Benny's father had once confided that Dai Li himself, the Nationalist chief of intelligence and feared spymaster, had promised that no harm would come to Pan Da, in exchange for a substantial sum. But Dai Li had died in a mysterious plane crash in 1946. No harm had come to Benny's father, it was true. But who could say what would happen if the Communists took over?

Pan Da walked out, back straight and head forward, and disappeared with the other prisoners into the maw of the cavernous jail.

Outside, the afternoon shadows had grown long. Families strolled by under the watchful gaze of old men sipping coffee at a sidewalk café. The wedding party was streaming out of the synagogue. Benny felt lighter, grateful for his father's words.

AS THE WESTERN NEW YEAR passed and the Lunar New Year celebrations for the Year of the Ox approached, the question of whether to run away or stay in Shanghai became ever more pressing. Members of Shanghai's elite fought over getaway tickets like an unruly mob. Benny's closest friends urged him to leave, saying that the Communists would treat families like his even more harshly than the Nationalists had. At school, the empty desks multiplied.

Benny had had chances to flee before. One of his best friends had invited him to join his family's escape. And his sister Cecilia continued to implore him to go with her airman husband to Hong Kong. A radio operator with the China National Aviation Corporation, he could smuggle Benny into his cockpit, or so she claimed.

Throughout the semesters, the *St. John's Dial* had been publishing the names of students, faculty, and staff who had departed. Some argued that fleeing was unpatriotic; philosophy professor E. Hsu told his students, "Nobody should run away from our country and from the responsibility of being a Chinese citizen." Nevertheless, the *Dial* reported, "The library is filled with worried students, anxiously poring over newspapers and discussing the latest news. Rumors circulate in the air, growing in proportion. The main topic of conversation is the question: 'Are you leaving Shanghai?' It may be some time before the turbulence will calm down and things will return to their normal course." The student paper implied that normalcy would soon be restored—yet what would that look like when nobody wanted to be left behind?

His own classmates were vanishing without a word of warning—or goodbye. Perhaps they hadn't even known they were leaving. Richard Lin Yang, who lived in Benny's dormitory, left suddenly one afternoon when a servant was dispatched to fetch him. Richard's father had ordered him to attend a special family dinner aboard a boat on the Huangpu River. Richard didn't return to campus that night, leaving all his belongings, even his prized stamp collection, in his room. No one could believe that Richard would have willingly left his rare Qing dynasty stamps behind. Richard's friends said that his father had used the ruse of a dinner to get his extended family onto the boat and spirit them out of Shanghai, knowing that some family members would otherwise have refused to leave.

Good for Richard. Good for them all, Benny supposed.

But what should *he* do? So far he had declined the offers to help him run away, more confident of his future in China than as a refugee in points unknown. He was haunted by the skeletal refugees he'd seen living in the streets of Shanghai since his childhood, by the men marking time in Little Vienna, and by countless others. Richard and his schoolmates had parents who would make the difficult decisions and figure everything out for them. If Benny's father weren't in prison, it would have been the same for him.

Instead, Benny was facing his future alone. His father had said that he would have tough choices ahead. Maybe he had been referring to his own decision to work with the Japanese enemy. Benny mused that his choice might be equally ambiguous.

He weighed the pros and cons. Hong Kong and Cecilia beckoned, and he could live with his sister. But so many people were fleeing to Hong Kong that the British colony was teeming with refugees. He'd be one in a million.

Then there was Taiwan. Hordes of Shanghainese were heading to that tiny island off the southern coast. Yet the Nationalists were the ones who had imprisoned his father. It was foolhardy to think Taiwan would welcome Benny. He wouldn't stand a chance there.

With no money and no *guanxi* connections for a traitor's son, his only asset would be his St. John's education—and he needed one more term to graduate. Without a college diploma, he'd have nothing. As a penniless refugee, he could even be forced to join the Green Gang, whose chiefs, including the "honorable uncles" to whom he owed his college debt, were already fleeing to Hong Kong. The best way to avoid that fate was to stay in Shanghai and get his diploma.

HANGZHOU, LATE 1948

ONCE IN A WHILE, ANNUO HAD TO PINCH HERSELF, JUST TO make sure that this postwar peace wasn't a dream. After enduring the treacherous four-month trek across rugged terrain to escape the bombers over Shanghai, she had to admit that her life in Hangzhou was so calm and pleasant, it seemed unreal, as though she'd been plucked from a cauldron and plopped into a painting of this celebrated city on the shores of the West Lake.

At first her father's decision to move the family to Hangzhou while he stayed in Shanghai had visibly upset her unflappable mother, especially when he arranged to give away all her hard-earned savings. Meanwhile, he could enjoy himself in Shanghai while he restarted his civilian life as a salt merchant. But for Annuo, these past three years in Hangzhou had provided a welcome stability. Her Nationalist father had been assigned a Western-style house that was bigger and more beautiful than anywhere else they had lived. Ever since ancient times, Hangzhou had been beloved for its scenic beauty. It was quite a recognition of her father's loyal service that her family could live in a fine war-requisitioned home with such a prestigious location. Even the eldest son of Generalissimo Chiang, Major General Chiang Ching-kuo, had moved his own family to Hangzhou.

The presence of so many high-ranking Nationalists—and their

children—brought greater acclaim to Hangzhou's famous Hungdao School, already nicknamed "the School for Nobility." The grandchildren of the generalissimo himself were among its students, and that's where Annuo's mother wanted her daughter to go. But Annuo had missed nearly three years of school after contracting diphtheria. Before that, she had attended school sporadically. By absorbing all of Charley's books and comics, Annuo had kept up her reading skills, but her grasp of mathematics was atrocious. Nevertheless, her mother signed her up to take the entrance exam for the girls' middle school and confidently accompanied her to the test. During a break Annuo confessed that she'd skipped nine of the ten math questions. Her mother was so distressed by the thought of losing face from Annuo's failure that she left in a huff. Annuo had to finish the test and find her way home by herself. To the girl's surprise, she passed the exam and was admitted to the School for Nobility at the end of 1945, when she was ten. Other students' math skills must have been even worse than hers.

LITERATURE WAS ANNUO'S FAVORITE subject. By 1948, when she was thirteen, she had read almost every classic in the school library. She was still a shy girl who preferred to sit by herself with *Anna Karenina* or the *Tale of the Three Kingdoms*. In school, she filled her notebooks with dreamy poems and pencil drawings of her classmates. At home, she'd sit under the graceful magnolia tree next to the house, reading or watching the light dance on the pink blossoms in the spring. Their home was so spacious that her two grandmothers and some cousins moved in as well. When the magnolias bloomed, her usually dour paternal grandmother would chortle with delight and gather some blossoms, instructing the cook to lightly batter and fry each fresh petal. Annuo's mouth would water at the very thought of their delicate flavor.

Her latest treasure was *Gone with the Wind*, translated into Chinese. She had used some of her *hong bao* from New Year's to buy this book that was an instant hit in China. Annuo felt a connection to the central character, a haughty young woman on the losing side of the

Thirteen-year-old Annuo (second from left) with her extended family at their Hangzhou home in 1948. Standing to her left are her mother and father; Charley is second from right. Sister Li-Ning is in front of her father and between both grandmothers, seated. An uncle and two cousins are also pictured.

American Civil War. China, too, was being ripped apart by civil war, right on the heels of the long struggle with Japan.

For Annuo, life in Hangzhou was best when her father was away. Fortunately that was most of the time. When he came to Hangzhou every few months, he always brought an entourage to keep him company. He enjoyed nothing more than entertaining his big city friends with an impromptu feast. By the time they arrived after their four-hour train ride from Shanghai, they'd be in high spirits. The whole house would fly into a frenzy, with everyone rushing around to please her father and his retinue. Her mother, the gracious host, never failed to make the house hospitable, organizing the unplanned banquets with whatever food they could whip together.

Annuo, however, had realized for some time that she could not please her father. Though he had hardly seen her in the years since her birth, he never failed to find some fault with her. She was too sensitive—

or not sensitive enough. She wasn't giggly and cute like Li-Ning. She reminded her father of his homely younger sister, whom he disliked. Once, in Hangzhou, Annuo had played a silly prank on her brother and cousin. Her father had been home and had flown into a rage at her, shouting, "You'll never have happiness in your life or amount to anything. No man will want you when you grow up! If you get married, your marriage will fail!"

Stung, Annuo couldn't imagine what she had done to deserve such outsized anger. Her father hated her, she concluded, and she resolved to stay out of his way. She absorbed his harsh pronouncement that she would never find happiness. Already a quiet girl, she withdrew further into herself—not quite glum, but rarely happy.

Her father's spontaneous parties presented her biggest challenge. She disliked having to sit, prim and proper, sometimes forced to speak to adults who had no interest in her or what she might have to say, all under her father's critical eye. Not only was she afraid that she'd irritate him, but she also couldn't fathom why some of the women, as educated as her mother, spoke in little-girl voices like her ten-year-old sister's. Or why so many of the men puffed themselves up as though they had the answers to everything. Annuo envied her sixteen-year-old brother, a boarder at his middle school, who didn't have to endure these dinners. She couldn't wait to be dismissed and sent upstairs to bed, where she could retreat with her books to a fantasy world far away.

BUT THANKS TO A STRANGE new contraption, Annuo's attitude toward the parties shifted. On one visit, her father brought home a gramophone. After the adults had finished eating and talking, someone mentioned having "itchy feet." The servants pushed the furniture aside in the parlor, rolled up the carpet, and talced the floor. Her father cranked up the gramophone and put on some popular band music. Then everyone *danced*. As if possessed by spirits, the properly formal men and women jumped up and moved about while *touching* one another. The first time Annuo saw the adults dance, her jaw dropped. Opposite sexes touching in public? Stunned to see even her parents embrace as they danced, she found this utterly contrary to everything she had been taught about acceptable Chinese behavior.

To Annuo's great surprise, her father decided that she and Li-Ning should learn to dance, since there were never enough female partners for his friends. Soon Annuo was dancing the fox-trot, tango, and swing to popular Shanghai band music. American tunes like "Tennessee Waltz" got everyone onto the dance floor. Annuo began looking forward to her father's surprise visits, hoping for the music to start up after dinner. Her feet were itchy—and she was happier.

But lately, outside, the mood had begun to sour. The Americans were leaving Shanghai—a discouraging indication of the U.S. president's flagging support for the Nationalists. Inflation and economic instability added to the broad chorus of discontent with the government—at marketplaces, on streetcars, even at school. Though Annuo's father had traded his military uniform for a business suit, he was still loyal to Chiang Kai-shek. He despised the Communists not just for their politics but also because of his personal experience with their guerrilla attacks against his troops. He agreed with Chiang's perspective that their treachery had undermined the Nationalist efforts against Japan.

As the weather turned cooler in the autumn of 1948, the exchanges at her father's parties grew more heated and more urgent. Increasingly, his guests discussed the need to flee. The Communists, they said, had grown stronger in Manchuria and the northeast provinces after their important military victories against the Nationalists. Each victory brought the Communists important infusions of captured arms and soldiers—defectors absorbed from the demoralized Nationalist armies. The Communists would surely drive southward to Beijing, Nanjing, Suzhou, Hangzhou—and the grandest prize, Shanghai.

As Annuo sat at the top of the steps, beyond the view of the adults, she'd wait for the debates to end and the music to start. During one especially lively discussion, she heard one man say, "The situation in the north seems more dire every day. How much longer should we wait to see if the generalissimo's troops can turn things around?"

"Running away undermines the Nationalist army when it still has a chance to win," chastised another. "We have superior American weapons and training. The Americans will never let China fall into Stalin's hands."

Her father's booming voice rose over the chatter. Eloquent and commanding, the former magistrate rendered his judgment. "Let's face the facts: The generalissimo has lost three major campaigns, and the Red Bandits have seized control north of the Yangtze River. A stallion can't outpace an ox if his leg is lame." The room was quiet as her father continued. "As a loyal Nationalist, it pains me to say that our stallion seems to have three lame legs. Once the Red Bandits cross the Yangtze River and take Shanghai, all of China is lost."

A sharp voice asked, "If that's the case, should we all start packing now?"

Annuo fidgeted as the question hung uncomfortably in the tense air.

Suddenly everyone was talking at once, dropping the names of far-away places like hot mah-jongg tiles. Hong Kong. Taiwan. Singapore. Indonesia. The Philippines. Malaya. Indochina. Brazil. A woman's voice rejected Europe, still in shambles from the war, and argued: "Going there would be worse than staying in Shanghai."

The mere mention of Australia and America triggered a snort. "Wake up! No one can get a visa to Australia with their 'whites-only' policy. And America just takes Chinese who are as rich as the Big Four families or as famous as the writers Hu Shih or Lin Yutang."

Every middle school student could recognize those names, Annuo included. The Big Four ruling families of China were the Chiangs, relatives of Generalissimo Chiang Kai-shek; the Soongs, relatives of Soong May-ling, the generalissimo's wife; the Kungs, whose tycoon patriarch was a direct descendent of Confucius and married to a sister of Madame Chiang; and the Chens, loyal and superrich allies of Chiang. All had amassed unfathomable wealth and power in the war years. It was rumored that the glamorous American-educated wife of the generalissimo and her relatives had skimmed money from their country's treasury and stashed it away in secret U.S. bank accounts. As General George Marshall had once reported, "A plane dispatched from [Chongqing] for Washington, D.C., with 'important secret documents' had to ditch in the river. When salvaged, what it proved to have was U.S. currency which the Soong family was sending to the U.S."

Nationalists like Annuo's father and his dinner friends were part of Shanghai's middle class and nowhere close to that elite stratosphere. But compared to proletarian workers, farmers, and foot soldiers of either army, they seemed rich, living well without fear of starvation. However, they were hardly wealthy. Even so, the accusations of the Chiangs' nepotism and corruption couldn't dampen her father's support for the Nationalists. As far as he was concerned, it was all Communist propaganda against the generalissimo and Madame Chiang.

ONE EVENING TOWARD THE END of 1948, the dinner guests were especially somber, preoccupied by the latest Nationalist defeats. As Annuo sat on the staircase hoping the music would begin, she recognized two loud voices rising above the noisy chatter. They belonged to her father and her seventh uncle, her mother's rich cousin. They were arguing about the island of Taiwan.

"You must take this threat more seriously, Cousin!" Annuo recognized the no-nonsense tone of her father's voice. "I can get all of us safe passage to Taiwan—we can be settled in before the Nationalist government finishes moving there."

"Taiwan? I've been to Taiwan. It's a backwater!" Seventh Uncle countered. "People there still think they're a Japanese colony. They speak Japanese, not Chinese. And they eat raw fish! They dress like Japanese and sleep on straw mats. No cars, no streetlights, no toilets! You have to squat over a hole in the ground. It's impossible for Shanghai people to live in such an uncivilized place with a bunch of country bumpkins!"

Annuo stifled a giggle at the thought of her portly uncle squatting.

Her father answered with an urgency in his voice that she hadn't heard before. "Cousin, I'm begging you to think of your family, your children. You know what the Communist bandits will do to a rich capitalist like you. You don't stand a chance if the Red Bandits cross the Yangtze River!"

"I survived the war and occupation under the heel of Japan's boot,"

Seventh Uncle replied. "At least the Communists are fellow Chinese. What can the Reds do that's worse than the Japanese? We'll survive this crisis as well."

"I hope you'll change your mind. I'm making preparations to leave for Taiwan—you're welcome to come with us," she heard her father reply emphatically.

"You should save your effort to get tickets for yourselves instead of wasting it on me. From what I hear, it's getting impossible to find tickets to Taiwan or Hong Kong. Better yet, buy all the tickets you can— you'll get rich by selling them to other scared rabbits."

Annuo's head began to spin. Were they going to run away again? To this backward place full of pro-Japanese people? Annuo felt as though a heavy weight had landed on her. But then again, so many of her schoolmates were already gone. General Han Deqin, her father's friend and superior, had already packed up his family for Taiwan, leaving his grand piano with her family for safekeeping. But Seventh Uncle made the place sound like some dreadful rice paddy stuck in the middle of the ocean. What would Scarlett O'Hara say if she had to give up her beloved Tara for some primitive island?

THE NEXT DAY HER FATHER and his entourage returned to Shanghai. Not long after, Annuo saw her mother sorting through clothing, photos, and other possessions. Ordinarily, Annuo would have said nothing, as it would have been impertinent to question her mother. But with such a big change on the horizon, Annuo broached the subject.

"When are we going to Taiwan?" she asked, trying to sound nonchalant.

"We will have to leave soon. It won't be safe to stay here."

"But how can we leave so many family members and friends behind?" Annuo blurted out, unable to stop herself.

Her mother didn't look up from her task. Her voice calm, she replied, "You're not a child anymore. In the new year, you'll be fourteen, the same age as your grandmother when she got married. Sometimes you must do what must be done, no matter how distasteful.

Besides, we will only be gone for six months—a year at most. Then we'll be back."

Only six months in Taiwan? Annuo immediately felt better.

BY EARLY 1949, AFTER the Lunar New Year, Annuo's father had given up trying to persuade relatives to leave with them. As the panic to flee raged into a frenzy, he needed to focus on his own family. Securing a passage to Taiwan was becoming nearly impossible, even for a former Nationalist official. But with General Han's influence, her father managed to get five plane tickets. The general clearly held her father in high regard, for he could have given those tickets to his own relatives. Going by airplane would be better than going by ship, her father said. A few overloaded passenger ships had already sunk en route to Taiwan, with thousands dying at sea.

The task of packing up the children and household once again fell upon Annuo's mother. Their family had run from danger so many times that packing up to flee was almost routine. This time, Annuo's mother said that each child would carry one small bag of essential items. To bring more clothing, they would have to wear extra layers on the day of the trip. They could each bring along one special object.

Annuo carefully examined the trinkets and charms she had saved. How could she choose just one? She decided to hide the treasures she couldn't take so they'd be waiting for her when she came back. Her mother had said that their trusted amah, Zhongying, refused to come to Taiwan but would stay behind, watching the house and caring for their relatives. Although she had been through so much with the family, Zhongying said that Taiwan was just too far away. She added that a lowly amah would have nothing to fear from the Communists.

After days of mulling over her one special item to take to Taiwan, Annuo finally decided: She'd bring her favorite book, *Gone with the Wind*. Thinking of Scarlett made her feel better about fleeing. After all, she repeated to herself, tomorrow is another day.

———

THE MOMENT ARRIVED WHEN there could be no more worrying, bickering, discussing, or planning as Annuo clambered onto an over-loaded train for Shanghai with her brother, sister, and mother. They would meet Annuo's father there and take an airplane to Taiwan.

An airplane! That exciting prospect almost took her mind off the unbearable slowness of the train. They had left Hangzhou at such a turtle's pace that they seemed to be moving backward. The crowded aisle was packed with people and their worldly goods. Annuo imagined them to be crabs in a pot ready to boil with everyone climbing over one another to escape.

She watched a corpulent man standing near her. Rivulets of sweat slid down his round cheeks to his chin. Periodically he lifted his fedora to wipe his damp head with a handkerchief. Like everyone else on the train, he was no doubt wearing extra clothing that couldn't fit into his bag. Annuo, too, was warm from the layers of underwear and dresses under her winter coat.

Across the aisle, her mother sat with ten-year-old Li-Ning on her lap. Muma and Charley had rushed onto the train in Hangzhou to nab two seats, pulling Annuo, Li-Ning, and their bags along behind. The 110-mile trip that usually took four hours would take all day at the rate they were moving—assuming there were no problems that delayed them further. Annuo had squeezed into a single prized seat with Charley. She had never seen such an endless crush of people trying to jump onto a train, not even during the Japanese war.

As the cars somehow grew even more crowded during their slow journey, desperate people grabbed onto the outside shell of the train and hung on, cramming their bodies onto every available space. Some sat on the open window ledges, legs dangling inside while the rest of their bodies hugged the outside. It looked so uncomfortable and dangerous. Still, those window sitters were better off than the people who stood on outside footholds with only their arms reaching into the train cabin. Most precarious were the ones sitting on the roof. With every sudden lurch, low-hanging tree branch or cable, some hapless souls were swept off the train, plummeting to a chorus of horrified shrieks.

Annuo tried to shut out the thought of people clinging for their lives. It brought back the terrible memories of her own frightening efforts to keep from falling headlong down a sheer cliff during their wartime trek. Around her, anxious people eyed one another warily. Some snapped at anyone who accidentally touched their belongings, while others sniffled through tears of excitement or distress—Annuo couldn't tell which. Unpleasant odors swirled through the car: the stink of sweat and adrenaline, fear and panic. And the cloying scent of mothballs from clothing stored away, too good to be left behind and now worn in heavy layers. To Annuo, these were the familiar sensations of a childhood spent running from war.

*By 1949, Chinese, desperate to flee to anywhere,
packed every train car, riding on the roofs, clinging to sides,
even hanging on to the locomotives.*

———

THE SKY WAS DARK when they pulled into Shanghai. It seemed that they had been aboard for days, not just the better part of one. The crowded cars came alive as people rushed toward the doors, everyone hoping to find passage out of China or at least to get somewhere safer than the place they had just left. Muma gathered the three children close to her and instructed them to hold tight to their bags, admonishing them, "Stay together, be quick, and look for your father."

When the tangle of people finally thinned, Annuo gulped the cool evening air as they stepped onto the platform. She hadn't been back to the city of her birth in four years and had forgotten how bustling it was. In a few moments, her father and uncle found them. Her father grabbed Muma's bags and took Li-Ning by the hand, leading them to a waiting car. "You're so late! We must get some rest," he urged. "Our flight is early in the morning."

As they settled in for the night at the apartment of Uncle Shu-shu and Aunt Yiniang, Muma's sister, Annuo's father tried one last time to convince Uncle Shu-shu to bring his family to Taiwan. Uncle simply replied, "I'm just a lawyer working for an American company. I wasn't a Nationalist, and I'm not a capitalist or a landlord. The Communists won't bother with me." He went on to explain that even if he had wanted to go, it would be impossible. As an eldest son, he was responsible for taking care of his parents in their old age. They refused to leave Shanghai, and Uncle could not leave them behind.

In the dark of the next morning, their families said goodbye.

"We won't be gone long," Annuo's mother promised.

"We'll be back before the year is out," Annuo's father assured them.

Inside the crowded airport, Annuo and Charley stood by the windows and stared in silence at the deep craters in the runway, evidence of the latest Communist bombardments. Could the plane really fly from here? Charley wondered aloud. Annuo said nothing, taking her cue from her tight-lipped mother. When they climbed aboard the military transport plane, Annuo and Charley had to sit on their suitcases because the space was so packed. Everybody seemed certain they'd be back within six months. Annuo already pictured herself back at her desk at her middle school.

Annuo could feel the sensation of speed and the roar of the engines at lift-off—but she was hemmed in too far from the tiny windows to see anything but strangers pressed tightly together. So much for her first plane ride. As the too-familiar stench of perspiration, tobacco, garlic, and mothballs enveloped her once more, she worried that Charley would get sick, as he had on the boats during previous escapes.

The airless flight would be short, someone said, lasting only a few hours. A baby started wailing behind her toward the back of the plane. Nobody paid any mind. A woman seated nearby wept quietly for the entire flight, upset that she'd left two of her young children and her elderly mother in Shanghai. Her husband tried to comfort her. "We'll only be gone for a short time; we'll see them soon," he said, repeating the words that everyone else wanted to believe. Annuo glanced at her mother, knowing that she regretted leaving her own mother behind in Hangzhou. But her face revealed nothing.

After flying four hundred miles due south, following the mainland coast along the East China Sea, the cargo plane was nearing the island of Taiwan. Annuo braced herself as the propellers made a high-pitched whine during the plane's descent. Even sheltered schoolchildren like her had heard the gruesome tales about overloaded planes crashing and colliding in the rush to escape from the Communists. Prominent Americans had died in some of the crashes, including Quentin Roosevelt II, the grandson of the American president Theodore Roosevelt. Scavengers reportedly took jewelry and valuables from luggage and even from body parts that washed ashore.

With each bump and jolt, Annuo fretted that they would join the grim statistics. She peeked at Charley, who seemed buoyed that the flight was nearly over and he had managed not to get sick. He flashed Annuo his impish *it's all okay* smile. Charley's confidence was infectious, and she slowly exhaled.

Not far from her, she could hear her father and other men on the plane vigorously discussing what to expect during their short stay in Taiwan.

"We have an obligation to teach the Taiwanese how to be Chinese again," said a man who described a previous trip he had taken there. "Japan brainwashed them to forget who they are!"

Another man scoffed. "Who cares about the local bumpkins on this little island? Our only priority should be to regroup and defeat the Red Bandits."

"With what?" derided someone near her. "Without Truman's support and America's military, it'll be hard enough to keep the Reds from invading Taiwan."

Annuo ignored the men. She was trying to conjure up something, anything, that would help her envision this unfamiliar place. Her mind simply drew a blank. She'd studied at one of the top schools in China, yet she couldn't recall a single lesson on Taiwan, its history or its people—not even when her fellow students were fleeing to the island with their Nationalist families.

As the plane skidded onto the airstrip, Annuo held Charley's arm tight in case they crashed. When they didn't, she let out a sigh of relief and turned toward her parents. As usual, her father was bantering with other passengers while her mother's face was calm. The scene resurrected a buried memory of another uncertain time years before when her mother had fallen out of a bus and Annuo had thought she was dead. That moment of terrible dread suddenly gripped her again. This time she shook it off. Facing the airplane door, eyes wide with anticipation, she waited to get her first look at this strange, backward place.

SHANGHAI, LATE SUMMER 1948

AFTER STAYING AT THE WEIDA HOTEL ON AVENUE DU ROI ALBERT for nearly a year, Bing had grown accustomed to the large single room. Elder Sister, Kristian, and Peter slept on a bed and cot in one corner, while Bing unfurled her bedroll at night and slept on the floor by the makeshift kitchen next to the bathroom. There was still enough room for Bing and Ah Mei to play with Peter and Ole, now five and nine. During the day, Kristian and Elder Sister were usually away—he at Texaco's Caltex offices and she socializing with friends. After the evening meal together, Ma would take a reluctant Ole with her to stay the night at her small room in a nearby *lilong*.

A few months earlier, Ah Mei had married a portly Jewish man from Iran. He was part of Elder Sister's circle of friends who enjoyed going to clubs and dance halls. Occasionally he'd stay for dinner. No one suspected a romance until he and Ah Mei surprised everybody by eloping. In the evenings, Ah Mei would stay with her new husband. Bing was happy for her and glad that she had found someone who treated her well. And she could still see her friend every day.

After Ma, Ah Mei, and Ole left for the night, Bing would ready Peter for bed. Then she'd relax and listen to Elder Sister and her husband launch into the same ongoing debate: When should they leave? Where could they go? How would they start again? They'd managed to pull through the long occupation years. Like so many others, they wondered, could the Communists be worse than the Japanese?

"The Russians who waited too long lost everything. When they got to Shanghai, they could only find work as bodyguards and dance-hall girls," Elder Sister would sniff.

"At least they were alive, unlike the ones who didn't leave and were slaughtered by the Bolsheviks," her husband would remind her. Here was the heart of the quandary: No one in Shanghai wanted to risk death, nor did they want to follow the path of the humbled White Russians to become lowly "White Chinese."

As a Danish citizen, Kristian expected no problems in getting the visas to repatriate to Denmark with his wife and sons. Those plans did not include Bing, nor would she have expected them to—of course an adopted sister-in-law counted for nothing. She'd be left behind, just as when Mama Hsu went off to Chongqing. But now she was older and more confident, able to maneuver around Shanghai and to stick up for herself. At least Ma and Ah Mei would still be there. Though Bing would miss Elder Sister and the boys, they could be back within the year, after the Communist government collapsed—that was what everybody said.

On this much Elder Sister and her husband agreed. But they could not decide where to go. Kristian did not want to return to Denmark; it would be too stifling after forty years in China. Besides, Elder Sister and the boys spoke no Danish. He had his eye on Australia instead. "It's a modern country, and English is the common language," he'd venture once again. Bing would groan to herself. The mere mention of Australia made Elder Sister bristle.

"How many times do I have to remind you that Australia is for whites only?" she would scold. "That's okay for you, but what about me? And our half-Chinese boys?"

America was also high on Kristian's list. It was on everyone's wish list, especially with much of Europe and Asia still recovering from the war. But while a Northern European like Kristian Jarldane could get a visa, prospects for Elder Sister and the boys were dim. The U.S. Congress had recently authorized entry visas for several thousand stateless Jews and European refugees, but Chinese were another story.

"Don't you know that America had a law to keep Chinese out—just Chinese! Even now, only a hundred and five Chinese people are allowed to immigrate each year—no matter where in the world they're from," Elder Sister would sputter indignantly. "Only the richest Chinese with the best connections will get those slots." If they decided to take their chances and apply for the necessary visas, the process could take weeks, perhaps months. By then it might be too late to get out.

Hong Kong was just across the border from Guangdong Province and would be relatively easy for them to reach. But it would also be easy for the Communists to take Hong Kong. On the other hand, Elder Sister had heard rumors that certain employees at the U.S. consulate in Hong Kong could be bribed—and were selling visas to the States for three thousand U.S. dollars apiece. For four of them, that would be a huge amount to bet on a rumor. If it turned out to be a trick to take their money with no visas forthcoming, they'd be stuck in Hong Kong and heavily in debt.

They nixed Singapore, the Philippines, Malaya, and other points in Southeast Asia because too many other Chinese were fleeing to those countries and Kristian might have trouble finding work. With the massive influx of Chinese and others, the swelling antiforeign resentment was also a consideration. At least the two of them agreed that Taiwan was a place for Chinese Nationalist diehards, not for people like them who found politics and corruption to be different sides of the same filthy coin. Brazil, Argentina, and Peru were possibilities with more relaxed immigration requirements. Brazil encouraged skilled people from China, Germany, Italy, and elsewhere to immigrate. But South America was so remote and undeveloped—and neither of them could speak Spanish or Portuguese.

The next day, they'd pick up the debate where they'd left off, adding new intelligence from the latest rumors. But as the summer of 1948 pushed on, their nightly exchange took on a more urgent tone following a spate of Nationalist defeats in Manchuria and three northern provinces—the Communist-"liberated" areas were now encircling Beijing. Communist commanders under Chairman Mao had successfully transformed their guerrilla campaigns against the Japanese into larger units. The Red Army had become capable of beating back the

Nationalist troops by integrating large numbers of defecting enemy soldiers. In addition, their land reform efforts throughout their liberated zones were winning the Communists significant local support. The Nationalist armies, demoralized and stretched too thin over large expanses of territory, were losing up to half a million troops in each major battle as the Red Army advanced southward toward the Yangtze— and toward Shanghai, only four hundred miles from the main battle zones.

WITH THE LOCAL ECONOMY spinning further into chaos, Bing found new and technical-sounding words in Kristian's English newspapers. *Hyperinflation* was one. As Elder Sister explained, "It means that prices are going up like crazy—even faster and higher than the price increases during the Japanese occupation. No end in sight." Bing nodded. Everyone in Shanghai had had the unsettling experience of looking in a shopwindow as a clerk reached in to cross out one price and scrawl a new, much higher price, often x-ing out prices several times in a single day. Not even the belt-tightening inflation during the war had prepared them for costs that seemed to multiply by the minute. In June 1948, a sack of rice had cost 6.7 million yuan; within a few weeks, the price had reached 63 million.

To address the massive discontent over the crushing inflation, on August 19, 1948, Chiang Kai-shek appointed his thirty-eight-year-old son, Major General Chiang Ching-kuo, to fix the worsening financial crisis. The young Chiang, born of his father's first marriage, used his authority as a finance commissioner to announce new policies to end hoarding, stock manipulation, black-market speculation, and price gouging. He told a nervous city that the new rules would apply to everyone, including the rich, powerful, and well-connected, who were known to be the most egregious speculators. They amassed vast fortunes by creating shortages through hoarding, driving up prices to then make huge profits by selling the hoarded goods.

Diverging from the usual topic of conversation at the hotel room, the grown-ups' discontent turned to these economic developments. Kristian hoped the Chiang government was finally getting serious about the out-of-control inflation. Elder Sister and Ma remained skeptical—especially when chaos erupted over Chiang Ching-kuo's most dramatic edict.

The newly appointed finance commissioner ordered citizens to hand over to the government all of the gold, silver, foreign currency, and the old version of Chinese yuan in their possession. Scofflaws would be executed, he declared. But the middle class and wealthy closely guarded their savings of precious metals and stable foreign currency, their main protection against the rampant inflation. To allay those fears, young Chiang guaranteed that his freshly minted currency would hold its value. To persuade the doubters, he dispatched trucks with loudspeakers throughout the former foreign concessions to blare his harsh warnings: "Those who hoard are public enemies" and "Those who damage the new gold-based currency will have their heads chopped off!" The government claimed to have special metal detectors that would root out any gold, silver, or other metal hidden in walls or floors, sending shivers of fear through the city.

At first, it seemed that Chiang Ching-kuo's economic reforms had some teeth. He arrested a number of businessmen and, with much fanfare, executed some low-level black marketers. Fearing the government's threats, many middle-class Shanghainese turned over their life savings to the government. Even Ma considered it, but couldn't bring herself to part with her small savings.

However, the well-intentioned younger Chiang went too far when he jailed the son of powerful Green Gang boss Du Yuesheng. If that wasn't enough to show he was serious, Chiang Ching-kuo also arrested David Kung, the nephew of his stepmother, Madame Chiang. Upon learning that her favorite nephew was in jail, Madame Chiang stormed into her stepson's office and slapped his face. Then she wired her husband, the generalissimo, who reportedly walked out of an important meeting with his generals in Beijing to address the family crisis.

Chiang Ching-kuo's reputation was in shambles after he'd suffered this major loss of face at the hands of his stepmother. Forced to abandon his currency reform program, he released the wealthy cheaters from jail. His monetary conversion plan crashed in a spectacular fiasco when it became clear that the government would not stand up to the wealthy and corrupt who were fleecing the failing economy. The newly issued currency collapsed, becoming instantly worth less than the paper it was printed on. Everyone who had obeyed the government's orders to use the new currency lost everything; their assets of gold, silver, and foreign currency were now locked in Chiang Kai-shek's treasury—and lining the pockets of profiteers.

China's economy resumed its rapid plunge, while Ma was overjoyed that she hadn't been duped. "Never trust politicians who grow fat when everyone else is lean," she warned Bing.

As hyperinflation careened out of control, it became common on Shanghai streets to see people with baskets, handcarts, and pedicabs overflowing with near-worthless paper yuan to buy a few vegetables. Anyone on fixed salaries paid in Chinese yuan had to spend their pay as soon as they received it, before it lost more value. Workers went on strike, demanding to get paid in rice and commodities, not in cash.

For many of Shanghai's wealthy capitalists, the economy's collapse was the last straw. It was now riskier to stay in Shanghai than to leave. The most prescient had already made arrangements to flee, renting space in Hong Kong and moving their chief assets there: bank accounts, factory equipment, key employees, eldest sons—hoping to salvage what they could from a country in free fall.

Kristian was fortunate to be paid in U.S. dollars, better than gold against the collapsing new Chinese yuan. But his Chinese colleagues faced financial ruin. Shanghai's middle classes were outraged, saying that Chiang's government had once again used lies and trickery to steal from hardworking people. The middle classes were stripped bare while ordinary workers and the poor were flayed to the bone. Strikes and work stoppages by employees of all kinds disrupted the city daily, as ordinary people could no longer afford basic necessities. From day to day, it became impossible to know if streetcars, buses, and other city services would still be operating.

It reached the point where Shanghailanders no longer discussed *if* they planned to leave but rather *when*. Chiang's days were numbered, they all agreed. Many regretted not having fled as soon as General

George Marshall left Shanghai to become President Truman's secretary of state. Marshall, having witnessed the Nationalist government's incompetence and corruption, opposed any further American military support for Chiang, in spite of Madame Chiang's concerted lobbying of Congress with the aid of her influential American friends, such as the publisher of *Time* magazine, Henry R. Luce.

In the face of the growing unrest and military defeats, the Nationalists imposed martial law over Shanghai in late 1948. They enforced a curfew and sent censors to newspapers and radio stations to screen all news, including both foreign and Chinese media. Newspapers appeared with blank spaces showing the caption "Removed by censor." But it was impossible to suppress the news of one huge military defeat after another—not when hidden contraband radios told of the millions of Chinese soldiers and civilians dead. Though the Nationalists insisted they would defend Shanghai to the bitter end, no one believed them. Every office worker overlooking the Bund could see long lines of coolies chanting, "Hey ho, hey ho" as they hauled China's entire treasury of gold, silver, and foreign currency onto Nationalist ships docked on the Huangpu River, all bound for Taiwan. The ships were also carrying nearly four thousand crates of China's greatest art treasures to the island. Nationalist officials packed up or destroyed documents, equipment, vehicles, lightbulbs, toothpaste, screws—anything of possible use—to keep them out of the hands of the Communist "bandits."

By November 1948, newspapers were headlining the mass exodus under way:

CHINESE RUSH TO GET OUT OF SHANGHAI: The stampede to get out of Shanghai gained momentum yesterday. . . . At the North station an unprecedented crowd fought to purchase tickets and get aboard trains which were already jam-packed. . . . In the afternoon four persons were trampled to death during the rush to board the train. On the Bund, crowds were prevented from climbing aboard overladen ships by seamen with firehoses who played streams of water and kept them back.

AS THE NEW YEAR APPROACHED, Elder Sister and Kristian decided it was time to go. They ended their debate and opted for Denmark, their surest path. They'd go by boat to the States, then by train to New York and take another boat to Denmark. There was a lot to be done: Find tickets for a ship out of Shanghai; obtain Danish passports and U.S. visas; purchase a required five-hundred-dollar bond for each of them in case the U.S. government needed to deport them.

Getting their Danish passports and U.S. visas from the consulates in Shanghai was easy, while getting tickets out, even for a foreigner, was near impossible. Ticket agents at the train stations, airports, and shipping docks were mobbed with people fighting for a seat to anywhere. "Who do you know?" became the most valuable currency of all as desperate people sought help from every friend and acquaintance.

Bing read articles in Kristian's English newspaper about panic selling:

MOTORCARS, APARTMENTS, CHEAP, BUT NO BUYERS

The steadily worsening political and military situation has brought a sharp increase in the local supply of apartments, houses, motorcars, electric refrigerators and household goods. Many Shanghai residents who are in a hurry to leave before the storm breaks have found that their properties formerly valued in the thousands of American dollars have suddenly melted away.

Panic filled the hotel room when, on January 31, 1949, the Red Army seized Beijing not long after taking the nearby port city of Tianjin. Bing had never seen Elder Sister so anxious. Now there was nothing to keep the Communists from pushing south to the capital in Nanjing—and then to Shanghai.

In a great stroke of good luck, the next day Elder Sister connected with a business agent she'd known during the occupation. In exchange for almost two thousand U.S. dollars, some fine English furniture that she procured from a vacant apartment, and several bolts of cloth, she bartered and bought four first-class tickets on the *General Gordon,* departing on May 4, 1949, bound for San Francisco.

As the family celebrated its good fortune, Elder Sister whispered to Bing, "Don't worry. I will find a way to bring you too." Bing shrugged, not knowing how she could get a passport when she didn't even know her own birth date. But Elder Sister surprised her by producing a blue Republic of China passport—with her name and photo in it! It listed Singapore as her birthplace and a birth date that added a year to her age. Elder Sister said one of her dance-club friends had helped her get the passport as a special favor.

Inside the passport was another surprise: a tourist visa for America! Elder Sister bragged that to get the visa she had visited another dance-club friend—an American who worked at the consulate. The midlevel clerk had invited Betty and her girlfriends to parties at his apartment a few times—and sharp-eyed Elder Sister had noticed that he brought the visa stamps home each night for safekeeping. She arranged another visit to his place, and while her girlfriends distracted him, Elder Sister stamped Bing's passport with an official visitor visa. "Now I just need to find a ticket for you—and I will!" Elder Sister declared. Though Bing remained skeptical, she couldn't help feeling an electric thrill.

But Elder Sister and Kristian still had more to do for their own exits. Getting the required five-hundred-dollar bond through an agent recognized in the United States was proving more difficult than getting the tickets. With time growing short, Kristian decided to trust a European friend who said his relative could get the bond. Kristian gave a few thousand U.S. dollars to the friend's relative. Then the man disappeared. After a frantic search, Kristian could only conclude that his friend's relative had absconded with the cash. Bing had never seen him so furious, his pale face bright red, with his veins bulging out of his neck. After many angry words, Kristian's friend paid back half of the stolen funds. The rest was lost, but at least the family eventually managed to obtain the necessary bonds.

The Communist forces had almost reached the Yangtze River by April 1949. Nationalist general Tang Enbo, the Nationalist commander in chief of the defense of Shanghai, decided to build a ten-foot wooden wall around the city's perimeter. The beleaguered citizens scoffed at such folly, saying the only purpose of the fence was to enrich Tang's friends in the lumber business. It was evident to all that a wall would do nothing to stop the Communist advance.

By May 2, the panicked clamor to escape had become so intense that the China National Aviation Corporation announced that it had suspended its flight schedules, allowing passengers to board almost immediately and planes to depart as soon as they were full.

As the family's departure date approached, the Red Army captured several nearby cities including Suzhou, Hangzhou, and Nanjing. Elder

As the Communist armies made their way south toward Shanghai in 1949, boats large and small were overloaded with people and cargo on the Huangpu River along the Bund, trying to get out of the city.

Sister and Kristian anxiously awaited their May 4 sailing date, as the Communists now seemed poised to encircle Shanghai.

BING PREPARED HERSELF TO be left behind again. She didn't care, she told herself. Still, she was aware that Elder Sister continued searching for another ticket even as she prepared to leave, asking everyone she knew if they had a single ticket on the *General Gordon*. Bing never expected Elder Sister to find one.

Then just a day before the ship was due to depart, the telephone rang. One of Elder Sister's contacts had a relative who had changed his mind about leaving and was having trouble finding someone with a passport and visa to buy his ticket. Elder Sister snatched it up for three hundred U.S. dollars. When she returned with it in hand, she was ebullient. "I got you a ticket—you're coming to America with us; start packing!" she shouted.

Bing couldn't trust herself to respond to Elder Sister's announcement. Incredulous, she could only ask, "But what about Ma?"

Elder Sister had a ready answer. "Everything is set. Ma has her sisters here. She thinks it's a good idea for you to come along with me, to help me with the boys."

It was true. When they went to Ma's place that afternoon, she was waiting for Bing. "You should go with Elder Sister. You can help take care of each other." Then she reached under her bed and pulled out a small weathered valise. "I carried this when I first came to Shanghai. Now I give it to you."

After so many harsh words from Ma, Bing was unprepared for this kindness. In the ten years that Bing had lived with her, there had been only a few moments of softness when she had shown that she cared. Then again, the mother who had given birth to Bing in Changzhou had abandoned her. And so had Mama Hsu. Ma was the one who had not only kept her but also taken her back after she ran away. Bing felt a twinge of sadness at leaving, but at least Ma wouldn't be alone.

Then there was Ah Mei. Saying goodbye to her one and only friend would be the hardest. Bing would not only miss the birth of her best friend's child, but the two might never see each other again, since Ah

Mei and her Iranian Jewish husband were planning to go with other Jews to Israel after the baby came. But Ah Mei was happy for Bing's good fortune, chiding her friend, "Don't be sad—we're both starting our new lives."

Bing had few regrets about leaving Shanghai and China. She knew that once she was on the ship she would never see her *baba* again. Bing felt that familiar stab to her heart. But now she had to think about herself. She had never dared to dream before. In Denmark, or America, or wherever she landed she'd make a fresh start. Now it was time to leave the bad luck behind. The very thought offered her an unfamiliar feeling: hope.

The next day, everyone rose early on their final morning in Shanghai. They had to get to the American President Lines docks on the Huangpu River with enough time to get through customs. Ma said goodbye to them at the apartment. She patted the boys on their heads and nodded to Kristian. She told Elder Sister to write and send money when she could. Then Ma surprised Bing by reaching for her hand. "I know you only remember the times that I cursed you," Ma said. "It was for your own good. Don't forget what I taught you. You've been a good daughter; take care of yourself."

Bing tried to say something back, but her words stuck in her throat. She nodded goodbye to the only mother she'd really known.

With that, Elder Sister, the two boys, and Kristian piled into the car that he had arranged. The four had so much luggage that there wasn't room for Bing. Instead, she took her valise and climbed into a pedicab headed toward the Bund.

BING ARRIVED AT THE SHANGHAI Hongkou Wharf late and flustered after almost getting struck by a car driven by some college boy on his way to Taiwan. When she found Elder Sister, just in time to check in for the voyage, Bing could finally calm herself. Standing in line to check in, she scanned her surroundings slowly, trying to etch these last moments in Shanghai into her memory. Everyone looked charged with emotion—alive with excitement for the imminent journey, anxious for an uncertain future, relieved at the chance to escape.

Kristian was actually jovial to be leaving the chaos of Shanghai. "It was a great city, but it's become a hellhole," he declared, his parting words.

From out of nowhere, Ah Mei and her husband appeared. Somehow Bing's heavily pregnant friend had managed to make her way through the crush until she found Bing and the family. Bing and Ah Mei clasped hands and remembered how they had held each other tight during their first years together as two lonely, abandoned girls. They promised to meet up again one day, knowing it would probably never happen.

Once on the deck of the *General Gordon*, Bing could see the skyline of the Bund stretched before her. She almost expected to be put ashore and told that there had been a mistake. Before that could happen, she found her way down to the third-class deck, where there were only hammocks left to choose from. She didn't know how she would manage to climb into one. Deciding she'd worry about that later, she took the stairs to the first-class level to see Elder Sister's cabin. Like the third-class deck, it was cramped, with six others in the small room in addition to Elder Sister and Peter: a German matron and her three half-Chinese daughters, plus a Chinese woman from the Philippines with her daughter. Kristian and Ole went to their similarly crowded cabin in the men's section.

Standing back on the main deck near Elder Sister, Kristian, and the boys, Bing was surrounded by a jubilant crowd of Europeans, Americans, and Chinese. To the shy teenager, the other passengers seemed so sharp and sophisticated, speaking English, French, and Mandarin in cultured, high-class tones. There were Americans on their way home, some born and raised in Shanghai, others who had come seeking fortune and adventure in the arms of the Paris of the Orient; nuns dressed in long black habits that looked so heavy and hot, leaving behind a lifetime of missionary work; Jewish refugees from Europe who had escaped the gruesome Nazi death camps only to find themselves in Shanghai, now finally on their journey to freedom in America. And so many fancy-looking Chinese in Western suits and beautiful dresses.

The captain sounded several deep, plaintive bellows of the ship's horn, and the *General Gordon* pulled away from the dock. Bing mustered a halfhearted wave toward shore.

"Goodbye, Baba." Bing felt her chest tighten in that empty place. "I'll never find you now," she whispered.

"Goodbye, Mama Hsu. I hope you made it safely through the war years.

"Goodbye, Shanghai."

Bing's eyes grew watery, but no tears fell. She wished to leave behind the bitterness and struggle, bad luck and loss, that she had known in Shanghai. No one would ever call an abandoned girl like her lucky, yet good fortune must have touched her. After all, she had made it this far, she mused, squaring her shoulders. Shanghai had offered her a refuge from the worst cruelties of the war years. Now it was time to go.

THE MORE THAN THREE WEEKS at sea passed by in one sickening blur. Each morning, Bing gingerly climbed off her hammock after a fitful night of swaying to the roll of the ship. On good days she managed to swallow some hot tea and a bite of the unappealing foreign food in the third-class mess hall. Then she headed to the first-class level for a woozy day with Elder Sister and the boys. By dinnertime, she was ready for her hammock deep below the main deck.

Bing couldn't wait to reach land. But when the ship pulled into San Francisco Bay, the immigration inspectors took her to the purser's office and refused to let her disembark. Bing felt her body freeze in fear. Did they notice that her passport and visa were fake? Would she be hauled off to jail in America? Or worse, sent back to Shanghai?

When Bing failed to appear at the departure area, Elder Sister stormed through the ship until she found her. Flashing her friendliest smile as she sized up the immigration agents, Elder Sister said in her most dulcet tones, "My young sister's English isn't so good, sir. Can I help you in any way?"

Unimpressed, he answered brusquely: "We have no record that your sister possesses the five-hundred-dollar bond required to enter the United States. She's young and Chinese—if she goes illegal, we'll catch her and need the five hundred dollars to send her back. Without it, she can't get off the ship."

Suddenly the problem was clear: Bing's ticket had been purchased in such haste that there had been no time to get the bond in advance of sailing. Elder Sister had hoped the oversight would go unnoticed. Now they needed to get a bond for Bing as soon as possible, before the ship headed back to sea. If they didn't, Bing would have to stay on board, sailing on to points unknown.

Kristian was dispatched into the city to find an agent who could issue the five-hundred-dollar bond. Purchasing the bond for Bing would require digging into the family's limited cash. Elder Sister and the boys waited on shore while Bing was detained on the ship.

Hours later, as the sun fell behind the towers of the Golden Gate Bridge, Kristian returned triumphant. Bing was unceremoniously released after the immigration inspector marked her passport with a visa for a six-month stay. "Welcome to America," one agent offered flatly.

Elder Sister had not sat idle. As her boys chased seagulls nearby, she had managed to strike up conversations with friendly men eager to assist a beautiful damsel in distress. Through their leads, she learned of an inexpensive rooming house on nearby Columbus Avenue where the family could spend the night.

When they reached the house, Bing was surprised to find that the proprietors were Japanese. At first Bing tensed up. The terrible memories of war were still fresh in the mind of every Chinese. There had been few Japanese left in Shanghai once they were rounded up and repatriated. But these Japanese were American, speaking English with American accents. Elder Sister and Kristian didn't seem worried. Bing relaxed.

After dropping off their bags and freshening up, they set out for dinner. Passing by a newsstand, they were stunned to learn that two days earlier the Communists had taken over their city. Shanghai had fallen! Elder Sister kept repeating, "Oh my God!" and Kristian kept muttering in Danish as they pored over the reports. They gave thanks upon learning that the takeover had been largely peaceful. Bing closed her eyes with thoughts of Ma and Ah Mei, grateful that the city had been spared the mass destruction it had suffered during the Japanese war.

They soon found themselves in an area called Chinatown. Bing admired the strangeness of America: Compared to Shanghai, the streets were clean, and the air smelled fresh, and when she had stepped off the ship, the sun had been so strong, her eyes had hurt. There were no crumbled buildings, no bomb craters, no façades riddled by machine-gun bullets. Not a single hint of war.

Pulling herself from her thoughts, she held on to Ole's and Peter's hands. "Can you see how different this place is from home? Not even this Chinatown is like China. Welcome to America," she said, smiling at their bright-eyed faces.

ANN ARBOR, JUNE 1948

FROM THE MOMENT HO CHOW ARRIVED AT THE UNIVERSITY OF
Michigan in September 1947 to pursue a PhD in engineering, his life
in Ann Arbor had gone smoothly, *almost* without a hitch. Having met
several other graduate students on his ship from Shanghai, Ho rented
an apartment with five other Chinese students at 428 Cross Street,
near the campus. Then it was every man for himself, since neither he
nor any of his roommates had ever cooked or cleaned for themselves
before.

Within a record time of nine months, Ho had completed all of the
requirements for his master's degree, earning A-pluses in most of his
courses. Though the classes were taught in English, he had managed,
since the math and science provided a common language. His lowest
grade was a single A-minus. He didn't brag or gloat—he expected
excellence from himself and had applied the same laser focus since his
middle school days in Shanghai.

Yet a nagging worry continued to threaten his years' worth of careful planning for graduate school and the car factory he hoped to build
in China. Money—or more specifically, his family's difficulties in getting foreign exchange—could derail everything. As soon as he'd arrived, he'd opened a bank account with the one thousand U.S. dollars
he'd brought from Shanghai, obtained after his family received spe-

cial permission to convert Chinese yuan into U.S. dollars. In theory, when his money ran low, his family would get another authorization certificate to convert yuan and to wire him dollars.

But according to his family's letters, it was getting more difficult and costly to exchange the needed funds. Back in 1946, before Ho had even applied to schools, for every one U.S. dollar, his family would have needed to convert about thirty-four hundred yuan. By the spring of 1947, one dollar cost fourteen thousand yuan. In 1948, a single U.S. dollar cost a million yuan on the black market. If he ran out of money, he'd be in serious trouble, because U.S. law prohibited foreign students from working. That was his biggest worry. That was why he'd pushed himself to complete his master's degree as soon as possible. It was his lack of money, not vanity about getting top grades, that compelled him. The sooner he finished, the sooner he'd end this vexing burden on his family.

Ho followed the routine that had stood him well in Shanghai, cutting a triangular path between his room, his classes, and the library. His daily fare consisted of boiled noodles with a few vegetables tossed in, fried pork chops, and eggs—without variation. His sole adventure was a visit to the nearby city of Ypsilanti, to see how cars were produced at the Willow Run auto plant. He didn't go to parties or dances. Dating was out of the question. There were too few female Chinese students—and the ones he knew were already spoken for. Michigan admitted more overseas Chinese students than other schools, but most were men. Still, on his transpacific voyage, Ho had enjoyed the company of a few women students. He knew that his mother would approve of those young ladies because they came from well-heeled families who could afford to send their daughters abroad.

Without any new Chinese women to meet, Ho's main pastime was fraternizing with the other Chinese engineering grad students—all male. They discussed ways of navigating school, America, and how to meet Chinese girls. Sometimes they gathered over a cheap dinner at a local Chinese restaurant serving "Chinese American cuisine." They all lamented that the Americanized food bore little resemblance to the home cooking they missed.

By far, their most frequent topic of discussion was the situation back home. Because American news carried little meaningful information about China, the students depended on letters from their families for updates, sharing what they learned with the group. Ho received so much mail that he was the envy of other students. Some weeks, he received several letters, each filled with family gossip and news of the rapidly declining political situation.

Ho's letters from home added fuel to his motivation to finish his doctoral program as swiftly as possible. His family often spoke of the extreme inflation and how difficult it was for them to pay for their essential needs, let alone to send U.S. dollars for his studies. His sister, Wanyu, wrote in 1948:

DEAR YOUNGER BROTHER,

THERE IS NO BIG NEWS FROM CHANGSHU, BUT INFLATION
HERE IS TERRIBLE, EVEN WORSE HERE THAN IN SHANGHAI.
LOTS OF THINGS ARE MORE EXPENSIVE. WE HAD TO RENT OUT
MORE LAND TO FARMERS. PRICES ARE RISING LIKE CRAZY.
PEOPLE LIVING ON FIXED WAGES CAN BARELY SURVIVE. . . .

As each letter from home underscored the mounting difficulties, Ho agonized over the strain he was placing on his family. He decided that he had to earn some money—in spite of being forbidden to do so by his visa restrictions. In the spirit of the Chinese proverb "Heaven is high and the emperor is far away," Ho was certain he could find a solution that didn't exactly violate the rules. By carefully searching university bulletin boards and making inquiries of other students and professors, Ho learned of something called an "internship" that would give him practical experience with the university's approval. If he could find an internship that provided a stipend for his living expenses, he could save money by living cheaply, and it wouldn't be a prohibited *job* under Immigration and Naturalization Service (INS) rules. Ho was thrilled to find such an elegant solution to his problem—worthy, he felt, of a clever Shanghainese. All he had to do was find a company to offer him such an internship.

Through his student network, Ho learned of a newly established company called China Motors, founded by Chinese American businessmen and funded by New York's Chinatown merchants. The company had opened a factory in Linden, New Jersey, just outside of New York City, to produce cars and other machines to be sold in China. It was the kind of company he'd dreamed of starting himself.

After writing to the company, Ho was overjoyed to receive an offer of an internship as an engineering trainee in the Production Engineering Department. He would assist with tool design and selection, plant operations, and blueprint controls, with a stipend for living expenses of $180 per month. That was a huge amount by Chinese standards. He wrote to his family with the good news. Elder Brother Hosun, who lived at the family house in Shanghai, sent a letter in response that arrived soon after Ho's graduation:

10 June 1948:

You're so young and bright. Keep working hard— don't let us down.

I've heard of China Motor company. It's good for you to work there. You can build a good relationship with the Chinese there and get to know lots of foreign big shots. When you come back, it will all come together.

If you go to a foreign factory, be careful in case there is discrimination against Chinese or possible problems with the immigration bureau.

Inflation in China is very serious, lots of increases every day. Things from overseas are even more expensive, so send some silk stockings. The Wembley neckties you sent me cost a lot, so I don't dare to wear one often.

in the summer of 1948, with his master's diploma in hand, Ho left Michigan for New Jersey and quickly found a cheap room in Elizabeth, an old industrial city near Linden. It was a short bus ride down Route 1 to the factory.

After receiving his graduate degree from the University of Michigan in 1948, Ho started his dream internship with China Motors in Linden, New Jersey.

Ho eagerly started at China Motors, excited that it was near a giant General Motors auto assembly plant. His first project involved refrigeration units, not cars, that China Motors was contracted to produce. After living expenses and rent, Ho had about ten dollars a week to spare. From his first paycheck, he sent five dollars to his mother. She chastised him in her next letter, telling him to keep the money and to eat better.

The letters from home included requests to buy items for his family that he could ill afford. Ho shook his head at some of the requests. Do they think I'm rich because I'm making a little money in America? he wondered. The wish list included a wireless radio, a watch with a nightlight on the dial, silk stockings, a camera flash attachment, subscriptions to *Life* magazine for acquaintances, a microscope, a Rolleiflex camera, Botanaire ties, and a new needle for a phonograph.

To save more money, Ho found a cheaper rental. He didn't tell his family about the peeling paint in the dark hallways or the industrial soot and smell. The run-down area was depressing compared to the elegant buildings of Shanghai and even his attic room on Medhurst Road. He didn't mention that he was paring down his living situation to pay for the items he sent home along with the occasional five-dollar bill. The airmail postage took an additional bite, and he could never be sure that his parcels would reach his family.

Now that he was a bit less worried about money, Ho found the reports on the rapidly declining situation at home to be unnerving. His family regularly reported on conditions in frightening detail.

A letter dated July 6, 1948, from his brother-in-law living in Huainan, a city in Anhui Province about three hundred miles northwest of Shanghai, said:

THE COMMUNIST ARMY HAS TAKEN KAIFENG [AN ANCIENT CAPITAL OF CHINA, APPROXIMATELY FIVE HUNDRED MILES NORTHWEST OF SHANGHAI]. THE COMMUNISTS NOW USE ROCKET CANNONS, VERY DIFFERENT FROM BEFORE. THEY ALSO LET YOUNG PEOPLE LEAVE TO MAKE COMPARISONS IF THEY WISH TO GO TO THE NATIONALIST-CONTROLLED AREAS. MANY OF THOSE RELEASED STUDENTS BECOME PROPAGANDISTS FOR THE COMMUNIST PARTY. RIGHT NOW ONE U.S. DOLLAR IS WORTH ONE MILLION YUAN, SO YOUR PAY IS HIGHER THAN THAT OF THE OFFICIALS IN THE GOVERNMENT. IF YOU'RE ABLE TO STAY IN THE USA, YOU'RE VERY LUCKY.

Ho's sister added this note:

I'VE HAD TO RETURN TO CHANGSHU BECAUSE OUR HOUSE IN HUAINAN IS NOW OCCUPIED BY NATIONALIST SOLDIERS. I ASKED THEM TO LEAVE ME SOME SPACE IN MY OWN HOUSE BUT THEY WON'T. I'M SO ANGRY ABOUT THESE BAD NATIONALIST SOLDIERS. EVERYBODY HATES THEM. SOME EVEN WISH FOR ANOTHER WORLD WAR TO GET RID OF THEM.

The letters also detailed the many problems in exchanging Chinese yuan into U.S. dollars. It was necessary for Ho to first apply for the government in China to issue a certificate, which that office would send to him. Then he had to mail the certificate to his family in China, allowing them to exchange their money and wire U.S. dollars to him.

On July 12, 1948, his brother, Hosun, wrote:

> I HAVE RECEIVED APPROVAL FOR THE FOREIGN EXCHANGE
> APPLICATION, SO I CAN EXCHANGE THE MONEY VERY SOON. BUT
> ACCORDING TO THE NEWSPAPER, THE NEW PROCEDURES FOR
> FOREIGN EXCHANGE SALES ISSUED BY THE ADMINISTRATION
> ARE VERY DIFFICULT, AND THE RATE IS NOT THAT GOOD. I'VE
> TOLD MOTHER ABOUT THE SITUATION, AND WE WILL TRY OUR
> BEST TO GET MONEY TO YOU. IN THE FUTURE YOU CAN REPAY
> US SINCE IT'S A LOT OF MONEY.

This was the first time that Ho's family mentioned the need for him to repay them. That had always been his intention, but with the exchange rate now increasing to about 4 million yuan per dollar, his brother wanted to make that expectation perfectly clear. On the black market, the rate was even more shocking, about twice the official rate. By prevailing on their tenants for the rent, Ho's mother gathered more than 2.5 billion yuan to exchange, but even that wasn't enough to send him another one thousand U.S. dollars to cover his anticipated tuition.

Two weeks later, on July 30, 1948, Ho's brother wrote:

> THE STRIKE IN OUR AREA HAS BEEN SETTLED, AND THE BASIC
> SALARIES ARE BEING ADJUSTED TO THE COST OF LIVING AND
> THE RAPID INFLATION. I WILL GET PAID ONE HUNDRED
> MILLION YUAN, AND THAT WILL BARELY SUPPORT MY FAMILY.
> IF I EXCHANGE THE YUAN ON THE BLACK MARKET, MY SALARY
> IS FIFTEEN U.S. DOLLARS PER MONTH.

Soon came the news Ho had hoped never to hear: The civil war had arrived at his family's doorstep in Changshu. Twenty thousand Nationalist troops were billeted in his hometown and were eying the Chow family home. In spite of the frightening news, his mother reassured him: "Don't worry; if it isn't safe here, we will leave. Stay happy always, Mother." Ho was more worried than ever.

A letter of August 10, 1948, from Hosun described the disastrous efforts of Chiang Ching-kuo, the generalissimo's son, to solve the terrible inflation in Shanghai:

> THE CURRENT SITUATION MAY IMPROVE, BECAUSE THE
> NATIONALIST GOVERNMENT SAYS THAT AMERICAN
> REINFORCEMENTS WILL COME SOON. THE NATIONALISTS
> [UNDER CHIANG CHING-KUO] ARE ISSUING SOME NEW
> ECONOMIC REFORMS. THE GOVERNMENT WANTS TO TAKE
> CONTROL OF ALL THE GOLD FROM ALL THE PEOPLE FOR THE
> STATE, AND THEY SAY THAT THEY WILL REFORM THE CURRENCY.
>
> OUR NATIONALIST ARMY IS TRYING TO KILL THE
> COMMUNIST BANDITS, BUT THE SITUATION IS NERVE-
> RACKING BECAUSE WE LOST KAIFENG AND WE ARE LOSING
> THE IMPORTANT CAPITALS [OF THREE PROVINCES]. THE
> ECONOMY CAN'T STABILIZE WHILE THE MILITARY SITUATION
> DETERIORATES.

As the Nationalist government spiraled out of control, Ho's family sent him a flurry of anxious letters about Chiang Ching-kuo's economic reforms and currency adjustments that forced citizens to turn in their savings of gold, silver, foreign currency, and old yuan. Like others in Shanghai, the Chow family faced the agonizing decision of whether or not to comply.

A letter from Ho's mother dated August 14, 1948, said:

> HO, MY SON, YOU NEEDN'T SEND MONEY TO US, THOUGH I
> AM STILL NOT CONFIDENT ABOUT BEING ABLE TO COLLECT
> OUR RENT. YOU SHOULD JUST KEEP IT. DON'T WORRY TOO
> MUCH FOR ME; I CAN LIVE A SIMPLE LIFE. YOU MUST BE
> WORKING VERY HARD. PLEASE DO TAKE CARE, AND TRY TO
> EAT WELL.

In a letter of August 16, 1948, Hosun wrote:

THE FOREIGN EXCHANGE FINALLY CAME THROUGH, AND I
HAVE CONVERTED NINE HUNDRED DOLLARS OF U.S. CURRENCY
THIS MORNING. I'LL SEND THE MONEY TO YOUR ADDRESS IN
ANN ARBOR, MICHIGAN. IT ISN'T POSSIBLE TO SEND THE
MONEY TO YOUR FACTORY. THE SITUATION HERE IS REALLY
BAD; THE COST OF LIVING IS GETTING HIGHER AND HIGHER.
INDUSTRY AND COMMERCE CAN'T FUNCTION ANYMORE.

Another letter from Hosun, dated September 4, 1948, said:

DID YOU RECEIVE THE USD? SINCE THE AUGUST 19
CURRENCY REFORMS BY CHIANG CHING-KUO, INDIVIDUALS
ARE PROHIBITED TO HAVE GOLD OR U.S. DOLLARS. PEOPLE
ARE RUNNING TO THE BANKS TO WITHDRAW THEIR MONEY.
THE CROWDS ARE ENORMOUS! ALL THIS INSTABILITY IS
DRIVING PRICES HIGHER AND HIGHER, AND PEOPLE ARE PANIC
BUYING. CHIANG CHING-KUO IS ARRESTING THE
SPECULATORS AND BAD BUSINESSMEN, BUT PEOPLE DON'T
TRUST THE NEW CURRENCY SYSTEM.

A letter dated September 9, 1948, from Wanyu, who was staying
with their mother in Changshu, reported:

WE'VE LOST HALF OF OUR COTTON HARVEST BECAUSE OF
HEAVY RAINS. MOTHER IS WORRIED ABOUT IT. I TRY TO
COMFORT HER, BUT DON'T WORRY TOO MUCH. MOTHER IS
CONCERNED THAT YOU WILL WANT TO CONTINUE WITH YOUR
EDUCATION AND THEN WE WILL NEED TO SEND MORE MONEY
TO YOU. WE ARE NOT SURE IF WE WILL HAVE ENOUGH,
BECAUSE OUR INCOME THIS YEAR IS BAD. WE ARE WORRIED.
MOTHER'S TEMPER IS LIKE A HOT PEPPER THESE DAYS, SO I
TOLD HER YOU HAVE A SCHOLARSHIP TO MAKE HER FEEL
BETTER.

On October 10, 1948, his brother-in-law in Huainan wrote:

THE SITUATION IS WORSE THAN BEFORE. PEOPLE ARE AFRAID
AND THE NATIONALISTS ARE LOSING THE CITIES ONE BY
ONE. IT'S GETTING DANGEROUS AND DIFFICULT BECAUSE
THOUSANDS OF PEOPLE ARE OUT OF WORK AFTER THE LATEST
DEFEATS. YOU GUYS WHO LIVE ABROAD ARE INCREDIBLY
LUCKY.

THE TWO STREAMS OF THE COMMUNIST ARMY IN THE
NORTH ARE A BIG THREAT TO THE NATIONALISTS, BUT NOT
MANY PEOPLE ARE FLEEING YET. ON THE ONE HAND, IT IS
HARD TO EARN A LIVING IN ANOTHER PLACE. ON THE OTHER,
MAYBE THE COMMUNIST PARTY ISN'T AS BAD AS THE JAPANESE.
THE NATIONALISTS SPREAD A LOT OF PROPAGANDA, AND
EVERYONE KNOWS THERE'S A BIG DIFFERENCE BETWEEN THEIR
WORDS AND THE TRUTH. BUT WITH ALL THIS CONFUSION,
ORDINARY PEOPLE WILL SURELY LOSE EVERYTHING THAT ISN'T
ATTACHED TO THEIR BODIES.

On October 22, 1948, Hosun reported from Shanghai:

THE GOVERNMENT HAS TAKEN SO MUCH GOLD AND FOREIGN
CURRENCY FROM THE PEOPLE. IT ALSO RAISED THE TAXES
FOR CIGARETTES AND ALCOHOL, SO NOW THE PANIC BUYING
IS EVEN WORSE. THE CHEAPEST ITEM IN THE WHOLE CITY IS
A TICKET TO THE MOVIES: IT'S ONLY 0.4 YUAN TO GET INTO
THE GRAND THEATRE. THE MOST EXPENSIVE ITEM IS A
PEDICAB—THE GOVERNMENT CAN'T LIMIT WHAT THE
DRIVERS CHARGE. CURRENCY REFORM MAY JUST BE AN
EMPTY DREAM. WE WISH YOU COULD COME HOME AS SOON
AS POSSIBLE, BUT THE SITUATION IS REALLY, REALLY BAD.
MANY PEOPLE HAVE DIED IN THE BATTLES THAT THE
GOVERNMENT LOST. IN MY OPINION, THE COMMUNIST BANDITS
ARE GETTING STRONGER AND STRONGER, AND IT IS NOT SAFE
IN SHANGHAI.

———

EACH LETTER'S DISTRESS ENGULFED Ho in a new tempest, pulling him down and sending him gulping for air. He struggled to stay focused on his work—what else could he do? As the Nationalist government sank deeper into the abyss, he and his coworkers at China Motors despaired over a possible devastating battle and revolution that could destroy Shanghai and everyone in it. The frenzied exodus from China—and from Shanghai in particular—had begun in earnest. As time went on, Ho's family wrote that they, too, were considering an escape.

In a December 10, 1948, letter, Hosun wrote:

IT'S BEEN A WHILE SINCE I SENT YOU A LETTER. HOW ARE YOU DOING? DO YOU MISS HOME? THERE'S A LOT TO TELL YOU ABOUT THE WAR. THE SITUATION IN CENTRAL CHINA IS VERY GRIM. THE NATIONALISTS SEEM TO LOSE EVERY BATTLE AND WILL BE DEFEATED BY THE RED BANDITS SOON. BEIJING, SHANGHAI, AND THE CAPITAL ARE IN DANGER, SO THE SITUATION IS SCARY, AND LOTS OF PEOPLE ARE CONSIDERING LEAVING. THERE ARE HUGE NUMBERS OF REFUGEES ON TRAINS AND BUSES. IT'S SO CONGESTED, I CAN'T EVEN DESCRIBE IT. THE PRESENT MILITARY CAMPAIGN IS FOCUSED ON HUAI-HAI [A REGION NORTH OF THE YANGTZE RIVER]. BOTH ARMIES HAVE LOST MORE THAN EIGHT HUNDRED THOUSAND LIVES; IT'S THE MOST TRAGIC SLAUGHTER IN OUR COUNTRY. THE FUTURE BODES ILL FOR THE NATIONALISTS. MAYBE THE CIVIL WAR WILL LAST SEVERAL MONTHS BECAUSE THE BANDITS HAVE LOTS OF SUPPLIES. MAYBE THE NATIONALIST AIR FORCE CAN MAKE A DIFFERENCE.

I HAVE MADE MY DECISION TO STAY IN SHANGHAI UNLESS IT GETS REALLY, REALLY BAD. STAYING TILL THE END CAN'T BE WORSE THAN BECOMING A REFUGEE. MANY RELATIVES HAVE MOVED IN WITH US. I HEARD THAT THE BANKS AND GOVERNMENT BUREAUS IN SHANGHAI ARE ALL SHIPPING IMPORTANT DOCUMENTS OUT. THE WHOLE SITUATION IS

TERRIBLY BAD. WHAT IS THE FUTURE FOR US SHANGHAINESE
PEOPLE? I THINK THERE IS LOTS OF BITTERNESS AHEAD.

On December 11, 1948, Wanyu wrote:

THERE HAVE BEEN LOTS OF RUMORS IN CHANGSHU IN THE
LAST FEW DAYS. PEOPLE'S HEARTS ARE WEIGHING WHETHER
TO FLEE OR TO STAY. LOTS OF PEOPLE IN OUR PROVINCE
ARE RUNNING TO SHANGHAI, WHILE THE RICH PEOPLE IN
SHANGHAI ARE RUNNING TO HONG KONG, TAIWAN, OR EVEN
TO AMERICA. MOTHER AND I HAVEN'T LEFT CHANGSHU YET.
IT'S NOT BECAUSE WE AREN'T SCARED, BUT (1) WE HAVE
PROPERTY IN OUR HOMETOWN; (2) IT'S VERY EXPENSIVE TO
MOVE OUR BIG FAMILY TO ANOTHER CITY; (3) I AM HOPING TO
FIND A JOB IN SHANGHAI; (4) MY HUSBAND IS WORKING IN
NANJING TEMPORARILY. HE MAY HAVE A CHANCE TO GO TO
TAIWAN, BUT THE ODDS ARE SLIM.

As 1948 came to a close, the letters from Ho's family continued to
chronicle the last gasps of Chiang Kai-shek's army and government.
In the northeast, the Communists surrounded two Nationalist armies
that had retreated to the city of Changchun, laying siege to the walled
city for months, starving an estimated 100,000 soldiers and 150,000
civilians to death and forcing those remaining to surrender. At the
same time, the Communists had gained the support of millions of
farmers by promising land reform—to redistribute the acreage from
rich landlords to poor farm families. The Red Army, now called the
People's Liberation Army, had killed or captured more than a million
Nationalist troops, taking critical firepower from the defeated army's
tanks, heavy artillery, ammunition, and other weaponry, much of it
from the United States. Hundreds of thousands of Nationalist troops,
from foot soldiers to generals, were defecting to the Communists. Re-
plenished, the Communists were ready to advance south to the Yangtze
River and the city of Shanghai.

Ho's heart sank as he imagined the soldiers bivouacked in the Chow
family compound, helping themselves to whatever they wanted. He

could picture the panicked buying sprees and bank runs in Shanghai, workers getting paid and then rushing out to buy anything they could grab that would hold its value better than the near-worthless paper money. Most of all, he could feel his family's pain as the Nationalist government continually raised taxes on everything, on top of the sky-high inflation. He knew that it would be impossible for his family to send him more money.

The troubles back home meant that Ho's internship was more important than ever. As much as his heart ached for his family, Ho needed to focus on learning how to take an engineer's design into production, from blueprints and machining the tool-and-die works to producing a finished product. Together with some other engineers, he built a prototype of a simple car, a three-wheeled motorized vehicle that could be mass-produced in China. Inside the immense industrial building that housed China Motors, Ho and his colleagues drove around in their little car. They nicknamed it "the Playboy."

When Ho wrote home, he kept his letters upbeat to assure his family that he was fine. There was no point in adding to their concerns when he was safe in America and they were facing disaster. He painted a rosy picture of the factory, its prospects for business, and his experience of building a prototype car. He was making progress, he averred, toward his dream of opening a factory of his own. As often as he could, he'd send a five-dollar bill to his mother along with photos of himself at the factory or in New York City.

But in fact all was not good at China Motors. The company was relying on Chinatown merchants in New York, Los Angeles, and San Francisco to fund its vision of selling manufactured goods to markets in China. With the Nationalist economy in a nosedive, the business model was collapsing, and investors were abandoning the venture.

For Ho, the first sign of the company's troubles came when payroll was delayed by a week in early December. Then the paychecks stopped completely. Without his stipend, Ho couldn't pay his rent. He quit his rental and moved into the cavernous factory, where he slept on an old couch in the frigid, unheated building.

The new year began with Ho caught in his own crisis, while the economic turmoil in Shanghai was so desperate that his sister and brother were advising their mother to sell some of the family's land. In the countryside, the growing land reform movement in Communist-influenced areas made it difficult to collect rent from tenant farmers as well as harder to find buyers for their choice farmland. More relatives from the extended Chow family in Changshu had moved to the house in Shanghai, all crammed together. No longer able to afford domestic help, they let their servants go. Even more shocking, one of Ho's uncles, a big landlord, had killed himself, unable to bear the pressures of the Communists' land reform measures. Chairman Mao had declared landlords to be the class enemies of the peasant farmers.

Other students in Ho's circle shared letters telling of mass meetings in rural farm areas that targeted rich landlords. In Communist-liberated areas, landlords were being "liquidated" in the name of land reform and their confiscated land redistributed. Norwegian missionaries observed landlords and other targets being severely beaten, tortured, sent off as beggars, with a death sentence for anyone offering them aid. Some reports estimated that one in six landlord families had had at least one family member killed in these political movements as the Communists gained strength in northern China. Ho realized that none of this could bode well for his family.

Then Hosun wrote on January 1, 1949:

PLEASE IMMEDIATELY SEND NINE HUNDRED U.S. DOLLARS TO
US OR AS MUCH AS YOU CAN DEPENDING ON YOUR SITUATION.
MOTHER AND I ARE ANXIOUS DAY AND NIGHT. THIS TIME IT'S
THAT THE GOVERNMENT HAS ASKED FOR MORE TAXES. IF WE
DON'T PROVIDE IT, WE COULD BE ARRESTED.

Ho's brother wanted back the nine hundred dollars that he had sent only a few months earlier. Ho had been counting on that money for his doctoral studies, but he knew that his family must have been desperate to ask for it back—especially when their losses in transaction fees would be doubled. Scrambling to find out how to send money to his family in Shanghai, Ho followed the advice of his Chinese colleagues—he wired the U.S. dollars to his family via the Xinhua Bank in Shanghai, for conversion into Hong Kong dollars. He sent all that he had.

By early 1949 the great flight out of Shanghai was in full swing—industrialists, intellectuals, businesspeople, the middle and affluent classes, Nationalist loyalists, foreigners, landlords, missionary converts, Eurasians, the frightened and the anxious. Those who lived in the rural countryside headed to regional cities, where they felt they would be more secure from advancing soldiers. Meanwhile, those in the provincial cities with the means to reach Shanghai fled there, hoping to find safety in its large numbers, and of course those in Shanghai with a reason to fear the Communists were rushing to get out of China. Everyone was looking to escape to a safer place. Ho's family, with its large landholdings, would undoubtedly encounter the wrath of revolution. Yet it was still unthinkable that a peasant army could take control of a city like Shanghai, let alone all of China.

Ho felt utterly helpless, unable to do anything to assist his family and struggling to sort out his own tangle of problems. To maintain his student visa status, he needed to be enrolled at a university, especially since his internship at China Motors was in trouble. He made an urgent appeal to the University of Michigan for a fellowship to continue his studies, but immediate funds weren't available. He frantically began to search for alternative schools that could enroll him and sponsor his visa. Desperate, he persuaded a mechanical engineering professor at New York University to take him on as a doctoral student. Ho would receive no financial aid, but he had just enough cash from his internship to register. At least he'd keep his student visa and not face deportation.

Amid this swirl of uncertainty, Ho learned that on January 21, 1949, Generalissimo Chiang Kai-shek was forced to resign from the presidency of the Nationalist government, ceding his title to a political rival, General Li Zongren. The news was a shocking confirmation that Chiang's military was in retreat and his government doomed. His resignation was headlined on the front page of *The New York Times:* CHIANG RELINQUISHES POST.

Ho and his fellow students were so unnerved that they conferred daily to glean any information that might help them piece together what was happening to their own families. The tectonic shifts back home were so stunning that Ho's hands shook whenever a thin blue aerogram arrived.

With Chiang's resignation, Communist leader Mao Zedong temporarily ceased fire, attempting to reach a settlement with the new president, General Li. But Chiang still held the real control of the government and its treasury. With little power and no money to pay his soldiers or officials, Li was in no position to bargain. His peace talks with Mao failed, and the Communist advance toward the Yangtze River continued.

On January 22, 1949, the day after Chiang Kai-shek resigned from the presidency, China Motors shut down. Ho was owed more than a month's back pay. He was not only out of work; he was homeless.

ALL HIS LIFE, HO HAD relied on his mother, elder sister, and brother to make the important decisions for him, to guide him on what to do. Should he rejoin his family in Shanghai? At least then they'd be together in this disastrous time. Where in America could he find help? Ho turned to the list of Jiao Tong students that he had volunteered to compile on his transpacific voyage just sixteen months earlier, when his future had seemed so bright. This social network of Jiao Tong alumni was becoming a lifeline for students like him who were caught up in China's upheaval. He contacted some Jiao Tong graduates in the Morningside Heights neighborhood of Manhattan near Columbia University, an area popular with former residents of Shanghai and northern China. They offered him a place on the floor of their small apartment on West 114th Street, just as families had done in wartime China. Ho gratefully accepted.

At the same time, Ho needed cash to support himself, as well as to answer his family's request for money. But he was torn. He had come to America with the expectation of returning with a PhD. Wasn't his family depending on him to accomplish that goal? Ho had penned a letter with his conflicted feelings and his questions to his mother, asking if he should continue working toward an engineering PhD, keep working in America, or possibly return home. Even with her world collapsing around her, Ho's mother sent an immediate reply.

In a letter dated January 23, 1949, Ho's mother wrote:

> SON, YOU ASKED WHETHER YOU SHOULD GO FOR FURTHER
> EDUCATION OR FIND A JOB. IT IS GOOD FOR YOU TO WORK.
> FURTHER EDUCATION IS NOT THAT URGENT. WE DON'T KNOW
> WHETHER WE CAN DO THE FOREIGN EXCHANGE ANYMORE. IT
> IS SCARY TO LOOK TO THE FUTURE NOW. WE ARE QUITE
> PESSIMISTIC. DON'T PLAN TO COME BACK. ONE DAY WHEN
> THE SITUATION IS SAFE, YOU CAN RETURN.

At the end of his mother's letter, Ho's brother had scribbled a somber postscript:

> WHEN YOU RECEIVE THIS LETTER, WE DON'T KNOW WHERE
> WE'LL BE. EVERYTHING IS CHANGING RAPIDLY. THIS IS A
> TRULY CATASTROPHIC TIME, AND WE DON'T KNOW WHAT LIES
> AHEAD. WE SHOULD EACH TAKE CARE OF OURSELVES. I HOPE
> WE CAN MEET AGAIN SOMEDAY.

Ho felt as if his blood were draining from his body as he read his family's messages. Would he see them again? Was his brother saying goodbye? Tears welled up in his eyes. What should he do? What *could* he do? Every instinct in his body said to rush home, to be with his family, and to comfort the mother who had always sacrificed for him. But his mother had told him not to come back. Ho agonized over his impossible choice.

He learned that a hundred or so students were trying to return to China: Some wanted to go home to reunite with their spouses and children; others had run out of money and thought they'd be better off in Shanghai; still others wished to join the Communists to rebuild their homeland. His few acquaintances in this latter group seemed motivated more by their zeal to aid the long-suffering Chinese people than by any love of Communist ideology. None of those rationales were compelling to Ho, but they added to the churn within him as he lay on the floor of the crowded apartment, unable to sleep. One night he realized, with a start, that he'd begun to rely on himself as he forged a life in America.

DESPERATE FOR MONEY, Ho heard that other China Motors employees had hired a lawyer to get their unpaid wages. He, too, filed a claim, for back wages of $312. He followed his mother's advice and decided not to return to the University of Michigan to complete his doctorate, even though he'd been surprised to learn that he'd receive a fellowship after all. That came too late; he had already decided to register with New York University as its first mechanical engineering doctoral student. Ho figured that New York was a better place to be during this crisis, since he'd be less isolated and might find a job more readily there.

Ho's other vexing worry was how to maintain his student visa status when he couldn't pay for tuition. If he messed up with immigration authorities, he could face deportation. Unsure of what to do, he wrote to the INS office in Detroit, telling them of China Motors' collapse and his enrollment at NYU with the possibility of a return to Michigan one day. He didn't mention that he was looking for work or that he was suing China Motors as his former employer, which could also get him in trouble with the INS.

After several nervous weeks, Ho landed a part-time job thanks to his Jiao Tong University network. Lin Yutang, the renowned Chinese intellectual in New York whose popular books on China were acclaimed in America, was looking for a clever engineer to help him design a Chinese typewriter. Ho got the job at two hundred dollars per month—a welcome increase from his stipend at China Motors. Now that he had an income, Ho rented an apartment with some friends at 620 West 115th Street, still in the Columbia University neighborhood where many other Chinese lived.

By April 1949, the Communists had swept over Beijing and Tianjin, unstoppable in their drive southward. Much to Ho's surprise and relief, the news reported that no looting or mass destruction had occurred in those big cities. Even so, the panicked exodus from Shanghai swelled to epic proportions. Every petty official seemed to find an excuse to use official transport out of the city. Shanghai's American-educated mayor, K. C. Wu, who had previously urged calm, announced his own sudden illness requiring treatment outside of China—and that he was unlikely to return.

Ho received word that his sister and her husband were on the run somewhere to the west of Shanghai in Anhui Province. They had managed to send a hasty letter to Ho while fleeing from Communist troops in a desperate effort to find a passage to Taiwan. Their stark message, dated April 2, 1949, read:

DO NOT COME BACK TO CHINA. THE SITUATION IS REALLY BAD. ARE YOU GETTING ACCURATE REPORTS IN AMERICA? NORTH OF THE YANGTZE RIVER, THE COMMUNIST PARTY IS EVERYWHERE. WHAT HAPPENED IN NORTHEAST CHINA IS REALLY SHOCKING. THE NATIONALISTS' STRONGEST ARMIES—THE NEW FIRST ARMY AND THE NEW SIXTH ARMY—COULDN'T DEFEAT THE COMMUNISTS. IF THE AMERICANS DON'T HELP, I'M SURE THAT THE GOVERNMENT WILL COLLAPSE IMMEDIATELY. IT IS BEYOND OUR WILDEST IMAGINATION.

THE NATIONALIST GOVERNMENT HAS BEEN LYING TO THE PEOPLE BY PRETENDING THAT THE SITUATION IS GOOD. THEY HELD A LEGISLATIVE SESSION AS THOUGH ALL IS NORMAL, AND THEY EVEN ELECTED A NEW PRESIDENT. IT'S SUCH A PRETENSE, LIKE THE END OF THE SONG DYNASTY IN HANGZHOU. GREAT PARTS OF THE COUNTRY ARE LOST, AND THEY STILL PRETEND THAT EVERYTHING IS OKAY. WE WILL NOT BENEFIT FROM THE COMMUNISTS, BECAUSE WE ARE LANDOWNERS AND PETITE BOURGEOISIE.

Don't go back? How could he stand by in safety when his beloved family and everything he held dear was on the brink of destruction? Ho could only share his worries with his fellow students, meeting up with them at every opportunity to discuss the latest news published by China correspondents and newswire reporters. Ho was glad that he had decided to stay in New York where there were many other students in his situation. At least he could always find a *New York Times*, with its frequent coverage of China's crisis.

On April 21, 1949, the People's Liberation Army crossed the Yangtze River, the vast natural barrier that had kept hostile armies away from the prosperous southeastern region for centuries. No longer. Two days later, there was worse news: The Communists had seized Nanjing, the Nationalist capital. Government officials had already fled the country—in spite of public vows that they would make Shanghai "their Stalingrad" with an all-out defense.

By month's end, the Nationalists were so afraid that the ordinary people of Shanghai could turn against them with riots to protest the worthless yuan, the food shortages, and their inability to govern, that they mounted machine guns on top of the city's landmark skyscrapers, turrets pointed at the residents below. Raw recruits in full field gear stormed through the fine restaurants of the Park and Cathay Hotels, startling guests who were dining and setting up their billets inside the luxurious hotels. Other soldiers were so awed by the elevators at the Broadway Mansions, home to many foreign reporters, that they rode up and down for hours, refusing to get off for the residents.

More frightening was the action on the streets as Nationalist soldiers summarily executed dissenters, black marketers, and suspected Communists right on major downtown sidewalks and intersections, including outside the American Club as the lunchtime crowd watched. Nationalist troops dug foxhole trenches at the Bund's Public Garden next to the British consulate in anticipation of the coming battle.

To Ho, each day's news was more unsettling. He worried constantly about his mother or brother getting struck by a stray Nationalist bullet or trampled at the market, if they had money to buy anything at all. By mid-May, embassies issued final warnings to evacuate for Americans, British, and other foreign nationals, while Operation Flying Dragon airlifted Shanghai Jews to Canada. The Nationalist police in Shanghai were using martial law to clamp down hard on those who remained. With the government's arrests and executions, requisitions of property, tight censorship on local and foreign reporters, and destruction of villages and homes, many were more afraid of the Nationalists than the Communists.

On the night of May 24, the residents of Shanghai climbed onto rooftops to watch the sky light up with missiles and firepower aimed at the Bund by Communists in Pudong. The *New York Times* headline of May 25, 1949, brought the news that Ho dreaded: "Red Troops Enter Shanghai, Seize West, Central Areas; Nationalist Forces Flee."

HO HAD NEVER FELT so unhinged. Like their fellow Chinese students throughout the United States, Ho and his friends gathered together, seeking comfort from one another as they scoured the papers and radio reports, parsing each word as though that could help them comprehend the magnitude of this "liberation" and its impact on their families, their country, and themselves.

In Shanghai, the Communists hastened to announce that life would go on in the city—business as usual. To slow the brain drain and flight of capital, to calm the wealthy and middle classes who had not yet fled, the Communist Central Committee announced a policy of "evolution, not revolution" to make the "rational reforms" they envisioned sound less drastic and frightening.

Many of Ho's fellow students were overjoyed that the Nationalists had been driven out. Chinese students in America were well aware of the Nationalists' corruption and had little sympathy for the retreating army. They believed that a new dawn was breaking for the beleaguered Chinese people. But Ho remained skeptical. Influenced by his elder brother's and sister's opinionated letters about the shifting political winds, he knew it was safest to steer clear of politics and politicians. In spite of their criticism of the Nationalists, his family had stood with the old regime. His brother-in-law had worked for the Nationalists as an engineer—and, having heard nothing from his sister in some time, Ho could only hope that her family had made it to Taiwan.

Most maddening of all, Ho hadn't received a single letter from anyone in his family for several weeks, during the worst of the turmoil. It was the same for the other students. Those with extra money tried wiring relatives in Hong Kong or Singapore, grasping for any bit of information, sharing their news, as they all longed to learn the fate of their families.

A few weeks after Shanghai fell, a thin blue letter finally arrived for Ho. It was from his brother and dated June 9, 1949, two weeks after the Communists had taken over the city. Ho realized with a shock that this letter from his brother was quite different. The handwriting was Hosun's, but the tone was unfamiliar. For one, he no longer referred to the Communists as "bandits," as he always had before. Ho had to wonder if someone had dictated the letter:

MY DEAR BROTHER:

THERE IS LIBERATION HERE. AFTER LISTENING TO THE SOUND OF GUNSHOTS THROUGHOUT THE WHOLE NIGHT OF MAY 24, SHANGHAI WAS LIBERATED. WE ARE FINE, JUST A LITTLE FRIGHTENED. MANY ESTATES NEAR HONGQIAO HAVE BEEN DESTROYED. STORES, FACTORIES, AND BANKS HAVE ALL REOPENED, BUT BUSINESS IS BAD.

EVERYTHING IS UNDER THE SUPERVISION OF THE "MILITARY CONTROL COMMITTEE." I DON'T KNOW THE FUTURE NOW. WE ARE TRYING OUR BEST TO LIVE OUR LIVES. THE PEOPLE'S LIBERATION ARMY HAS REALLY GOOD PRINCIPLES, AND THEY HAVE THE SPIRIT OF WORKING HARD. NOW THE WHOLE COUNTRY FEELS LIKE BUILDING THE COUNTRY AFTER THE WAR. I THINK IT'S GOOD.

OUR HOMETOWN, CHANGSHU, HAS BEEN LIBERATED FOR TEN DAYS. IT'S GOOD THERE TOO. SECOND AND THIRD UNCLES ARE IN CHANGSHU. YESTERDAY ANOTHER UNCLE CAME TO SHANGHAI AND SAID HE WANTED TO CONTRIBUTE A LARGE AMOUNT OF RICE TO THE COMMUNIST PARTY. MOTHER IS HAPPY NOWADAYS, SO YOU TAKE GOOD CARE. YOU KNOW OUR PEOPLE'S GOVERNMENT CHERISHES THE PEOPLE WITH TECHNICAL SKILLS. DON'T WORRY ABOUT COMING BACK. I KNOW FROM YOUR FORMER LETTER THAT YOU GOT A SCHOLARSHIP. I'M VERY HAPPY FOR YOU. YOU CAN DECIDE FOR YOURSELF WHETHER TO STAY IN NEW YORK OR TO RETURN TO MICHIGAN. OUR SISTER AND HER HUSBAND ARE IN TAIWAN; I CAN'T REACH THEM FROM SHANGHAI. CAN YOU

TELL THEM HELLO FROM ME? MOTHER IS HEALTHY AND THE
KIDS STILL THINK OF YOU.

Ho's world was spinning out of control. Had his brother had a
change of heart, or was he too afraid to write the truth? Ho hadn't
heard from his mother and didn't know the whereabouts of his sister.
His entire network of Chinese students was seized by panic, everyone
asking themselves the same nervous questions. Where were their families? Were they safe? Should they return to China? If they stayed in
America, how could they survive?

With so many questions and so little information, Ho felt stymied,
stuck. He was a man of science, not a soothsayer. But one thing seemed
clear: Whatever path he chose would determine his future in ways that
he couldn't anticipate or fathom.

SHANGHAI, MAY 1949

ALL THROUGH THE SPRING OF 1949, SHANGHAI HAD BEEN in a state of imminent apocalypse. Even at the insular St. John's campus, Benny was on heightened alert, awaiting the presumed Communist takeover of the city. Any Americans and foreign nationals who had not yet evacuated received "last chance" warnings from their governments. But not everyone at St. John's was disheartened by the turn of events. It was an open secret that his campus, like many others, had underground Communists and sympathizers among its students, even those from wealthy families. Those hidden Communists didn't dare reveal themselves, knowing they'd face summary execution.

Still, the biggest concern in Shanghai was not the Red Army's approach but the crippled economy. Life for the city's six million residents had grown increasingly harsh under the rigid martial law imposed after the Nationalists' string of defeats. A strict curfew prohibited going outside for any reason between 6:00 P.M. and 6:00 A.M., whether to tend to a sick family member or to get some hot water from the corner tiger stove. Violators could be shot. Shanghai's famed nightlife ground to a standstill, further sinking the economy. Only Nationalist soldiers were out past curfew—which gave necessary cover for them to move machinery, antiquities, goods, documents, and China's entire treasury onto ships headed for Taiwan.

After the Communists crossed the Yangtze River on April 21, Benny had to scramble for a place to stay when the Nationalists ordered fifteen Shanghai universities shut down, including St. John's, Jiao Da, and Fudan. Though the Nationalists claimed the closures were for students' safety, no one believed them, and news reports said the authorities anticipated that students would rally in support of the Communists.

Benny found temporary shelter with the help of his buddies and the few relatives who would still speak to him. Thankfully, St. Mary's Hall wasn't shut down, and Doreen was safe there. But he had no idea how his father was doing; Benny hadn't visited him in months because of the fighting near Tilanqiao. Benny hoped that the Nationalists' wave of street executions hadn't spilled over into the prison.

The closer the Red Army came to Shanghai, the more bizarre the news seemed to Benny. On May 24, with the Communists surrounding the city and ready to attack at any moment, the British consul general R. W. Urquhart and other British diehards celebrated "Empire Day." The once-powerful overlords of the foreign treaty ports toasted the shrinking British Empire over lunch at the Long Bar of the elegant Shanghai Club, at number 2 on the Bund.

A few blocks away, an even more surreal event was taking place. The Nationalist garrison in Shanghai was staging a colorful, flag-waving "victory parade" from Nanjing Road through Hongkou Park. Caravans of jeeps rolled by, and soldiers marched along, distributing handbills urging all to "resist the aggression of the Communists to the bitter end." Benny and his friends dubbed it a "retreat parade": At the end of the route, the troops and vehicles kept right on moving toward the Wusongkou wharves, where they boarded ships headed to the East China Sea and Taiwan.

All that night, the sound of bombs and machine-gun bursts punctuated the darkness, the acrid smell of gunpowder and burning rubber filling the air. By the next morning, on May 25, the city's eerie silence was broken only by the occasional boom of distant explosions. Shanghai awoke to find its main avenues lined with thousands of Communist troops—country boys in tattered green uniforms. They had marched into the city quietly, no pounding footsteps coming from their cloth or straw shoes. By 7:30 A.M., they made their way to the Bund, running on the double-quick through the major thoroughfares of the former French Concession. The only opposition arose in a few areas near the Embankment Building and the post office by Suzhou Creek from rear-guard Nationalist soldiers who seemed unaware that their comrades were already in retreat at sea. General Tang Enbo himself, the Nationalist commander in charge of Shanghai's defense, who had declared that he would fight to the last man, was on his way to Guangzhou by the time the Red Army marched into the city.

When Benny stepped beyond the quiet lane where he was staying and onto the wide main streets fresh with spring foliage, before him were endless rows of sleeping soldiers. Thousands of men and boys, many appearing much younger than he, lay on the sidewalks like so many neat wooden staves. After weeks of fighting, they slept despite the bright sunlight and the morning's traffic.

At a nearby intersection, Communist soldiers with green caps accentuated by red stars stood watch at blockades that the Nationalists had held only the day before. Benny watched as a small crowd of local residents edged closer, curiosity eclipsing their caution. Benny, too, wondered if these were a different breed of soldier, men who could seize a grand city without pillaging, raping, and killing civilians. There was no wave of terror, which had been the hallmark of both the Japanese military and the retreating Nationalists. To the surprise of onlookers, foreign journalists among them, the tired soldiers politely rejected offers of hot tea, food, even hot water. "The People's Liberation Army does not take anything from the people," replied a snappy young soldier.

If the Shanghainese locals were bewildered by the disciplined rag-tag soldiers lining their streets, those bleary-eyed country boys were equally stunned to awaken in the Paris of the East. Few had ever seen such towering skyscrapers, grand mansions, fine motorized vehicles, or Westernized Chinese who looked to them as alien as the foreigners.

At St. Mary's Hall, Doreen and several other girls had spent the night at a teacher's cottage, huddled on the floor and out of the path of stray bullets. After Benny found her safe and unharmed, he couldn't resist checking on his own nearby campus. A sea of soldiers greeted him: two thousand Red Army troops asleep on the grassy commons by the landmark old camphor tree. He would have stopped to pray at the Pro-Cathedral, but it, too, was occupied by soldiers sleeping on the pews and floor. In contrast to the chaos and looting of the retreating Nationalists, the Communist victory was almost peaceful.

Some fighting flared up outside the city proper, in Pudong and Woosung in the east and by Hongqiao in the west. After a small Nationalist unit put up a last-ditch fight near the Bund, they surrendered once they realized they'd been abandoned by their fellow soldiers. Other Nationalist troops who had been left behind simply shed their uniforms and disappeared into the teeming city, clad only in their underwear.

CURIOUS TO SEE WHAT other changes came with the liberators, Benny made his way to Nanjing Road, not far from his late grandfather's former house on Tibet Road. The city's center had broken out in wild celebration, welcoming the victorious Communists on the same blocks where the Nationalists had held their victory parade fewer than twenty-four hours before. Nationalist flags were swiftly replaced by red banners with yellow stars. Troops of enthusiastic youths paraded by, chanting anti-imperialist slogans, shouting to bystanders about the benefits of Communism. "May the People's Liberation Army live ten thousand years! Welcome, People's Liberation Army!" they shouted. Giant portraits of Mao Zedong had materialized overnight, covering the sides of Shanghai's tall buildings, evidently the work of countless underground Communist supporters who had been secretly preparing for this moment. Boys and girls from the Communist Democratic Youth League put up thousands of colorful posters welcoming the troops. Teenagers with armbands stood in for the traffic cops who'd fled with the Nationalists. Girl League members, carrying big baskets of red carnations, put them in the buttonholes of the Red Army soldiers.

Benny watched from the sidelines as university students, including some he recognized from St. John's, swayed to the *yang ko,* a familiar line dance popular with peasant farmers, the backbone of the revolution-in-progress. They snaked through the streets in long triple lines that foreigners called the "Communist conga." Though the festivities seemed never ending, Benny didn't participate, not with his father in prison—and he wasn't the only one to hang back. Others who tired of the continuous celebration could duck into movie theaters that stayed open while schools and other businesses were closed: *Deception*, starring Bette Davis, was featured at the Majestic Theatre off Bubbling Well Road, while *I Wonder Who's Kissing Her Now* was at the Cathay. Benny didn't dare waste any of his small earnings from tutoring on a movie. He'd have to keep closer tabs on his spending now that the economy was sure to be in even greater flux.

More than anything, Benny hoped the Communists would allow students to graduate as scheduled. He gave a silent prayer of gratitude when classes resumed at St. John's on June 13. New rules went into effect immediately—such as suspending morning prayers at the chapel. Startled but not surprised, Benny knew not to protest. A pro-Communist assembly was held instead to thank the soldiers of the People's Liberation Army who had bivouacked at the campus during the weeks of Liberation. The students in charge praised the soldiers' dedication to the people's revolution. Benny held his own worship, praying alone in his room.

A pro-Communist group emerged as the new student leadership on campus. Students like Benny were surprised to learn who among their classmates had been secret Communists. It had been rumored for some time that the women's dormitory was a hotbed of radicalism. Schoolmate Tao-Fu Ying, whose family came from a long line of compradors like Benny's, learned that his own sister was an underground Communist. The now openly pro-Communist campus group proclaimed its first priority: to bring the missionary school in line with the party's political principles. English would no longer be spoken in the classrooms, ending one of the hallmarks of a St. John's education. The dominance of the language at St. John's was condemned as a part of the "slavery education" promoted by the missionaries.

All over the country, the Chinese language would henceforth be taught as the language of learning and commerce. All classes, including his courses on American politics, were to be conducted in Chinese.

Benny didn't care. He could easily complete his course work in either language. By summer's end, he'd have all the college credits needed to get his diploma at the September graduation. Then he'd be through with college, and he, too, might consider leaving.

MARSHAL CHEN YI, SHANGHAI'S newly appointed Communist mayor, hastened to calm the city's skittish residents, urging them to conduct their lives as usual while cooperating with the People's Liberation Army. Within days, trolley and tram service resumed; electricity and water flowed. Train rails and bridges damaged in the fighting were repaired and street blockades quickly dismantled. River traffic started up again, and a few ships were allowed back into the once-bustling port. Thousands of mines left by the Nationalists in the waterways and government buildings had to be disarmed as the Communist Party leadership moved into the massive municipal government complex by the Bund on Hankou Road, once home to the British-dominated Shanghai Municipal Council.

A new currency, the renminbi, was being introduced to replace the Nationalist gold yuan. Some clever Shanghai counterfeiters went to work on the new bills right away but were swiftly caught and arrested. The red flag with a large yellow star and four smaller ones flew over the Bund atop the Custom House, the Harbor Office, and General Post Office, which issued new postage stamps commemorating the Liberation of Shanghai and Nanjing. In one of their most popular moves, on June 24 the Communists eliminated the much-hated curfew and *baojia* system of neighborhood snoops, saying that the Nationalists had violated the rights of the people.

With much fanfare, Communist commissioners handily accomplished what Benny's father had failed to do as police commissioner: They quickly and efficiently shut down the vice industry of the Badlands. Prostitutes, dance-hall girls, gamblers, opium dealers, and addicts had to attend mandatory Communist reeducation sessions. Authorities slapped stiff fines on the owners of ballrooms, gambling halls, and other businesses for tax evasion. Uncooperative owners and managers were arrested and punished. The tightening vise of regulations and entertainment taxes gradually drove many out of business.

As the weeks progressed under the new regime, to Benny it seemed possible that the Communists could move Shanghai in a positive direction. Many welcomed those early measures as necessary and good, especially because of the economic stability that had been so absent under the Nationalists. But Benny was still worried about his father and had to wait for revised visiting procedures to be issued at the Tilanqiao Prison before he could venture back. In the meantime, he hoped that the Communist government would release his father and other prisoners.

Although Shanghai had been liberated at the end of May and the Nationalists were in retreat, the Communists did not yet have control over all of China's vast territory. Clashes between the two armies continued in the south and west. The Nationalists even launched air attacks on Shanghai from Taiwan, sending bombers in their American-made planes to strafe the city, killing Chinese civilians in Zhabei and Nantao, the same areas that had been leveled by the Japanese. The Communists had neither an air force nor antiaircraft defense, giving Chiang Kai-shek's military unfettered ability to bomb the port of Shanghai and to gun down civilians on the streets below. Not even the Japanese "Zeros" had done that to Shanghai—a point that the Communist-controlled press emphasized. A Nationalist plane mistakenly bombed the British ship *Anchises,* a commercial vessel that had been allowed into Communist waters. Luckily, all passengers and crew were rescued, but the incident made it clear that the civil war was not yet over.

BENNY'S HAPPIEST MOMENT IN four long years came when he held his St. John's diploma in his hands on September 14, 1949. He had graduated at last. There was no ceremony, no one to cheer him, none of the pomp and circumstance of past years when graduations had been held at such lavish venues as the Grand Theatre. Missionary-founded schools like St. John's now faced great uncertainty. Benny was just grateful to have obtained his coveted diploma before his college might be forced to shut down.

Finally he could look toward his future. Benny quickly landed a job with the National YMCA in Nanjing. Dr. Tu Yu-Ching, the former president of St. John's, had become the secretary-general of the YMCA in China. Dr. Tu offered Benny a job as his secretary.

Benny was excited to be of service to the church. Nanjing was only a couple of hours away from Shanghai by train—near enough to visit his father occasionally. It was a hopeful sign that the leaders of the Christian churches were willing to stay in China under Communist rule. If they weren't afraid to stay, why should Benny worry?

No matter what God had planned for him, Benny was sure he'd land on his feet. After all, he'd made it through these last rough years. But there remained one gnawing worry that he couldn't shake: his sister Doreen. If he took the job in Nanjing, she'd be on her own in Shanghai. His trusting sister always seemed so vulnerable. If only he could take her with him. But she had no interest in going to Nanjing, and he couldn't support her anyway. Still, he couldn't leave the naïve and sheltered eighteen-year-old behind in a big city like Shanghai with no one to count on for help. If something happened to her, he'd never forgive himself. Benny felt stuck, not sure what to do except pray for guidance.

The solution came in the form of a letter from his second sister, Cecilia, in Hong Kong. She was expecting another baby, her third, and wanted Doreen to come to Hong Kong and help with the children. That would solve everything, Benny thought excitedly. Doreen would be safe with Cecilia, and all his siblings would be accounted for.

In the weeks following Benny's graduation, the People's Liberation Army defeated the main opposition forces left in China's southwest. On October 1, Chairman Mao Zedong stood before a sea of millions at Tiananmen Square in his chosen capital of Beijing and proclaimed, "The Chinese people have stood up!"

The Communist government swiftly imposed new rules for the country—including procedures that would make it more difficult to leave China. Previously, anybody with a ticket could leave for Hong Kong. Now all persons wishing to leave Shanghai had to apply for an exit visa. Under the Nationalists, it had always been possible to bend the rules, for a price. There would be no such slack with the Communists. Already it was growing difficult to get the required exit visa. On top of that, Hong Kong was so overwhelmed with refugees that the British authorities were restricting the entrance of Chinese into the colony—something they had never done before.

As Benny made preparations to leave for his job in Nanjing, he realized that he needed to send Doreen to Hong Kong soon in case further restrictions were imposed. But his sister was suddenly balking. She was getting nervous about being so far away from Benny—and her parents. In spite of her family's problems, she wanted to be near them.

With no time to lose, Benny decided to apply for Doreen's exit permit anyway. It wouldn't be possible to buy a train ticket out of Shanghai without one, so he'd have to buy the train ticket afterward. In case he couldn't convince her to leave, he applied for an exit visa for himself too. One of them would use the ticket.

Soon Benny had the official response: His visa application had been denied—too many intellectuals were fleeing from Shanghai. But Doreen's exit permit was approved.

Benny made his way through the railway offices, as hundreds of others pushed and clamored to buy train tickets for their escape.

Armed with the official exit permit and the money he had saved up from his odd jobs on campus, he hurried to the Shanghai North railway station. Everyone in the city seemed to have the same idea. Still muscular from his boxing lessons of long ago, Benny made his way through the crowd to the ticket counter. He barely had enough money for the ticket for a train from Shanghai to Guangzhou, leaving in two days. "Don't complain; you're lucky you got one," barked the gruff agent as Benny emptied his bagful of cash. The ticket would take Doreen about nine hundred miles closer to Cecilia. Once she was in Guangzhou, the border crossing to Hong Kong wasn't far, and he had church connections there who could help.

Benny didn't have much time to persuade Doreen to leave. "We have no good family connections here in Shanghai, no *guanxi* for your future," he argued. "In Hong Kong, you won't have to marry a Communist. When things settle down in Shanghai, you can always come back." Eventually, he convinced her.

On the morning of Doreen's departure, Benny helped her pack. Along with her clothes and identification papers, she took the last of Benny's cash and a few small pieces of gold jewelry from before their father's arrest. It all fit into a small bag. She tucked the ticket into a pocket.

When Benny and Doreen arrived at the Shanghai North railway station, they were stunned to find their mother waiting for them. There she was, her features as fine as ever, looking elegant in her high heels and high-necked silk *qipao*. Somehow she had learned that Doreen was leaving. She pleaded with her daughter to stay.

"Come live with me in Suzhou," she begged. "If you go, we'll never be together again!"

Benny hadn't seen his mother since the day he had left his two youngest siblings with her. He didn't believe that she cared about Doreen, not after the way she had abandoned them all. He figured she needed Doreen to help her with her new babies. He had to counter her entreaties, or else his sister might waver. "You're young, and you have a chance to have a life," he told Doreen. "Take it!"

The train was boarding at the platform. Before Doreen could get on, she had to present her exit permit to Communist customs inspectors and submit to their questions. On the platform, she went into the "Red House"—nicknamed for its color as well as the new regime's politics. Benny and his mother waited in uncomfortable silence.

Inside, a scornful inspector rummaged through Doreen's bag, zealously searching for contraband. As he dug through her things, he pontificated, saying that anyone wanting to leave the new People's Republic must be a counterrevolutionary. The inspector found her gold jewelry and accused her of hiding it for illicit purposes. The officials seized all of her possessions and pushed her out of the Red House. She ran to Benny in tears, relaying that the inspectors had taken everything.

As Doreen stood crying, the train engineer tooted the horn, and the conductors announced the last call to come aboard.

Benny shouted a single question: "Where is your train ticket?"

Suddenly Doreen remembered and reached down to her hip. "It's in my pocket!"

"That's good enough!" Benny exclaimed, almost carrying her to the departing train. As Benny hustled his sister toward the car door, his mother clung to the girl's arms, imploring her to stay, pleading that she needed Doreen to care for her as she grew older.

"No, you mustn't leave! I'll never see you again!" she screamed, trying to dig her high heels into the platform as she tugged on Doreen.

Benny was stronger. He managed to push his sister onto the train just as it began to pull away.

From the open door, Doreen called out to him. "I have no money, no clothes. Nothing! What should I do?"

"Go to the YWCA in Guangzhou!" he yelled to her. "I'll contact them."

Doreen stared back at him in silence, her eyes wide with disbelief, as Benny waved goodbye.

"I'll never see you again!" their mother wailed.

Benny spotted Doreen's ashen face at the window where she was seated, and continuously waved to her as the train advanced. He tried to ignore his mother, appalled that she would try to keep her own daughter from her one chance at a better life. At least his mother had failed. He felt a twinge of sadness too, realizing that he no longer recognized the mother he had once adored.

When the wisp of engine smoke dissipated in the gray sky, Benny finally stopped waving. He glanced at his mother, quiet at last. She was on a bench, rocking as if propelled by a metronome. She glared back at him.

"You—my firstborn son—how dare you break your mother's heart?" she cried.

Swallowing hard, Benny couldn't answer. Each word from his mother felt like a dagger into his chest.

With Doreen gone, there was nothing else to say. For a moment, his mother glanced in his direction. He half thought she'd ask about his university studies. When he was a boy, she had tracked his schooling closely, praising his smallest progress and assuring him that he would one day follow his father's footsteps. But now she only craned her long neck to check on the next train to Suzhou.

"Goodbye, Mother," he said gently, shrugging off her silence as he turned to leave, wondering if he'd see her again.

PART FOUR

WAR'S LONG
SHADOW

HO

Age 25

NEW YORK, 1949

AFTER HO RECEIVED HIS BROTHER'S CRYPTIC LETTER expressing enthusiasm for the Communist Liberation of Shanghai, he had no further communication from his once prolific family. Overwhelmed with worry for their safety and the staggering guilt he felt over his inability to help them, Ho could focus on little else as he assembled tidbits of information, whatever he and his compatriots could glean from news and letters.

If that weren't enough, another disaster came crashing down on him: In July, the U.S. Immigration and Naturalization Service sent him a notice to appear for a hearing. Ho had sent a letter to the INS requesting permission to work part-time. If he failed to go to this hearing or if he went and said something wrong, he could be deported. If the INS had discovered that he was already working, he could also be deported. What if someone turned him in? Had it been a mistake to sue China Motors for back pay?

Ho knew of other students who had been detained by the INS and threatened with Federal Bureau of Investigation (FBI) interrogations, imprisonment, and deportation. Ho tried to swallow his panic, knowing that his family was being blown around China like leaves in the Communist wind. He desperately needed their advice, but he didn't even know where they were. Just thinking about his predicament sent him into a nervous sweat.

He had to consider the possibility of deportation from the United States—but to where? To China and into Communist hands? Or to Taiwan, where he'd never been? On the other hand, if he managed to stay in the United States, he could be dragged down by the anti-Communist tide that was rising in America, targeting anyone Chinese. His family had never favored Communism. Last he'd heard, his sister and her husband were trying to get away from the Communists, to flee to Taiwan. But that might not count for much when most Americans seemed to think all Chinese were alike—and no different from Japanese, Koreans, or anyone from Asia, for that matter.

Most of the five to six thousand Chinese students in America were in the same dire straits, dependent on their families in China for financial support. The students had to find a way to subsist but were prohibited from working. In addition to the students, another three-to-four thousand Chinese professionals on temporary visas were stranded in the United States as well.

A few sympathetic Americans wrote to newspapers and politicians, urging Washington and the INS to allow the students to get jobs. As early as January 1949, the U.S. National Student Association in Cambridge, Massachusetts, asked the INS assistant commissioner for rule changes to permit Chinese students to work part-time. In addition, it recommended that the INS lift the requirement that students carry a full course load, so that they would have time to work. Sororities, church groups, and college administrators made similar appeals.

But there was nowhere for Ho to get basic information on this complicated dilemma. Once again, he turned to his most reliable source of help: other stranded Chinese students. There were nearly three hundred of them in the New York area, attending various colleges and universities. The largest concentration was at Columbia, which was one of the reasons Ho had chosen to live near the university. He'd meet with his compatriots at the student union, the International House, or any available space where they could gather informally and commiserate. Students whose families had fled to Hong Kong were the most likely to receive letters with useful details, since communications from the British colony were unhindered and the steady influx of refugees there brought constant updates on the situation in China. Letters from Shanghai and Taiwan, in contrast, were scrutinized by censors, forcing the senders to share only the blandest of niceties.

To bypass the censors, some correspondents resorted to code. One educated member of Shanghai's social set, having decided not to leave his home, arranged to send a message in a photo to his family, who had fled overseas: If he was standing, all was well. If he was sitting, things were bad. When he finally sent them a picture, he was lying down.

Some students received news in the form of a rebuke. Chinyee, a painter studying fine arts at the College of Mount Saint Vincent in New York, never imagined that her family would lose its comfortable standing. She had a rude awakening when she wrote to her mother in the spring of 1949 asking for some new *qipao* dresses. Her mother sent a curt reply: "You don't know what's going on here in China. Life in Shanghai has turned upside down. Don't think of coming back here or to Taiwan either; everything is chaotic. Be happy with what you have, and don't ask for such petty things."

The students were by no means unified in their views about the volatile events back home. One organization at Columbia, the Chinese Students Club, had existed as a social group for a number of years. Some members argued that the club had a moral obligation to speak up about China, while others wanted to keep politics out. The openly pro-Communist students decided to organize their own campus group, naming it the Chinese Students Association. Confrontations between the two groups grew so heated that Columbia's administration intervened and refused to continue recognizing either organization, denying use of campus facilities to both.

When Ho arrived in the United States for study, he had joined a group called the Chinese Students' Christian Association. One of the largest Chinese student organizations in the United States, the CSCA had been sponsored by the YMCA since the early 1900s. Though Ho had eschewed politics, as his family had often admonished, he'd figured that a Christian organization was innocuous enough—and a good place for him to meet Chinese girls. The national leader of the CSCA

In the early morning hours of May 25, 1949, the People's Liberation Army marched into Shanghai, passing in front of the iconic Park Hotel.

in early 1949 also made frequent appearances at Columbia, a Chinese Canadian named Paul Lin. It soon became evident that Lin and his wife Eileen were ardent supporters of the Communist government, encouraging students to return home to help build the new China.

After the Liberation of Shanghai, when there was little doubt that the Nationalist era in China was over and the Communists would soon control the country, fear of Chinese Communist infiltrators quickly grew inside the United States. The FBI increased its surveillance of Chinese students and sought out "friendly" ones who might serve as informants. The Chinese Students' Christian Association that Ho had joined came under intense FBI scrutiny as federal agents fanned out across the country, investigating Chinese student groups and their leaders. Paul Lin was tagged with the FBI label of "rabid pro-Communist."

The FBI's surveillance was hardly a secret, as the agency interviewed a broad range of students and Chinese scholars. Everybody knew someone who had been interrogated by the FBI—or had been contacted themselves. Prominent Chinese faced questioning as well, including Dr. Paul Chih Meng, director of the China Institute in New

York, whose board chair was Henry R. Luce, an influential member of the pro-Nationalist China lobby. In a declassified confidential interview, Meng told the FBI that he believed more than 80 percent of Chinese students in the United States were sympathetic to the Communist government but noted that this did not mean they were all Communists. Other FBI sources estimated that at least 90 percent were sympathetic to the Communist government, again cautioning that this was more indicative of their rejection of the Chiang Kai-shek regime, which many viewed as hopelessly corrupt. To uninformed FBI agents and American politicians, however, the political distinctions between anti-Chiang and pro-Communist viewpoints mattered little. To them, all Chinese were potential Communists.

The volatility of the American political climate only made matters worse for the students. Congressional debates on what to do with the Chinese added to the tension as their fates swung in the wind. Under the terms of the Immigration Act of 1924, a student visa status expired upon completion or termination of studies. A debate ensued in Washington over whether to allow Chinese students to return to China—and what to do with their visa status if the students were forced to stay in the United States. Some politicians felt that the students should be barred from returning to China to prevent them from aiding the Communists with their American educations. Others, in the tradition of anti-Chinese exclusionists who tried to drive out all Chinese from the Americas, were afraid of any increase in the "Yellow Peril" population. They strongly opposed granting any form of residency to the estimated ten thousand stranded Chinese students and nonimmigrants, a number which far exceeded the official quota of only 105 Chinese immigrants allowed into the United States per year.

This then was the conundrum: America's decades-long racial exclusion aimed at keeping Chinese out of America was at odds with the preference of politicians now opposed to sending American-educated Chinese into Mao's embrace. Ho knew he had to tread very carefully as he weighed his limited options, especially as stories of missteps by other students began to circulate. Maria Lee Koh, for example, had given up her student visa in order to register as a refugee—only to find that the minuscule quota for Chinese refugees had been filled.

Suddenly she was on the docket to be deported. Through her un-flinching determination, she succeeded in persuading an Ohio repre-sentative to introduce a private immigration bill in Congress that allowed her to stay in the United States. About a hundred other Chi-nese managed to seek similar private congressional bills enabling them to remain.

AFTER WEEKS OF WORRY and consultations with his trusted friends, Ho decided he'd be better off answering the INS inspectors forth-rightly rather than offering some convoluted excuses. Since it was his own letter requesting permission to work that had prompted the hear-ing, perhaps they'd view him favorably. By the time Ho forced his leaden feet to the INS office at 70 Columbus Avenue for his hearing, he had decided to tell all. He disclosed that he had been working—at least he wouldn't have to worry about the INS finding out. The hard-eyed agent glared at him and asked for details, sternly informing Ho that he now faced punitive action and possible deportation, pending the agency's investigation and deliberation.

Ho prepared himself for the agency's judgment. He knew he could be jailed, deported, or both. He wasn't sure which fate would be worse.

A week after his hearing, he received a letter from Edward J. Shaughnessy, the acting director of the INS New York District, who minced no words about Ho's previous denials about working:

ON THE BASIS OF THE RECORD IT APPEARS THAT YOU
VIOLATED THE TERMS AND CONDITIONS UNDER WHICH YOU
WERE ADMITTED TO THE UNITED STATES AND THAT YOU
DELIBERATELY ATTEMPTED TO CONCEAL THAT VIOLATION BY
MAKING FALSE STATEMENTS UNDER OATH. DESPITE THE
FOREGOING YOUR REQUEST FOR PERMISSION TO ACCEPT
PART-TIME EMPLOYMENT IS GRANTED SINCE IT APPEARS
THAT YOU REQUIRE SUCH EMPLOYMENT IN ORDER TO
MAINTAIN YOURSELF BUT YOU ARE ADVISED THAT IN
THE EVENT YOU SHOULD COMMIT ANY FURTHER VIOLATION

OF THE CONDITIONS UNDER WHICH YOU WERE ADMITTED
TO THE UNITED STATES APPROPRIATE ACTION WILL BE
TAKEN.

Ho had to read the letter a few times before he was certain that he was in the clear. Even though he had committed violations, he now had permission to work part-time. He realized that he could finally get a job without fear. Yet he felt little joy, because he still had no word from his family. They would be glad for him; of that he was certain—if they were alive and well.

Other Chinese students were not as lucky, Ho knew. The FBI had even called one of his roommates to its office for questioning. Ho and the other roommates tried to reassure him—after all, Ho's INS outcome had been favorable. But when their friend didn't return from his interrogation, the roommates grew anxious. They made discreet inquiries, but the young man seemed to have vanished. Soon they discovered that he had been arrested and detained on Ellis Island, within view of the Statue of Liberty. As they pieced together the chain of events, they concluded that a tipster had contacted the FBI, naming the roommate as a security threat. It turned out that the snitch was the jealous ex-boyfriend of their roommate's girlfriend. He had called the FBI out of spite.

Ho and his friends were stunned that such a scurrilous accusation could lead to their friend's arrest. No one was surprised when such things happened in Shanghai—after all, their entire generation of students had been wrongly labeled as collaborators. But Ho had expected America to be different from China. Instead, a chorus of powerful Americans claimed that all Chinese in America comprised a "fifth column" of enemy infiltrators. U.S. senator Joseph McCarthy accused American diplomats with expertise about China of being Communist sympathizers—only one aspect of his claim that government employees, teachers, homosexuals, and Hollywood writers and actors posed dangerous national security threats and therefore needed to be investigated and purged.

EVEN THOUGH HO'S LEGAL status in the United States was now relatively secure, his place as a stranded student and refugee was still difficult to navigate. Most Americans assumed that every Chinese immigrant worked in a restaurant or laundry—the limited job options available to earlier generations of Chinese in America. At every turn, Ho and his compatriots were asked if they were waiters or washers. Armed with PhDs but no jobs, they were offended by the constant assumption that all Chinese were laborers.

Of course, there were complexities and differences among the Chinese exiles. Though many stranded students were in financial straits, the American news media seemed interested only in the wealthiest elite in the United States, such as Madame Chiang Kai-shek and her relatives. Her brother, T. V. Soong, the former finance minister, had a posh address at 1133 Fifth Avenue. Madame Chiang Kai-shek often stayed at 10 Gracie Square on the East River, one of the most prestigious residences in New York, where her sister Ai-ling and Ai-ling's supremely wealthy husband, financier H. H. Kung, owned a home.

Such superelites occasionally appeared in New York's society gossip columns: David Kung, Madame Chiang's favorite nephew, who had been jailed back in Shanghai for corruption, was rumored to be gay, while his sister Jeanette always dressed in men's clothing and reportedly had two "wives." Some members of Congress had suspected Madame Chiang of being a lesbian because of her cross-dressing niece.

Since most of these elite exiles entered the United States on diplomatic passports, they were shielded by diplomatic immunity from the FBI and INS investigations encountered by the other Chinese in America, yet even they could not always escape the prejudicial stereotypes. In order to buy his apartment on Fifth Avenue, wealthy T. V. Soong had to obtain a letter from no less than Henry Morgenthau, a former secretary of the treasury, guaranteeing that Soong would not open a Chinese laundry on the premises. Still, most of the students had nothing but scorn for those wealthy Nationalist exiles, derisively calling them the "White Chinese," like the tattered White Russians of Shanghai.

BUT FOR THE STRANDED STUDENTS of every economic circumstance, the uncertainty and confusion took a toll. Students from families far better off than Ho's were in trouble. Richard Lin Yang, the St. John's student whose father had whisked him out of Shanghai using the ruse of a family dinner on a boat, had made his way to the University of California at Los Angeles but became so unnerved that he spent his time waiting tables, pumping gas, betting on horses at the racetrack, and finding bit parts in Hollywood war movies. Jack Tang, the eldest son of P. Y. Tang, one of the most successful textile manufacturers in Shanghai, floundered at MIT as his father's China holdings were wiped out. Before the Communist revolution, Jack's life had been mapped out for him. As the Number One Son, he was expected to take over the thriving family business, one day to become the next patriarch. He had pursued his studies with that future in mind. Now there was nothing. His father had to rebuild the family textile business in Hong Kong. With all the stress, Jack fell ill and was confined to bed rest for several months. As he struggled to reimagine his place in a world outside of China, 1949 became a lost year.

Ho couldn't afford to abandon his studies or to get sick. But with his life spinning in a swirl of uncertainty, his grades plummeted in his science classes—for the first time ever. His flagging performance only added to his dismay and disorientation.

The harsh Cold War reaction to the stranded students stoked their internal debates over whether to return to China. Those with fiancées or spouses and children or aging parents could only despair as the INS, FBI, and State Department, having been purged of knowledgeable "China Hands," imposed rules and procedures that made it more difficult to return to China. Some wished to go home simply because they found the financial strain and limited job prospects for Chinese in America too daunting, while others, inspired by vocal idealists and pro-Communists like Paul and Eileen Lin, were eager to help build a bright future for China. With numbers of Chinese students clamoring to return home, the FBI and INS worried that they comprised an influential mass movement planning to repatriate.

In response, the State Department established a Chinese Assistance Desk to take requests from students seeking to return—with the names of requesters promptly sent to the INS for investigation. Those who had studied science and technology in particular were barred from repatriating on the grounds that it could be "inimical to national security." Even scientists and engineers who had committed serious immigration violations, like Ho, would not be sent back, while students of arts and letters, humanities and social sciences, were quickly approved for return and shipped at State Department expense to Taiwan or Hong Kong, the nearest locations to Shanghai with diplomatic ties to the United States.

Meanwhile, as American politicians debated what to do with these stranded students and scholars, China's new Communist government was reaching out and appealing to them to come home. The Beijing government organized a letter-writing campaign to Chinese students abroad, exhorting them to return to their motherland to help chart the course of the new China. A few of the letters came from Premier Zhou Enlai himself, while most came from students' family members, reassuring the students that the Communist regime would welcome them back with open arms. Every batch of returning students was vigorously lauded in the Chinese news.

No such letter arrived for Ho. He almost envied the students who received them—at least they knew that their families were alive. But he and his friends began to suspect that those letters were written under duress when some received follow-up messages from their families on the heels of the invitational letters. The new messages from home urged them to ignore the prior appeals and rosy promises.

Of the five to six thousand Chinese students in the United States in 1949, only about one hundred received permission to return to China. Untold numbers were rumored to have left surreptitiously, without State Department approval, by taking circuitous journeys through Europe, since the United States government blocked all travel to the Communist country. Still others made their way home by crossing, undocumented, into Canada, which had established diplomatic relations with the new People's Republic. In spite of his conflicted feelings, Ho couldn't seriously consider returning, not when his family had made it so clear that he should stay put.

Finally Ho received a new letter, from his brother. Ho had to calm himself as he carefully handled the tissue-like paper, afraid he might tear it in his nervous haste. The message was somber, from Hosun, in Shanghai, and dated September 20, 1949:

> IT IS MORE THAN FOUR MONTHS SINCE WE'VE BEEN IN TOUCH, AND IT SEEMS LIKE A CENTURY. MY WIFE DIED ON JULY 20 FROM TUBERCULOSIS. I HAVE BEEN VERY SAD. . . . DON'T WORRY TOO MUCH FOR US. IT'S A REALLY HARD TIME, BUT I'M SURE WE'LL MANAGE. HAVE YOU EXCHANGED LETTERS WITH OUR SISTER? YOU CAN TELL HER MY NEWS AND SAY HELLO FROM ME. AFTER THE WHOLE COUNTRY IS LIBERATED, MAYBE WE CAN BE TOGETHER AND NEVER BE SEPARATED AGAIN.

News of his sister-in-law's death came as a shock. She was not much older than Ho and had a young child with his brother. Ho could feel Hosun's pain in the brief note and wished he could somehow comfort his brother. He was powerless to do anything when he was so far away and the mail delivery between China and America was so unreliable. He wanted to send a few dollars to help with the funeral costs. But he couldn't even do that when his student network advised that the new Communist government was screening all mail, especially from the United States. Anything American, including money, could be considered subversive. In addition, the FBI and other U.S. authorities were surely monitoring correspondence to and from China as well. Ho had to be doubly careful.

It was another month before Ho heard from his sister. She and her husband and children had somehow reached Taiwan.

On October 22, 1949, his sister, Wanyu, penned a letter from Jilong, Taiwan, where her husband had found a job:

> THE SITUATION IN CHINA IS WORSE DAY BY DAY. TAIWAN IS BAD TOO, BUT AT LEAST THERE IS NO WAR HERE. GUANGZHOU AND XIAMEN ARE BOTH TAKEN. THE NATIONALISTS AND COMMUNISTS ARE STILL FIGHTING OVER [THE ISLAND OF] JINMEN. IF TAIWAN IS LOST, WE WILL HAVE NOWHERE TO GO.

BUT HERE IN TAIWAN, WE NOW HAVE ANOTHER CONCERN.
THE LOCAL PEOPLE ARE ANGRY AT THOSE OF US FROM OTHER
PROVINCES. TAIWANESE PEOPLE CALL US *WAI SHENG REN*
[OUTSIDERS]. THE LOCALS ARE AFRAID THAT THERE WILL BE
ANOTHER MASSACRE LIKE 2-28 IN 1947. IF THAT HAPPENS, WE
MAINLAND PEOPLE WILL ALSO SUFFER.

YOU KNOW WHAT HAPPENED TO MY HUSBAND? SOME OF THE
LOCAL PEOPLE HATE HIM, AND HE CAN'T DO HIS WORK WELL.
SO WE *WAI SHENG REN* ARE SUFFERING DISCRIMINATION HERE
AS WELL. LOTS OF PEOPLE WISH THAT THE AMERICAN ARMY
WOULD COME AND PROTECT US. WE DON'T HAVE THE STRENGTH
TO PROTECT OURSELVES. WE CAME TO TAIWAN FOR A BETTER
LIFE, AWAY FROM THE COMMUNISTS. WE DON'T WANT TO BE
ALWAYS RUNNING AWAY, ALWAYS FLEEING SOMEWHERE.

The letter from his sister added to Ho's anxiety. Like most Chinese,
he was unfamiliar with Taiwan or its history, but her reference to a
massacre was worrisome. Ho learned from more knowledgeable students that the Nationalists had killed thousands of Taiwanese in a 1947
uprising called "2-28," having occurred on February 28. He feared his
sister's family could face more turmoil in Taiwan, but at least they
were alive. Ho took on a new role in his family from his distant but
stable outpost in New York. Now his dispersed family members were
turning to him for information, advice, and support. It was a strange
reversal for him, the youngest child who had always followed the
guidance of his elders.

A regular mail service was soon in place between Taiwan and the
United States, and letters began arriving from his sister much more
often than from his mother or brother in Shanghai. Wanyu and her
husband had always provided Ho with full details about the goings-on
in China, readily offering their opinions. But the Chinese student network in the United States, highly critical of the Chiang Kai-shek government in Taiwan, warned that the Nationalist secret police were
extending their draconian reach to the United States. Many believed
that the Nationalists had spies in America to keep watch on the students. More than once, Ho advised his sister to be more discreet in her

letters to him, out of concern that the Nationalists and the U.S. government were monitoring their mail.

On December 2, 1949, a longer letter arrived from Wanyu and her husband, again from Jilong:

WE ARE FINE, THOUGH THE SITUATION IS WORSE DAY BY DAY, AND TAIWAN IS VERY NERVOUS. WE MISS HOME VERY MUCH. WE ARE STUCK HERE, CAN'T GO AHEAD AND CAN'T GO BACK. OUR LIFE IS SO TEDIOUS AND BORING. SOMETIMES I THINK THERE IS NO HAPPINESS IN LIFE ANYMORE. WE ARE BOTH FAR AWAY. WHEN WILL THE DAY COME TO RETURN HOME?

OUR BELOVED MOTHER HAS WORKED HARD ALL HER LIFE, WORRYING ABOUT US ALL THE TIME. SHE RAISED US BY HERSELF, AND NOW WE CAN'T TAKE CARE OF HER. I CAN'T EVEN SEND LETTERS TO HER. DO YOU HAVE ANY WAY TO LET HER KNOW THAT WE ARE ALL RIGHT HERE? I WANT TO GIVE HER SOME COMFORT, BUT I DARE NOT SEND LETTERS TO HER, IN CASE IT WILL CAUSE HER SOME TROUBLE.

WE ARE GOOD BUT THE PRICES ARE HIGH HERE. WE CAN BARELY GET THE MONEY WE NEED. RECENTLY, TAIPEI WAS FILLED WITH SHANGHAI BUSINESSMEN. ALL THE FAMOUS OLD SHANGHAI BRAND STORES ARE OPENING NOW IN TAIPEI. SHANGHAI FOOD SHOPS ARE POPPING UP. EVEN THE FAMOUS SNACKS FROM OUR HOMETOWN HAVE BEEN APPEARING.

FROM TAIWAN WE HEAR THAT THE SITUATION IN THE MAINLAND HAS CHANGED DRASTICALLY; IT IS AS BAD AS WE IMAGINED. LOTS OF PEOPLE HAVE NO CONFIDENCE. THE COMMUNIST PARTY ARRESTED FIVE HUNDRED PEOPLE IN THE HOMETOWN OF ONE OF MY COLLEAGUES AND KILLED TWENTY-TWO. THEY ARE SAID TO BE THE LANDOWNERS AND "BAD ELEMENTS." ALTHOUGH THEY KILLED THE RICH PEOPLE UNDER THE AUTHORITY OF THE COMMUNIST PARTY AND TRANSFERRED POWER FROM ONE GROUP TO ANOTHER, THE SITUATION OF THE POOR FARMERS IS THE SAME. MANY DYNASTIES THROUGHOUT HISTORY HAVE COLLAPSED BECAUSE OF THE HUGE GAP BETWEEN RICH AND POOR. PEOPLE SAY

THAT THERE IS NO CORRUPTION INSIDE THE COMMUNIST
PARTY, BUT WHEN THE HONEYMOON IS OVER, THE GOVERNMENT
WILL BECOME LAZY AND DO EVERYTHING FOR ITS OWN
BENEFIT. IT IS THE EXPERIENCE OF OUR HISTORY FOR
THOUSANDS OF YEARS. MAYBE I AM TOO PESSIMISTIC, BUT IT
IS THE TRUTH.

With the U.S. government barring scientists and engineers like Ho
from leaving the United States and his family insisting that he stay
away, Ho had to face the possibility of remaining in a country that he
had never intended to make his home.

Ho examined his situation squarely: He was now cleared to get a
job, but he noted that he was twenty-five and that it was time for him
to think about marriage. Among the Chinese students in America, he
estimated there were almost ten men to every woman—without a single woman in his engineering circles. Some of the men joined Chinese
fraternities with names like Alpha Lambda Phi, "FF," and Phi Lambda,
but Ho had no interest in them.

A Chinese graduate student in New York, a social scientist, completed his master's thesis on the dating habits of Chinese male students. His findings became a major topic of conversation among Ho's
compatriots: 45 percent of the male students surveyed believed that
"most of the Chinese girls [students] in the U.S. are conceited" and
play "hard to get." On the other hand, the female students polled in-
dicated by a large margin that they were interested in finding potential
marriage partners. The researcher concluded that a large proportion
of the men were daunted by the overwhelming odds against them.

Ho was determined not to become one of those discouraged men.
As he analyzed his situation, he felt that he was a strong contender in
the high-stakes competition for eligible Chinese women: He was intel-
ligent; his visa was clean; he had a job with a bright future as an engineer. He came from a good family. Had he been in China, his mother
and other family members would have already vetted potential mates,
possibly even making the selection for him. But stuck in America, he
would have to find a wife without family assistance or interference.
On this matter too, he was truly on his own.

TAIWAN, EARLY SPRING 1949

FROM THE MOMENT THAT HER PLANE LANDED ON THE AIRSTRIP of Songshan Airport on the northern edge of Taipei, the island's capital, Annuo had the uneasy feeling that things might not go as well as they all hoped. The sighs of relief after the airless flight on the cargo plane turned to gasps of dismay when the airplane door opened to a suffocating gust of hot, humid air. Annuo began peeling off the many layers of heavy winter clothes she had donned in Hangzhou's cold March weather. Her seventeen-year-old brother, Charley, and little sister, Li-Ning, ten, were doing the same, along with everyone else on the plane. The sudden shock of intense heat seemed to catch the grown-ups by surprise too.

Outside, the wilting sun beat down on Annuo as steam rose from the tarmac; the damp air on her clammy skin leached away the joy she had felt for their safe landing. What else should they have known about this place? Even the remote village in Jiangxi Province after her family's four-month trek five years earlier had seemed more inviting than this.

At least her father's former superior officer, General Han Deqin, was waiting for their arrival. He had been the governor of the Nationalist resistance forces in Jiangsu. Annuo had known his children from the days after the Japanese war when they, too, had lived in Hangzhou.

Her father had become a civilian then, but General Han had stayed in Chiang's government and was now an official with the Nationalist regime in Taipei.

Good luck now touched Annuo's family: General Han had found a house for them to rent, when so many newly arrived refugees had nowhere to live. On that first hot car ride from the airport, Annuo found that the heavy scent of earth, flowers, and greenery reminded her of the West Lake in Hangzhou on a steamy summer day. But she was shocked to see thousands of idle soldiers huddled by tents and lean-tos along the roads and railway tracks, many clad only in their undershirts and rolled-up khaki pants. This is the defeated Nationalist army, she realized, hunkering by their makeshift shelters, smoking, playing cards, swatting at flies and mosquitoes.

As the family drove through Taipei, the houses at the city's edge were unlike anything she had known before—small one-story frame houses with curved, Japanese-style roofs and windows. The local people looked even more alien to her, dressed in baggy, shapeless clothes that she associated with Shanghai's rickshaw pullers and coolies, not smartly dressed city folks. They had sun-browned skin and wore wooden sandals on bare feet, their legs without stockings to cover their red mosquito welts. Annuo stared in surprise, unable to find any similarity to her previous life. She had not known what to expect, but it would not have been this.

ANNUO'S FIRST IMPRESSIONS WERE no different from those of hundreds of thousands of other refugees from the mainland who were arriving in hordes and overwhelming the six million locals who lived on the island. Four hundred years earlier, Portuguese traders had dubbed the lush tropical island *Ilha Formosa* or Beautiful Island. *Formosa* was the name the other Western imperial powers adopted. To the local people it was simply *Taiwan*.

Most of Taiwan's residents were ethnic Chinese from Fujian Province, who had been crossing the hundred-mile strait for generations. They subsisted on the fertile green island by farming and fishing. After the First Sino-Japanese war ended in 1895, a defeated China had ceded Taiwan to Japan, which planned to turn the island into a show-case of its expansionist designs on the rest of Asia. Imperial Japan built schools, railroads, coal mines, factories, and hospitals, raising literacy rates and living standards. It also banned the local language and culture, forcing the Taiwanese to adopt Japanese language, hous-ing, clothing, and customs. Japan controlled the government and in-dustry with close oversight of people's lives. Taiwanese who cooperated with their colonizers were rewarded, while those who resisted were crushed.

Annuo's family, like many newly arrived refugees, was completely unaware of the simmering resentment by the local Taiwanese toward the Nationalists. Upon Japan's surrender in 1945, Chiang Kai-shek's Republic of China had taken over control of Taiwan. The Taiwanese had initially welcomed their Chinese brethren, but the victorious Na-tionalists came to the island as conquerors, treating the locals as enemy subjects. The new masters from the Chinese mainland proved harsher than the Japanese, setting off a firestorm one day by cracking down on a woman peddler, then shooting into a crowd of protestors. A mass uprising began the next day, on February 28, 1947. In the days that followed, the Nationalists killed thousands of Taiwanese, inflicting "a reign of terror, probably unequalled in the history of the [Nationalist] government," according to Shanghai newspaper editor John W. Pow-ell. The Nationalist military imposed martial law on Taiwan, just as it later would in Shanghai—arresting and executing Taiwanese leaders, teachers, and intellectuals, shutting down newspapers and suppressing dissent. By the time Annuo's family arrived in 1949—two years after 2-28—more than a million Nationalist loyalists, family members, and supporters had already fled to Taiwan in their desperate retreat, with many more on the way. Most were too immersed in their own trauma to notice the island's tensions. In Taipei, an area known as *machang ding*—horse field—had been an execution ground for dissidents. That was where Annuo and her family would live.

THE HOUSE IN *MACHANG DING* was another shock. Annuo and Char-ley ran ahead of their parents into the small covered hallway and into two empty rooms. There were no closets, no chairs, just bare walls and thin sliding doors of wood and paper. The floors of both rooms were covered with a woven straw mat.

They listened quietly as General Han explained that this was a Japanese-style house with no beds or chairs. They would sit, eat, and sleep on the woven straw floor that the Japanese called tatami. A primitive charcoal fire burner in the outer hallway was for cooking and heating water. "After all," he reminded them, "this island suffered as a Japanese colony for fifty years. Many of the customs are more Japanese than Chinese." Annuo remembered the disparaging words of her seventh uncle, spoken months ago: The people in Taiwan still thought they were Japanese.

Then she recalled his other major complaint about Taiwan—in a Japanese-style house, there was no toilet or indoor plumbing. Outside, behind the house was a hole in the ground that served as a latrine. To use it, they would have to squat. Once a week, workers would come to clean out the waste, much as the night-soil collectors made their rounds each morning through the *lilongs* of Shanghai, taking the human waste for use as fertilizer in neighboring farming villages. According to her mother, this also spread contagion and parasites, and that was why nearly all children in China had to take giant pills to expel the worms that infected their bowels.

Cooking? How would they make do here with no servants and no money to hire any? Annuo wondered. She had never seen her mother cook or clean, except for the brief time when her father had left them to join the Nationalist resistance. Yet she seemed as unperturbed as always. Though the brunt of their many moves across China had fallen on Annuo's elegant mother, she never complained and would certainly have never caused Annuo's father to lose face in front of the general. The unspoken lesson for Annuo was that she should never voice her dissatisfaction. Her mother thanked the general with a demure smile and a gentle nod of her head. Not a hair was out of place, despite the warm, humid air and the long plane ride. She's the graceful swan, Annuo reflected. If only I could be more like her instead of the clumsy, ugly duckling. Then maybe my father would like me.

"No thanks necessary; don't be so polite," the general replied.

"Your husband has been one of my finest officers and a true stalwart of our Nationalist cause." Then he cleared his throat and looked at Annuo's father.

"There is one more thing: I'm sorry but I could not find employment for a man of your caliber—there are many educated and skilled men fleeing to Taiwan from all over China but not enough suitable positions."

For a moment, her eloquent father said nothing. It was true that more than a million Nationalists had retreated from the mainland, overwhelming the island's resources. Further, the entire Nationalist government was in disarray: The national administration on the mainland was disintegrating but had not surrendered. Though Generalissimo Chiang had resigned from the presidency of China, he retained the title of supreme commander of the armed forces and party leader and had set himself up in Taipei with his closest circle—and almost all of China's treasury. A vast number of formerly high-ranking Nationalist officials and intellectuals from all over China had descended on Taiwan, an island smaller in area and population than most mainland provinces. The new government would have far fewer positions available. Already the party factions and competing military cliques were jockeying for power. General Han advised Annuo's father to wait and see what kind of patronage jobs would emerge.

But Annuo's family had left Shanghai with little money. Even when her father was working, money flowed so freely from his hands that his family was often living on the edge. To Annuo, it seemed her family's finances had been best with her mother in charge. In those days, they had sometimes even had money for special treats.

Her father spoke up. "Sir, you know better than anyone that I served during the war and sacrificed without any thought of material gain. In coming to Taiwan, I had to leave everything behind."

General Han raised his hand to interrupt. "No need to say more. I will lend you whatever money your family needs until an appropriate position opens up for you."

Before the general turned to leave, he offered the family an admonition: With so many refugees streaming in, they needed to be vigilant against the constant danger of Communist spies and subversives who were attempting to sneak onto the island. Passports and identification papers of new arrivals were being checked closely since most refugees were not well-known Nationalists like Annuo's father. In addition, some of the Taiwanese were malcontents, unhappy with the return of Chinese rule, the general warned. The Nationalists had been able to subdue the 2-28 Taiwanese uprising in 1947, but the military had had to impose martial law on the island to root out and eliminate trouble-makers. "You must all beware and stick with other trusted National-ists from the mainland," he cautioned.

ANNUO WATCHED IN ADMIRATION as her mother attacked the chal-lenge presented by their Japanese home. If any of the children dared to complain about the uncomfortable house or the primitive latrine, their mother reminded them they could have done much worse. "We're lucky that we're not living in a tent or lean-to shanty like the people along the roadside," she told her children. Annuo was old enough to appreciate her mother's ability to dig in and make the best of every daunting situation.

Venturing beyond the thin walls of their Japanese house was no less of a challenge. Mosquitoes, cockroaches, lizards, and snakes were everywhere. People clunked by, clip-clop, in their Japanese-style wooden sandals called geta. Those locals stared right back at Annuo and her family—their citified clothes, leather shoes, and pale skin broadcast "newly arrived mainlander" to all. The Taiwanese called them *wai sheng ren*, as they dubbed all outsiders, while calling them-selves *ben sheng ren*, meaning those who belong. Remembering Gen-eral Han's warning about possible local hostility, the new arrivals kept their distance and remained cautious.

In those first weeks in Taipei, Annuo stuck close to her mother when she went shopping each morning at the street markets. Although Annuo and her parents could speak a number of different Chinese dia-lects, none was of use at the neighborhood stores. The Taiwanese dia-lect was most similar to that of Fujian Province, the nearest part of the Chinese mainland to the island, and completely different from the northern dialects they knew. By using gestures and facial expressions to indicate what she wanted, Annuo's mother was able to buy the essentials: rice, eggs, some vegetables. A pot and some charcoal bricks.

Dinner at the little Japanese house posed a special challenge. Annuo's mother had never before cooked on such a primitive stove. As she fussed with the charcoal and matches, nothing would light. At some point she must have recalled some distant memory of Zhongying preparing the fire. She sent Annuo scurrying to collect some dried twigs and grass for kindling. Soon, the smell of fresh rice cooking permeated the two small rooms. But anticipation turned to dismay as dark smoke billowed from the pot with the pungent odor of burning rice. That night they ate in silence, chewing slowly as they scraped away the hard, burned grains.

As usual, her mother displayed neither distress nor disappointment. Breaking the awkward silence, Annuo's father suggested that they pretend they were munching on a succulent morsel of Jinhua ham.

Charley chimed in: "Mmmm, the rice is much more delicious than the mush we had to eat during the war."

Annuo offered, "This is almost as good as the hard-boiled eggs we ate along the mountain trails in Jiangxi."

Soon they were giggling over their first cooked meal in their Japanese house.

To everyone's relief, her mother mastered the stove, and they were soon eating fluffy white grains again. In a few weeks, edible and even tasty meals were coming out of their mother's tiny kitchen. Annuo recognized the look on her mother's face as she tackled the Japanese house—it was the same resolute expression as when she'd dispatched the Japanese soldiers who pounded on their door in occupied Shanghai. As then, Annuo's mother was determined to do whatever was necessary for her family's safety and well-being.

THE MOST DRAMATIC CHANGE in Annuo's family routine involved her father. He had been absent for most of her life, serving as the Nationalist magistrate in Guizhou, fighting the Japanese in Jiangsu and Jiangxi Provinces, and working in Shanghai as a salt merchant. Suddenly he was ever present. Whereas he used to direct his soldiers, now he lorded over his wife and children. Everything that Annuo and her siblings did came under his constant scrutiny, command, and control.

As the family's supreme commander, her father imposed rules and restrictions without explanation. Given Taipei's limited public transportation, many children rode bicycles to school. However, the Liu children were forbidden to ride bikes at all. It didn't matter that the bus system was undependable. They would just have to wait. Bicycle riding could lead to independence; independence could lead to disobedience and unacceptable dalliances.

In searching for schools for the children, Annuo's parents quickly learned that the most acclaimed secondary school for girls in Taiwan was the Taipei First Girls' High School, located in the heart of Taipei, next to the main government building. The beautiful school grounds were enclosed by a tall fence with access through a main gate, much like the finest private schools in Shanghai.

It was Annuo herself who decided that she wanted to attend the prestigious First Girls' High School. She couldn't stand her father's scrutiny and believed that this school could be her pathway to salvation. She had heard that its graduates were virtually guaranteed a spot at the top college, the National Taiwan University or Tai Da, as it was known. Graduates of Tai Da had the best shot at getting a visa to attend graduate school abroad. If only she could attend the First Girls' High School, she might be able to get away from this suffocating island of Taiwan.

Because Annuo's family had arrived in Taiwan near the end of the school year, she would normally have had to wait until school resumed in September. But because the exodus to Taiwan in 1949 had brought a deluge of school-aged children to the island, the Nationalists created an extra school term over the summer to accommodate the huge influx. Special midyear school entrance examinations were to be held to determine which schools the newly arrived students would attend. Only those who scored in the top 1 percent could hope to get into the best girls' or boys' schools.

Once again, Annuo's future depended on a test. To get into the First Girls' High School, she would be competing with other exiled students from all over China. On the day of the exam, Annuo swore to herself that if she was admitted, she would work harder in this school than she had ever done before.

Days later, Annuo took a bus to the school to see the posted results. She had to find her name listed somewhere on the long sheets of paper with students ranked in order, with the top scores first. To her astonishment, her name was near the top. She was one of the approximately one hundred who had made it into the special off-term session at the school of her dreams. Annuo rubbed her eyes, thinking that it might be a mistake. Then she looked again. Her name was still there.

Until this point, the fourteen-year-old had thought of herself as little more than a thistle burr, riding along to whatever place war and circumstance took her. But as her mother reminded her, Annuo was the same age as her grandmother at the time she had married and then learned to manage her own household. Now, Annuo told herself, it was time for her to have a hand in her own future. School would provide the means.

But she would have to bide her time. Meanwhile, her father drew the circle around her even tighter. She was not permitted to visit other children at their homes for fear that she could fall under bad influences. For the same reason, there could be no school trips with her classes or going out with friends. Without his vigilant presence, who knew what harmful spell might befall his children? She was not allowed to learn how to type—no reason was given. No listening to music, which could create a distraction and was a definite corrupting influence. No dancing or contact with the opposite sex for his now-teenaged children—it didn't matter that he had taught Annuo and her younger sister to dance.

The suffocating rules were bad enough, but her father's disapproving eye was especially drawn to her. She couldn't do anything right. Even when she did nothing, he found fault in her. Her lips were too thick, her nose ugly; her teeth were bad and her legs too short and stubby. "She just isn't right," her father would say about her. Annuo had heard it all before, but in Hangzhou her father had often been away. In Taiwan, her father glared at her constantly. She felt trapped in her own house. The martial law wielded over the entire island now permeated their home as her father channeled to his family, with Annuo as chief scapegoat, the fear and paranoia that had propelled the retreating Nationalists to the island.

WITH THE MASS EXODUS to Taiwan continuing unabated, Supreme Commander Chiang Kai-shek kept Taiwan on a constant state of high alert. As one newspaper reported, "Taiwan has seen perhaps the greatest influx of population in its history [with] high government officials, rich business men, landlords and precious cargo from panic-stricken Communist-threatened Shanghai [fleeing] to this island." Vigilance against Communist infiltration was essential, the Nationalist government warned, and every man, woman, and child had to be prepared to defend the island against a Communist invasion.

The ever-present threat of Communist infiltration helped to keep any discontent at bay, as did the fearsome secret police force, which crushed Chinese dissent and suppressed the local Taiwanese population with arrest, abduction, imprisonment, and execution. This harsh Nationalist police state became known as the White Terror, the same name given to Chiang's extermination campaign against leftists and labor leaders two decades earlier in Shanghai.

Annuo's father fell right in step with the Nationalists' obsession with Communist infiltrators and Taiwanese troublemakers. He informed his family that it would be better for them to die than to live under Communism. "If the Red Bandits come to Taiwan, I will kill myself," he declared. "I'll jump into the ocean and drown myself. And I will watch all of you jump in first," he commanded.

With news of each advance of the Red Bandits toward total victory on the mainland, the Nationalists tightened their military grip as the island exiles despaired that they would be next. Even the support of the American government was flagging. Secretary of State George Marshall, who had failed to bring the Nationalists and Communists to an agreement in 1947, had told Congress that it was "unlikely . . . that any amount of U.S. military or economic aid could make the [Chiang] government capable of reestablishing and then maintaining its control." Fortunately for the Nationalists, the "China Bloc" of conservative Republicans in Congress tied the China Aid Act of 1948 to the Marshall Plan, procuring nearly $600 million in combined economic and military aid for Chiang's government.

But gone were the days when Madame Chiang Kai-shek had been invited to address Congress while staying at the White House to drum up support for the Nationalists. Annuo grew accustomed to both anger and despair filling the rooms of their little house: on the one hand, her father's bitter denunciations of the hated Communists; on the other, her mother's regret for not persuading her own mother to come with them to Taiwan.

Surrounded by pessimism and gloom, with displaced refugees like her parents mired in their yearning for the life they used to enjoy in Shanghai, Annuo and other young mainlanders could draw only one conclusion: There was no future for them in Taiwan.

ANNUO HAD TO WAKE up extra early to wait for a public bus to go to school. If she was lucky, eventually one would stop that had room for her to stand amid the sweaty crush. Though she would rather have been riding a bicycle, she was glad to get away to school. Her uniform that proclaimed her admission to the First Girls' High School was her proud badge of distinction: green blouse with a red tie, black skirt, jacket, and shoes, hair cut short to the ears. Her fellow students came from all over China—and several spoke her native Shanghai dialect. They were easy to spot. Theresa Chen-Louie had skillfully sewed her black skirt from an old pair of her brother's pants. Its A-line style *with pockets* was the envy of the school. Theresa, a McTyeire girl, had used her Shanghai style, everyone said. Still unintelligible to Annuo was the local dialect that the several Taiwanese girls spoke, though fortunately for her, classes were taught in Mandarin. The Nationalists had long ago designated the northern dialect as China's national spoken language. At the end of the day, Annuo would wait for another sweltering bus to take her on the hour-long ride back to *machang ding*. Many of her classmates visited one another's homes, but that was still taboo for Annuo.

Her jobless father connected with other idle warriors. They'd spend each day going over the news from the mainland, ruminating over the continuing civil war with the Reds, sharing gossip about the latest arrivals and which factions were in or out of Chiang's favor. Annuo's father had plenty of company. By the fall of 1949, General Bai Chongxi and his troops had retreated to Hainan Island; then they dispatched to Taiwan. That was the final defeat, for the mighty Muslim general from southern China had led one of the Nationalists' fiercest armies. Yet when General Bai arrived in Taiwan with his extended household of seventy-some people, even he found himself adrift on the small island because he was not in the generalissimo's close circle of trusted confidants. The general's son, Pai Hsien-yung, who witnessed Shanghai people like his once-powerful father reduced to aimless, dissolute lives, chronicled Taiwan's displaced and dispossessed in his acclaimed works, *Taipei People* and *Crystal Boys*.

New mainlander exiles to Taiwan arrived by boat and plane each day, stoking fears of Communist infiltration. Here, arrivals line up in Jilong, waiting to be vetted, processed, and, with luck, admitted. Many are rejected and sent to points unknown.

Annuo's father and his cronies constantly discussed possible escape routes off the island in case the unthinkable happened and Taiwan fell to the Communists. Hong Kong and Southeast Asia were too close to China. Hawaii was a favored possibility, but it would be too difficult to get a visa to the American territory. Her father talked about moving the family to Brazil, whose government seemed to be extending open arms to skilled and educated people, including Chinese. Some families left on freighters bound for Singapore, Mombasa, and Cape Town, eventually reaching South America. A girl of Annuo's age, Vivian Hsu, left with her parents and ten siblings on a two-month journey to São Paulo, intending—but not succeeding—to learn Portuguese while at sea.

Upon hearing of each potential haven, Annuo's father and his friends hatched new plans. Annuo's heart sank as her father grew excited about Brazil. How could her escape plan work if they moved yet again, this time to an area even more distant and strange? She hoped it was just bluster, the talk of men with nothing better to do. Her family barely had money to pay for groceries and bus fare, let alone passage to Brazil.

Machang ding was filled with mainlander families like hers. Some claimed that they could hear executioners' gunshots in the area. Newer arrivals still came every day, packing into already crowded homes with relatives and friends. All were marking their time on an island they had never cared for, nervously waiting for the decisive battle with the Communists that could end in their own annihilation. Countless men, who, like Annuo's father, had once held prestigious jobs, desperately schemed to get lucrative employment, get the mainland back, and get out. When more enterprising Shanghainese opened small teahouses serving *xiao long bao* and other regional foods, the exiles spent their days there, drowning in the everlasting sorrow of loss and separation from loved ones, old glory and all things familiar.

AN OPPORTUNITY AROSE OUT of this dissolute time—for Annuo's mother. With the millions of refugees on Taiwan, there was a critical shortage of doctors. To keep the lack of medical personnel from becoming a health disaster, a special program was launched to retrain doctors and other nonpracticing health professionals. Friends and acquaintances urged Annuo's mother to use her medical training.

In the Japanese-style house with its paper walls, Annuo lay on the tatami late one night, unable to sleep in the heat. Her parents were talking, and she strained to hear her mother's low voice. "My beloved father sent me to school to do some good," she said, adding, "and we could use the money."

Annuo had no problem hearing her father's response. It was immediate, angry, unequivocal. "If you start working, I will divorce you."

After that, there was only silence. Annuo wished that her mother would challenge her father's threat. She recalled her mother's stories—how she had stopped the foot-binding process that had already damaged her feet and how she had begged to go to school with her brothers. Annuo's mother had fought to become a doctor, then stifled her dreams to appease Annuo's father. Yet they had survived the many war years when he was away only because her mother had managed to find work in occupied Shanghai.

But once again, Annuo's mother acquiesced to her father. He instructed her to learn mah-jongg so that she could better entertain his many guests, and she became addicted to the game. On doctors' recommendations, she took up smoking to improve her weak heart. Annuo's father demanded her mother's constant attention. She seemed to shrink in stature, becoming little more than Annuo's father's helpmate. Annuo resolved that she would never let her potential become so diminished. She wanted to use all her talents, whatever they proved to be.

THERE WAS ONLY ONE THING that her mother couldn't accept in silence: She couldn't tolerate sitting on the floor. With surprising insistence, she'd complain that she needed a chair. Every day, at every mealtime, she twisted and fidgeted, looking awkward and uncomfortable. Her legs were too stiff; her broken feet swelled; her dresses were unsuitable, she said. Being forced to sit on the floor, Japanese style, was not only uncivilized but also unacceptable for Chinese who had risked everything to defeat that terrible enemy. She wanted a chair.

Annuo's father refused to allow her mother to get one, arguing that they wouldn't be in Taiwan long enough to justify spending their limited money on furniture. It was the only time Annuo saw her mother openly disagree with her father. His unchanging rebuttal: "There's no point in wasting money when we'll be home soon."

One day, Annuo returned from school to a big surprise: On the tatami of the main room were some wicker chairs. Her father had brought them into the little Japanese house. As usual, neither of her parents said a word about it. They acted as though the chairs had been there all along. But Annuo sensed her mother's satisfaction. She couldn't remember when her reserved mother had ever looked so pleased.

Annuo and her siblings took turns flopping onto the seats, laughing at the wonderful stiff chairs as they dangled their legs. In the midst of her fun, Annuo suddenly realized that the chairs could mean only one thing. Despite the official propaganda that a Nationalist victory was imminent, her father must have decided that they wouldn't be leaving Taiwan soon. She would not be returning to her school in Hangzhou. They would not be reuniting with their amah, Zhongying, or other family members. The sobering thought deflated her excitement.

Finally, though, Annuo's father found a job—to be the director of the fisheries bureau of an American organization. He would be paid in U.S. dollars and would even have the use of a car and driver. Her family's fortunes greatly improved and they could start repaying their debt to General Han.

ON OCTOBER 1, 1949, Mao Zedong announced the founding of the People's Republic of China. The Union of Soviet Socialist Republics (USSR) immediately recognized the Communist government, while the United States continued to treat the Republic of China on Taiwan as the sole legitimate government of China.

So it was to Chiang's great surprise and disappointment that on January 5, 1950, Truman bluntly clarified his position on China and Taiwan:

[The United States does not] have any intention of utilizing its armed forces to interfere in the present situation [in Taiwan].

The United States government will not pursue a course which will lead to involvement in the civil conflict in China. Similarly, the United States government will not provide military aid or advice to Chinese forces on Formosa [Taiwan].

The generalissimo and Madame Chiang's powerful friends in America's China lobby roundly attacked what they saw as Truman's abandonment of China to Mao's Communists. General Douglas MacArthur disagreed openly with his commander in chief's unwillingness to attack China. At the same time, Senator McCarthy began to rock the United States with rhetoric that singled out the State Department's "China Hands" for suspected Communist sympathies.

Truman's rebuff intensified the Nationalists' isolation and fears of Communist infiltration. The vise of martial law further tightened as Taiwan became an overt police state. With the island full of soldiers, the hunt for possible subversives was relentless, tightening the generalissimo's iron grip. Foreign journalists had their visas revoked if they deviated from the official line. There was no room for dissent. The label of "pro-Communist" spelled certain death.

On March 1, 1950, Chiang Kai-shek announced his return to the government's presidency, forcing out the acting president and further consolidating his control. He declared Taipei to be the "temporary capital of China." Chiang re-created his mainland government in Taipei, as though the exiled bureaucracy were still running all of China instead of a small island. With ex-governors, high-ranking officers, scholars, and officials lining up for spots on the government payroll, Chiang brought on his own trusted people at every level, pulling the military, party, and government under his authority. The local Taiwanese population found itself even more displaced. A large political prison was built on Green Island, off Taiwan's eastern coast, to lock up Taiwanese leaders far from their communities. As one businessman declared, "We Taiwanese have been made to feel like slaves to the Nationalists; we represent four-fifths of the population and have little or no say in setting our policy or choosing our leaders." With their vision of an imminent return to the mainland dashed, the Nationalist government could no longer put off housing the hundreds of thousands of soldiers and their families who huddled in makeshift tarp shelters. Chiang reorganized his army-in-retreat, building large urban residential sectors that his government called "military dependents' villages." Each military family was allotted about two hundred square feet, with thousands of them packed into flimsy, boxlike structures.

By concentrating his soldiers and their families into such military dependents' villages, Chiang was able to claim that his battle-ready troops were set to spring into action and "retake the mainland" at a moment's notice—with America's aid. Thousands of Nationalist soldiers began digging fortifications on the small island of Jinmen, barely a mile off the Chinese coast near the port city of Xiamen. From there, the Nationalists could launch their great offensive—and perhaps draw the Communists into a confrontation that would force Truman's hand.

President Chiang was biding his time, certain that the Cold War between the United States and the USSR would heat up. If another war broke out, he'd use that opportunity to obtain American support and relaunch his armies to retake the mainland. No matter how much Truman disdained the Nationalists, Chiang believed he was America's only alternative to the Chinese Communists. The island of exiles prepared to wait for America to back them up in an all-out attack on their mutual enemy.

Annuo could see signs of the growing tension everywhere. Nervously, she wondered if another war was coming. On the bus to school, she passed endless streams of patriotic banners exhorting, "We will return to the mainland fighting!" Slogans alluding to classical Chinese literature promised to "return the mountains to the water!" Though the hope of a victorious return to the mainland seemed hollow, Generalissimo Chiang continued to send bombers to attack Shanghai and other coastal cities.

Nevertheless, America under Truman was cutting its losses in China and withdrawing. Chiang's Republic of China on the island of Taiwan would have to fend for itself. With the loss of American support, a constant worry gnawed at Annuo: Her father's threat to drag them all with him into the cold, dark ocean loomed ever possible.

BING MOVED BRISKLY THROUGH THE COOL SUMMER AIR ALONG busy Columbus Avenue in San Francisco. With a tight grip on five-year-old Peter's hand, she was headed to the sidewalk greengrocers of Chinatown to get some inexpensive food to tide them over until Elder Sister could find a solution to their latest predicament.

A few days earlier, Kristian and ten-year-old Ole had boarded a train to New York, where they would transfer to a Denmark-bound ship. The family was nearing the end of its cash, and Kristian needed to tap into his pension and bank account in Denmark. Once he arrived in Copenhagen, he would wire the money for the others to join him. Before he left, Kristian had reached into his thin leather wallet and handed Elder Sister fifty dollars.

"What is this?" Elder Sister had asked, incredulous. "How long do you think this will last us?"

"I'm sorry, darling, but that's all I can spare," he answered calmly. "Ole and I have to get all the way to New York, then Denmark, with barely enough for the tickets. If anyone can make a go of it, you can. At least the room is paid up to the end of the month."

Elder Sister made no further protest. Kristian was right—she had supported seven family members through the wartime occupation with only her Shanghai charm and savvy. Bing wasn't worried either—her supremely confident elder sister could do anything.

On her way back to the rooming house, Bing took a route along Stockton Street into the Italian area of North Beach. She noticed that there were few Chinese beyond Columbus Avenue. People glared at her with long hard looks that made her uncomfortable. It was different from the admiring stares she got in Chinatown, where men rushed to the doors and windows of every restaurant and shop to gawk as she walked by. She ignored them all, tossing her permed hair back and keeping her head high, as any Shanghai miss would.

Bing was equally curious about these inhabitants of Chinatown. If it weren't for their faces, the calligraphy on shop signs, and a few fake-looking pagodas, Bing wouldn't have recognized anything Chinese about the place. Moreover, the majority of residents were from the Taishan region of Guangdong Province, far to the south of Shanghai. Bing couldn't make sense of their Toisan dialect. To communicate, Bing was forced to use the bits of English she had picked up from Kristian and Elder Sister. At first, Bing felt self-conscious about it, but soon she realized that she knew enough to get by.

Elder Sister hadn't been idle either. With only a few days' rent left at the rooming house, "Betty Woo" had gone to work in search of eligible bachelors for Bing—at the better restaurants and business establishments, family association halls and social clubs, even some fancy nightclubs. It wasn't hard to find them. The draconian Chinese Exclusion Act of 1882, which had barred most Chinese from entering the United States, had been repealed in 1943 to keep China in the Allied fold. But a quota was immediately imposed that limited immigration to 105 Chinese each year—from any country in the world. But the decades of restrictive laws had forced Chinatown to be a bachelor society by excluding almost all Chinese women, and barring Chinese men already in the United States from becoming citizens or marrying American women. Still, Elder Sister didn't want just any bachelor for Bing. He had to have a future, U.S. citizenship, or a green card—and enough money to repay Elder Sister for Bing's passage to America. On her very first foray, Elder Sister found a prospect and invited the young man to the rooming house to meet Bing.

AT THE APPOINTED TIME, Bing waited nervously in the front hall of their building. Because she had entered the United States on a visitor visa, she knew that she would have to find a man to marry within six months if she wanted to stay in the country. She wasn't as picky as Elder Sister, but she had standards too. She made a hasty appraisal of the young Chinese fellow who approached the door: He was tall and slender with his hair slicked back, neatly dressed in a buttoned cardigan sweater over his shirt and slacks. He looks pleasant enough, Bing thought. And very American.

"You must be Bing," he said with an easy smile. "I'm Raymond. Your sister said to come by and meet you."

Bing nodded. "I'm very pleased to meet you." She spoke slowly and carefully in her best English.

He looked relieved. "Good, you speak English. Can you speak Toisan?" he asked.

"No. I speak Shanghai dialect. And some Mandarin. Do you?"

When he shook his head, she added, "That's okay. I understand your English. You sound just like an American."

"Well, I'd better talk like an American," he laughed. "I was younger than that little guy when I got here." He nodded toward Peter. "Say, would you like to go for a walk and some lunch?"

With Peter as her chaperone, Bing walked with Raymond to Portsmouth Square, a pleasant little park at the edge of Chinatown. They strolled to the Ferry Building, where Raymond pointed out the graceful Bay Bridge. "I stood right there along the Embarcadero when the bridge opened in 1936," he said proudly.

Back in Chinatown, Raymond took Bing and Peter to a luncheonette on Waverly Place that was busy with local Chinese. Raymond ordered a "combo" lunch—a new word for Bing—with thick pieces of tenderized beef in heavy brown gravy, fried rice, an egg roll, and wonton soup. Bing noted that she'd never seen such food in China. Amused, Raymond explained that in America, Chinese had to make do with the local ingredients to prepare food that non-Chinese would eat. "*Bok wai* are afraid to try food that is too different," he said, using the Toisanese word for "white devil." Bing liked his forthright manner, how he told her about America without showing off, the way some Shanghai boys might. "If the *bok wai* didn't eat Chinese food, we would starve to death. Even educated Chinese can't find work in America except in laundries and restaurants." Raymond himself worked as a waiter in Chinatown, on the evening shift that didn't end until late at night, after other Chinatown workers finished their workdays and grabbed some supper at the local restaurants.

With her arrival in San Francisco, on May 28, 1949, Bing hoped that her life would be better in America—or Denmark—than it had been in China.

Raymond walked Bing back to the rooming house. After Bing thanked him and took Peter to their room for his nap, Elder Sister asked Raymond to chat.

"My sister is a wonderful girl, don't you think?" Betty purred in honey-laced tones.

When Raymond agreed, Betty pressed on. "A lot of young men will be interested in marrying her, but I want to make sure she finds a good man with a future in America. Do you have a job? A green card?" After he nodded yes to both, Elder Sister smiled and told him how pleased she was. She lowered her voice conspiratorially. "We have a problem. Because of the Communists, we left China in such a hurry that we have very little money to live on. Any man who is serious about my sister must first pay me back one thousand dollars for her boat ticket and the bond."

Raymond gave a long low whistle. "You might as well ask for the moon! Not many guys in Chinatown have that kind of money."

To keep from losing Bing's potential suitor, Elder Sister changed her tone to cushion the blow. "Don't worry about it now; maybe you have some friends who can help you out if you really like her. But don't wait too long. We could be deported if I don't get some financial help soon." Looking up at Raymond through her eyelashes, she had an idea. "Maybe young guys like you don't have much money, but do you know of any older men? I'm going to divorce my old man. Maybe there's someone you can introduce me to?"

At first Raymond said nothing and sucked on his teeth. Then he offered, "I know a fellow who's Cantonese, but I've heard him say he'd like to meet a Shanghai lady. His name's Lee Chou. He's kind of flashy, but you might like that." He took a good, long look at Betty, assessing her carefully. "I'll find out if he'd like to meet you. Maybe he can help you out."

Raymond decided not to pursue Bing, but he kept to his word about Lee. Within days, a mustachioed Chinese man in a zoot suit, looking to be in his forties, came to visit Elder Sister. She was ready for him, dressed in her most alluring red *qipao*, complete with padded bra, girdle, handbag, and matching red high heels.

"Elder Sister, you look like a movie star," Bing said admiringly before going to answer the door. She knew that she'd never come close to achieving her sister's special appeal.

Betty touched up her lipstick. "Thanks, Bing. Wish me luck," she said with a wink.

If Lee was looking for a Shanghai bombshell, Betty was TNT. He took her to the Forbidden City, Chinatown's swanky nightclub, for dinner and a show. Before the evening was over, he asked Betty to marry him. Betty was ready with her pitch: She liked him plenty but couldn't marry him until she divorced her husband in Denmark, which she intended to do after he sent for her. In the meantime, she could be deported because in a week they'd run out of cash and had nowhere to go.

Without hesitation, Lee offered to find a place for her, Bing, and Peter if Betty would marry him after her divorce. She agreed.

The next day, Lee rented a three-room cottage on Broadway, a few blocks beyond the north edge of Chinatown. He outfitted the place with furniture, dishes, and cookware, whatever they needed. Bing, Elder Sister, and Peter took two rooms, while Lee slept in a small room off the kitchen. He even gave Elder Sister cash for groceries.

With their rental at the rooming house coming to an end, Lee's timing was perfect. Bing was astonished that he was so generous with them—and that he had accepted Elder Sister's terms. He demanded nothing and was never at the cottage except to sleep—in his own room. He didn't seem to have a job, yet he always had money. Bing wondered if he was a gangster. She kept her speculations to herself, though, not wanting to be disrespectful to Elder Sister.

With their living arrangements secure, Betty forged ahead to snare Bing a husband. "If your visa runs out before we find you a man with a green card to marry, you'll have to come with me to Denmark. There, you'll have to get married too—and in Denmark, there are only white men to choose from." Bing agreed that she'd be better off with a Chinese husband in America. She would accept whatever fate had in store, as she had always done. "Don't worry," Elder Sister said. "You're young and pretty. Men are like dogs; they'll come sniffing. I'll find you a nice one."

Raymond continued to stop by on occasion, just as a friend. Sometimes he'd take Bing and Peter out for a matinee at the Great Star Theater in Chinatown or for lunch at Clinton's Cafeteria, a popular place for *lofan*—meaning non-Chinese or "foreigners" in Cantonese. Bing enjoyed his insights on America. It was well known in Chinatown, he told her, that many Chinese were "paper sons" or "paper daughters" with questionable immigration documents. In the big San Francisco earthquake and fire in 1906, all the city birth records had been destroyed—creating an opportunity for a few generations of Chinese, mostly from Guangdong Province, to claim an American-born Chinese father whose wife had been forced to stay in China because of the exclusion laws. This allowed the reputed offspring to be admitted into the United States as citizens—if they could convince immigration inspectors. It was a difficult route into the United States, involving lengthy imprisonment with many months of grueling interrogations at Angel Island Immigration Station in San Francisco Bay. But it was worth it for those who passed the questioning and were allowed to enter the country. According to Raymond, many of the people in Chinatown had this kind of paper trail.

No one Bing met would ever admit to being a paper son, not when the INS was eager to deport almost every Chinese. But several suitors cautioned her to be wary as she went about her quest for a citizen or permanent resident to marry before her visa expired. Some of the stories they told her sent chills down her spine—about Chinese who had been targeted and lynched by mobs of angry white devils in California and elsewhere; about harsh, selective enforcement by immigration agents against Chinese and other Asians, often leading to imprisonment and deportation. She had to be alert, some warned, because INS snitches were everywhere, ready to pounce on any Chinese with false papers. Bing began to wonder if she'd be better off in Denmark.

Raymond admonished her to stay away from Chinatown slicks who ran illegal gambling parlors. These gangsters kidnapped girls to work as prostitutes, he said, and they had guns. "You're a sweet kid, and people may take your kindness for weakness. Your sister knows how the game is played. Stick close to her. If you get in trouble, don't bother with the *lofan* police. They won't help a Chinese," he added. Raymond offered to help Bing get a job harvesting flowers at farms in San Jose. "They're always looking for field workers. The pay is seventy-five cents an hour. Off the books," he told Bing, lowering his voice.

Bing listened politely to Raymond's ideas, but she couldn't risk getting caught by the INS. Besides, a proper Shanghai girl wouldn't work as a field hand, to become as stoop-backed and brown-skinned as farmers in China. Hearing the difficulties of other Chinese in America made her both anxious and grateful that her own dubious papers hadn't been detected on the ship. Bing had her paper secrets too. Elder Sister warned her never to utter a word about her forged passport to anyone.

Elder Sister also reminded Bing to keep her adoption a secret. But

Bing already knew too well the stigma of being abandoned and adopted. She had been the empty bottle, not worth keeping. Who would want to marry a girl who didn't know her parents' names or her birth date? Bing was immeasurably grateful to Elder Sister for treating her like a real sister and presenting her to the world as her own flesh and blood. Of course Bing would never reveal this secret.

Some of the suitors caught her attention. Bing especially liked one handsome fellow who took her and Peter to lunch at Woolworth's, in fancy Union Square, just beyond Chinatown. Almost all of the people in that busy square were *lofan*. Bing was charmed by the young man's kind disposition. He worked at a restaurant and seemed to like her. After "the talk" with Elder Sister, Bing was surprised that he still wanted to see her. Could it mean something more?

On their next date, he took her and her ever-present young chaperone to an ice-skating show in downtown San Francisco. Bing had a fun afternoon with him, and on the way back to the cottage on Broadway, they stopped and sat in a park while Peter chased pigeons.

"I like you a lot, Bing," he said, "but what your sister is asking for is impossible. This is our last time out. I thought I'd show you a good time because I won't be coming back."

Bing looked down at her feet. "I'm sorry," she said. "You've treated me very well. Thank you for everything."

Before he left, he offered a parting thought. "You know, a lot of guys say to watch out for Shanghai girls; they're out to hustle you. You're not like that at all. But your sister is something else."

Bing didn't mind saying goodbye to him—or any of them. She had learned years before not to get too close to anyone. Still, she was beginning to worry that the price Elder Sister was asking of her suitors was too high. Or could her bad luck be following her from Shanghai?

Elder Sister, however, wasn't waiting for luck to find them. "You make your own luck," she insisted. Instead of resting on the largesse of Lee, her unwitting benefactor, she'd been conducting her own reconnaissance to follow the money in Chinatown. Early in Chinatown's history, having been largely ignored and disenfranchised by the city's politicians, the Chinese had developed their own network of governance, with powerful associations organized by occupation, ancestral hometowns, and family clans. Betty sashayed her way through the various headquarters, which were almost entirely male.

One of the most influential organizations in Chinatown was the Chinese Consolidated Benevolent Association, which handled the community's relations with San Francisco's mainstream society. It was staunchly loyal to the Nationalists, whose defeat in China only intensified the organization's anti-Communist fervor. Chiang Kai-shek's portrait hung inside its main hall, along with a prominent display of the Nationalist flag. Signs of the civil war and ideological divisions were ever present in Chinatowns everywhere. The blood feuds, internecine accusations, political surveillance, and gang thuggery reminded Betty of occupied Shanghai. She was on familiar ground.

Mustering all the appeal of a sophisticated Shanghai lady, Betty charmed and teased the prominent elders of Chinatown. One, a lawyer with the surname Yee, belonged to the large Yee Family Association. Betty wasted no time in telling him about her beautiful, innocent, and marriageable sister—and the quandary of her visa. "She has big eyes, full lips, and a nice shape—and she can cook! She'll be a great catch for some lucky guy," Betty assured him. The lawyer happened to know of a fellow clansman, John Yee of New York City, who was visiting relatives in neighboring Oakland, across the bay. According to the lawyer, John Yee was a fortyish widower who worked for a bank and was looking for a wife.

Betty arranged for John to meet Bing at the cottage. When the portly, balding man approached, Bing felt a moment of panic. He looked old enough to be her father. If he was truly forty, he was twice her age. As Elder Sister went to the door, she reminded Bing that Kristian was thirty years older than she. Bing calmed herself and looked more closely. The man had a genial smile. He was wearing a suit, something none of the other men she had dated owned, and he brought her flowers. Since he spoke Chinese in the Toisan dialect, they conversed in English.

"I'm very glad to meet you, Bing," he said, bowing slightly. "Would you care to join me for lunch?"

Bing suppressed a giggle. He was so formal. "I'm happy to join you for lunch. Would you mind if my nephew Peter joins us?"

"Of course," he replied with a cheerful smile.

They went to Sam Wo, an inexpensive eatery where Bing had gone with other suitors. But John Yee seemed different. Unlike many of the other men, he didn't just talk about himself—he wanted to know about her. Bing painted a bright but vague picture, careful not to hint at her difficulties. She learned that John Yee's wife had died years before and they'd had no children. He had lived in New York's Chinatown for many years, working as a teller with the Bank of China. He was taking a month's vacation to visit his sister and brother who lived and worked in Oakland. He told her stories about New York and asked her about her life in Shanghai.

When lunch was over, he asked Bing if she'd like to see him again. She paused. She liked his gentle personality. He seemed kind and cheerful, with a ready smile. His employer was one of the biggest banks under the Nationalist government. That seemed more promising than a restaurant or laundry. Bing answered that she'd be glad to see him again.

They met the next day for lunch. Bing felt safe and secure in his presence. Since he was staying with his sister in Oakland, he had to take a ferry or a bus all the way to San Francisco to meet her. That impressed Bing as well. Timing was a problem, though, as his vacation would end soon, and he'd have to return to New York.

At the end of the second date, Elder Sister pulled him aside: If he wanted to marry Bing, he would have to pay two thousand dollars for the travel costs plus the immigration bond. Listening in the next room, Bing stifled a gasp. That was double what Elder Sister had told the other men!

John was taken aback. Two thousand dollars was a huge sum. He was a frugal man who had worked hard to save his money as a bank teller, not a Bank of China magnate like T. V. Soong or H. H. Kung. He told Betty that he wasn't sure and would consider her terms on his way back to New York. When he said goodbye to Bing, he spoke gently but didn't mince words. "I like you a lot, but I have to think about it. Is your sister marrying you off or selling you?"

———

ELDER SISTER HAD A sixth sense about people—and she could smell money. She had instantly sized up John Yee: He was older than the others who were interested in Bing; he had worked for years at a bank, which had to pay more than a Chinese restaurant; and he was a Cantonese, as notorious for their thrift as Shanghainese were for their extravagance: He had surely saved plenty.

There was another reason why Betty had doubled her price. She hadn't received a single letter from her husband or son to confirm that they had arrived safely in Denmark. Kristian was supposed to wire her money to pay for her travel to Denmark—and they might need a ticket for Bing as well if they hadn't found a suitable husband by then. Betty couldn't string Lee along forever. It was only a matter of time before he tired of waiting—and supporting them. She needed a fall-back strategy, just in case.

A month went by, and there was no word from John Yee. Bing figured that Elder Sister had asked for too much. She hadn't told Elder Sister what he had said about her, but she hadn't forgotten either. To dispel any doubts, Elder Sister insisted, "He'll come around. You'll see."

In the meantime, other suitors continued to call on Bing. Word was out that she was still available. But Bing wasn't interested. She didn't want to start seeing someone new without knowing if she should wait for John. She liked his easy and pleasant manner. That he was older no longer concerned her. Rather, his age brought more security and stability, something she'd never known.

Bing didn't know what she'd do if John Yee declined. She had learned of another young Chinese woman in her neighborhood who was struggling with her visa situation. Margaret Soong, a flight attendant with CNAC, the Chinese airline, had landed in the United States just after the Communist victory in Shanghai. Several CNAC pilots had defected to mainland China with the airline's planes, but Margaret faced deportation as a stranded crew member. Luckily for her, another guest at her hotel was a well-known Catholic priest, Reverend John T. S. Mao, who tirelessly worked to find scholarships for Chinese

Christian students to attend American colleges. He was helping Margaret to stay, but college wasn't an option for Bing, whose formal education had ended in third grade.

ONE DAY IN MID-SEPTEMBER, a telegram arrived at long last. It was from Denmark—but sent by Kristian's brother. Elder Sister's husband had fallen ill on the transatlantic ship to Denmark. He'd been hospitalized as soon as the ship reached Copenhagen. Poor Ole, not knowing a word of Danish, had been living with his uncle's family for more than two months.

The telegram ended with: COME TO DENMARK. DO NOT DELAY.

Elder Sister had to act quickly. She didn't have enough money to get to Denmark. But her best prospect was John Yee in New York. She went to a pay phone and called his sister in Oakland. "Hello, Florence? This is Betty—you remember me, Betty Woo from Shanghai? Your brother John was interested in marrying my sister? We have to leave for Denmark soon. Can you let your brother know? If he wants to marry Bing, he better not waste any time, or she'll be gone."

John Yee got the message. Bing seemed like a sweet girl. She was more beautiful and had a nicer disposition than he'd hoped for. She didn't mind if he took her to cafeterias and other cheap places and didn't seem like the pampered wives of rich Chinatown merchants who played mah-jongg all day and flaunted their wealth. But two thousand dollars was an incredible sum. It couldn't possibly have cost that much to bring her to the United States. That was almost his entire life savings in America, squeezed from decades of work in the menial jobs relegated to Chinese. He'd gone to night school to learn basic bookkeeping and to improve his English. Only after that had he been able to work his way into a teller's job.

On the other hand, he had been widowed for so long, and there were few potential Chinese brides in the United States. He liked the way she treated her nephew—she'd be a good mother if he was lucky enough to have children. But she was so young. Would she really want to be with a man more than twice her age? He had lied when he'd told the elder sister that he was only forty.

John turned to his boss and closest friend—Berne Lee, the manager of his bank branch—for advice. Berne had given him the chance to work there when it had first opened in New York many years earlier. Back then, Chinese hadn't trusted banks and had been especially hesitant about one headquartered in China. Chinese-language newspapers, even in faraway America, ran stories about China's bank failures, currency collapses, and rampant corruption. To win over customers, John and Berne had gone door to door, tenement by tenement, educating restaurant workers, laundrymen, sailors, and merchants in Chinatown about banks and how their money would be safer in one—and earn interest. The two men succeeded in getting enough deposits to sustain the Chinatown branch of the Bank of China on the Bowery. Moreover, Berne was one of the few married men in Chinatown. He would know what to do.

John presented his worries to his good friend: the money, Bing's youth, the domineering sister. The fact that he had already used up all his vacation time on his recent trip. Berne addressed each point. If John needed more money, Berne would help him out. In the special case of an employee's marriage, the bank would give him another month off. As to the sister and Bing's age, Berne asked John: "Do you love her? Could you love her? If you love her, you'll be able to work things out."

His friend's questions gave John pause. Yes, he could love her. In fact, he must have had feelings for her if he was still considering the outrageous demand from her sister, plus the additional cost of going back to California. He was a cautious and thrifty man—for any other girl, he would have walked away without a moment's thought.

The next day, John called his sister with the following message: Tell Bing he would like to marry her. He could get back there in two weeks.

BING WAS THRILLED. It was already October, and her visa would be expiring on November 26. Now she didn't have to go to Denmark. At least in America, she could get by in English. She didn't know John Yee well enough to *love* him, not the way people did in the movies, but she liked him. She hadn't expected much in this search for a husband, and she could have done worse. Here was somebody who really *wanted* her. Her own father and mother hadn't wanted her. Her first adoptive mother, Mama Hsu, hadn't wanted her. John Yee wanted her enough to pay two thousand dollars. Yes, she could marry him.

Elder Sister seemed more excited than Bing—she grabbed the bride-to-be and danced around singing, "Happy days are here again!" while Peter doubled over in laughter at the sight of them.

Suddenly the cottage on Broadway was abuzz with activity. With the cash she had on hand, Elder Sister began to assemble Bing's modest trousseau: new shoes, nightgowns, lingerie. A coat for the cold New York weather. They found a tailor to sew some new dresses for Bing. A wedding gown to be worn only once would be too extravagant. Instead, they selected a special fabric for a dress that she could wear again.

Travel plans, too, had to be made. Elder Sister reserved a passage to Denmark for herself and Peter. They'd take a train to New York and from there board the ship to Copenhagen. She didn't know what she would discover there, whether Kristian would be too ill to leave Denmark. But war and chaos had taught Elder Sister to prepare for the worst, just in case. She needed an alternate plan.

If things didn't work out in Denmark, Elder Sister decided she would return to America. But she learned that a bank account in the United States with at least two thousand dollars was required for an immigrant visa. John Yee's "dowry" would buy her tickets to Denmark, but it was not enough to gain her reentry into the United States. She would have to sell some of her jewelry. She picked out her most expensive piece: the diamond solitaire that Kristian had given her before they were married. She hated to part with it, but this wasn't a time to be sentimental. Refugees everywhere had to barter and sell whatever they had in order to survive. And she was a survivor.

Elder Sister knew exactly whom to approach about her ring: "Sugar Daddy" Lee. Since he was supporting her on the promise of marriage once she divorced Kristian, he'd be glad that she was getting rid of the wedding ring.

When Lee returned to the cottage that night, Betty was dressed to kill.

"Lee, darling, I have good news," she purred. "My dreadful husband has finally wired me that he's ready for the divorce." She'd be leaving for Denmark soon, she explained, and when she returned, she'd marry him. She also told him about the two-thousand-dollar requirement for the return visa. "Can you help me to get a good price for my wedding ring? I won't need it anymore." The big diamond flashed brightly as she showed off the ring. "We paid five thousand U.S. dollars for it ten years ago," she said, inflating the price with her Shanghai bravado. "Can you get that for me, darling?"

Pleased to hear that her divorce was on the way, Lee examined the ring closely and grunted. "Five thousand dollars? Is it the Hope Diamond? Don't worry; I have some pawnshop pals who know diamonds. Leave it to me."

The next night, Lee returned. "My buddies say that you were snookered if you paid five grand for this ring. The best they can do is twenty-five hundred dollars."

Betty appeared to mull this over. She objected briefly at the prospect of such a loss. After pausing a beat, she agreed to sell. Bing knew that under her poker face, Elder Sister was pleased. Lee left, promising to sell the ring the next day. Alone with Bing, Elder Sister shared an excited whisper. "He got a good price. Now we're in business!" The next day, Lee came by and plunked down twenty-five hundred dollars in cash. Elder Sister promptly opened a savings account, crossing that big hurdle for a return to America if she wished.

THE GOLDEN MID-OCTOBER SUNLIGHT streamed into their cottage as Bing answered the knock on the door. It was John Yee, standing outside with a suitcase in one hand and a bouquet of daisies in the other. He had just arrived from New York, and his first stop was to see Bing.

Without even a hello, he looked at her intently. "Are you sure you want to marry me and live in New York?" he asked almost shyly.

Bing returned his gaze without flinching. She nodded and replied in a firm voice, "Yes, I'm sure."

John smiled broadly and handed Bing the flowers.

By then, Betty had rushed to the door. John reached into the inside pocket of his coat and pulled out a fat envelope, handing it to her. "Here's two thousand dollars. Please count it," he requested. "I don't want to hear that I shortchanged you." When she'd finished counting and was satisfied, he asked, "Do I get a receipt?" His tone was jovial, but Bing sensed he was only half joking.

Elder Sister replied, "She's all yours—after the wedding."

"Then let's not waste time," he said, taking Bing by the hand and leading her to get blood tests, then to city hall for the marriage license. They would go to Reno, Nevada, where they could get married without delay by a justice of the peace. Bing packed a small bag and headed out the door.

Before going to Reno, they stopped in Oakland to see John's sister Florence. In anticipation, Florence had spent days preparing a traditional Taishan herbal concoction to enhance the young bride's health and fertility.

Florence handed Bing a cup filled with dark, thick fluid. "Just drink it fast," Florence instructed. "It will help make things easier for you. Tonight." She gave Bing a knowing smile.

Bing hesitated. She wanted to please her soon-to-be sister-in-law. She had no choice but to raise the foul-smelling liquid to her mouth. She downed it. Almost immediately, Bing became woozy and started gagging. She remembered that she had experienced this once before.

"Is there alcohol in the drink?" Bing gasped in between spasms. "I'm very allergic."

"Only a half bottle of whiskey," Florence replied. "Not much."

Bing's skin broke out in an itchy rash. She felt ill during the entire trip to Reno. She could barely remember how she got there or the marriage ceremony itself. That night at the hotel, Bing felt miserable, her wedding night a bust. The special Chinese concoction had made nothing easier for her, no matter what Florence believed. The next day, Bing and John went back to Oakland to visit his extended family for a few days. A relative who owned a Chinese restaurant held a big wedding banquet. Two hundred members of the large Yee family came, but Elder Sister couldn't get there from San Francisco. The only people Bing knew were John and Florence. She couldn't talk with her wedding guests because everyone spoke in the Toisan dialect.

Another bride might have pouted, but Bing didn't mind. She was used to being on the margins, and it didn't bother her, not even at her own wedding party. Her every smile and nod was a genuine reflection of her happiness: She'd have her own home, her own place with John Yee. Soon she and John would leave for New York. Bing had spent all her life following the wishes of others. Now she would make her own path.

CHAPTER
23

DOREEN
AND
BENNY

Ages 19 and 22

A LARGE SMUDGE OF DRIED TEARS BLURRED THE TRAIN window next to Doreen where she had pressed her damp cheek to catch a final glimpse of Benny and her mother before they disappeared from view. Her mother had chased after the train, not stopping until she reached the very end of the platform, her arms outstretched as if to pull Doreen back.

Doreen had had to fight the desire to run through the train, toward the retreating figure. What kind of daughter was she to spurn her mother's wrenching appeal, especially when her mother had never before asked anything of her? She had managed to calm herself by resting her gaze on Benny as he waved her on. His reassuring smile seemed to telegraph that she was doing the right thing. That she'd be okay.

As the steady chug of the train lulled other passengers to sleep, Doreen imagined the other life she might have had, unblemished by war and treason. Now nineteen, she'd have been heading off to college and, one day, would have had a beautiful wedding. Her smart and charming elder brother would have been a doctor, a statesman, or possibly one of Shanghai's notorious playboys, the spoiled sons of the rich and mighty who had no purpose in life but to revel in the city's decadence. Instead of living that fanciful dream, she was sitting on this train packed with other refugees from the Communists. Instead of lightness and joy, she felt weighed down by the guilt of leaving her mother and for taking Benny's ticket—his chance to make a new life for himself.

How would she manage on her own? She'd been the pampered third daughter, cared for by servants. Even after her father was jailed and her mother left them, Doreen had never had to shoulder any responsibility. Benny had watched out for her. Now she was headed to a foreign place to stay with a sister she hadn't seen in four years, a brother-in-law and children she'd never met.

Alone and penniless on this train full of strangers, without food or a change of clothing, Doreen was finally running out of tears. She sat staring out the blurry window during the three-day trip, oblivious to all but the lurch of the train, her regrets, and her doubts. But Benny had told her to go to the YWCA. She would do as he'd said.

By the next day, a family seated nearby took pity on the sad girl traveling alone. Their hunchbacked grandmother with kind eyes handed Doreen a cold yam. She hadn't realized how hungry she was until she devoured it, skin and all.

Doreen wondered what would become of her family. Everyone she knew had always referred to the Communists as "Red Bandits" or worse. Her father's White Russian bodyguards warned anyone who would listen about the evils of Communism. The Nationalists blamed Communists for everything bad in China. And now the Communists had actually taken over.

As the train pulled into Guangzhou, Doreen tried to shake off her melancholy. She had to figure out how to get to the YWCA. At least this train station was smaller and less overwhelming than Shanghai's. Doreen still possessed the big-city savvy of a Shanghai girl. Speaking in the Guangzhou dialect she had learned from her grandparents and extended Pan family, she asked some railway clerks for help. With their directions, she climbed into a pedicab, hoping her face wouldn't reveal that she didn't have a single yuan.

When she arrived at the Y, Doreen asked the driver to wait while she ran inside for help. A Chinese woman in plain Western clothes was expecting her. "You must be Doreen," the woman said in English. "I'm Miss Ling, the YWCA director. Your brother called me. I'll take care of the pedicab. And don't worry; you'll be safe here."

Miss Ling explained that Benny had gone to the Shanghai YMCA office and, from there, contacted the YWCA in Guangzhou about his sister's dire circumstances. After paying for the pedicab, Miss Ling took Doreen to the large kitchen. The cook prepared a simple meal for her. Though Doreen was famished, she tried to eat politely in front of Miss Ling, to show that she wasn't like a hungry beggar. As she summoned all her willpower to keep from gulping her soup, Miss Ling spoke. "You can stay here as long as you need. I'm sure we have spare clothes that will fit you. After you've rested, I'll show you some work you can do in our office to earn your keep." Soon Doreen collapsed on a cot in a large dormitory room inhabited by other women like herself who had nowhere else to stay. But thanks to Benny, she was now only a few hours by train from her sister in Hong Kong.

WITH DOREEN SAFE AND NEARLY to Hong Kong, Benny prepared to move to Nanjing for his job at the National YMCA office. His boss and benefactor, Dr. Tu Yu-Ching, had been criticized by some of the foreign Episcopal staff at St. John's for his time as president of the university. They felt he had been too acquiescent toward the more radical students as the Communists took power. But now Benny's colleagues at the YMCA hoped that his boss's prior "soft" treatment of Communist students would help keep their Christian organization in the good graces of the new regime. Benny was glad to be moving to Nanjing. No one would know of his family's history there, and there would be fewer painful reminders of what once was.

Shanghai's constant state of political agitation was another reason Benny wanted to leave. Everyone was on high alert as Nationalist forces continued to terrorize the city with air strikes from their island bunkers in Taiwan, using American-made planes and bombs. The Communists had depended on guerrilla warfare and received little material aid from the Soviets. Even in victory they had neither an air force nor an antiaircraft program. By February 1950, the steady bombardment of Shanghai by the Nationalists was so severe, at times the city lost electricity and water.

Instead of diminishing the revolutionary fervor, however, the attacks only further inflamed the outrage and clamor for radical change. The new Communist government publicized its efforts to ferret out any remaining Nationalist assets and secret opposition forces. The Avenue Pétain mansion of former finance minister T. V. Soong became the Communist Party headquarters. Benny had often gone past the imposing villa. Newspapers recounted that the "imperialist running dog" Soong had fled to Paris and New York with his wife and aides, while Chiang Kai-shek and his wife had reportedly taken millions of dollars in cash to the United States for safekeeping, angering many Chinese. Other reports said that the Chiangs, the Soongs, the Kungs, and other high-profile Nationalists had misused diplomatic passports and skimmed millions of U.S. dollars intended as aid for the relief of war-stricken Chinese.

Benny feared that the constant stoking of hatred against the old guard didn't bode well for his father. Each day, news stories reported on atrocities committed by the Nationalists in the last days of their rule, such as the many arbitrary executions. The Communists had captured more than a hundred thousand Nationalist soldiers, placing the higher-ranking ones in the hulking Tilanqiao Prison—the same location as C. C. Pan.

A people's tribunal was reviewing backlogged cases of criminals charged with various offenses, from black-marketeering and theft to possession of Nationalist assets. Almost daily, accused counterrevolutionaries were being paraded before jeering crowds in Shanghai's parks and public grounds. The huge Canidrome in the former French Concession and the British racecourse in the former International Settlement became arenas for public recrimination, judgment, and execution. Each time one of these spectacles was announced, Benny cringed and asked himself, Is it my father's turn?

When it was finally time for Benny to leave Shanghai, he took the train to Nanjing. The station was almost calm, without the frenzied crush to escape he'd experienced when he was last there with Doreen and his mother. Nanjing, the former Nationalist capital, was China's second-largest city, but its population of 2.6 million seemed placid compared to Shanghai's 6 million. Benny moved into a room at the YMCA, where he found both camaraderie to ease his newcomer status and anonymity to mask his family shame. In his job as secretary to Dr. Tu, his English skills grew sharper from typing reports and correspondence. He could even save some money. Most gratifying of all, he was doing God's work to help the Christian movement in China continue. This way, he hoped to make some small atonement for his father's sins.

In the first several months after the founding of the People's Republic, the government struggled to keep the economy and essential services running while consolidating its control over public order. The new regime hastened to assure frightened capitalists that their factories and shops could continue without disruption. Similar promises were made to intellectuals and skilled professionals of the petite bourgeoisie. Communist or not, the country could not afford to lose the entire class of professionals, technicians, business owners, and managers to the panicked exodus well under way. Even foreign missionaries with the YMCA and other Christian groups were told they could keep their church doors open—at least for the unspecified future.

But with each passing month, the revolutionary government grew more stringent and demanding. The new regime needed money to run the country. Under the Marxist principle "from each according to their ability, to each according to their need," the bourgeoisie had to carry the heaviest load. Hefty taxes and higher wages for their employees were imposed on business owners at hearings conducted by indignant workers' committees. Afraid to reduce their operations and face recrimination at worker-run tribunals, businessmen were leaping to their deaths from Shanghai's tall buildings in shocking numbers. Pedestrians on the streets below hugged the buildings to avoid the crumpled bodies and to prevent themselves from becoming casualties. At schools throughout Shanghai, students were required to take new courses on political thought, while applied sciences were emphasized over the arts. At St. John's University, its formerly prized English-language curriculum was no more.

Attendance at Benny's fellowship meetings and Sunday church services steadily shrank. As more Western missionaries departed from China, the future for the Y and other Christian institutions was dimming. When Benny had graduated in 1949, 33 of the 177 teachers at St. John's had been foreign. Less than a year later, only five Western teachers remained.

In Nanjing and other cities, enthusiastic revolutionaries organized rallies to conduct mass "trials" of big landlords and capitalists who were forced to wear dunce caps that listed their offenses, intended to "educate the laboring people" on the crimes of "running dogs of the imperialists." The accused had to face public criticism to reform their thinking. To help them change, their wealth was seized and redistributed. In the rural countryside, China's vast population of poor farmers also held mass meetings to "speak bitterness" and confront despicable landlords with their crimes and cruelty. Many were beaten to death when the big rallies turned violent. In the months following the revolution, more than a million landlords are estimated to have been killed as part of this land reform movement.

Through his job at the YMCA, news of these events crossed Benny's desk. With each new report, he felt ever more certain that he had done the right thing in sending Doreen to Hong Kong. For that, he was most thankful.

AT THE YWCA IN GUANGZHOU, Doreen had sent an urgent letter to her sister in Hong Kong almost immediately after arriving, asking for money to buy the train ticket for the short distance from Guangzhou to Shenzhen, where she could cross the border into Lo Wu, the first rail stop in the British colony of Hong Kong. Cecilia had written back saying she couldn't afford Doreen's ticket. Financial uncertainties were roiling her husband's company, the China National Aviation Corporation, a distinguished airline that had flown airlifts over the Himalayas to supply the Nationalists during the war against Japan. Since the Communist victory, businesses in Hong Kong had faced constant labor disruptions due to the economic uncertainty. Several of CNAC's pilots had even commandeered planes and defected to the

Communists. According to Cecilia, her husband's work was so erratic that they barely had money to feed their children. It would take time to scrape together the cost of her ticket.

Doreen didn't mind waiting. Miss Ling, the director, had plenty for her to do at the Y. Grateful to be of use, Doreen was pleased that her English skills were an asset. Living at the Y was a far cry from her life as a boarding student at St. Mary's Hall, but she knew she was lucky to have this safe place to bide her time.

Guangzhou continued to swell from the huge numbers of refugees pouring in, all with the hope of crossing into Hong Kong. Many had no place to sleep but on the streets. As one of the last major cities under Nationalist control, Guangzhou had also been one of the last places on the mainland to issue Republic of China passports. Refugees from all over had poured in to get the travel documents they needed to flee China, since the United States and many other countries still recognized the Republic of China as the only legitimate government. Even a year after the revolution, Guangzhou and Shenzhen continued to be the gateways to the British colony of Hong Kong and the Portuguese colony of Macao. But rumors swirled that those gates might soon close, as those colonies were overwhelmed by more than a million refugees. Doreen could only hope that the border would stay open long enough for her to cross.

Within a few months, Doreen heard from her sister: She was sending the train ticket. Bidding a tearful goodbye to Miss Ling and her new friends at the Y—aware that they, too, would soon depart— Doreen left for the Chinese border village of Shenzhen, where she would cross to Lo Wu on the British side of the border and meet her sister's husband.

The train was choked with people and luggage, an unpleasant reminder of her wrenching train ride from Shanghai. At least this time Doreen felt hopeful. She was looking forward to college and the chance to study overseas—maybe even in America. When the train reached its last stop at Shenzhen, all passengers had to get out and walk the final stretch. Doreen had been warned by her friends at the YWCA that she'd have to pass by some border police before she would be allowed to walk across a small bridge marking the border.

Then she'd be in Lo Wu, located in the sparsely populated New Territories beyond Kowloon and Hong Kong Island.

Even though her friends had coached her on what to expect, Doreen grew nervous as she joined the long queue to reach the border guards. The Chinese exit police were inspecting everyone's bags, just as the horrid inspectors at the Shanghai station had done. She watched as inspectors seized money, gold, and jewelry from travelers who hadn't hidden their valuables carefully enough. Exiting Chinese were permitted to take only the equivalent of five Hong Kong dollars in cash out of the country. "These belong to the people of China, not to the running dogs of imperialists and their lackeys," the inspectors said. Doreen had nothing left for them to take. She was quickly waved on.

As she continued toward the Hong Kong side, Doreen soon encountered another set of guards, both English and Chinese, all wearing British uniforms. Instead of checking packages, these guards asked questions—and depending on the answers, they were turning some people back. Even from the end of the long line, Doreen could hear the anguished cries and entreaties of those who had been barred from entering: "We've come from so far. You must let us through!" "My mother is gravely ill. I must go to see her!" The guards were unmoved. No one had mentioned this step to her—was this a new trap?

As she reached the front of the queue, Doreen squared her shoulders and murmured a little prayer. The soldier asked her, in English, if she could speak Cantonese.

"*Hai-yaah!*"—yes!—she replied firmly, in the Cantonese accent she had carefully honed during her stay in Guangzhou.

"Where will you stay in Hong Kong? Tell me quickly," he shot back.

Doreen fired off her sister's address in rapid Cantonese. With that, the Hong Kong guards allowed her in. They didn't ask for her papers or proof of her intended destination. The British wanted to admit only those already from the area—and to bar any more refugees from distant regions like Shanghai. Woe to those who couldn't answer in Cantonese—they were summarily turned back. Until this new requirement, there had never been restrictions on ethnic Chinese entering or leaving the colony. Now, to keep both refugees and Communists out, that had changed.

AS DOREEN ENTERED LO WU, she murmured her thanks to her Cantonese great-grandparents for keeping their ancestral tongue alive in Shanghai. Other Chinese walked quickly, as if to get away before the guards could change their minds. Some in expensive-looking Western clothes appeared crumpled and haggard; Doreen guessed that they'd had to sleep on the station grounds until approved for exit—and they, too, had to carry their own bags. Looking at the ground as she walked, Doreen suddenly realized that she had crossed the border out of China and was in British Hong Kong! She scanned the waiting crowd and spotted a man in a CNAC uniform. Rushing over to him, she saw it was indeed her brother-in-law! With difficulty, she restrained her excitement, greeting him with a demure nod in the formal Chinese way. He gave a reserved nod back but offered, "You made it—welcome to Hong Kong!" She followed him onto the next train from Lo Wu to Kowloon, the peninsula across from Hong Kong Island, and sat quietly with a big smile of relief across her face. Soon she would be in the safe embrace of family again.

After they reached Kowloon station, the two walked through curving streets and alleys that were even more crowded than the lanes of the Dasheng *lilong* where her family had once lived in Shanghai's former French Concession. The concrete apartment buildings seemed taller and narrower than any she had known, while overhead shop signs and bamboo poles with drying laundry jutted over the roadway. Her brother-in-law turned in to one of the buildings, and they trudged up several flights of a dark, narrow stairwell. Entering one of the small apartments, Doreen was overjoyed.

"Big Sister, I've been waiting so long to join you!" she exclaimed as Cecilia introduced her two daughters, aged one and two, who shyly clung to her skirt.

"It was hard for us to save money for your ticket, Younger Sister," she replied. "I wrote you that my husband doesn't have steady work. It's a good thing you're here to help. The new baby is coming soon."

Doreen gulped. "You know I couldn't buy the train ticket from Guangzhou because the immigration police in Shanghai took everything."

"That was your own fault—why didn't you hide your money better? You and Benny should have expected their thievery," Cecilia snapped.

Cecilia led Doreen to an area off the tiny kitchen. "This is where you'll stay—together with the maid." As soon as Doreen put her bag down, her sister made her expectations clear. "You'll help her with the children and her chores."

Suddenly the nineteen-year-old noticed the faded wallpaper, peeling in some places, and the discolored, moisture-stained ceiling of the cramped apartment. She'd never been in such a narrow, crowded building.

"Of course I'll help your amah with the children. Perhaps I could go to school for a few hours each day?" Doreen ventured.

"School? What does a girl like you need with more schooling? Eldest Sister Annie and I were married by your age. You have your St. Mary's diploma; that's plenty." Cecilia practically spat out the words. "Don't you see all the refugees here in Hong Kong? You don't have money to pay for school, and neither do we." She closed the subject with an emphatic "Humph!"

Doreen was surprised by her sister's harshness. Though she had known that she'd have to help, she hadn't expected this. But she could also see that one maid couldn't handle all the cooking, cleaning, and laundry. Instead of continuing her education at a Hong Kong school, Doreen began spending her days watching over her sister's two girls and helping the maid with the wash and whatever else she needed.

Doreen knew she should be grateful to have a bed and a roof over her head—with more refugees streaming in each day, everyone talked about Hong Kong's terrible housing shortage. According to local newspapers, more than a million Chinese had entered the colony, doubling its population almost overnight. At the end of World War II, Hong Kong had a population of 600,000. By 1950, it was bursting, with an official population count of 2,360,000. Having arrived by

The massive refugee crisis and squatter slums in Hong Kong included the notorious Shek Kip Mei slum, pictured here, which left more than fifty thousand refugees homeless after a catastrophic fire on Christmas Day 1953.

plane, boat, train, and foot, many of the new refugees became destitute after spending all their money on a short-term place to stay while searching for someplace cheaper. Many ended up as squatters in makeshift encampments on muddy hillsides.

At the same time, the Hong Kong government was afraid that both Communist and Nationalist agitators would stir up political discontent and turn the colony into a battleground. Crippling strikes and labor unrest caused constant disruptions. With Hong Kong's economy dependent on trade with China, any economic embargo against the Communist mainland would have had an immediate and disastrous effect on the colony. And if the Red Army crossed the border into the New Territories, Britain was in no position to defend Hong Kong militarily.

IT WAS A TERRIBLE BLOW to become her sister's menial housemaid, but Doreen didn't dare voice her dissatisfaction. Cecilia's worries over money made her ill-tempered. After the birth of her third child—yet another girl—Cecilia's mood soured even more. At every opportunity, she picked on Doreen.

"Why don't you hurry up and find a husband who can pay us for the room and board you owe us?" Cecilia would say. "You're an old maid already, and if you don't get married soon, it'll be too late for you!"

Doreen could feel her ears and cheeks turn red whenever her sister nagged her about this. But she was different from her elder sisters. Annie and Cecilia had both gotten married by the time they were seventeen. Cecilia hadn't even finished her middle school studies when she eloped. Both of Doreen's sisters had always been more interested in fashion and social status—window-shopping with their mother, associating with the popular girls, and seeking the attention of rich boys. When the family's status plummeted after their father's arrest, Cecilia ran off to Hong Kong with her aviator husband rather than face social humiliation.

Status and money hadn't been so important to Doreen. She wanted to be educated, to use her mind. In that way, she was much more like Benny. She remembered fondly how the two of them would trade quips during the fancy Sunday parties while Annie and Cecilia looked for rich playboys to flirt with. Now Doreen had to listen to her sister's constant rants. If she wasn't pushing Doreen to find a rich husband, Cecilia harangued her about money to help with household expenses.

"Why can't you go to one of the nightclubs or dance halls and make a few dollars each night?" Cecilia would ask. "Lots of Shanghai girls are doing it, even girls from high-class families. Too proud to sell a few dances? Who do you think you are? If it weren't for us, you'd have to sell a lot more than that!"

There was nothing Doreen could say in reply. Everyone in Hong

Kong knew that Shanghai girls were considered hot commodities among the sailors and other men on the prowl. Doreen was sickened by her sister's attempts to steer her in that direction. In the gritty parts of Hong Kong, *Shanghai nui* had become almost synonymous with *prostitute*. In Wan Chai and near the docks of the busy port city, it was true that plenty of desperate Shanghai women had no other way to survive. Gossips whispered the family names of Shanghai women rumored to be selling their bodies. Was that what Cecilia wanted her to become?

I will never sink to that, Doreen vowed to herself. I will never sell my smile or my soul in a dance hall—or worse. Never!

To keep her sister at bay and to try to make a life for herself, Doreen began searching for a job. When she could get away, she'd head to Hong Kong Island on the Star Ferry, the dependable green-and-white boats that cost only a few pennies for a ride on the second-class deck. She would always jockey for a spot with a view of the Customs House clock tower and the Peninsula Hotel so that she could watch them recede as the ferryboat chugged across the wide shipping lanes to Central, the main administrative district of the British colony.

Hunting for work, Doreen quickly learned to keep her Shanghai background and attitude to herself. The vast majority of the Hong Kong Chinese were Cantonese from Guangdong Province—and they thoroughly disliked the refugees from the north, especially those from Shanghai. Their reasons were wide-ranging: There were just too many refugees; the city was already too crowded; the very character of Hong Kong was changing because of these outsiders. Every day, Doreen passed news hawkers shouting headlines "Shanghai Exodus Continues," "Two More Ships Come to HK with Refugees," "HK's Growing Population Reflected in Traffic Accidents."

Moreover, the Shanghai migrants simply rubbed many Hong Kongers the wrong way. Locals considered them to be show-offs, arrogant braggarts, and spendthrifts who offended Cantonese values of thrift and modesty. A common saying summed up the local attitude: "When Cantonese have a hundred dollars, they act as if they only have one dollar. Shanghainese with one dollar act as if they have a hundred."

Hong Kong natives tended to lump together the migrants from the north as though they were all the same, labeling them all as "Shanghainese" no matter what part of China they were from. Everything wrong with the refugees was blamed on the Shanghainese: Beggars on the street who scrounged for coins or scraps of food had to be Shanghainese; prostitutes were Shanghainese; the aggressive beggars who threw themselves onto the hoods of cars and refused to move until they received a handout—they were most definitely Shanghainese. Some Cantonese made a game of wrapping their leftovers and trash in newspaper and tossing them out of their upper-story windows to watch the "Shanghainese" beggars scramble for the contents on the street below.

Hong Kong's refugee crisis was exacerbated by the British colonial government's decision to do nothing to aid the overwhelming number of new arrivals. Instead, the British overseers deferred to wishful thinking—that the problem was temporary and the million-plus refugees would soon leave. Indeed, many of the refugees wanted to leave. But most had nowhere to go. The colony's governor, Alexander Grantham, opposed large-scale relief efforts to provide basic sanitation or housing, saying there was "no reason for turning Hong Kong into a glorified soup kitchen for refugees from all over China." Hong Kong's British authorities resisted using the very word *refugee*, as refugees would require some kind of international humanitarian response. Instead, the colonial government referred to the critical situation as a "problem of people." Geopolitics further complicated the crisis: Both the People's Republic of China on the mainland and the Republic of China in Taiwan claimed to be China's sole legitimate government, yet neither was willing to acknowledge the mass exodus or provide assistance for the refugees. Caught in the crosscurrents of global interests, the "problem people" languished in their Hong Kong no-man's-land.

Doreen's ability to speak passable Cantonese was enough to get her into doors as she inquired for work at every opportunity. But as soon as she was pegged as a *Shanghai nui*, she was finished. With a million new refugees looking for work in Hong Kong, unemployment was at astronomical levels. Searching bulletin boards, shops, and gathering places for possible leads, she realized that so many other Shang-hainese were far more experienced or skilled than she. For example, John Chan, one of Benny's St. John's schoolmates, once ran his fam-ily's hundred-year-old stevedore business. It took him more than a year to land a job with a group funded by the U.S. government called Aid Refugee Chinese Intellectuals, created to help the most educated refugees. Doreen couldn't qualify for their assistance. She couldn't even compete with Shanghai teenagers like biracial Myra dos Reme-dios, who had taught herself to type and learned stenography—and was desperately searching for work while living at the dog racetrack in Portuguese Macao, now converted into a refugee camp. Migrants like Myra were even hungrier for work than Doreen. With so much competition, Doreen fell into despair.

Sometimes, before heading back to her sister's place in Kowloon, Doreen would make her way up to Victoria Peak. Walking around the park near the summit, she'd descend into such deep thought that she'd barely notice the famous view.

Was it a mistake for me to come to Hong Kong? she asked herself. There's no life for me here and no hope. Doreen felt lost, just one of more than a million refugees from China, gasping for air and a place in the clogged colony. Sometimes she closed her eyes, thinking that her best option was in the deep blue sea surrounding her.

TAIPEI, 1950

F URIOUS AT BEING ABANDONED BY THE UNITED STATES IN HIS quest to retake the mainland, Generalissimo Chiang continued the bombing sorties over Shanghai and the mainland coast. His air force not only inflicted heavy civilian casualties, but Chiang also targeted two of the American companies still operating in the city, Standard Oil and the Shanghai Power Company, on the grounds that their fuel and electricity aided the Communists. A few Americans who remained in Shanghai witnessed the attacks—and the irony that Chiang had bombed them with American-supplied planes and ordnance. Though the U.S. government protested Chiang's actions, it could not stop his attempts to push Washington to the brink of war with Communist China. The people on Taiwan, living under military control, braced themselves for the impending showdown between the mainland giant and the tiny island. Even schoolchildren like Annuo were gripped by fear and dread. To reinforce its control over the terrified populace, the Nationalist government further tightened martial law.

That fear drove yet more desperate refugees onto Taiwan, arriving by overloaded boats and planes, at their peril. Chiang's military and his secret police, now under his son's command, turned many away after subjecting the new arrivals to extreme screening, ostensibly to root out potential Communist infiltrators, spies, terrorists, dissidents, and anyone who was not in lockstep with the regime. Somehow two of Annuo's maternal uncles managed to make their way onto the island: her mother's eldest brother as well as a younger brother, his wife, and daughter. They had escaped separately from Shanghai to Hong Kong, then to Taipei. One after the other, they found Annuo's family. Now every inch of tatami matting in the small house was occupied.

A FEW ANXIOUS MONTHS after President Truman's abandonment of Taiwan, everything abruptly changed again. On June 25, 1950, a new war broke out in Korea, seven hundred miles to the north. Annuo, now in her second year at the Taipei First Girls' High School, was in class when the school principal assembled the entire student body to announce the alarming development: The North Korean army had invaded South Korea. There was war on the Korean Peninsula.

Annuo's teacher explained how, after Japan's surrender in 1945, the United States and the Soviet Union had arbitrarily divided Korea, a Japanese colony since 1910, into two parts at the thirty-eighth parallel north. The Communist North was aligned with the Soviets and Communist China while the South was allied with Washington. North Korea's leader, Kim Il-Sung, had launched the attack to unify the peninsula under his rule, aided by military support from Stalin and Mao. It seemed that the world was on the brink of another global war.

More war? Annuo and her schoolmates listened in stunned disbelief. War had defined their lives, and they knew too well the turmoil and devastation that would follow. Annuo worried about her brother, Charley, who was turning eighteen and would soon have to report for service in the Nationalist army. Every male in Taiwan was required to serve for one year. Images of low-flying bombers and soldiers with bayonets came rushing back to Annuo. She instinctively shut her eyes as if to block the memories of the violence she had already seen and to shut out what was yet to come.

At home that night, Annuo learned more details of the attack by listening to the adults' animated talk. North Korea had crossed the thirty-eighth parallel with 89,000 assault troops and 150 Russian tanks, taking the American-supported South by surprise.

Although the civilian population was fearful that the nearby war could engulf Taiwan, many of the island's thousands of idle soldiers seemed energized by the news. Annuo's father and his Nationalist friends hoped that the war in Korea would compel the American military to stand against the Chinese Communists. It could be the break Taiwan needed.

On June 27, 1950, two days after North Korea's invasion, President Truman made an about-face from his speech abandoning Taiwan, just six months earlier: "I have ordered United States air and sea forces to give the Korean government troops cover and support." He followed his announcement with a longer statement about Taiwan:

> The attack upon Korea makes it plain beyond all doubt that Communism has passed beyond the use of subversion to conquer independent nations and will now use armed invasion and war. . . . The occupation of Formosa [Taiwan] by Communist forces would be a direct threat to the security of the Pacific area and to United States forces. . . . Accordingly, I have ordered the Seventh Fleet to prevent any attack on Formosa.

Concerned that Chiang Kai-shek would inflame the conflict with Communist China, Truman also called on the Nationalists to cease their provocative air raids and other military operations against the mainland. Undeterred, Chiang promptly offered to send his army's "fighting force of thirty-three thousand Nationalist soldiers" to Korea. Pentagon generals rejected his proposal, questioning its real value. But any offense Chiang might have taken was more than mitigated by the long-hoped-for influx of American aid. The U.S. Navy was returning to the East China Sea. Taiwan's Nationalists fervently hoped that American military and economic aid would pour into their coffers once again.

In Washington, talks were under way to provide $300 million to Taiwan to help keep the strategically located island out of Communist hands. Within a few years, the total aid would reach $2 billion. The Yanks were back. Before North Korea had crossed the thirty-eighth parallel, there had been fewer than a hundred Americans in all of Tai-

*With Taiwan's new strategic significance to the United States, in 1950,
infusions of American arms and aid boosted the Nationalists' military,
reinforcing their rule by martial law.*

wan. Now thousands were on their way, to use the island as a base for
their efforts in Korea. With the massive injection of U.S. support,
overnight Chiang's control over Taiwan became stronger than ever.
Annuo's father and other Nationalist *wai sheng ren* could rest more
easily on the island while still holding tight to their dream of taking
back the Communist mainland.

WITH HER FATHER'S NEW job and Taiwan's security assured, Annuo's family finally moved to a larger house in Taipei. This one had a
real kitchen and three bedrooms, and to the great relief of Annuo's
mother, there was furniture. By then, another uncle—her father's
younger brother—had joined the household, with his wife and two
teenagers, whom Annuo was to address as Elder Brother and Elder
Sister. With the addition of a live-in cook and a maid, the household
swelled to fifteen. The crowded living arrangements were typical of

most every mainlander family on the island. For Annuo, the additional relatives pushed her further to the side. Elders, including siblings and cousins, were first in line when it was time to eat, bathe, or even to use the toilet. At mealtimes, the adults helped themselves first. Next came her elder brother and the teenaged cousins. By the time Annuo could reach into the serving bowls, any tasty morsels were gone. There would not be a trace of egg yolk left to add color or flavor to her small bowl of rice. After breakfast, she had to wait for the elder children to prepare their lunches for school first, leaving little for her by the time she had her chance. When it was her turn to bathe, the bathwater had turned cold and gray, already used by nearly everyone else.

Annuo's sister, Li-Ning, was younger, but she was also her father's favorite. He made sure to set aside some of the best food for her. Annuo was the small and ugly daughter who would never amount to much, as her father often pointed out. In the pecking order under her father's ironfisted control, Annuo came last.

IN SPITE OF HER unhappiness at home—or perhaps because of it— Annuo blossomed at school, outshining her cousins and siblings. With more arrivals from the mainland every day, there were many more girls from backgrounds like hers. In her second year, about 30 percent of the students at the First Girls' High School were *wai sheng ren*, many from Shanghai; the following year, it was more than 50 percent. The school's student body grew more familiar to her, its sequestered grounds her refuge. There, Annuo was special, one of Taiwan's top students. Her school years passed quickly, though not fast enough for her.

Annuo adored literature and the stories that transported her to czarist Russia, medieval France, the American frontier, or imperial China. She began writing poetry. When she was sixteen, she placed second in a national essay contest, behind an accomplished and much older writer. At dinner that night, Annuo eagerly told her extended family about winning the high honor—and her father promptly used the opportunity to ridicule her. She had used the pen name "Zi Ruo," meaning *self-confident*. In front of everyone, he mocked her by twisting her pen name into "Zi Ku"—*self-tortured*. When any family member attempted to praise her work, her father contorted his face as if he had swallowed a bitter pill. Annuo's extended family erupted in laughter at her expense. What was supposed to be a proud and happy moment for the quiet teenager turned into profound humiliation. Annuo didn't dare to write again. In her imagination, she was a weed in the cracks of Taipei's harsh concrete, stepped on with every flowering.

But outside of her home and away from her family's derision, Annuo's efforts at school paid off. She graduated at the top of her class and was admitted to the elite and highly competitive National Taiwan University or Tai Da. Her escape plan was still intact.

Instead of being pleased, Annuo's father piled on more criticism and pressure. Entering college students had to declare their intended majors before they started school. Annuo wanted to study English literature, to immerse herself in the books that lifted her from her grim reality. Her father insisted that she study medicine instead, to care for him in his old age. Annuo, the best student in the family, was his only hope for a doctor in the family.

"English literature? What possible use will come of that?" he asked. "You should think of how you will help your family. I absolutely forbid such a selfish act. If you wish to remain my daughter, you will study medicine!"

Annuo listened to her father's angry words without comment, but this time she was unable to choke back her defiance. She simply couldn't do as her father commanded. After witnessing illness and death as a child, she couldn't bear the sight of blood. The thought of being in a hospital again nauseated her.

Never before had Annuo refused to obey her father's command. A taut and smoldering silence settled over their house as Annuo and her father remained deadlocked. Her father was the supreme commander in their home, and no one ever challenged him—not even her mother or uncles. Annuo trembled at her own audacity.

Near Annuo's house, one of Taipei's major waterways coursed by. For many hopeless refugees, the river offered a tempting end to their misery. Lifeless bodies were fished out with numbing regularity. Annuo stared hard at the waterway and its promised release from her father's pressure. She could almost imagine the peace she would feel as she slipped into the deep waters. But then she'd remember her plan to escape, maybe even to America. She could never get there by studying medicine. Yet her father would berate her till her dying day if she chose the humanities. She would have to decide soon or else forfeit her acceptance to Tai Da.

By the end of the third day of their impasse, Annuo had an idea. She could offer her father a compromise: She would study law—as her father had. How could he denigrate his own field? She first broached the idea with her mother: "I'm willing to study law instead of literature. I cannot choose medicine." With her mother as go-between, her father grudgingly agreed. It wasn't what Annuo wanted, but at least she would end up with a diploma. In the fall of 1953, Annuo entered the undergraduate program of Tai Da's law school.

Annuo (right) takes a break from her undergraduate law studies at Taiwan University with one of her cousins, circa 1955.

MEANWHILE, THE WAR IN KOREA had led to an open feud between Truman and General Douglas MacArthur, whom the president had appointed supreme commander for the Allied powers. Taiwan figured prominently in their public schism, since MacArthur opposed Truman's hands-off policy toward Taiwan and Communist China. By the time the United States and the People's Republic of China were confronting each other in the Korean War, MacArthur was making public statements in direct contradiction to the president. Whereas Truman was determined to keep Korea from becoming another world war, MacArthur wanted to use Chiang Kai-shek's troops to attack China, even to use nuclear weapons at the risk of drawing the Soviet bloc into a full-scale nuclear world war.

On March 24, 1951, MacArthur torpedoed Truman's efforts to end hostilities by unilaterally declaring his intention to expand military operations against China. Two weeks later, Truman fired him.

A cease-fire in the Korean War was finally brokered in 1953, though the war did not officially end. The border dividing the two Koreas remained at the thirty-eighth parallel, just as it had been before the war. The peninsula, however, had become a cratered moonscape from the intensive bombings. Some five million soldiers and civilians had been killed. General Dwight D. Eisenhower swept to victory as president of the United States, and with a Republican administration in office, the conservative China lobby that supported Chiang Kai-shek regained its influence. One of Eisenhower's first actions in office was to remove Truman's ban against the Nationalist military attacks on the Communist mainland. The Nationalist army was now "unleashed," as Chiang put it, while his stronghold on Taiwan was secured indefinitely under the protection of the United States. Generalissimo Chiang and his son Chiang Ching-kuo vigorously crushed any dissent from Taiwanese *ben sheng ren* and mainland *wai sheng ren* alike. Though the existence of the Republic of China in Taiwan was ensured by the U.S. Seventh Fleet, the price to the republic's citizenry was high.

The war in Korea and the threat of Communist invasion only further solidified the stranglehold of the military and secret police. Annuo's generation was inured to obey rules, to avoid conflict, and to stay off the government's watch list. Like other college students in

Taiwan, she had heard of government raids on campuses. Students suspected of subversive activities or Communist sympathies often disappeared and were never seen again.

Annuo avoided such dangers and did her best to plod through the undergraduate law program. She was completely uninspired, forced to study a subject she disliked. But it was her means to an end, she kept reminding herself: She needed the college degree to apply to graduate school, to get away from this suffocating island. She went through her college years in a daze, as though she had shut down the better part of herself.

Annuo had started at Tai Da when she was almost eighteen. Her bus trips to reach the distant campus took hours each day, and her father's stifling rules from her middle school years still applied: no bicycle riding, no visiting friends, no trips away, no dating, no boyfriends. Although boys were forbidden, she was also warned that she could marry only an engineer or a scientist. How will I ever meet anyone to marry? Annuo fretted. Maybe my father's old condemnation is right—no one will want to marry me.

By the time she was ready to graduate, Annuo felt more lonely and isolated than ever. At twenty-two, she didn't have many girlfriends and wouldn't dare to try to meet boys. She was squelching her dreams—just as her mother had done with hers—to satisfy the demands of her father. It dawned on Annuo that she was becoming the person she never wanted to be. She had to get away.

NEW YORK, 1950

THE CLOUD OVER HO'S LIFE BEGAN TO LIFT AFTER THE INS HAD decided that he could work without fear of deportation. Meanwhile, the political storms affecting the lives of all the stranded Chinese had only intensified from the anti-Communist and isolationist whirlwinds emanating from Washington.

In 1950, a former State Department official and suspected Communist named Alger Hiss was convicted of perjury and imprisoned. American scientist Harry Gold, along with engineer Julius Rosenberg and his wife, Ethel, were charged with spying for the Soviet Union. While Senator Joseph McCarthy launched a hunt for Communists in the State Department, Congress considered ways to limit admission of all immigrants except for those from Northern Europe. The proposals before the American public included the exclusion and deportation of potential Communists and subversives, "psychopathic personalities," and "homosexuals and other sex perverts."

The spreading phobia of foreigners and Communists included suspicions that all Chinese were threats to national security, leading Ho and his fellow students to question their long-term prospects in America. Every three months, Ho was required to report in person to the INS regional office at 70 Columbus Avenue in Manhattan to surrender his passport and confirm that his immigration status was unchanged.

Other Chinese students across the United States faced more onerous monthly personal appearances before the INS. Ho was more fortunate than the students in Buffalo or other distant locations who had to travel several hours each way by bus with school chaperones for the brief appearance. Once the INS bureaucracy reviewed each case, the passports were returned by mail with the new extensions. Then the process would begin again.

Unlike Ho, many of his compatriots were still barred from working. Unexpectedly, a window of possible relief appeared in 1950 when more politicians in Washington realized that they could not coerce Chinese students to stay in the United States while at the same time forbidding them to support themselves—especially when those policies were being used as propaganda by the Chinese Communists. Congress passed the China Area Aid Act of 1950, providing six million dollars to assist the stranded students. In addition, the Displaced Persons Act of 1948 and later the Refugee Relief Act of 1953 allowed for a few thousand Chinese and "Far Eastern" refugees to apply for visas and for permanent residence status—similar to provisions that had allowed some two hundred thousand Europeans to enter America as refugees under the Displaced Persons Act, though in far fewer numbers.

Unsure of what to do, many students were hesitant to apply for assistance. After all, they had come to the United States as students, not refugees. Some refused to apply because they objected to the refugee label, which conjured images of impoverished beggars, White Russians, and Ashkenazi Jews in Shanghai.

After weighing the options, Ho warily applied for refugee status. However, global events once again threw the Chinese students and their families, wherever they might be, into turmoil. When North Korea invaded South Korea in June 1950 with support from the Soviet Union, America entered the war two days later, to prevent the spread of Communism. As the new global crisis exploded, Ho and the other stranded Chinese watched closely, unsure how this new war would affect their families, the region, or their own tenuous positions.

When Communist China entered the war, sending two million troops to aid North Korea, Washington's spotlight was back on China.

Congressional hawks, joined by American commander in chief of the United Nations Command, General Douglas MacArthur, seemed intent on total war with the Communists. MacArthur sent U.S. warplanes to rain napalm on nearly every town and hamlet in North Korea and notoriously declared his willingness to use nuclear warheads to create a radioactive wasteland along China's border with North Korea.

Truman rejected MacArthur's bravado, fearing that such an attack against China would draw the Soviet bloc into a nuclear world war, but the possibility of employing nuclear weapons horrified Ho and his friends. With the images of the nuclear holocaust in Hiroshima and Nagasaki fresh in their minds, they knew that a single atom bomb over China's densely populated cities would be deadlier yet, incinerating millions of people, including, perhaps, many of their families.

The exiles met in private, worried huddles, well aware that they had no voice in America. On the one hand, if they opposed an attack against Communist China, they might be labeled as pro-Communist and face arrest and imprisonment by the U.S. government—or by the Nationalists, if they ended up in Taiwan one day. But if they criticized the Communists, their families in China could be harmed in retaliation. Several dozen stranded Chinese students became so frustrated by what they viewed as a forcible detention in the United States that they appealed to Communist China's premier Zhou Enlai to intervene; it is not known if Zhou took action, but their letter and the names of the student signatories immediately entered FBI files. Others posted anonymous letters to American officials, complaining of the detentions as well as the prohibitions against returning home. All such activities became subject to FBI investigation.

Already, it was whispered through the Jiao Tong student-alumni network that one of the school's most prominent graduates living in America was accused of being a Communist. Qian Xuesen, renowned as a leading rocket scientist, had served with the U.S. military during World War II, holding the rank of colonel, after his training at MIT and California Institute of Technology. Qian helped create the U.S. missile program and, after the war, became a professor at Caltech. Qian had sought permission to visit his aging parents in China, but the U.S. government blocked his request, stripped him of his security clearance, and forbade him to leave the country, in spite of the insistence of Qian and many of his American colleagues that he was not a Communist. Then came the shocking news that the INS had arrested the esteemed scientist in September 1950 and imprisoned him on Terminal Island in Los Angeles. Ho and other stranded Chinese scholars were stung by Qian's mistreatment. If a world-famous scientist with a history of loyal service in the U.S. military could be accused and jailed, what could save them from the same treatment or worse?

Qian was the most distinguished Chinese in America to be so accused, but the FBI used harsher tactics against the working-class Chinese in Chinatown and other "downtown" neighborhoods. The INS conducted three "lightning raids" in Brooklyn, arresting eighty-three Chinese suspected to be "aliens," imprisoning them on Ellis Island. Newspaper articles declared that "a great amount of Chinese Communist literature" was seized. A "Confession Program" was being prepared for Chinatown, promising amnesty to anyone who admitted their own illegal entry—and who would snitch on others. The INS and FBI investigated groups like the Chinese Hand Laundry Alliance, which had been critical of Chiang Kai-shek. Chinese as young as eleven years old were being detained for up to a year on Ellis Island.

In defense of such actions against the Chinese in America, John F. Boyd, district director of the Seattle INS branch, later wrote in a memo to the INS Central Office:

> One of the most alarming aspects of the situation . . . is the danger to national security. Most of China is Communist dominated. Some of the Chinese . . . show evidence of indoctrination. These persons will be potentially dangerous in the event of outright war with China. Certainly this is no time to relax the control over them as they seek to enter the United States. The Service would likely be censured by Congress should such relaxation come to attention.

WITH THE KOREAN WAR under way and the angry talk of using nuclear weapons against China, Ho was in for another shock: He received a draft notice for military service from his draft board in Elizabeth, New Jersey. He had registered with the Selective Service System when he went to work for China Motors, as was required of all males in the United States between eighteen and twenty-six. In July 1950, the Selective Service had classified Ho as 1-A. He would be among the first in line to be drafted to fight in Korea. Ho was in disbelief. How could he possibly fight against China? He prepared a letter to his draft board informing them of his impending refugee status and inquiring if that would change his draft classification. After posting his letter, there was nothing to do but wait. Young American men around him were being pressed into military service and sent to Korea. Ho wondered if he might be joining them soon.

Just when matters couldn't get worse, the FBI contacted Ho. They wanted to interview him. Would he be shipped to Ellis Island like his former roommate, or imprisoned like rocket scientist Qian? On the appointed day, he nervously entered the FBI office in downtown Manhattan. The FBI agent asked him to explain his involvement with the Chinese Students' Christian Association. Ho's answers were straightforward and without hesitation: He had only attended the group's social events. He had never been part of any political activity and had no information about it. The FBI agent let him go, but Ho was unnerved by the experience. In the past, he had listed the group on his résumé. Never again.

With Senator McCarthy and the House Un-American Activities Committee widening their witch hunt to target almost anyone, no one in America seemed safe. Like many others in the United States during the 1950s, Ho and the Chinese exiles just wanted to blend in and stay out of trouble.

AFTER A YEAR'S WAIT, in 1951 Ho was approved for refugee status. The new designation came with a bonus: He'd receive a stipend of $150 per month in government assistance for as long as he remained a student. The money couldn't have come at a more critical time. His project to engineer a Chinese typewriter was being shelved, and he would have to find another job.

The newly enacted federal assistance turned visa holders like Ho into "professional students," as they jokingly called themselves. In order to receive the refugee stipend, they had to continue their studies, whether or not they cared to. Because most had entered the United States as graduate students, they had to stay enrolled in a university program. There was another compelling reason to maintain their status: Every Chinese student was well aware that most American companies would not hire a Chinese, regardless of education, skills, or talents. There were plenty of stories of Chinese American graduates with advanced degrees who could find work only as waiters or laundry workers. Ho's $150-per-month refugee stipend was definitely better than the pay at a menial job.

Luckily for Ho, he was still a graduate student at NYU. To get his doctorate, he would have to complete a dissertation. Ho accepted the topic suggested by his adviser—attempting to prove a theory about the effects of vibration on material plasticity. The subject intrigued him, and he'd collect his stipend for as long as it took him to complete his thesis.

Later that year, Ho learned of a small engineering company that was looking for a draftsman. He applied and was offered the low-paying drafting job. As a mechanical engineer, Ho was qualified to do far more advanced work. But knowing that few, if any, American companies were hiring Chinese engineers, he took the job. Fortunately, Ho's new boss soon recognized his talents and encouraged him to adjust his immigration status and obtain a security clearance that would allow him to work on more challenging projects. His company provided Ho with a letter of recommendation to the INS:

MR. CHOW IS AN ESPECIALLY TRAINED MECHANICAL
ENGINEER AND HIS SERVICES WITH OUR COMPANY WILL BE
OF GREAT BENEFIT TO OUR NATIONAL DEFENSE PROGRAM
TODAY. . . . OUR FIRM HAS MADE EVERY EFFORT TO ACQUIRE
AND TRAIN PERSONNEL OF MR. CHOW'S CALIBER, BUT WE
FIND THAT IT IS ALMOST IMPOSSIBLE, IN VIEW OF TODAY'S
CONDITIONS, TO DO SO AS QUICKLY OR EFFICIENTLY AS
HIRING MR. CHOW TO DO THIS WORK. . . . WE REQUEST THAT

MR. CHOW'S APPLICATION BE PROCESSED WITH UTMOST
SPEED SO THAT OUR COUNTRY CAN BENEFIT IN SOME MEASURE
FROM HIS ABILITIES.

The company's efforts paid off. By the end of the year, Ho received approval to work on military projects classified as "confidential" and undoubtedly bound for use in the Korean War. Nevertheless, the INS was never far away, as Ho was reminded each time he reported in person.

By the fall of 1951, new government procedures allowed Chinese scholars and students to apply for a special immigration status as "displaced persons." Such a status was almost as good as a green card and would remove the constant threat of deportation that his temporary status as a refugee student carried. Only a relatively small number of the "most desirable" stranded Chinese scholars would be admitted as displaced persons. In September 1951, Ho applied for displaced person status.

THAT SAME YEAR, by sheer happenstance, Ho met a remarkable woman. One of his friends wanted to drop something off at another friend's apartment on Riverside Drive. Ho tagged along. The location was a pleasant walk to the Hudson River from Ho's place near Columbia. The building was fancier than anything he knew in the student ghetto where he lived. While the friends chatted by the door of the apartment, a young woman came out of another room to meet the visitors.

"This is my younger sister, Junlin Wong," said the host. "She's new to New York—just graduated from Meredith College in Raleigh, North Carolina."

Ho gave her a respectful nod and murmured some congratulatory words. She had a ready smile that dimpled her cheeks like Shirley Temple's. Her eyes, bright and inquisitive, sparkled with friendliness. She was fashionably dressed, and she had an educated and sophisticated demeanor. He sensed at once that she was from Shanghai. When she greeted them in the dialect of the Shanghai region, he was happy that he'd guessed right. Then, in English, she said that in America, she went by the name Theresa.

Ho instinctively smoothed out his shirt and slacks, straightening his back to look taller. He introduced himself, hoping not to sound foolish.

"I'm Ho Chow, and I'm very pleased to meet you. I'm a doctoral student at NYU. Mechanical engineering." He wanted her to know that he was in a desirable field. "How long have you been in New York?" Ho avoided any sensitive subjects, such as when and how she managed to leave China. "You're from Shanghai? My family lives in the former International Settlement on Medhurst Road," he offered. She replied that her family was in Hong Kong but had once lived not far from his home, on Jessfield Road.

Smiling, she answered his questions without a trace of shyness. Ho liked Junlin immediately and knew that he wanted to spend more time with her. But his friend's business with her brother was done, and Ho could think of no good excuse to linger.

"Nice to meet you," Ho heard himself say. "And welcome to New York."

Afraid she would find his comments awkward, he stole a glance as he exited and thought he saw a smile on her face.

Back outside, Ho peppered his friend with questions about the young woman and her family. Her father was a high-level business-man with the Bank of China. He had left China for Hong Kong when the Communists took over. Her father had managed to send his children, including a son, a physician daughter, and Junlin, to school in the States. That was all Ho could learn.

But he was in luck, as he soon ran into her at the China Institute in its building donated by the Luce family at 125 East Sixty-fifth Street. High-society Americans like the Luces supported the institute's programs—and the China lobby to aid the Nationalists. Sometimes the stranded Chinese students held social activities in the organization's basement. Junlin was a volunteer there. As she helped serve tea and cookies, Ho reintroduced himself to her.

Laughing, she said, "I remember you very well, Mr. Chow. I saw you only a few days ago!" Then she turned to greet the other guests.

There were several other bachelors like himself at the event that afternoon. Ho knew he was bound to have competition for Junlin's attention. He would have to be bold. Going back for another cookie, he asked, "Would you like to join me for a walk or at least allow me to escort you home after this party?"

She looked at him quizzically for a moment, then met his gaze. Tilting her head, she said, "I'll have to let my brother know, but yes, that would be lovely."

Ho grinned as he sipped his tea and waited for the event to end. One of his friends noted his buoyant mood and asked, "Did Junlin add something to your tea?"

On their way home, Junlin and Ho went to the park and talked all afternoon. He learned that she had lived at the Bank of China's compound on Jessfield Road in Shanghai, next to the notorious 76. She had been there when the dreaded puppet police from 76 shot three accountants to death in the driveway because of the bank's affiliation with the Nationalists. Afterward, her family had fled with the rest of the bank staff to Kunming. There, she'd had to be ready to run to an air-raid shelter at any moment. Often, she could see the bombs fall from the sky as she ran. When the war was over, her family had returned to Shanghai, and she had attended Aurora College for Women, run by the French Sisters of the Sacred Heart. When the Communists came, she'd fled with her family to Hong Kong. After trying for six months to get a visa to study in America, she had finally entered the United States a year before, in June 1950.

Ho was entranced by this bright and beautiful twenty-two-year-old woman. He told her of his family home in Changshu and his harrowing escape to Shanghai during the war. He was not one to brag, but he wanted her to know that he was a top student, a country kid who had worked his way up to being the number one mechanical engineer at Jiao Tong, and that his prospects were good. Ho tried to sound casual in mentioning that he had a good job—and that, one day, he intended to provide financial help to his family in Shanghai and Taiwan. Shyly, he even shared with her his dream to build cars in China and that he had several inventions in mind.

To Ho's delight, they hit it off. Junlin wasn't put off by his commitment to his family. Although her family in Hong Kong didn't need her to send money, she was determined to support herself by looking for work and was soon hired as a file clerk at Oxford University Press.

They met again. Ho told her how his five housemates at Michigan had rented one cap-and-gown set and taken turns wearing it for the all-important photos to send home. She laughed at herself while recounting her first night at Meredith College, where she had arrived after a long train ride. The housemistress had handed her some sheets for her bed—and Junlin had had no idea what to do with them. She had never made a bed before. He shared his amazement at seeing so much food wasted in America, while Junlin described the dismay she felt about racial discrimination. She'd seen segregated restrooms and water fountains marked "Whites Only" and "Coloreds" while attending college in North Carolina. Being Chinese, she hadn't known which to use.

In late 1951 his draft board wrote to him stating that, because he had turned twenty-seven, he was over the draft age. To his tremendous relief, he would be reclassified as Class 5-A and was unlikely to be called to duty for the war in Korea.

But then came some disappointing news. Ho's doctoral adviser informed him that a PhD candidate at another school had submitted a dissertation solving the exact problem Ho was focusing on. His work had been for naught. If he wanted a doctorate, he'd have to find a new dissertation topic—and to start again. Ho had set his sights on getting a PhD ever since his vocational school teachers had encouraged him. But at his age, he didn't want to start again, especially not when he had a more important goal—he had met the woman he wanted to marry.

Determined to show Junlin that he was such a good catch that she couldn't possibly want to marry anyone else, Ho searched for a better job. He got a driver's license. But his biggest challenge was learning to dance. Junlin was a wonderful dancer, while Ho had never ventured a single step. He took a few lessons and dared to ask her to go dancing, hoping she'd overlook his clumsy feet. In August 1952, he was offered an engineering position with the Celanese Corporation of America at more than four times his draftsman's salary.

Ho's campaign to charm Junlin was a success. He telephoned her

*With a corsage and dinner at a restaurant proffering white
tablecloths, its own photographer, and no Chinese food,
Ho tries to sweep Theresa Junlin Wong off her feet.*

father in Hong Kong at considerable expense for permission to marry
his daughter. She had already told her family all about Ho in the two
years they'd been dating, and her father approved. But with the continued embargo against Communist China, Ho was unable to call his
own mother in Shanghai. Still, he was sure that she would be happy
for him.

On April 5, 1953, Ho Chow and Theresa Junlin Wong were married. About two hundred guests celebrated with them at the Hotel
Greystone on Broadway and Ninety-first Street, a popular venue for
Columbia students. At the simple reception, they served sandwiches
of chopped egg, chopped liver, ham, and sardines. On Ho's happiest
day, his only regret was that no one from his family attended his wedding. His life in America would be perfect if only his family could be
together.

NEW YORK, 1950

AFTER THE WEDDING FESTIVITIES IN OAKLAND, BING AND her husband, John Yee, headed to New York by plane. The roller-coaster flight made several stops to refuel before landing at Idlewild Airport on Long Island. Elder Sister and Peter had taken a transcontinental train to New York. The plan was for Bing to meet up with them before they boarded their ship to Denmark.

John had hired some painters to spruce up his apartment in anticipation of Bing's arrival, but since they hadn't finished in time, he rented a cheap hotel room in Times Square for a week. During the long days while he was at work, Bing explored midtown Manhattan, admiring the skyscrapers and bustling city. There was even a Chinese restaurant in Times Square—Chin Lee's—but unlike the eating places she had known in San Francisco's Chinatown, the customers were American, not Chinese. When she saw the high prices, she didn't eat there either. Instead, she walked and gawked. New York was bigger, taller, brassier than Shanghai, but the energy was instantly familiar and reassuring. Where San Francisco was comfortable and friendly like Suzhou, New York was electric, just like Shanghai. Times Square resembled the more risqué sections in the Badlands and near the Bund, complete with bright lights, prostitutes, and beggars—though instead of the downtrodden being Chinese, here they were all Americans—a strange reversal to the young woman from Shanghai.

When Elder Sister's train arrived, she booked a room at the Hilton near Times Square, where she and Peter would stay a couple of nights before crossing the river to New Jersey for their ship. Stepping into the palatial lobby to meet them, Bing had to smile: Of course Elder Sister would pick a fancy hotel no matter how tight her finances, never the modest place that John had chosen. Elder Sister spotted Bing first and bellowed, "You're so thin! What's wrong with that husband? Is he starving you? I warned you that Cantonese men are cheapskates!" Bing grinned broadly, glad to see Elder Sister and already sad to have to wish her a bon voyage, not knowing if they'd see each other again.

By the end of the week, Elder Sister had departed, and John's apartment on the Lower East Side was ready. The taxi stopped at a six-story walk-up at 32 Henry Street, on the edge of Chinatown. When they stepped into the old, dark building, Bing thought there was some mistake. John unlocked the door to an apartment on the ground floor. Bing looked around in disbelief: The rooms were small and cramped. A covered bathtub sat in the middle of the kitchen, doubling as a table and lit by a circular fluorescent light that cast an eerie glow on the tin-type ceiling. The ill-fitting windows in the front rooms did little to block the sounds and soot from the busy street. Bing straightened her back when she realized there was no bathroom. Before she could ask, John cleared his throat. "The bathroom is down the hall. We share it with the other tenants."

At first Bing said nothing. Finally, she spoke. "The worst place I ever lived in Shanghai was better than this. Must we stay here?"

John gave her a pleading look. "The rent is only eleven dollars a month; that's how I saved two thousand dollars to pay your sister. Please give it a try. That's all I ask."

Bing gave a reluctant nod. Her new life would not be as she had hoped, but she would try to make the best of the situation.

———

NEW YORK'S CHINATOWN WAS smaller than San Francisco's, with far fewer Chinese people. Yet it seemed more congested, hemmed in by Little Italy and the tenements of the Lower East Side, home to generations of immigrants from all over. Each morning after John walked to the Bank of China branch at Chatham Square, Bing went about her own routine. As in San Francisco, most of New York's Chinatown residents were from Taishan and elsewhere in Guangdong's Pearl River Delta. During her months in San Francisco, Bing had already begun picking up some Toisan dialect, which was more useful in America than her own. And as in San Francisco, wherever Bing went, the Chinese workers in the restaurants, shops, and laundries stuck their heads out to get a glimpse of the *Shanghai nui*.

One day, as Bing walked across Doyers Street, an older woman leaned out of the corner curio shop and exclaimed loudly, *"Nung Shanghei-ni?* Are you from Shanghai?"

Bing swung around, startled. This woman spoke her own Shanghai dialect! Excited, Bing went over, and the two began chattering in rapid-fire Shanghainese. Her name was Mrs. Fung, and she claimed she could spot fellow Shanghainese just by the way they carried themselves. She was married to the Cantonese merchant who owned the curio shop and, having lived in New York's Chinatown for several years, could speak the Canton, Toisan, and Shanghai dialects as well as English.

"I didn't think there were any Shanghai people in Chinatown," Bing confessed.

"Oh, there are quite a few," Mrs. Fung said. "On weekends there are even more—the high-nosed 'uptown' Shanghainese only come to Chinatown to eat or buy groceries. But a number of Shanghainese live here, mostly young—like you. They stop at my shop for tea in the afternoons. Come by and meet them."

Soon Bing was a regular at Mrs. Fung's curio shop at the corner of Doyers and Pell, becoming fast friends with the circle of other displaced Shanghai exiles. Some, like Bing, had fled China because of the impending revolution. Others had gotten out during the tumultuous

(From the left) Bing in New York's Chinatown at the curio shop with her downtown friends: Mary Yu, holding her new baby, Maybing and her husband, and the Fungs, the store owners.

war years. Unlike the stranded students and intellectuals, these "downtown Shanghainese" weren't inclined to leave America for a revolution-in-progress—and few could have afforded to go back in any case, or their travel documents might have been too irregular to risk leaving. Bing's circle included Mary and Maybing, two sisters who had married brothers, all from Shanghai. The brothers both were Chinatown waiters who worked at fancy Jewish resorts in the Catskills during the summer. One of the brothers had served as a GI in the Pacific, and thanks to postwar federal legislation, could marry a "war bride" from China without having to apply for one of the 105 immigration quota slots allotted to Chinese. The other brother was a merchant seaman who had jumped ship and bought the paper name of Sing.

Then there was Vicki, a nurse, who had come to America after the

Japanese war and married a Chinatown merchant, and Suzanne, divorced from her diplomatic-corps husband and overstaying her visa; she worked at the Bulova Watch Factory. These downtown Shanghainese had become friends, taking day-trips together to Jones Beach and Coney Island. Like Bing, most were in their twenties. None made enough money to pay uptown rents—and in any case, few landlords beyond Chinatown were willing to rent to Chinese. Chinatown was affordable, and they formed a downtown Shanghai community of their own.

Like the Chinese exiled in the United States, everyone in the downtown Shanghai group had family members in China. They anxiously awaited any word from home, glad to receive even the most cursory news confirming that their families were okay. Sometimes the letters included tiny black-and-white studio portraits. Bing wrote letters to Ma in the painstaking calligraphy she had practiced since the third grade, her last year of formal schooling. She told Ma of her marriage to a good Cantonese man and her life in New York. Bing treasured each missive from home and sometimes caught herself missing Ma, relieved to know that she was safe and well cared for by other relatives.

Yet even as these Chinese looked back to Shanghai, they were putting down roots. By the early 1950s, the women of the postwar marriage boom were having babies. That nasty "love potion" from John's sister must have worked, for Bing was pregnant too. She felt lucky to have such a kindhearted and easygoing husband. When he complained about her cooking, she answered tartly, "Then you cook." And so he did, preparing their dinners from then on. He was delighted to become a father at his age. As Bing's pregnancy progressed, she had to stumble through the dark hallway at night to reach the communal toilet. John promised that he would look for a new place after the baby came.

When their son was born, John named him Henry, the same name as their street. A girl would've been named Catherine for the cross street. Little Henry was as chubby and cheerful as Bing and John were proud and doting. When Henry turned one month old, they had a red-egg celebration at a restaurant. Bing's Shanghai friends came, many with their own small children in tow.

———

IT HAD BEEN MORE than a year since Bing had last seen elder sister Betty. Bing missed her but was glad to have finally set up her own household. Every day, Bing took Henry around Chinatown in his carriage, joining other young mothers out with their children at Columbus Park on Mulberry Street. She ended her daily outing at Mrs. Fung's shop to see her downtown Shanghainese friends. There, Bing caught the latest news about the situation back home and the need for Chinese to be cautious in America. Her friends talked about the clean-cut *lofan* FBI agents, who stuck out like stinky tofu as they surveilled Chinatown, seeking Communists, potential deportees, as well as possible informants. On her way home, she'd pick up some fresh groceries for John to cook for dinner. Her life fell into a pleasant rhythm that offered more contentment than she'd ever dared dream of.

Then came the letter from Elder Sister. She was returning to New York—alone. Her two boys were moving to Australia with their father. Because the mail delivery had been slow from Europe, Bing and John calculated that Elder Sister's ship would arrive in just a few days.

They flew into a frenzy of preparation for Elder Sister's return. Bing couldn't wait to show off her new baby and new life to her sister, but John was in a panic. "Oh, that sister of yours," he moaned. "She'll have nothing good to say when she sees this place."

John was right. Even as Elder Sister's taxi pulled up to their building, Bing could hear the distinctive, booming voice: "Are you sure this is the right place? What kind of a dump is this?" Elder Sister stood outside the building in her leopard-skin coat and French high heels, with several leather suitcases. She practically bowled over John with her energy. "Is this where you brought my sister? No Shanghai woman would want to stay in a place like this." Inside the apartment, she lectured Bing nonstop in Shanghainese, repeating the same basic message: You must learn to control your husband and get him to move into a more suitable location. Though John couldn't understand every word, Elder Sister's meaning was unmistakable.

Pausing occasionally between volleys, she'd stop to look at the baby. Then she'd start again. Bing said nothing, suddenly flashing back to her days as a young girl trying to survive Ma. I don't miss this about Ma—or Elder Sister, Bing realized.

When Elder Sister finally calmed down, she told Bing that Kristian had convalesced slowly while she waited in Copenhagen with Ole and Peter. It hadn't taken long for Betty to conclude that she could not possibly live in Denmark. "The food is terrible; the weather is bad; it's dark all day long in the winter. That's why the people are pale as ghosts. I can't live like that—and I won't."

Kristian didn't want to stay in Denmark either. He feared that the Cold War with the Soviet Union could heat up into another war in Europe. He'd always wanted to move to Australia—and so they'd hit the same impasse as when they'd plotted their escape from Shanghai. This time they'd decided to split up. Kristian would take the boys to Australia, and Betty would return to the United States. He wouldn't contest a divorce should she seek one.

Bing was stunned to learn that Elder Sister was actually going to end her marriage. Bing had thought Betty had been bluffing all along with Lee, the San Francisco man who had paid their expenses for months. In a small voice, Bing asked if this meant Elder Sister was going to get together with Lee. Elder Sister looked blank. "Oh, him? He'll get over it." Bing marveled at Elder Sister's ability to land on her feet, whether in San Francisco, Denmark, or occupied Shanghai. Now she was going to take on New York.

Kristian and the boys left Denmark for Australia via Italy. As Elder Sister had predicted, Kristian was allowed ashore when the Italian liner pulled into Sydney Harbour in January 1951, but his biracial Eurasian sons were not. One Australian newspaper headline queried: "CAN THESE TWO STAY HERE? Immigration officers today temporarily banned from landing two Danish-Chinese children who arrived by ship from Genoa with their Danish father."

Australia's white supremacist policies were so politically charged that the arrival of Peter and Ole, seven and eleven, had violated those race laws. It was big news. After some bureaucratic juggling because of the boys' youth, the national government in Canberra decided to allow them to join their father temporarily until the national government could decide whether to let the half-Chinese boys remain. When

Elder Sister learned of her sons' ordeal, she was incensed—and vindicated. "Can you believe how those Australians treated my boys? They'd never have let me off the ship. And I'd never let them treat me like a second-class person. I was right not to go there!"

Elder Sister rented an apartment on the Upper West Side of Manhattan, near Columbia University and the cluster of educated uptown Shanghainese. This came as no surprise to Bing, knowing how much appearances mattered to Elder Sister—she could never live downtown. Bing was pleased that Elder Sister was close enough to visit and far enough to keep John calm.

Bing was caught unaware, however, by the stream of surprised questions from her Chinatown friends after they met Betty. "Are you really sisters?" they asked. "You're so different in every way." Yes, they were sisters, the two assured everyone.

Elder Sister reminded Bing not tell anyone—not even John—that she was adopted: "People can be cruel. Don't give them reasons to look down on you. Me and you, we're as good as blood sisters."

With all her heart, Bing felt that Betty was a true sister. When friends got a bit too curious, she'd throw them off with a quick answer. Bing's close friend Maybing especially liked to probe.

"Where in Shanghai did you live?" she asked.

"Off Avenue Joffre," Bing had answered truthfully, naming the biggest and longest street in the former French Concession.

"Which school did you attend?"

This was harder to answer because Maybing had been a teacher in Shanghai.

"I had to start and stop school several times during the war," Bing said.

Bing was accustomed to saying little when conversations got personal. She'd been so invisible as a child, it wasn't hard to make herself small. When she couldn't evade a question, she gave a casual shrug and said, "Those are bad memories of wartime."

That was an answer that would stop even the most curious questioner. Every Chinese knew how devastating the eight-year war with Japan had been. Few had been untouched by the suffering, misery, and loss. Among Bing's circle of Shanghai friends, no one wished to rekindle wartime nightmares. Not even her husband. After those tragic war years, everyone had painful stories they'd rather forget. This was the time to look to the future.

IN THE SUMMER OF 1951, John surprised Bing by coming home from work at lunchtime. He knocked on the door, and Bing was puzzled as to why he didn't use his key. When Bing opened it, he staggered in and collapsed on the bed. Bing couldn't rouse him. Panicked, she didn't know what to do. Finally, she put the baby in his crib and ran to the nearest doctor's office, a few blocks away. The doctor was in, and he rushed back with her to Henry Street. The baby was crying, and a neighbor had come into the unlocked apartment to comfort him.

John had suffered a massive stroke. He was alive but unresponsive. The doctor called an ambulance to take John to nearby Gouverneur Hospital in Chinatown. Three weeks later, John died. From his death certificate, Bing learned for the first time that her husband had not been in his forties but in his fifties. Still, it was a shocking death for a seemingly healthy middle-aged man.

An onslaught of emotions swept over Bing: grief, anxiety, fear. Some of John's friends blamed her for failing to call an ambulance to take him to Bellevue Hospital, which they viewed as much better. But Bing knew nothing about American ambulances, hospitals, emergency rooms. Then came all the people who claimed to be friends and associates of John's. She'd never heard John mention most of them, but because he had worked at the Bank of China, they all seemed to think he had a lot of money. Now they contacted his widow, saying that John owed them.

Bing's friends stood by her, helping her with the baby. John's boss and close friend Berne Lee was John's executor and Henry's godfather. He helped Bing sort out John's finances. Elder Sister comforted Bing and watched out for her interests too. John had owned a life insurance policy, a savings account with a small amount of cash, and some stocks—mostly worthless. After paying for the hospital, funeral, cemetery, and various debts, there was enough to put aside a couple thousand dollars for Henry's education and for Bing.

Widowed at twenty-one, in a strange country, with a child not even a year old, Bing faced her new reality. Some people in Chinatown clucked that she was unlucky, that fate was unkind to her. Bing didn't care—they had no idea how much bad luck she had already overcome, and it had made her strong. Now she was grateful for their tenement apartment. She wouldn't have to worry about paying the eleven-dollar rent.

But there were other problems. Everyone in Chinatown knew how the INS and the FBI were hunting for Chinese to arrest and deport. Under orders from Director J. Edgar Hoover, the FBI conducted raids on Chinatown organizations and publications while openly tailing suspected Communists throughout Chinatown. At Mrs. Fung's curio shop, the Shanghainese worried that Chinese like themselves would come under greater scrutiny. News reports said that some Chinese were being held on Ellis Island. What if they were deported—and to where? Back to Shanghai to live under the Communists?

Bing's friends asked her if John had taken care of her immigration status. John had been a naturalized American citizen and everyone, including Elder Sister, had figured Bing would readily become one too. John had even hired a Chinatown lawyer to apply for her permanent resident status as the wife of a U.S. citizen. Concerned, Bing's friends urged her to straighten out her status. But with so many other more pressing matters to attend to after John's death, her immigration matters had to wait.

A FEW MONTHS AFTER John's death, Bing ran into a Shanghai man named Frank Hsieh at Columbus Park, where she often took little Henry to play. She and John had purchased a crib from Frank, the owner of a baby-furniture store in New Jersey. Frank spoke flawless English, having studied at St. John's University, and had lived in America for more than a decade. He had been a translator at the United Nations for a time and held a number of odd jobs before buying the baby-furniture store.

Bing was impressed by how much Frank Hsieh knew about America. He began to call on the young widow. When Bing told him about Elder Sister's plan to get a divorce, he suggested that she file in Florida. He had been through a divorce himself and knew that courts moved faster in Florida than New York. Frank offered to take Elder Sister and Bing to Florida in his car for a short holiday. Elder Sister encouraged Bing: "Why not? He's sweet on you, and if he'll take us there for free, let's go!"

Bing, Elder Sister, and baby Henry piled into Frank's Studebaker. After a two-day drive, they were in Miami, basking in the sun. It was fun for Bing, the kind of trip she'd seen in magazines and movies. They found two rooms at a cheap motel, with Bing, Elder Sister, and Henry sharing one. Frank had been right—Elder Sister's divorce sailed through. To celebrate, they went to a little diner near the motel on their last night. Everyone was in great spirits—until Frank and Elder Sister started talking about China.

"That Chiang Kai-shek has never worked for the best interests of the Chinese people," Frank argued. "He robbed China blind and let the people starve to death while lining his pockets with American dollars. No wonder so many Chinese turned to the Communists."

"What? How dare you say such garbage about the generalissimo!" demanded Elder Sister. "You must be a Commie pinko!"

Bing listened helplessly with Henry on her lap as the conversation rapidly spun out of control. In Chinatown, tempers flared whenever the issue of the "two Chinas" arose. Now her sister and her suitor were going at it. Bing knew that Elder Sister would never back down— and soon it was clear that Frank wasn't about to either. Their voices grew louder as they began cursing in Shanghainese.

"You college boys think you're so fucking smart," spat Elder Sister. "You're no better than dog shit."

"Goddamn you, big-mouth whore. What do you know?" he shot back. "I was in Chongqing during the war; I saw it all firsthand when you were screwing white devils in Shanghai. How dare you!"

Suddenly they were throwing things. Frank tossed his drink at Elder Sister, then heaved the glass, shattering it. She slapped him, knocking his wire-rimmed glasses to the ground, breaking them. The police came and hauled Frank to the station. Elder Sister jumped up to leave, practically dragging Bing and her baby with her to catch the first bus back to New York.

On the long ride, Elder Sister fumed at Bing. "If you ever see that useless mule penis again, we can't be sisters. It'll be over between us!"

FRANK MADE IT BACK from Florida and began calling on Bing again. When he was with her, he was charming and gentle. He recited couplets by China's great poets, and Shakespeare sonnets. He wrote beautiful love letters and poems to her. There were no signs of the angry man she had seen in Miami. They didn't talk about the ugly incident and never mentioned Elder Sister.

Some of Bing's friends in her Chinatown community knew Frank. As word got around about the fight in Miami, her friends warned her to stay away from him. "He can't control his temper," they said. "Don't get involved with that guy."

Frank kept stopping by. Bing had never had such attention lavished on her, not even from John. Whereas John had been hesitant to marry her, Frank was smitten and eager to wed. John had been cautious about spending money, while Frank wanted to take her places and

True to her haipai *Shanghai spirit, Betty (right) was always fashionable and perfectly coiffed, even on a visit to Chinatown to see Bing and her baby in their tenement flat in 1951.*

didn't worry about the expense. He was handsome and athletic, with big ideas about China, politics, world peace. Though Frank was older than Bing, he was much younger than John had turned out to be. He made her feel beautiful and wanted. Special. That was something new—and Bing liked it.

Moreover, Bing was a young single mother. What about her son's future in this foreign land? Others warned her about Frank, but would they be around to help her when the insurance money ran out? Frank might not have been perfect, but he was educated. After dating so many waiters in San Francisco, she wasn't sure that she'd find anyone better. Maybing's husband had turned out to be a gambler who squandered his children's food money at the racetrack. Elder Sister was still looking for her next husband. Even if Frank had a bad temper, she had seen his kind and loving side. Surely he would be different with her.

When Frank asked Bing to marry him, he said he'd treat Henry as his own. Bing wanted to say yes, but how would she win over Elder Sister? She knew she had to make her own decisions rather than always following the commands of the two women who had dominated her life. But then the choice was made for her: Bing discovered she was pregnant. They went to a justice of the peace and were married in late 1951, with Bing radiant in a borrowed wedding gown. Frank was overjoyed to marry this beautiful young woman—and to be an expectant first-time father.

BING'S NEW LIFE WAS off to a good start: Frank rented an apartment in a brand-new high-rise, complete with an elevator and basement laundromat, in Irvington, New Jersey. She was finally able to move out of the tenement with the communal toilet down the hall. Elder Sister had found a Chinese businessman to marry; she put aside her differences and invited Bing to the wedding, without Frank. Elder Sister repeated her admonition to Bing: Don't tell anyone, especially not Frank, that you're adopted. Even without the warning, Bing had no intention of telling Frank: She figured that if he knew that they weren't blood sisters, he'd never let her see Elder Sister. Whenever Frank asked her a question about her life in China, Bing gave her stock answer: "The war years are bad memories that I try to forget." Soon he stopped asking.

Just when the couple was settling down after Bing had given birth to a baby girl, she received a notice from the INS ordering her to appear at a deportation hearing. Bing tried not to panic. Her marriage to Frank, coming only eight months after John's death, had drawn considerable disapproval in her close-knit community. Had someone reported her? Frank took Bing to the Chinatown immigration attorney whom John had hired to adjust her immigration status. The lawyer had done nothing. Now the INS was accusing her of overstaying her visitor visa, which had expired two years earlier in November 1949, right after her marriage to John. His American citizenship should have led to her permanent residency, but his death had thrown her into jeopardy. Worse yet, with the Korean War under way, Communist China was America's enemy. Politicians in Washington were raising alarms about the Chinese threat in America. Surveillance, arrests, and deportations in Chinatown continued unabated.

At least Bing didn't have to face the immigration court on Staten Island by herself. Frank was with her at every step, able to navigate the court with his fluent English and knowledge of American ways. He testified that she was his wife and that they had two native-born American children. The immigration officials ruled that the U.S.-citizen children would be harmed if their mother were sent away. Bing's deportation was suspended, and she was granted a green card to stay in the United States as a permanent resident.

But now the INS fixed its spotlight on Frank. He had entered the United States on a diplomatic visa and then stayed under the radar when he left the United Nations. By defending Bing, he had made himself vulnerable. The INS launched an investigation into his status and found that he had not worked at the UN in years. Federal agents went to their apartment, arrested and detained him.

With help from John's life insurance proceeds, Frank posted the required five-hundred-dollar bond and was released from immigration detention in Newark. However, the INS launched a "special inquiry" investigation because Frank had written numerous articles about China and was outspoken in his criticism of Chiang Kai-shek.

After more than two years of hearings and legal limbo with no end in sight, Frank and Bing expected to be deported to Taiwan, a place neither had ever been. The journey would be all the more difficult because they had a third child—and another on the way.

Worn down by the stress of the immigration proceedings and exhausted by so many pregnancies in a short time, Bing became ill and was diagnosed with tuberculosis. The cost of his immigration case and expenses for the children had drained Frank's finances, leaving him little money to pay for doctors. Most upsetting of all, health officials were threatening to take her children away. What more could happen? It seemed ages ago that she had left Shanghai convinced that her bad luck as a twice-abandoned girl was changing. Now she had to wonder—if good fortune ever came her way, would she have any strength left to hold on to it?

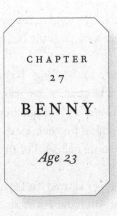

NANJING, 1951

IN MAY 1951, THE PINK-TINGED MAGNOLIA BLOSSOMS WERE IN full bloom, and Benny was enjoying his second spring in Nanjing. He had been working at the National YMCA office for more than a year when a telegram from Annie, his elder sister, arrived. Benny braced himself.

The message was brief:

FATHER IS DEAD. GO TO THE PRISON, GET HIS THINGS.

Benny felt as though his heart had stopped momentarily. Then he said a silent prayer for his father. Benny had feared that this day would come. He left immediately for Shanghai, where he learned that his father had been executed at Tilanqiao Prison. That was all he needed or wanted to know. He had to acknowledge that it was a miracle his father had stayed alive for so long. At least I'll never have to go into that shameful place again, he told himself.

Just beyond the immense prison gate, Benny collected his father's worldly goods from the surly guards—some articles of clothing and his wire-rimmed spectacles. There was no body to collect; it had already been disposed of.

Is this all that's left of him? Benny wondered. He choked back his remorse for failing in his duty to give his father a proper burial. He asked for his father's forgiveness as the heavy door slammed behind him.

When Benny returned to Nanjing, he received more shocking news. His mother, too, was gone. After learning of the execution at Tilanqiao Prison, his mother's lover apparently had concluded that the Communists were coming for them next. Rather than face arrest, imprisonment, and execution, he had shot Benny's mother dead, then killed himself.

Shutting his eyes, Benny pictured his beautiful and gentle mother. He could almost feel her soft hand reaching out to him, brushing his hair out of his eyes, as she had done so often when he was a boy. He had been her favorite then. She had made no secret of that, indulging his every wish. He had adored her too. Before the ugliness of his father's arrest and his mother's departure, nothing pleased him more than bringing a smile to her face.

After all their misfortunes, now this. Hot tears rolled down his face as he choked back a sob. The ominous prophecy his mother had flung at Doreen had come true: They would never see her again. No one would. His father's decision to work with the Japanese had come at a terrible price. Now both of Benny's parents were dead under odious circumstances. None of the extravagant pleasures they had enjoyed were worth this, Benny decided. His head bowed under the weight of his sorrow. In the quiet of his room, he dropped to his knees and prayed for his parents and once proud family.

BENNY FOUND HIS RELIEF in solitude. During lunch breaks, he'd walk along the Qinhuai River or the shaded streets near the Temple of Confucius, where the heavy fragrance of osmanthus soothed him. At work, Benny concentrated on his daily tasks as a secretary at the YMCA headquarters as well as his Christian outreach work. Talking to others about God's mercy brought him comfort in the face of his own losses. He was grateful to be in Nanjing—not just for his anonymity, but also because in Shanghai the Communist Party seemed especially determined to keep watch over the city's huge and volatile population. His Christian colleagues there seemed more on edge. At least in Nanjing he could suffer through his grief in private, safe from the judgment of others.

During his trip to recover his father's effects, Benny hadn't visited his sister or other relatives. With their father labeled a counterrevolutionary and traitor of the worst order, they tacitly agreed it would be unwise to see one another. Benny didn't dare to look for his youngest siblings, Edward and Frances. They were now wards of the Communist government, and it could be harmful to them to have someone from their father's family add to their stigma. At least they were teenagers, he reasoned, hoping they could fend for themselves.

The Communist Party had begun instructing the general population to root out Rightists and counterrevolutionary behavior. Benny had heard the stories of neighbors, coworkers, family members, even children, being enjoined to report on anyone they suspected of being an enemy of the state. Kenneth Wang, the president of Aurora College for Women and a Harvard Law School graduate, had planned to stay in Shanghai with his wife, Mary, and their three young sons. But they knew it was time to leave their beloved city when their seven-year-old challenged their "incorrect behavior" for listening to Voice of America on the radio. Vem Chuang was eight years old when his prominent Shanghai family was held under house arrest in their luxury Embankment Building apartment as Communist officials subjected the children to a "struggle session," exhorting them to speak up against their adult family members. Eventually, one child reported that his uncle had committed crimes against the revolution; the child was praised and his uncle executed.

Yet in the two years since the Red Army marched into Shanghai, the city had changed for the better in notable ways. Pedicabs, carts, lorries, and trams still fought for space on the crowded streets, but the beggars, prostitutes, black-market peddlers, and opium dens that were once deemed permanent fixtures in Shanghai had virtually disappeared. This impressive feat instilled a certain public confidence in the new regime. In addition, the trains between Nanjing and Shanghai were running on time, and prices for tickets and other goods had finally stabilized after the years of wild inflation under the Nationalists, improving everyone's lives. Shopkeepers' doors were open for business, though with noticeably fewer goods to sell, a situation that the new government blamed on the imperialist bombings and embargo by the Nationalists and Americans.

AFTER THE LIBERATION, the workers, peasants, soldiers, and others on the "red" proletarian side of the class spectrum had taken to the streets in wild celebration of the revolution that was supposed to break the chains of their oppression. On the opposite "black" counterrevolutionary side, the capitalists and landowners who hadn't fled in the exodus were nervously hoping to ride out the storm, praying that the upheaval would soon pass.

Between those extremes was the middle class—the petite bourgeoisie of skilled professionals, small business owners, and intellectuals. Premier Zhou Enlai himself issued assurances that they had

Prisoners, en route to be executed, are paraded through crowds lining the main streets of Shanghai.

nothing to fear, that a peaceful transition to socialism would keep them unscathed, and that they should call on their sons and daughters studying overseas to return and rebuild China. Zhou promised that they would be welcomed back with open arms.

However, less obvious to Benny and other observers of the new regime were the decisions of the Communist Party Central Committee in Beijing to consolidate its power. Having gained control over national security and essential services, the government began extending its reach into other aspects of everyday life. At work, Benny noticed that more worried letters were coming to the YMCA national office, asking for guidance on how to handle the increasing demands and pressures on church groups—such as the heavy tax levies imposed on schools, churches, and businesses. The Sisters of Loretto, who had operated schools for girls in Shanghai and elsewhere in China since 1923, were drowning under the onslaught of new taxes. The remaining American administrators of St. John's University discovered it was nearly impossible to exchange monies sent by the American Episcopal Church Mission to pay for an unexpected government assessment of eighteen million renminbi (approximately four thousand dollars).

A number of missionaries intended to stay in China "for the duration." To allay their concerns, they pointed to a letter by Premier Zhou Enlai signed on February 26, 1949, stating, "The faith of the Christian churches and our party's ideology may differ, but we are one in service of the people. The Christians' love for the common folk, their nurture of human personality and boundless efforts for the common good especially, have won our party's high esteem."

But that was before the revolution was completed. Now many who stayed in China found themselves in an impossible position: The government ordered them to pay higher wages and heavier taxes while drastically limiting their ability to cut costs. To keep the precarious economy from being flooded with more jobless workers, the new government forbade employers to lay anyone off, from clerks and factory workers to domestic household servants. Employers would first have to provide expendable workers with severance packages in amounts to be determined by the Communist government. In the meantime, employers were still required to pay the rising taxes.

The changes worried Benny. The rhetoric had grown more fever-ish after the United States entered the Korean War in June 1950 and sent its Seventh Fleet to support Taiwan, then threatened to drop atomic bombs on China. In response, a mass force of People's Libera-tion Army troops had headed into the frigid Korean Peninsula. Some Chinese soldiers had no weapons or ammunition and were instructed to get their weapons by killing enemy soldiers.

Just as in the United States and Taiwan, the government in main-land China further tightened its control in the name of national secu-rity. Chairman Mao had written, "Who are our enemies? Who are our friends? This is a question of the first importance of the revolution." The Communist leadership launched a new mass movement against internal enemies called the "Campaign to Suppress Counterrevolu-tionaries." Its targets included formerly respected leaders of a more traditional and "feudal" Chinese society who were now deemed "counterrevolutionary" and "Rightist." Extending the campaign to the cities, Communist officials organized mass meetings to "struggle against" those "bad elements" and teach them the errors of their old and backward ways. Previous land reform campaigns hadn't touched the urban capitalists and middle classes in cities like Shanghai or Nan-jing. With a war going on against the American imperialists, this cam-paign would put Shanghai's urban elites on a tighter leash.

Religious organizations, too, were declared counterrevolutionary. In April 1951, the government in Beijing had called together a "Con-ference of Christian Institutions," during which prominent Commu-nists leveled devastating accusations at leading missionaries and Chinese Christians. Overnight they were labeled agents of American imperialism. It was a signal that the Communist Party was ready to take on religion—what Karl Marx had called the "opium of the masses." Benny and other YMCA workers could feel the earth trem-bling beneath their feet.

At the conference, a bishop, Francis Xavier Ford, and his secretary, Sister Joan Marie Ryan, of the Maryknoll Society, one of the largest American Catholic missions remaining in China, were denounced for engaging in "espionage activities behind a false missionary front." The two had already been arrested and were imprisoned. Seven other leaders of various denominations were accused of being "tools of American imperialist aggression." Some leaders within the National YMCA itself attacked the Y's international leadership for doing "undercover work" in the service of their "American masters." In each case, the accused were denounced by close friends and former colleagues. The message was clear: Independent religious organizations were no longer welcome in China.

BENNY'S QUIET LIFE IN Nanjing was endangered—the YMCA had become unsafe for the son of a traitor. In his St. John's network, other graduates reported being shamed for having attended a "black imperialist university." While red symbolized everything good and revolutionary under the Communist government, black signified everything counterrevolutionary and bad beyond redemption. The harsh words worried him.

Though Benny had endured fewer fellowship meetings and worship services, now the Christian teachings themselves were being changed. The Communist Party launched the "Three-Self Patriotic Movement" to bring foreign missionary teachings in line with party ideology. Christian churches were required to adopt the Three Selfs: self-governance rather than foreign church leadership, self-support rather than foreign financing, and self-propagation—no missionary proselytizing. Foreign religious doctrine, including the Bible, was suspect.

Benny knew that it was time to leave the YMCA. If he stayed, he too might be singled out as a *yang nu*—foreign slave—or a *zou gou*—running dog. He made discreet inquiries about other work and learned of a position at the Nanjing Agricultural University. Its library needed someone to type index cards in English for their card catalog. With the exodus of so many foreign residents and educated Chinese, a large number of English-language books had been collected by the library and needed to be cataloged. How ironic, Benny mused, that his English education at the "black imperialist school" landed him the job.

The library offered exactly the obscurity Benny had hoped for. Wartime politics had condemned his parents, and he was determined not to let that happen to him. If he had learned anything from his family's catastrophe, it was to lie low. He was glad to learn that the library had a vast number of books to catalog. It would take him a long time to plod through them, typing one card at a time.

Benny moved from the YMCA in the commercial center of Nanjing to the university on the quiet outskirts at the base of Purple Mountain, its peak graced by Sun Yat-sen's mausoleum. It all suited Benny just fine. He wanted to get away from the mass movements and public denunciations that disrupted the busier parts of the city.

With every turn of the Cold War, China was becoming more isolated from the rest of the world, to the alarm and dismay of the cosmopolitan Shanghainese and educated elites who had remained. U.S. efforts to "contain" China and block its recognition in the UN further limited its international contact. But in Benny's quiet corner of the library, he had access to English-language publications and news. There he learned that thousands of Tibetans had fled into exile after Tibet's annexation by China in September 1951. He read about General MacArthur threatening to use nuclear weapons and wanting to send Nationalist soldiers in Taiwan to attack China—acts that could lead to a new world war, with China in the crosshairs.

Benny had quit the YMCA just in time. In 1952, the Communist Party initiated another mass political movement, this time against Rightist thinking. Virtually all foreign religious institutions were finally shut down, with any remaining missionaries charged with various crimes and ultimately forced to leave China. The Sisters of Loretto had to shutter their schools under the watchful eyes of police so that they would not steal "the people's property." McTyeire School for Girls was converted into a public school with the proletarian name Shanghai No. 3. St. John's University was dismantled: Its medical school and departments of agriculture, architecture, and engineering were absorbed by other universities. Some of its notable alumni were listed as criminals; campus buildings were reborn as the East China University of Political Science and Law. After seventy-three years in Shanghai, the beloved school that had educated three generations of Benny's family had vanished.

Each political firestorm and mass movement was followed by another campaign more disruptive and vehement than the last. The Three Anti campaign targeted corruption, waste, and bureaucratism to tighten the reins on party members. This was followed by the Five Anti campaign—a full broadside aimed at the evil ruling class that Benny was part of. The bourgeoisie was under attack with the goal of purging its five poisons: bribery, tax evasion, stealing of state property, cheating on government contracts, and insider trading. Once again, the entire population was mobilized to search for the poisoned ones in their midst, to publicly struggle with them, and to make them confess and reform.

This intense new political movement gave Benny another reason to be grateful that he was out of Shanghai. If he'd stayed there, the son of the traitor would have been hauled in front of a mass gathering to be criticized and humiliated into confessing his sins. In Nanjing, he could still be relatively anonymous. But even in Nanjing, Benny had to answer to the Five Anti campaign. As a graduate of the black imperialist school, he faced interrogation to root out his "bourgeois thinking." There was nothing he could do but grit his teeth and cooperate by confessing to everything he could think of.

If they say one plus one is three, I, too, will say three, he told himself. He relied on advice that his dear grandfather dispensed during sessions with his opium pipe: "A dog who can tuck his tail between his legs will live to be an old dog." With this latest political upheaval aimed at people of Benny's background, he did his best to keep his tail down.

Benny didn't try to hide his father's collaboration with the Japanese or his connection to 76. They'd have found out anyway. He told them that he had ridden his bicycle at 76. His questioners were appalled and disgusted, but they had to concede that he had been only twelve years old then. Benny managed to avoid getting labeled as a counterrevolutionary or Rightist. Fortunately, he had never spoken out on political issues and was too young to have done anything questionable during his father's days as a collaborator. He was released from his interrogations without incident.

Benny retreated further into the bowels of the library to find shelter among the books. With no church services or fellowship gatherings available, he didn't dare show his Bible in public. Instead, he repeated the Lord's Prayer in silence. It was his way of "self-preaching," his private protest of the Three-Self movement. Yet he was lonely. He missed his friends and family but couldn't contact them. They were all from counterrevolutionary class backgrounds, and they might be accused of plotting and scheming together if they stayed in touch. He'd face even more trouble if he communicated with Doreen and Cecilia, for they lived among the imperialists in Hong Kong. He hadn't written to them since just after his parents' deaths, not even to give Doreen his new location.

At times he felt as if he were moving through life while standing still. He lived simply, staying in a single room in the staff dormitory and taking his meals at the communal canteen. He tried not to think of his family's misfortunes, but some memories still seeped into his thoughts. Glorious Sunday dinners in the big mansion on Jessfield Road. Annie's wedding at the Paramount ballroom; dancing on the glass floor with colored lights glowing from below. There were all those good times he'd had with Dennis and George in their BDG Club. It was another lifetime ago when they zipped through the streets of Shanghai, first on their bicycles, later on motorcycles, getting a steak with eggs and mashed potatoes at the Cosmopolitan for one U.S. dollar. Or hot chocolate at DD's. Benny could almost taste the creamy sweetness of the White Russian baker's cheesecake. Rather than cheering him, the once-happy memories now intensified his feelings of loss and regret.

CHAPTER

28

DOREEN

Age 20

HONG KONG, 1951

BENNY'S LETTER ARRIVED ONE SUMMER MORNING WHEN THE steam of Hong Kong's heat was already stifling. Doreen was at a low point, discouraged by her fruitless job search as ever more refugees arrived to compete for the lowest-paying jobs. With tensions high because of the war in Korea, Benny's letter had been delayed even more than usual. Mail to or from the Chinese mainland was screened twice, by censors on each side of the border scrutinizing for pro- or anti-Communist subversion, depending on which direction it was headed.

The Pan sisters hadn't heard from their brother in some time. As Cecilia scanned the letter's contents with nervous anticipation, she let out a terrifying scream. Doreen rushed over and read the shocking news: Both their mother and their father were dead. Killed under the most grievous of misfortunes. She collapsed with a protracted wail.

The news was almost too much to bear. Mother and Father both shot to death? The two sisters momentarily put aside their differences to clutch each other, as if to pull their parents back from the hungry ghosts. Doreen wept tears of regret and guilt. "If only I had stayed behind as Mother wanted," she cried, "perhaps she'd still be alive!" The next time Doreen went to Victoria Peak, she seriously contemplated flinging herself from the mountaintop. Maybe then she'd see her mother and father in the next world. Consumed with remorse,

Doreen fell into depression. She grieved for her parents and worried about Edward and Frances, who were not much younger than she. Benny had written that their welfare was now in the hands of the Communist authorities.

Walking with her eyes downcast one afternoon, Doreen had a chance encounter with fate. She'd come up empty after another day job hunting. Not eager to hear her sister's complaints, Doreen dawdled along the narrow, winding streets of Tsim Sha Tsui in Kowloon. Many Shanghai exiles lived in the tall apartment buildings there, crammed into rentals that had been divided and subdivided so many times, there was barely space for a cot. She found small comfort walking among the crowded buildings, listening to passersby speak the Shanghai dialect—a tiny slice of home. Suddenly she heard a familiar voice shout, "Doreen! Doreen Pan!" She spun around to see a well-dressed young woman about her age waving. It was Mamie Tong, her closest friend from St. Mary's Hall. Overjoyed, Doreen ran to Mamie, and the two friends clasped hands.

"I thought I recognized you—I've been running to catch up with you!" Breathless words spilled out of Mamie's mouth.

"I can't believe it's you! I thought I'd lost all my friends," Doreen exclaimed. Mamie was one of the few girls who hadn't shunned her after Pan Da's arrest, but Mamie had disappeared from school when her family fled Shanghai as the exodus reached full throttle in late 1948. Her father and brother worked in the shipping business and had left for Hong Kong months earlier, sending for Mamie and the rest of the family once they were settled. The two former classmates stood on the narrow street catching up in nonstop Shanghainese as other pedestrians streamed by.

Mamie had been in Hong Kong for over two years. She had a good job with a company that was well known in Shanghai, the Moller Shipping Line. The Mollers were a Jewish family who had arrived in Hong Kong from Sweden in the 1860s, later expanding to Shanghai and making their fortune in shipping, insurance, real estate, and other businesses. Everyone in the former French Concession knew the huge Scandinavian-style Moller castle not far from where Doreen's family had once lived. Mamie's elder brother James had told her about the Moller office in

Hong Kong—and that the relocated Moller managers from Shanghai preferred to hire other Shanghainese. They wanted employees who were sophisticated and would project the professional demeanor of Shanghai. All five of the office clerks were former St. Mary's girls.

After relating all this, Mamie shared the most important bit of information: Lowering her voice, she told Doreen that their classmate Isabel Chao was quitting Moller to take a job at the American consulate. Isabel had always been one of the sharpest and most poised girls in their class, Mamie noted. No wonder she'd been hired by the Americans. So there would soon be a job opening at the Moller company! The office hadn't started looking for a replacement, Mamie said. If Doreen needed work, she'd have a good chance.

"Do I need work?" Doreen's eyes widened. "Oh my, yes! I've been hunting for a job ever since I got to Hong Kong, and no luck! I've been so discouraged."

The next day, Doreen put on a dark, striped *qipao,* one of her few dresses—not too flashy, suitable for an office. In Hong Kong, it was easy to pick out the Shanghai women in a crowd: They were the ones with a confident flair, who could look fashionable in a plain dress. *Haipai,* some called it, the notorious Shanghai attitude. Hong Kong women resented those from Shanghai, but the local men didn't mind staring. Doreen managed to hide her nervousness as she followed Mamie to the Moller Shipping Line office.

Inside, Doreen saw women busy at work on what Mamie explained were Hollerith machines. As Doreen drew near, she recognized all of the young women. It made her so happy, seeing these women who once were like sisters, having boarded together from the time they were in junior middle school. Doreen fought the urge to rush over to them. Instead, she flashed her friends a discreet smile and waited primly for her interview. In the Shanghai dialect, a supervisor called her over. He fired off questions as he looked her over: "You went to St. Mary's too? So you know English and Western etiquette like the other girls? Can you type?"

Nodding vigorously, Doreen answered, "Yes, sir!" in English. "I speak English fluently. I'm a quick learner, and I can type fast in English. I'll get along well with the others too."

Doreen was hired on the spot. Mamie showed her how to use the big Hollerith card-punching machines. Doreen was thrilled to be working at a well-known Shanghai company, with the added benefit of being with her friends from St. Mary's. During their breaks, they told her the latest gossip about other Shanghai classmates who, like her, had once been pampered Shanghai princesses. They whispered about former Shanghai playboys who were now driving taxicabs or washing dishes—if they were lucky enough to have jobs. Even more shocking were the familiar names of young women from good Shanghai families who were making money as dance-hall or singsong girls in Hong Kong. Doreen decided not to tell the others about her sister's pressure to become one of those girls herself.

Doreen Pan (far left) and three of her St. Mary's schoolmates in Hong Kong visit with one of their former teachers (center) in the early 1950s.

DOREEN'S JOB AT MOLLER gave her more than an income. She gained back her confidence and reconnected with a circle of old friends who had known her in a happier time. In those long-ago days, she used to wear the latest styles, even sporting a mink coat at school. All of them had lived the luxurious life of Shanghai's Chinese elite. Back then, none of them could have imagined *having* a job, let alone *needing* one.

It didn't take Doreen long to master the office machines. She produced balance sheets and shipping reports with the punch cards, sorters, and collators. She was glad to learn the new skills when everyone was saying that computational machines were the wave of the future. And she could practice her proper American English with customers from around the world.

Her pay was 350 Hong Kong dollars a month—about 40 U.S. dollars. She gave 100 HK dollars to her sister Cecilia, who sniped and caviled that Doreen's office wage was small change compared to what she'd get at a dance hall. To Doreen, it was a fortune. She sent another 100 HK dollars to Benny as often as she could. The periodic letters from him contained only the most superficial and upbeat news. But newly arrived refugees from China told another story, about food rationing, continuing shortages, hunger. Pro-Nationalist agitators in Hong Kong spread stories about mass meetings where thousands of "red" workers and peasants were stirred up to demand confessions from the "black" capitalist enemies for their crimes against the working people and to humiliate, beat, even kill the counterrevolutionaries. Doreen knew she couldn't believe everything the partisans said about the Communists, but she had no doubts that Benny, with their family's background, would be considered very black. She knew that, in spite of his cheerful letters, his life could not be good. She sent him what she could, sometimes sending rice, oil, and sugar instead of money. She figured that he could use the little she sent.

With the remaining money from her paycheck, Doreen covered the costs of her bus and ferry fare. There wasn't much left for new clothes. She stopped eating meals at her sister's apartment so Cecilia would have one less cause for complaint. Fortunately, the Moller owners, themselves exiles from Shanghai, gave their employees food vouchers in addition to their salaries. The Mollers wanted their staff to have at least one decent meal a day. They knew that if they provided cash for food, their workers would likely scrimp on meals and spend the money on other necessities. The food vouchers, for use at Café Wiseman on Queen's Road Central, would buy a set lunch of soup, entrée, vegetables, and dessert, Western style.

Taking advantage of the Mollers' generosity, Doreen and her clever St. Mary's classmates found that by skipping lunch or sharing one meal between them, they could sell their weekly vouchers for 4.5 HK dollars each. If they sold six vouchers, they'd have enough to buy fabric and hire a tailor to make a new dress. A coat took a month's worth of vouchers. With better clothes and good friends, Doreen went out with her pals and started to meet young men. That also mollified Cecilia, who feared that her unmarried sister would be a burden forever.

Occasionally, Doreen ran into others from her past life in Shanghai. Some classmates had fared much better than she: While Isabel Chao's superb English had landed her a job at the American consulate, Diane Tang Woo, whose father had been killed by a bullet intended for T. V. Soong, moved in with an aunt on Robinson Road, one of the finest locations in Hong Kong's Mid-Levels and the highest point where Chinese were allowed to live. Doreen heard about others who were not doing as well, including some classmates of Benny's from St. John's: George Shen had arrived with only five HK dollars and was sleeping on a table in an auto parts shop run by a family friend. Ronald Sun's accounting degree from St. John's was deemed invalid by the British accounting firms where he sought work. Valentin Chu, who had been a journalist with the esteemed *China Press* in Shanghai, was given such demeaning work at the British *China Mail* paper that he announced he was going to quit. Shocked that a Chinese would speak out, his editor argued that he couldn't quit; he'd have to be fired. Defiant, Val said, "To hell with you" and walked out. His Chinese, Indian, and Filipino coworkers followed him to shake his hand—they had never seen anyone stand up to the British. "I'm from Shanghai," he replied. "I'm not colonized." Nevertheless, Val and the other St. John's men struggled, moving from one vermin-infested hovel to the next.

Once, as Doreen boarded a tram on her way home from work, she spotted a young man who looked familiar. As she looked in his direction, she saw him duck as if to avoid her. His skin was tawny brown from the sun, and he was wearing the janitorial uniform of the Ho Man Tin refugee resettlement authority. Then she realized with a start that it was Ben Char, another St. John's fellow who had once dated her sister Cecilia! When they both arrived at the depot to catch the Star Ferry, Doreen called his name. Looking sheepish, Ben took off his worn cap and greeted her. "Doreen Pan—you're looking well. How long have you been in Hong Kong?" While riding on the Star Ferry, the two shared sketches of their journeys.

Ben had taken his brother's car to Taiwan, almost running over several people in Shanghai when his brakes failed. On the ship, he'd had to sleep in the car on the open deck. Having no food, he ate with the crew from a communal pot of rice, with flies swarming so thick it was impossible to eat the rice without swallowing a few. "I was so naïve; I asked, 'How can people live like this?' The sailors called me '*xiao ke*'"—a worthless playboy. "But now I know. People do what they must to survive. That's what I've had to do."

In Taiwan, Ben had joined his brother and their father, who had been a prominent businessman in Shanghai. But he couldn't get a venture going in Taiwan, where commerce was limited and the best opportunities went to cronies of Chiang Kai-shek. Ben moved again with his father to Hong Kong, but his luck had been even worse here—his family had lost everything. Ben had to scrounge for any work he could find. He struck out on his own, moving into the kind of rough shanties that Doreen could see from the road. Ben described rats the size of dogs and rain gushing through his shack like a river. He finally got lucky, landing a job with the Ho Man Tin refugee resettlement authority, patrolling the housing projects. "At least it's something. I have a decent place to live," he confided.

Doreen matched his frankness and told him how she was little more than a maid to her sister and how she had found a job with other St. Mary's girls, skipping meals to pay for her dresses. By the time the ferry reached Kowloon, they were both laughing at the blind naïveté of their former privileged lives. With his cap in hand, Ben swept his arm in a deep bow. "Mademoiselle?" he asked. Giggling, Doreen curtsied. "You can tell your sister and the St. Mary's gals that Ben Char is doing well. I really am," he said, and smiled.

"See you again," they both said, parting ways and knowing that they probably wouldn't.

WHEN DOREEN WENT OUT with her friends on their lunch break in Central, men of all backgrounds stopped to admire the *Shanghai nui*. The young women kept their heads high as if not to notice their oglers. They went on outings together, to Ciro's, a popular Shanghai night-club, now reestablished in Hong Kong. Or to the Ritz, a fancy dance club in North Point, an area full of Shanghai refugees. With its Fili-pino big bands and large dance floor, the Ritz enabled the friends to pretend they were in old Shanghai for a few hours. It was even ru-mored that one of Du Yuesheng's henchmen from the notorious Green Gang was running the dance club. To Doreen and her friends, that familiar connection only added to its appeal.

One day, one of Doreen's coworkers invited her to come along on a group date, as a last-minute replacement for another gal who couldn't go. The coworker's boyfriend was bringing another bachelor. He worked at the Nanyang Cotton Mill, owned by a Shanghai industrial-ist. Hong Kong's newly established textile mills and factories had been introduced to the entrepôt by exiled Shanghai entrepreneurs, among them some of that city's most successful industrialists. They had moved their factories and other assets to Hong Kong as early as 1947, when they realized that the economy was collapsing and the National-ists could not prevail.

Doreen figured the date would be a Shanghai fellow and agreed to fill in. But Andrew was Cantonese—and the two of them were like oil and water from the first moment. They began arguing about every-thing: food, music, life in Hong Kong, the weather. Soon the two were yelling at each other. Doreen's girlfriend pulled her aside and asked her to calm down. "Do you have to make a scene? I invited you— please don't embarrass me; you're making me lose face in front of everyone." Doreen stopped arguing with Andrew, but she continued to deride him in Shanghainese, assuming that no one else but her friends could understand her. "This guy is so full of baloney and bullshit—a typical no-good Cantonese," she rattled on. "I hate Hong Kong boys, and I never want to see this guy again!"

For her friend's sake, Doreen made it through the evening. Andrew politely saw her out, and when he turned to say goodbye, he spoke to her in Shanghainese. He had understood every insult she had flung at him. Doreen figured she'd truly never see him again.

Some months later, a major typhoon struck Hong Kong, destroying most of the lean-to shacks of mud and sticks, homes to many thousands of refugees. Andrew drove his car to the building where Doreen lived with her sister to check on her. "How's the tough one?" he asked her in Shanghainese. Then he invited her to lunch.

At the restaurant, he tossed her a menu, saying, "You order."

Doreen, surprised, threw the menu back at him. "No, you order!" The two proceeded to spar with each other. Then they laughed and relaxed. After lunch, Andrew took Doreen on a ride through the New Territories, and they began to talk.

From Andrew, Doreen learned why local Hong Kongers had a terrible impression of Shanghai people. With their arrogance and fancy English, the Shanghai arrivals seemed to prefer the white foreigners to their fellow Chinese. But for all their flash, the Shanghainese couldn't outsmart the Hong Kong Cantonese. He told her about the rich Shanghai exiles who thought they could take control of Hong Kong's gold market just because they brought so many gold bars with them. But the Hong Kongers knew the local gold trade better, including alternate routes to smuggle in the precious metal from Southeast Asia, enabling them to circumvent customs duties and tariffs. The Cantonese held on to the gold market, and the upstart Shanghai traders lost everything.

Not to be outdone, Doreen shared the opinions that Shanghainese held about Cantonese. The men were domineering toward women, tradition-bound with their rules on when women should kneel and bow to elders and how far they had to walk behind their husbands. Cantonese were inflexible, unwilling to accept new ideas and modern ways, rejecting Western improvements simply because they were foreign. And if Shanghai people were extravagant spendthrifts, Cantonese were the other extreme—tightfisted skinflints.

They exchanged views on food: Shanghainese love delicious food, said Doreen. Cantonese love *healthy* food, countered Andrew, pointing out that Shanghai dishes were stewed in soy sauce, salt, and sugar until everything turned brown. Cantonese steamed their food and preferred clear sauces, using less oil and salt. "What's so great about those Shanghai hairy crabs?" Andrew asked Doreen. "Too much trouble for so little meat." Soon the two were joking about their own narrow-mindedness.

Andrew invited Doreen on drives around the colony, showing her the place through the eyes of the local people. The Chinese in Hong Kong had no say over their lives, he explained. Instead, they were treated as the inferior underlings of the British Empire, deemed incapable of governing themselves. "His Excellency the Governor" ran their lives while foreigners on the other side of the world at the Home Office in Whitehall made the rules.

The two drove around the shantytowns of Diamond Hill in Kowloon and North Point on Hong Kong Island—areas where there were so many Shanghainese that the refugees could get by speaking just their own dialect. Even in the more expensive neighborhoods in the Mid-Levels, there were pockets of Shanghai exiles, clustered together. The children of those Shanghainese could be found loitering in such enclaves: girls like Matilda Young, who chose to play in the streets rather than go to school because she couldn't understand a word of Cantonese; boys like Sydney Chang who became troublemakers in Hong Kong, setting fires simply to get out of school. Doreen knew that in Shanghai these former high-society youth would have spent their time going to tea dances and socials. In Hong Kong they were misfits without a society to connect to. They were as dislocated as she'd been.

At least she had Andrew to help ground her. He opened her eyes to the thousands of Nationalist soldiers retreating from the Communist forces across the invisible pencil-line border into Hong Kong's New Territories. Bringing another crisis to the colony, these defeated soldiers suddenly found that they were men without a country, unclaimed and unwanted by any state. Their former Nationalist commanders in Taiwan refused to take responsibility for them, unwilling to assume their costs and suspicious that Communists had infiltrated their ranks. Their former adversaries in the People's Republic considered them enemies who should be prisoners of war. Meanwhile, the British colonial administration didn't want to acknowledge or appear to harbor them, lest it provoke its giant Communist neighbor. The stranded soldiers sheltered themselves in ramshackle tin and cardboard encampments until the British administration finally moved them to Rennie's Mill, a remote, abandoned site in the New Territories.

The British colonial government continued to ignore the humanitarian crisis engulfing Hong Kong until a terrible fire on Christmas Day 1953 destroyed a huge squatter shantytown in the Kowloon area of Shek Kip Mei, leaving fifty-three thousand homeless. Finally the British had to acknowledge that the refugees in Hong Kong were there to stay. In the face of constant agitation from both Nationalist and Communist protestors, the Hong Kong government embarked on building large-scale public housing with running water and sanitary facilities to house the million-plus new residents.

It began to dawn on Doreen, too, that she might not return to Shanghai, the port city that had been her family's home for four generations. She'd never intended to stay in Hong Kong, but maybe there was some magic here after all. Thanks to Andrew, Hong Kong began to feel more like a home to her. In him she had found a beau and, perhaps, a future. Maybe she could make a life there—but how could she feel at home without Benny, the one family member she was closest to? All she had were his brief letters that contained nothing but platitudes. At least she knew he was alive.

With each passing year, even those letters came less often. She couldn't be sure that he received the money or packages she sent. Then his letters stopped.

ANNABEL
ANNUO

Age 22

IN THE SPRING OF 1957, ANNUO HAD NEARLY COMPLETED HER undergraduate law program at Tai Da, having spent four miserable years in a course of study that was of no interest to her except to keep her father at bay. With her college degree in sight, she could possibly leave Taiwan by going to graduate school abroad.

Brother Charley had already left to study in America two years earlier, after serving his mandatory year of military service. Luckily, the war in Korea had reached its stalemate by that time, and the continued American presence had discouraged an attack from the Communist mainland. Charley had yet another obligatory service to fulfill, this time mandated by their father: to bring the rest of the family to safety in America. "One by one, you children and cousins must leave Taiwan, like cars in a train," her father strategized. "Charley is the locomotive." Annuo, the second car in the train, was his main backup. This was an assignment that she embraced wholeheartedly.

But once again, her father intervened with his own idea. He saw an advertisement for nursing personnel in the United States. The ad claimed that, because of a nursing shortage in America, anyone who passed the nursing school admissions test would be guaranteed a spot in an American school.

Nursing fit perfectly with her father's grand design. A nurse would be almost as good as a doctor when he grew older and needed medical care. And of course it fell neatly into his plan to send his children to the United States as a means of escape for him one day. But to Annuo, the prospect of nursing school was as repugnant as medicine, and besides, she was sure that she could get accepted to a graduate school in a subject of her choosing. She bristled at her father's insistence that she take the upcoming nursing school test.

Ignoring Annuo's objections, her father registered her for the exam. To prevent her from finding an excuse to miss it, he sent his car and driver to pick her up at school and take her to the test site. Just like a prisoner, Annuo concluded bitterly. She took her seat in the test hall. When it was time to begin, she stared at the test booklet. Without answering a single question, she handed in her blank answer sheet and left. Days later, the results were posted in the newspaper. Annuo's name was dead last. Livid, her father accused her of sabotaging his plan, his face turning bright red. For once, she had prevailed over his authority. She said nothing, savoring her victory.

Annuo hurried to apply to graduate schools in the United States before a new battle with her father could erupt. The process of obtaining an exit visa for foreign study was unchanged from the days when the Nationalists had run all of China: She needed a bachelor's degree from a Taiwan university, an acceptance letter to a foreign graduate school, a passing mark on the Ministry of Education's patriotic "good citizen" test for study abroad, and enough money for tuition and living expenses. She hunted for the schools with the lowest tuition and fees that might accept her and then applied to several. Soon she heard from the University of Oregon: She had been accepted as a graduate student in journalism. It wasn't the literature that she had once hoped to study, but it would still make use of her love of writing.

The required Ministry of Education exam didn't faze her: Chinese history and general knowledge, Nationalist principles, English proficiency. Annuo passed easily. But she was less confident about the next test, the English exam required by the U.S. consulate. Like most other college graduates in Taiwan, she had a basic reading knowledge of English but with little opportunity to practice speaking, she was far from fluent. Still, she passed and was approved for a U.S. student visa.

Freedom was finally within Annuo's grasp. She couldn't wait to escape her domineering father and her stagnant life on an island ruled by military law. She felt no attachment to Taiwan. Having spent her entire childhood running from one hiding place to the next, she didn't call any place home, not even her birthplace of Shanghai. To Annuo, Taiwan was just another way station.

The last hurdle was the money. Annuo needed five hundred dollars to deposit in a U.S. bank as soon as she arrived in America, to show that she had enough money to support herself. Her father grudgingly loaned her the money—which she sent back as soon as her college paperwork had cleared, depleting her bank account. She also decided to take on a new name when she reached America. Instead of Annuo, she would call herself Annabel. She'd have a new name and a new life. At last.

IN SEPTEMBER 1957, ANNABEL arrived in Portland, Oregon, after a rough voyage on a Taiwanese freighter. It had been the cheapest passage she could find, with thirty other passengers, mostly students. A professor from the university met her and another female student at the dock. In exchange for light household chores, they stayed at his home temporarily while preparing for the English proficiency exam required by the university. Annabel cleaned while her classmate cooked, and they both slept on the floor of his apartment. One month after arriving, they took the scheduled English test. Annabel passed, but her roommate did not and had to leave school.

Annabel moved to a housing cooperative and quickly realized she had a problem. Though she had passed three English proficiency tests, she was struggling in school. English words flowed too rapidly, a fast-moving stream that she couldn't catch. When other students laughed at jokes, she stood by and felt stupid. But three months later, she began to find her roommates' chatter irritating. With a start, she realized that she could understand their inane conversation.

Yet Annabel found herself miserable and terribly alone. She had lived a tightly controlled life for so long that it was unnerving to be out of her cage and on her own. She didn't like martial law or the

Annabel Annuo in front of her cooperative dormitory in 1957, at the start of her graduate studies at the University of Oregon. Though she could communicate in English, she was most comfortable wearing her qipao.

domineering rule of her father, but she missed the security and safety of that insular life. It had been familiar and safe. At school in Taiwan, she'd had a good name and reputation. In America, she was a nobody. It didn't matter to anyone if she existed or not. She went to a few school socials because she still loved to dance. But she was always the last girl to be asked.

Returning to Taiwan was out of the question. She couldn't afford a ticket and didn't want to face her father's scorn for failing to execute his grand plan. Mao and the Communists were as determined to take Taiwan as Chiang and the Nationalists were committed to taking back the mainland. Her father was equally adamant: Taiwan was a sitting duck, and he had to get his family away from the Communist threat.

To counter her loneliness, Annabel signed up for a program to welcome international students. She was matched with a "Friendship Family," a local couple and their young children, who volunteered to introduce her to American life. They showed Annabel many kindnesses, inviting her to meals and family occasions that helped ease her isolation. Their cute four-year-old daughter would take her by the hand, happy to see her. One day, they told her how they loved Chinese food and asked her to cook them an authentic Chinese meal. Caught by surprise, Annabel couldn't say no. After all, they had been so generous with her. She was also too embarrassed to admit that she barely knew how to boil water. With trepidation, she agreed.

Her Friendship Family eagerly awaited their Chinese banquet while Annabel grew more anxious. Her stomach was twisted into a knot for weeks. What could she possibly cook? Then she remembered the cookbook her mother had given her when she left for America. Annabel scanned the recipes and rejected any that called for "condiments readily found at any market in Shanghai." Finally she chose a recipe with just a few ingredients: "rock 'n' roll eggs," a famous Suzhou dish, the cookbook claimed. It seemed simple enough: Make a small hole in each egg, remove the contents from the shell, and mix with soy sauce, salt, sugar, minced green onions, and ground pork. Then replace the mixture into the shells, steam, and serve. Easy, she thought.

On the appointed day, Annabel brought two dozen eggs and other ingredients to her Friendship Family's home. Their table was set with flowers, candles, and polished silver. "We're so excited," her hosts told her, beaming with anticipation.

As they relaxed and watched TV, Annabel went to work in the kitchen. She encountered her first problem immediately: She had never cracked a raw egg before and didn't know how to do it. An hour later, the lady of the house peeked in. "Is everything okay in here?" In one swift glance, she saw broken eggshells and raw egg splattered all over her counters and floor. Her husband was dispatched to get another dozen eggs for Annabel while she began cleaning the mess.

Armed with more eggs, Annabel gamely tried again, this time piling the mixture into some eggshells. But she hadn't anticipated that the eggs would roll over, turning her concoction into a sloppy pudding. Hungry, the four-year-old cried, "Mommy, I don't want Chinese food. I want a peanut-butter sandwich!" Red-faced, Annabel feared that her first cooking foray had strained her relationship with the family—and forever ruined Chinese food for them.

IN TIME, ANNABEL ADJUSTED. After a year in Oregon, she decided to transfer to a school that would offer better job prospects. She was accepted into the noted journalism department at the University of Missouri. There, she honed her writing skills and grew more confident with the English language.

In 1960, with her master's degree in journalism in hand, Annabel headed straight to New York City. She was sure she'd find a job. Each day, she went from one publishing company to the next in search of work as a typist, unaware that staffs in journalism and publishing were almost entirely male. She was quickly shown the door at *Time* magazine, *The New York Times*, *Ladies' Home Journal*, Doubleday, Random House, and a host of other companies. Not long after, she was back, this time asking the same companies if they'd hire her to sweep their floors. She received the same unequivocal no.

Annabel thought of giving up. She'd had no idea that doors would be shut to her as a woman and an "Oriental." But then she'd remember her father's harsh words. "You'll never amount to anything," he'd said, voice full of disdain. She had to prove him wrong. Stiffening her back, she kept on looking.

Just as she was running out of money and hope, Annabel received a call back from Scholastic Magazines. They needed someone to work as a copywriter in their rights and permissions department. Her education in law and journalism was perfect. It wasn't on the creative side of publishing, where she'd hoped to be, but it was her chance. She took the job, right across Forty-second Street from the New York Public Library on Fifth Avenue. There was even a fancy Shanghai-style Chinese restaurant nearby on Park Avenue—not that she could afford it, but its presence was comforting. She had made it! She was working in the heart of the publishing world in New York City. She had done it on her own, and best of all, there was no one to disparage what she had accomplished.

Annabel didn't know many people in the big city yet, but she didn't feel alone. There was so much for her to explore in New York. And Charley, who was working on his doctorate in agricultural economics at Iowa State University, had once introduced her to a friend of his from graduate school. The young PhD—a physicist named Sam—was planning to move to New York for a job, and he seemed to enjoy her company. His family, too, had fled the mainland for Taiwan, and like her, he had no desire to return to the island. Sam would understand her father's plan to bring her family out. Annabel had a chance, she believed, to please her father at long last by helping to get her relatives away from the ever-present Communist threat. Then, maybe, she'd prove that she was a person of worth and substance.

NANJING, 1957

AFTER ENDURING THE REPEATED INTERROGATIONS OF THE anti-Rightist and *san fan* and *wu fan*—Three Anti and Five Anti— mass movements, Benny had retreated further into his solitary life. Apart from going to work at the library and taking his meals at the university canteen, he kept to himself. One day, as he approached the canteen for lunch, Benny noticed a young woman standing by the entrance, looking lost. She was a new teacher, about his age, and unsure how to get food at the canteen. Benny showed her where to hand in her meal chit, where to wait in line, how to order her food. Grateful, she flashed him a smile. When he invited her to sit at a table with him, she accepted. He felt his cheeks grow warm and was glad that she had gone to get hot water while his face blushed red.

Her name was Chen Ling, and she was from Hangzhou, the an- cient city built around the West Lake, long revered by poets and paint- ers for its scenic pagodas, arched bridges, and weeping willows. She had just joined the faculty of Nanjing Agricultural University, having graduated from Fudan University in Shanghai. Fudan was one of the top schools in China—without the missionary connection and bag- gage that St. John's had had. A biologist, she would be teaching em- bryology and histology to undergraduates. In the new China, the party and the constitution declared that women were no longer subservient to men, but were their equals. They were to work at the same jobs as men and receive the same pay. Chen was an educated woman of the new society, a full-fledged teacher in the natural sciences, a field designated as top priority by the Chinese leadership. She could look forward to a good future.

Benny liked her friendly, open face and the way her eyes sparkled when she smiled. With her permed hair, fitted clothes, and pumps with low heels, she had the Shanghai sense of style. He asked if he could join her at the canteen the next evening. She agreed, and it was then that Benny got his chance to learn more about her. Chen Ling also came from an educated family—not black like his, but not red either. When the Communists came to power, her father had run away to Hong Kong, leaving her mother to raise Chen and her brother.

In the next months, Benny and Chen continued to meet each other for meals in the canteen. Benny gradually told Chen about his family. Everything. He had been afraid that she would pull away and shun him. But she didn't. Instead, she showed empathy, understanding that the war had affected people's lives in complicated ways. When he was with Chen, he felt lighter. He had almost forgotten how to feel happy. Chen helped him remember.

Benny no longer buried himself in the library. He cast off his self-imposed solitude. When a colleague asked if he'd be willing to teach English and Russian, he accepted the position. He left the library, estimating that he had typed catalog cards for five hundred thousand books. During his many long days at the typewriter, Benny had assumed that he'd never get married. Who would want to marry him, the son of the worst possible kind of running dog? But Chen Ling didn't think of Benny that way. The fact that she could like him helped him slowly gain confidence. After a year of their deepening friendship, Benny asked Chen Ling to marry him. She said yes. He couldn't imagine anything more joyful.

Chen Ling and Benny Pan were wed in July 1957. Benny was almost thirty. In the new China, weddings were no longer big and ostentatious. They had a civil ceremony in Nanjing with no relatives present. In Benny's previous life, before all the troubles, his family would have planned a huge celebration to mark the marriage of the

Coming from a traitor's family, Benny hadn't dared to dream that he'd ever find someone as wonderful as Chen Ling.

Number One Son of his generation. His mother used to say that she'd have the marching band of the Shanghai Volunteer Corps lead the wedding party down Bubbling Well Road. Dennis and George would have been his groomsmen, and his parents would have held court, looking splendid.

Such extravagances meant little to Benny now. All that mattered was that he and Chen were making a new life together. They rented a white lacy wedding dress with a long train for Chen and a tuxedo for him, complete with cummerbund. The "masses" still looked to old ways to commemorate their weddings, and such bourgeois frivolities were still allowed. The photo of the radiant bride and the dashing groom could have been taken decades earlier.

After the wedding, they received time off from their work teams and took a train to Hangzhou, a few hours away. Benny met Chen's mother and younger brother, who had been unable to leave work for the wedding but happily gave the couple their blessings. Before returning to Nanjing, Benny asked Chen's brother to send a letter to his sister Doreen in Hong Kong to tell her of his marriage and whereabouts. Because Benny was labeled as black, he felt it would be too dangerous for him to write directly to his sister in the imperialist colony, especially with the "Anti" campaigns under way. The government postal censors would no doubt take notice. But Chen's brother lived in a different city and was younger, without a political history. It would be safe for him to send a letter.

Back in Nanjing, the newlyweds were off to a fine start. They both had good jobs as teachers. Neither noticed that their married life coincided with a new political wind: the Hundred Flowers Campaign, aimed specifically at intellectuals. They had been planning their wedding when Chairman Mao and the Communist leadership had encouraged intellectuals to criticize excesses of the party, to "let one hundred flowers bloom and one hundred schools of thought contend."

A torrent of pent-up criticisms came gushing from disenchanted intellectuals—criticisms of the party, its workings, and the revolution itself. Party leaders who had authorized the criticism, including Mao himself, were caught off guard by the vehemence of the critiques. They swiftly ended the campaign and turned the spotlight on the intellectuals instead, especially those who had spoken up.

As teachers, Benny and Chen were intellectuals, but neither had participated in the Hundred Flowers Campaign. Benny knew better than to open himself up to attack. But universities and schools became the targets of the new Anti-Rightist Campaign. No one was exempt. This time, the party mandated that intellectuals experience the hardship of the masses. Only then could intellectuals reform themselves, root out their bourgeois thinking, and embrace the revolution. Chen was sent to the countryside first—to a place called Yancheng, in northern Jiangsu Province, a few hours away. Many people in the urbanized southern part of Jiangsu, next to Shanghai, considered people north of the Yangtze River to be ignorant peasants. The area was very poor, and teachers were needed there. The couple would have to live apart, but they knew the assignment could have been far worse. Benny was relieved to learn that Chen was being sent to work in the rural town as a teacher, not a laborer, and they wouldn't be too far from each other.

For Benny, there were more interrogations. What were the names of the foreigners he knew from his days at the black imperialist training school? Were they spies? Did he have any more contact with them? In his English classes, why did he teach, "The sun *is* covered by clouds; the sun *was* covered by clouds; the sun *will be* covered by clouds"? Was he saying that Chairman Mao, the sun, would be covered up? Who were the clouds? How would they cover up the sun?

Like others who endured such "struggle sessions," Benny was ordered to put his confessions in writing. He had to list every place he had lived, everyone he had known. He repeated all that he had previously confessed about his counterrevolutionary father and family. No, he was not in contact with any foreigners. No, his foreign teachers at St. John's were not spies. He didn't know any spies. Benny confessed to what he could. Yes, Chairman Mao was the sun and light of China. Yes, it had been wrong of him to mention the sun and clouds when he was teaching the passive voice of the English language. He criticized himself for being born into a bourgeois family and denounced his counterrevolutionary past. He told his inquisitors what he thought they wanted to hear. He wrote and rewrote his confessions several times. Any deviation from a previous statement was additional fuel for more questions and criticisms.

After numerous struggle sessions and confessions, the verdict was rendered. Because Benny had done nothing his inquisitors could use to label him a Rightist, he was spared from a harsh punishment. But he would not be permitted to remain in Nanjing. Since he was an intellectual of the worst bourgeois sort, he was sent down to be a laborer in a village outside of Wuxi, a city not far from Nanjing. Benny was again grateful that the decision had not been more severe. Others he knew of were sent for indefinite periods to harsh regions in Xinjiang in the distant northwest beyond Mongolia, or the frigid northeast of Heilongjiang.

Not afraid of hard physical work, Benny threw himself into the farm labor of the peasantry. His tormentors allowed him to keep his Bible, his St. John's diploma, and his wedding photo with Chen. These were his companions. After a year, Benny was released and sent to Yancheng to teach again. And to be reunited with Chen.

In Yancheng, Benny and Chen could live a simple but comfortable life. The area was so desperate for teachers that the couple was treated with respect. In their teaching jobs, Chen and Benny each earned sixty renminbi per month, equivalent to less than ten U.S. dollars. Still, their combined pay placed them at upper income levels in a poor area like Yancheng. A half pound of beef or shrimp cost less than one renminbi.

Benny became the English instructor at Yancheng Middle School, where Chen had already been teaching biology and embryology. The families of their students aspired to send their children to college, an impossible dream before the revolution. But would-be students still needed to achieve a minimum grade on the national entrance exam. A foreign language like English could add critical bonus points to their overall score. Benny became so popular as an English teacher that the dean of the school asked him to serve as assistant dean.

In 1960 Chen and Benny had a baby girl. Her birth coincided with the start of a devastating famine in China after a terrible drought and a series of major crop failures. Basic food essentials were unavailable in towns and cities. Millions across China starved to death with no more than grass and tree bark to eat. Benny's family was able to make it through the famine years with the help of Doreen's packages of rice, powdered milk, and cooking oil from Hong Kong. Food essentials were more precious than the money she sent. He could thank her only in his prayers, for it would have been folly for him to write to anyone overseas. A few years later, Chen and Benny had a second daughter. Chen's mother came from Hangzhou to live with them and help care for the children. With the money from their savings and from Doreen, Benny bought the first television set in their neighborhood of Yancheng. The whole community would gather to watch TV at their small cottage.

That was the lull before the next storm. In 1966, when Benny's elder daughter was six years old, the Communist Party under the leadership of Chairman Mao launched a massive political campaign intended to change Chinese culture and traditional ways of thinking. Calling it the Great Proletarian Cultural Revolution, Mao shut down the universities and middle schools and radicalized a generation of youth into an army of Red Guards. These teenagers and children were unleashed to root out "capitalist roaders" from among intellectuals, bureaucrats, party members, neighbors, and family members. It was a way for the aging Mao to assert his power against opposing factions within the Communist Party. With the imprimatur of the Great Helmsman, Chairman Mao Zedong, the Red Guards broke into homes, destroying books, art objects, and personal property and attacking the occupants in their quest to eliminate the "Four Olds": old ideas, customs, habits, and culture.

At the middle school where Benny taught, all teachers and administrators came under attack. Teenaged Red Guards rounded up their school elders and locked them up separately in a few classrooms for an indefinite period. Benny was forbidden to leave the school with the struggle against him and the others under way. His file of previous confessions was brought before him again, and his home was searched. This time, his Bible, diploma, diaries, and various letters and photos were confiscated as evidence of his crimes.

Once again, Benny's life was scrutinized. This time the questioning was more aggressive and hostile than ever before. It was both terrifying and interminable. His bourgeois upbringing. His father. His family. Traitors and class enemies.

"You rode a bicycle on the grounds of 76—that enemy place of unspeakable evil?" the Red Guards asked, incredulous.

"Yes, but I was only a boy. I knew nothing about the place," Benny replied truthfully.

His accusers were relentless in their criticism of his education at the imperialist St. John's University, his belief in an oppressive religion, his acquaintance with foreigners. They grilled him on his sisters in Hong Kong. Why did Doreen send him money and food? Were his sisters spies? Was Benny a spy? He was ordered to list the names of everyone he had known—and the Red Guards sent investigators to check on them. One of the investigators went all the way to Guangzhou to dig up something on Benny. His interrogations in the previous movements had been mild in comparison to this. But the investigators could find nothing that proved him to be a capitalist roader.

He remained locked in the classroom, unable to see his family. One year stretched into three. Occasionally Chen could get a message to him. He was let out for interrogations, meals at the canteen, and to perform chores of sweeping and cleaning the school. No classroom teaching took place during the ten years of the Cultural Revolution.

When the Red Guards couldn't put a capitalist "hat" on Benny, they worked on Chen, pressuring her to divorce her imprisoned husband. Because she refused, they sent her away from Yancheng to work in a village where there wasn't even a cottage for her to live in. Accompanied by her elderly mother and two young daughters, Chen built a small hut out of twigs and mud with their help, using her bare hands. When Benny didn't hear from her after a long while, he was overcome with worry. Eventually, the Red Guards told him where his family was and that he would be permitted to see them once a year, three days per visit.

Though Benny hadn't been charged with any crime against the people, his captors weren't releasing him. Still, his incarceration was better than the fates of his colleagues at the school who were sent to faraway regions to reform their thoughts. Some had died from the harsh conditions and the stress of the brutal interrogations.

After a while, Benny was the only teacher remaining at the school. Three things kept him from sinking into despair: the image of Chen and his young daughters, always on his mind; the Lord's Prayer, which he repeated several times a day; and the knowledge that he had done nothing wrong. Sooner or later, this political movement would come to an end. He prayed that it would be soon.

One of Benny's Red Guard interrogators revealed some tragic news, apparently uncovered while digging into Benny's past. His childhood friend Dennis, one of his BDG Club pals, had been the son of a rich capitalist. After graduating from St. John's, Dennis had joined his family's business. According to Benny's captor, Dennis had jumped to his death from a third-story window after one of his struggle sessions. Benny was certain that his friend had been subjected to intense pressure. From the bits of information Benny could gather, the Red Guards in Shanghai were more radical and destructive than anywhere else. Benny had to wonder what might have happened to him had he remained there, where his father's crimes were well known. Would he, too, have been driven to suicide?

Alone in his classroom prison, Benny thought about his good friend, who had always been generous with him, welcoming him into his home when Benny had nowhere to go. Of the three boys in the

BDG Club, Dennis had been the most carefree, the one who had experienced little hardship, unlike Benny or George, who was a boy when his father was kidnapped and murdered.

Benny wondered if Dennis had killed himself because he hadn't known suffering and couldn't withstand the torturous assaults of the Red Guards. Benny reckoned that, in some strange irony, his family's troubles helped him to survive these new challenges. Like the Chinese people, he had been through the bitterness of war and invasion, economic and social chaos, abandonment and loss. Now revolution and revenge. The Red Guards weren't through with him yet, he knew, and he prayed that the merciful Christian God had not forgotten him. But if he could endure years of confinement, separation from his family, and continual harassment with no end in sight, surely he'd be able to overcome whatever trials the future would bring.

Sitting at the table covered by white linen in midtown Manhattan, Bing listened as Elder Sister spouted a litany of grievances against her second husband, a Shanghai-born businessman she had met and married in New York after her divorce. "That son of a rotten turtle egg" had lied to her about having a green card, she complained bitterly. The two women sat near the restaurant's sleek entrance flanked by floor-to-ceiling mirrors trimmed with red and gold accents. From this spot, the impeccably coiffed Betty could watch for any approaching customers.

With just one ear tuned to her sister's nonstop diatribe, Bing deftly aimed a pair of plastic chopsticks at a small dish of thinly sliced braised beef, served cold in its shimmering aspic. Her imitation-ivory utensils were imprinted in red with the words "Peking House Restaurant" in English and Chinese. The Peking House was one of the few eateries in North America where Chinese exiles from Shanghai, Beijing, and provinces north of Guangdong could taste the familiar flavors of their regional cuisines from home.

Bing lifted a sliver of beef to her mouth. She closed her eyes and for an instant was transported to Shanghai and Suzhou by its heavy salty-sweet flavors—until she was abruptly jostled into the present as Elder Sister cursed the "no-good smelly dog turd." At that very moment, the door to the restaurant opened, and a group of neatly dressed Chinese stepped in. Without skipping a beat, Elder Sister rose and smiled warmly. "Good evening. Welcome to the Peking House!" she purred in her genteel, honey-smooth English. "May I help you?"

Judging by the sophisticated air of the patrons, Bing guessed that they, too, were from Shanghai, but with high-class educations, unlike hers. The men sported business suits, and all the women but one wore beautiful silk *qipao*s. A man with thick wire-rimmed glasses responded to Elder Sister in equally confident English. "Good evening. We have reservations. Under Chow. Ho Chow." On his arm was an attractive, petite woman who, like Bing, wore a loose maternity top over a tapered skirt and high heels. The two expectant mothers exchanged smiles.

IN 1953, THE KOREAN WAR had ended in a cease-fire and stalemate. An estimated 2.7 million Koreans, or nearly one in ten, had died as a result of the war, with the civilian death rate rivaling that of World War II. After the inconclusive truce, Korea was still divided, while China and the United States grew more polarized than ever. In Cold War rationale, American leaders believed that China had to be "contained" to prevent Communist expansion. As a result, following Truman's stunning flip-flops in U.S. policy, Taiwan was resuscitated overnight and declared to be strategically important to the United States. It would retain its newfound protected status indefinitely. Hong Kong, dependent on trade with China for its financial health and choking with refugees, faced economic collapse when the United States imposed an international embargo against the Communist mainland. Disaster was averted with the help of industrial entrepreneurs who had fled Shanghai; with their economic and social capital, Hong Kong transformed from a trading portal to a global manufacturing center. Both Taiwan and Hong Kong found renewed purpose and stability after the Korean War, energized in no small part by the resourcefulness of Shanghai exiles who brought their expertise in manufacturing, shipping, and international commerce.

Back in Washington, Senator Joseph McCarthy's reign of anti-

Communist hysteria collapsed from its own excesses, his Red-baiting having gone too far in his ever-widening net of accusations, leading to his censure by the Senate. But the damage to U.S. foreign policy toward China had been done: The State Department and other influential institutions had exorcised their most seasoned diplomats possessing experience in China and Asia. The resulting void on the American side of the "Bamboo Curtain" clouded U.S. policy decisions for decades, persisting even into the present.

The targeting of Chinese in America continued in spite of McCarthy's fall. Powerful FBI director J. Edgar Hoover remained convinced that Chinese Americans were a fifth column of the enemy, Communist infiltrators on U.S. soil. In America's Chinatowns, federal agents mounted systematic raids on Chinese American organizations, especially pro-labor or "left-leaning" ones that dared oppose the racist inquisitions. The U.S. Department of Defense funded the noted anthropologist Margaret Mead to conduct an extensive ethnographic study of the stranded Chinese exiles in New York City. Throughout the latter part of the 1950s, Mead's research partner Rhoda Métraux studied over a hundred of these educated and newly displaced Chinese. Mead's team of anthropologists, psychiatrists, internists, and others collected data through extensive interviews and medical and psychographic tests to create a profile of Chinese political character—and the "Chinese mind."

It is no coincidence that so many Shanghainese found their way to New York City, where the number of Shanghai exiles grew. They were drawn by the inexorable pull of a city so like their lost home in its electrifying energy, cosmopolitan diversity, and endless possibilities for the enterprising. Not even London or Paris could offer Shanghai migrants a comparable familiarity.

Beyond New York, Shanghainese went wherever they could make a living—university towns like Champaign, Illinois, or other large cities such as Los Angeles, Chicago, and San Francisco. As they married and had children, many of the displaced Shanghainese followed the American middle-class movement to the suburbs.

Nor is it surprising that, after their escape from war and revolution, the refugees would want to fit in, to rebuild their lives in an oasis of calm. In that way, the Chinese exiles mirrored the conformity of Americans in the 1950s. Some educated Shanghainese felt compelled to differentiate themselves from members of earlier Chinese migrations to America, bristling when every conversation with Americans seemed to begin with the same question: "What restaurant do you work at?" The Shanghainese did not know of the struggles that earlier Chinese waged to be able to live in America. Instead, this new wave sought to establish that they were not proletarian waiters and laundry workers but rather were exceptional Chinese who could become model Americans. Indeed, in 1966 a *New York Times Magazine* article invented the notion of the "model minority" to praise Asian Americans in pointed contrast to African Americans amid racial tensions and calls for equality. Unfamiliar with the history of discrimination in the United States and unaware that the newly created stereotype pitted Asian Americans against other minorities, some of the Shanghai exiles welcomed the chance to be seen as the "good minority" instead of as enemy intruders.

YET FOR MOST EMIGRANTS from Shanghai, America's restrictive immigration policies toward Asians made it an unreachable haven. The vast majority of Shanghainese first headed to Hong Kong, Taiwan, Southeast Asia, and other more accessible ports. No one knows how many fled as the revolutionary tide swept their country, though it's clear that millions from all parts of China crossed its vast, porous borders. Even today, the Communist Party neglects to acknowledge two truths: first, that this mass exodus did, in fact, take place and, second, that China suffered immense losses of economic, social, and intellectual capital from Shanghai.

But some countries never accepted these new arrivals, and within a few years, many Shanghainese exiles would have to flee again, from anti-Chinese pogroms in Malaysia and Indonesia, for example. In Hong Kong, they clustered together in large enclaves, setting up their own schools, shops, and so many services that many could get by speaking only Shanghainese, without bothering to learn one word of the local Cantonese dialect. In Taiwan, the Shanghai exiles opened eating and drinking establishments, social clubs and mah-jongg halls, to ease their homesick yearnings, just as the European refugees in Shanghai had done with their cafés, *boucheries,* and bakeries.

While refugees, then and now, are often labeled in their places of refuge as freeloaders and parasites by hostile nativists, the experience of the Shanghai migrants provides a contrary vision. For example, the students and scholars who were stranded outside of China after the Communist revolution were among the best and the brightest of their generation, not unlike the German intelligentsia who fled Berlin as Hitler ascended to power and whose ranks included Albert Einstein, Thomas Mann, and Walter Gropius. For China, the exodus caused a significant brain drain that Premier Zhou Enlai himself tried to stanch. Those refugees were not merely China's loss; they became a tremendous boon to their new countries, contributing their knowledge, skills, and talents wherever they found themselves. Two future Nobel Laureates, Chen-Ning Yang and Tsung-Dao Lee, were among the stranded Chinese students and professionals in the United States, while the influx of Shanghai's engineering talent to Taiwan helped to fuel the electronics revolution there—Morris Chang, for example, founded Taiwan Semiconductor Manufacturing Company, the world's largest silicon producer.

It would be one-sided to highlight the achievements of highly successful Shanghai exiles while ignoring the tribulations of many others, particularly when the Shanghainese themselves tend to showcase their achievements and downplay their setbacks and losses. Yet Shanghai's international outlook and fluid coexistence of different cultures were high-value assets for less privileged Shanghainese as well—aiding the cooks, tailors, teachers, war brides, sailors, merchants, and others as they navigated new and alien environments. Some, such as documentary film producer Mi Ling Tsui's parents, came to the United States as servants to the wealthiest of the displaced; her mother, as the personal maid of T. V. Soong's mistress, and her father as her personal tailor, eventually landed in New York's Chinatown. Financially strapped members of the Shanghai diaspora found ways to set up small businesses in storefronts that doubled as their homes or to work as shop clerks, librarians, tailors, garment workers, and, yes, waiters—whatever jobs they could find at a time when Chinese Americans were limited to restaurants and laundries.

Even among Shanghai's elite social set, everyone knew of others who had fallen from grace, without the money, prestige, or influence they'd once had. For example, when the Nationalist embassy in Washington stopped paying salaries to its staff, Hsien Hsien Chow, a diplomat and China's star athlete, and his wife, Bae Pao Lu, tried to support themselves and their three young daughters by opening a small corner market in the district, with living quarters above the store. The former socialites learned to cut up raw chickens and stock shelves, but the venture failed because the soft-hearted soccer champion gave away his goods to customers who couldn't pay. In New York City, Richard King's father had to moonlight as a waiter at Betty's Peking House Restaurant even though both his grandfathers had been founders of the Bank of China. His family had lost so much money in the course of fleeing to Hong Kong and New York that his mother-in-law took in piecework from a sewing factory—"just for fun," as she told her circle of White Chinese émigrés.

Shanghai migrants who failed to regain their former status in brave new worlds could look to their children to recoup what had been lost. Some of those children were born in China and left when they were quite young, while the majority became the first generation to be born outside of Shanghai. Either way, their displaced parents, like immigrants from every shore, sought to imbue their offspring with their proud sensibilities of home. Indeed, the children of the Shanghai diaspora include many high achievers, though some scholars of immigration maintain that the academic attainments of Chinese American children are more due to their status as striving immigrants than to their cultural origins. To name just a few, the better known include:

Hong Kong Chief Executive Tung Chee-hwa; U.S. Cabinet members Elaine Chao and Nobelist Steven Chu; Ambassadors Julia Chang Bloch and Linda Tsao Yang; government executives Christopher P. Lu, Henry Ying-yen Tang, Christina M. Tchen; architect Maya Lin; Tony award winners David Henry Hwang and Ming Cho Lee; filmmakers Ang Lee and Janet Yang; authors Iris Chang, Gish Jen, Gus Lee, Bette Bao Lord, Adeline Yen Mah, Pai Hsien-yung, Lynn Pan

Ling, Amy Tan, Shawn Wong; advocates Ying Lee Kelley, Stewart Kwoh, Daphne Kwok, Francis Wang, Frank Wu; philanthropists Leslie Tang Schilling, Oscar Tang, Sue Van, Lulu Chow Wang, Laura Wen-Yu Young; business leaders John Chen, Philip Chiang, Charles B. Wang, Geoff Yang, Shirley Young; journalists Ti-Hua Chang, Steve Cheng, Frank Ching, Maureen Fan, Vic Lee, Dan Woo, William Woo; scholars Gordon H. Chang, Evelyn Hu-DeHart, Mae Ngai, John Kuo Wei Tchen.

This incomplete list of notable children of Shanghai migrants could go on, but the point is to show that the hardships and sacrifices of those who made the difficult exodus were not lost on their offspring— some of whom became vocal critics of the adversity they witnessed. Many took the lessons of their parents' lives and paid them forward, changing the landscape of their migrational homes with the voices, viewpoints, and character of the Shanghai diaspora.

THE EVENTS, DESCRIPTIONS, and dialogue recounted in this book are based on hundreds of hours of interviews with Annabel Annuo Liu, Benny Pan, Bing Woo, Ho Chow, and those close to them, as well as letters, photographs, and documents they generously shared. Numerous scholars have been consulted for their perspectives, as were research materials, oral histories, and private collections. More than one hundred other Shanghai exiles submitted to interviews as well; these were conducted mostly in English, though in some cases a translator assisted. Regrettably, it was not possible to include all their remarkable experiences in the confines of this book, but their sharp memories and observations grace each page. The names of only two people in the book, Doreen Pan and Frank Hsieh, have been changed due to family concerns. Though there wasn't room to include the complete stories of what later happened to the four main characters as they blazed their diasporic trails, here, in brief, is a summary of the next part of their very full lives:

AFTER HO CHOW SUCCEEDED in gaining security clearances to work on defense-related contracts, he found his way to Melnor Corporation, where he remained for most of his professional life, garnering more than sixty industrial design patents. He took a brief leave from Melnor to start his own company—thus fulfilling a boyhood dream.

Ho's brilliant work as an engineer bought him a comfortable home in the suburbs of New York, where he and Theresa raised a daughter and a son. They remained active in their community as well: Theresa served as president of the China Institute Women's Association, and Ho became national president of the Jiao Tong University Alumni Association of America, successfully spearheading a major campaign for a scholarship fund.

From all appearances, Ho's life epitomized the American ideal that new immigrants and refugees can only dream of. Yet a large hole remained in Ho's idyllic picture: He could not enjoy his accomplishments when he was separated from his mother, brother, and sister, knowing the difficulties they faced in China and Taiwan. Like so many migrants, Ho sent money to help out his family, never giving up on his hope of reuniting and bringing them out of China to join him in the United States. For years, he wrote letters on their behalf to the State Department and officials in Hong Kong and Taiwan.

In 1973, one year after President Richard Nixon's historic visit to China, Ho was invited to join a high-level delegation of American scientists and engineers to meet with their counterparts in China. Ho asked the hosts in advance if he could visit his mother. With the permission of both governments, Ho met his mother and brother in a tearful reunion after their twenty-six-year separation. His mother still lived in the same house on Medhurst Road, but it had been subdivided to add several other families that had moved in; the government had assigned additional occupants to residences deemed too large for just one household. An added bonus for Ho's family resulted from his visit: Shanghai authorities gave their rooms a fresh coat of whitewash, the first in almost thirty years.

When Ho returned to the United States, he kept up his efforts to get his mother and brother out of China, but both died before he could succeed. Eventually, Ho managed to bring his sister, Wanyu, and her husband and four children out of Taiwan. When he did, he set them up with jobs and a place to live. Eventually, he was able to sponsor some of his deceased brother's grown children to the United States as well. After Ho retired, he and Theresa moved to northern California to be near their children and grandchildren. Several of their New York Shanghai friends also relocated to their West Coast retirement community, where they have kept a busy social calendar and stayed connected to their ever growing extended family.

ANNABEL ANNUO LIU WAS working at Scholastic Magazines in New York City when she married Sam, the physicist she met through her brother Charley. After Sam went to work for IBM, Annabel found a job at nearby *Reader's Digest* in Westchester County. Then Iowa State University offered Sam a professorship in physics, and they moved to Ames. There, Annabel's journalism career took off. The first story she wrote was a feature-length article about a local sculptor, which appeared on the front page of the *Des Moines Register* Sunday magazine. The story won top honors in the annual Iowa Press Women awards. As Annabel stood to be recognized at the awards ceremony, she heard someone gasp in surprise, "She's an Oriental!"

After writing nearly ninety front-page feature articles, Annabel was invited to teach journalism at the state university. The young couple welcomed the birth of a daughter and a son, and the family followed Sam's research opportunities to Denmark, Germany, and finally Oak Ridge, Tennessee, where they stayed for more than a decade. Finding no publications to write for in Oak Ridge, Annabel took her creativity into another genre: humorous essays in Chinese. Her stories about life as a Chinese migrant in America were serialized on the front pages of the literary section of Taiwan's leading newspaper. She became a regular essayist for the *World Journal,* one of the most widely read Chinese-language newspapers in the United States. Not unexpectedly, her father disparaged her popularity, finding offense in his daughter's self-deprecating humor. But Annabel persisted. And, in spite of her initial disastrous effort in the kitchen, she became quite skilled as a cook and was the translator of Adelle Davis's popular *Let's Eat Right to Keep Fit* into Chinese—in part to keep her father in good health.

With her brother Charley, she helped bring her younger sister, Li-Ning, and two cousins to the United States, coaching them on the English proficiency requirements and secretly editing her sister's graduate school papers and doctoral dissertation into proper English. Eventually Annabel's parents joined their children in the United States after her father retired from a distinguished career in Taiwan, thereby fulfilling his master plan for their family.

For many years, Annabel tried to overcome her amnesia covering the period of the Japanese occupation when her mother had sent her to live with another family. She hungered for insight into that traumatic episode and the insecurities, self-doubts, and fears of abandonment that continued to plague her. Even after hypnosis, that period remains a disturbing void. However, other memories are so vivid that Annabel has refused to go back to Shanghai or to buy any major products from Japan. Just before she turned eighty, Annabel wrote and published two books of memoir and poetry in English. She adds these to the several popular books she has written in Chinese. Living near her daughter on Philadelphia's Main Line, she writes and lectures about her complex and conflicted life, in which every place and no place is truly home.

AFTER TWO YEARS OF immigration proceedings, Bing Woo and her husband, Frank, managed to stave off the INS and avoid deportation to Taiwan. By then they had four children. Finally able to settle down, they bought a house in a New Jersey tract development after getting turned away from a neighborhood of Philadelphia, where they were told that "Orientals aren't welcome." Bing was treated for her TB and on doctor's orders put her children into foster care. This rekindled the nightmare of her own abandonment, and she tearfully insisted on bringing them home. Bing's TB subsided, but her life wasn't easy. Her educated husband was a proud man and a dreamer, unwilling to be subservient or second-class. Thanks to the same opinionated temperament that got him arrested for fighting with Elder Sister in Florida, his conversations with employers, neighbors, and strangers often ended in angry curses.

To support their growing family, Bing's husband drove a taxi and sold Fuller brushes door to door. Then he started a home business producing baby-themed novelties to sell to florists, with Bing, himself, and their children providing the labor. After a long day of caring for the children, Bing would spend each night doing hours of piecework on the items that Frank later delivered to flower shops in the family car. The income from the business barely covered the groceries, but at least Frank was his own boss. In between sales trips, he wrote love poems to his wife, and several books and plays that were never published. However, his published articles and essays criticized America's China policy and attracted the attention of J. Edgar Hoover. FBI agents canvassed the family's neighbors about Frank, but the investigation led nowhere.

Bing found a few good friends in the suburbs. Once, as she pushed a shopping cart in a supermarket, with babies in tow, she locked eyes with another East Asian woman. Bing asked, "Are you Chinese?" at the same moment that the other woman asked, "Are you Japanese?" Sue Warren, the war bride of a GI who had been stationed in Japan, introduced herself and the two women became fast friends—just seven years after their two countries had been at war. Later, Bing's closest friend, Maybing Chan of the downtown Manhattan Shanghainese group, moved her family to Bing's New Jersey town. For years, their two families were the only Chinese Americans in town.

The abandoned girl who had always adored children found fulfillment with her own brood, which eventually numbered six. Bing kept her promise to her sister Betty: For decades she didn't tell her husband, her friends, or her children about being abandoned or adopted, tying her childhood anguish into the knot of her shameful secret.

In the years after Frank died, Bing became the proud grandmother of eleven. Watching them thrive in loving homes, Bing could no longer contain the harsh memories of her own childhood.

I know this because Bing is my mother. When she was seventy-four years old, she first shared the secret truths of her life with me. The details, locked away until that moment, came rushing out in a torrent of revelations. After getting over my own shock at her hidden history, I encouraged her to remember and, when my journalistic instincts took over, I began interviewing her. Gradually, she opened up to other family members and friends. With each telling, the pain that Bing had repressed seemed to loosen and her healing process could begin.

BENNY YONGYI PAN SURVIVED the ten-year span of the Cultural Revolution that separated him from his wife and daughters and subjected them to terror and torment. During President Nixon's visit to China in 1972 at the height of the Cultural Revolution, Chinese society was under maximum security. That year, Benny's captors canceled his annual three-day visit to his family and put him on lockdown, fearing that the former English teacher would somehow communicate with the visiting president. When the Cultural Revolution ended after the death of Mao in 1976, Benny was released from his decade-long detention. He rejoined his family and was no longer classified as a counterrevolutionary. His St. John's diploma, diaries, and Bible were returned—and he promptly burned them so they could never again be used against him.

Benny's sister Doreen married Andrew, her Hong Kong beau, in 1954. His early work with textile manufacturers from Shanghai blossomed into a successful business of his own, producing ladies' lingerie. By the time the Cultural Revolution began in 1966, Doreen hadn't heard from Benny in years and didn't know if he was alive or dead, but she faithfully continued sending him money. After his confinement, Benny received in a lump sum all the money that his sister had sent him.

Living together again with his wife and two daughters in a very poor rural area north of the Yangtze River, Benny fretted that his daughters would not get a proper education. He and his wife, both still teachers, tutored their girls at home, while also applying to the government to change their *hukou*, or designated residence, to his wife's hometown of Hangzhou. Eventually, they succeeded and were permitted to move and enroll their girls in the better schools there.

By 1980, after decades of the closed Bamboo Curtain and tight U.S. containment, China had begun to open up. When Benny's elder daughter placed high among university applicants, she was chosen to study in the United States. Benny instructed his daughter not to return. Ten years later, in 1990, Benny and his wife received permission to visit their daughter in America. Sadly, Chen died before the scheduled trip, and Benny went alone. During his visit, President George H. W. Bush issued an executive order in response to the 1989 Tiananmen Square uprising: Chinese who had come to the United States within a certain time frame were allowed to become permanent residents. To Benny's surprise, his visit fell within the executive order's eligibility dates. He became an American citizen in just a few years. Later, his younger daughter was also able to immigrate to the United States.

Armed with his U.S. passport, Benny returned to Shanghai many times. After decades of separation, he reunited with his brother and three sisters—and visited the former campus of St. John's University for reunions with his fellow alumni, including his BDG Club pal George. During his first years in the United States, Benny worked in Orlando, Florida, as a greeter for the China exhibit at Disney World. He later moved to Queens, New York, to be near his daughters. Active as a volunteer in his low-income housing project, he has been honored by the city council for his work with seniors. He remarried and for a number of years was president of the St. John's University Alumni Association, Eastern United States chapter.

Benny and his fellow alumni around the globe spent more than a decade trying to restore historical recognition to their beloved university. They mounted a major fundraising campaign to donate funds to the school that now occupies their alma mater's buildings. After years of effort, they hit an inexplicable roadblock. It was rumored that the Communist Party's Central Committee rejected any acknowledgment of the "black" university. The disappointed but devoted alumni turned instead to supporting St. John's University in Taipei and St. John's College of the University of British Columbia in Vancouver. Both schools have committed to keeping alive the memory, spirit, and motto of their former school: "Light and Truth." Benny has visited both locations with his old friends and schoolmates on several occasions, reliving the camaraderie they once had as privileged youth in the Shanghai of long ago.

IN 1953, BING'S SISTER, Betty, and three friends debuted a new kind of restaurant on Manhattan's east side with the financial support of her second husband and other Shanghai exiles. Located at 845 Second Avenue near the United Nations, the Peking House Restaurant was unlike those in Chinatown that largely served the hybrid "Chinese and American" fare invented by earlier generations of migrants from Guangdong Province. Betty's Peking House won rave reviews— and not solely for the different style of Chinese cuisine it offered. With its white tablecloths, modern look, and full bar with a liquor license to serve high-class cocktails, their Manhattan venture was infused with the sophisticated *haipai* style of swanky nightclubs that had once proliferated in Shanghai. Peking House was one of the first elegant Chinese restaurants in an upscale midtown location in Manhattan. Adventurous New Yorkers welcomed the northern Chinese flavors—as did the Shanghai exiles. The demand for "authentic" Chinese cuisine led to popular cookbooks, turning a few educated exiles into celebrity cooks, most notably Florence Lin in New York, Joyce Chen in Boston, and Cecilia Chiang in San Francisco. It also brought competition and inevitable imitation of the Peking House.

A few years after Betty's Peking House opened, the rival Peking Park Restaurant set up shop nearby, at Fortieth Street and Park Avenue, featuring a similar menu and ambience and a nearly identical name. The Peking Park had a better chef, a fresher décor, and the cachet of newness. Devotees of northern Chinese cuisine abandoned the Peking House for the Peking Park, which soon became a staple for social occasions. But for most of the Shanghai emigrants, even the uptown Shanghainese, restaurants like the Peking House and the Peking Park were a rare indulgence, since their prices and service were geared toward the higher-paid *lofan*.

Encompassing the uptown, downtown, and elite White Chinese, New York City's Shanghai exiles reflected the great diversity of their hometown and its residents—a cliché, perhaps, when thriving cities by their very nature attract people of many talents, skills, and backgrounds. In this regard, the exodus and diaspora from Shanghai has mirrored the pattern of other migrations in history where, for example, the first to flee have generally been those with the most money, connections, and options for locating a safe harbor. Only later does the fear of imminent doom drive those with far fewer resources to run from the unthinkable. This, too, was true for the Shanghai exodus.

Yet it is commonplace in the United States and elsewhere—including among Chinese—to dismiss the migrants and refugees of this exodus as "rich Shanghainese," as though they are all cast from the same mold. The vastly different lives of Annuo, Benny, Bing, Ho, and others in this book should work to dispel such one-dimensional mischaracterizations. Benny's comprador family, for example, got its start in the Cantonese enclave of Shanghai, one of many urban neighborhoods with roots in distant "native places." The families of Annuo and Ho, as well as the floating population of abandoned children like Bing and Ah Mei, illustrate the dynamic nature of China's domestic migrations. Sharp culture clashes ensued when Shanghai migrants encountered other regional Chinese cultures, whether in Hong Kong, Taipei, New York, or elsewhere, underscoring the fact that Chinese society is not monolithic. With China's ascendance on the world stage and the growing presence of Chinese beyond its borders, a more informed and nuanced understanding of its complexities—past and present—is needed.

Even though this book examines a singular period of history, it reveals the manifold differences and conflicts that exist within even a small segment of one city's population. As the stories of "hot" and "cold" war experiences show, to label all the people of a country or culture as the same is a folly with potentially global consequences. This alone is a valuable lesson of the Shanghai exodus, a simple insight that bears repeating, especially when migrants and refugees everywhere are still often painted in one dismissive stroke.

ABOUT TWO YEARS AFTER the rival restaurant opened, Betty's Peking House shut its doors, while the Peking Park Restaurant grew into a popular banquet venue. Despite the increasing numbers of Shang-hainese and other Chinese exiles, two northern-style restaurants could not be sustained. Betty seized the moment to divorce her second hus-band and launch her quest for a third.

Ho and Theresa Junlin Chow had occasion to patronize the Peking Park Restaurant over the years, especially since the China Institute held special events there. In 1960, Annabel Annuo Liu, the journalism school graduate, had found her way to Manhattan and was working a few blocks from the Peking Park. In time, Benny, his daughters, and Doreen made it to New York. Ho, Bing, Annuo, Benny, and Doreen might have encountered one another there at some point, just as they probably crossed paths in Shanghai's foreign concessions when they were youngsters in the besieged city.

This book is based on the journeys of these intrepid individuals, yet their stories contain what is universal among the people who en-dured this cataclysmic period of modern history. Where America's World War II generation is often lauded as its "greatest," these Chi-nese contemporaries of that generation deny any claim to such super-latives, especially when China's five-thousand-year history spans hundreds of generations. Nevertheless, this particular demographic, defined by exodus and liberation, possesses the greatness that they share with all who survive the savagery of war, social upheaval, vio-lent extremism, and the desperate scramble to find safe haven, any-where.

What other lessons can be drawn from their ordeals? Certainly what was true for the refugees and exiles of Shanghai remains true for people fleeing from catastrophe in contemporary times, whether these migrants are driven from Syria, Myanmar, Bosnia, Sudan, Somalia, Guatemala, or too many other places. These refugees have all faced the agonizing choice of whether to stay or to flee—a torturous deci-sion burdened with the guilt of leaving and the fear that the next boat, plane, train, or bus may be the last one out.

In a world fractured by turmoil, there is much to learn from the profound human experience shared by the uprooted and displaced, whether from Shanghai or Aleppo: their courage in setting forth on a course rife with danger; their steadfast will to survive the hardships of dislocation, often in unfriendly lands; their willingness to adapt to cultures quite unlike their own; and their ability to recognize and seize opportunity. They inspire with their resilience and teach that the human spirit is willing to risk all to find peace and shelter from harm, even if their sacrifices may not bear fruit until the next generations. There are many lessons to be learned from refugees and migrants that can contribute to the understanding needed to navigate the global tectonics, to bring people together, not drive them into flight.

For these Shanghai emigrants, the passage of seven decades has allowed the stories of their turbulent odysseys to reach light. As Annabel Annuo Liu replied when asked about her experiences, "I've been waiting for someone to tell our story." If told often enough, one day such stories may become lessons for historical reflection, not broken paths to be retrod.

ACKNOWLEDGMENTS

WHEN THIS BOOK WAS IN ITS INFANCY, YEARS AGO, I ENcountered some lukewarm reactions to it. One leading social scientist cautioned that "this topic is very controversial in China." More than a few Chinese Americans signaled negative feelings toward Shanghai people, referencing their stereotype as rich blowhards. Then there was the AIDS activist from Hong Kong who was doing human rights work in China; he struggled with what to say to me after learning of my book's subject, and he eventually blurted out, "But that's so . . . ordinary."

Looking back, I appreciate how such reactions helped me explore the events of this book from different viewpoints. I soon learned that the frenzied escape out of Shanghai had been so massive that in places like Hong Kong and Taiwan, the topic of those refugees from the Communist revolution was as ordinary as talk about the weather. I also discovered that, in the United States, this migration had been ignored by many who viewed all Shanghainese through the same lens, while, in China, the very existence of this exodus has been repressed.

Ironically, this was an "ordinary" and familiar story for me as well. From as early on as I can remember, my aunt Betty would solemnly declare that she and my mother had left Shanghai on the "last boat before the Communists." To her, nothing more needed to be said. In addition to my gratitude to Aunt Betty for showing me that there are no limits to what a woman could reach for, I thank her for this cryptic allusion that stayed stuck in my imagination like a mysterious black hole. In time, I met many other Shanghai exiles who grieved for children and other loved ones they'd been separated from for decades, unable to reunite with them in a world fractured by ideology. Later I encountered people like myself—the grown children of Shanghai migrants and refugees whose families had all escaped on the last boat, plane, or train. Yet, everyone had fled on different transports. Eventually, I realized that a much larger story lurked behind the proverbial "last boat," and I felt compelled to find it.

First and foremost, I give heartfelt thanks to the remarkable survivors of this exodus who generously shared their extraordinary lives. Most of my Shanghai interviewees were well over seventy when I met them, and some of their painful accounts were told through tears. I truly regret that I could not fit all of their stories onto these pages. These inspiring raconteurs include:

Betty Barr (Shanghai)
Deanna Chan (Palo Alto, California)
Florence Chang (Oakland, California)
Margaret and Bill Chang (San Francisco)
Sydney Chang (Shanghai)
William Yukon Chang (New York)
Yingying and Shaujin Chang (Milpitas, California)
Isabel Chao (Hong Kong)
Ben and Vivian Char (San Francisco)
Theresa Chenlouie (San Mateo, California)
Grace Chen (Shanghai)
Stanley Chen (Boston)
Julia K. Cheng (San Francisco)

Cecilia Chiang (San Francisco)
Rio Lieu Chiang (New Jersey)
Frank Ching (Hong Kong)
Chinyee (Princeton, New Jersey)
Evelyn Chong (Shanghai)
Bae Pao Chow (New York)
Gregory and Paula Chow (Princeton, New Jersey)
Ho and Theresa Chow (Walnut Creek, California)
May Wong and Bill Chow (Shanghai)
Philip and Sarah Choy (San Francisco)
John Chu (New York)
Kenneth Chu (Los Angeles)
Valentin and Vicky Chu (Walnut Creek, California)

Vem Chuang (Berkeley, California)

Ven Young and Jeanette Doo (San Jose, California)

Yuncong Du (Hong Kong)

Robert and Doreen Fan (Mill Valley, California)

Mary Fung Fulbeck (Covina, California)

Leah Jacob Garrick (San Francisco)

Gloria-Tao-t'ai Hsia (McLean, Virginia)

Betty Hsiao (Walnut Creek, California)

David Hsiung (Vancouver)

George Hsu (Shanghai)

Sophia Hsu and Alexander Yu (Vancouver)

T. C. Hsu (New York)

Vivian Hsu (San Mateo, California)

Jane Hsueh (Foster City, California)

S. Y. Huang (Walnut Creek, California)

T. Y. Jiang (Sydney, Australia)

Chris Kao (Taipei)

Richard King (San Francisco)

Maria Lee Koh (Seattle)

Rosalyn Koo (San Mateo, California)

C. F. Kwok (Annandale, Virginia)

Frank Kwok (Foster City, California)

Julia Lauh (San Mateo, California)

Lily Loh and Frank Lee (San Francisco)

Ming Cho Lee (New York)

Vera Lee (Shanghai)

Vic Lee (San Francisco)

Sueyung Li (San Francisco)

Zichong Li (Shanghai)

Kenneth C. Liang (Hawthorne, California)

Florence Lin (Walnut Creek, California)

Julia C. Lin (New York)

Annabel Annuo Liu (Wallingford, Pennsylvania)

Henry and Theresa Hsu Liu (Farmington Hills, Michigan)

Maria Liu (Shanghai)

Herbert Ma (Taipei)

Kenneth Pai / Bai Xianyong (Santa Barbara, California)

Benny Pan (Queens, New York)

Lo-Lo Zhang and Sandy Pan (Burlingame, California)

Y. C. Pan (Beijing)

Y. K. Pei and Mary Li Pei (Beijing)

Xiaohong Shao (Beijing)

George Shen (Atherton, California)

Linda Shen (Shanghai)

Yip Shen (San Francisco)

Charlie Sie (Palos Verdes Estates, California)

Margaret Soong (Riverdale, New York)

Myra dos Remedios Souza (San Francisco)

Mary Anna Sung (Hsi) (Berkeley, California)

Ronald Sun (Walnut Creek, California)

Mary Koo Tai (Kona, Hawaii)

Jack Tang (Hong Kong)

Nancy Tang Francis (Atherton, California)

Nellie Sung Tao (Vancouver)

James Tong (Shanghai)

Frances Tsu (San Francisco)

Miling Tsui (New York)

Tung Chee-Hwa (Hong Kong)

Reginald Van (Hong Kong)

Wang Yi-fang (Shanghai)

C. S. and Loretta Wang (New York)

Mary Wang (Oyster Bay, New York)

Jeannette Wei (Foster City, California)

Margot Chou Wei (Silver Spring, Maryland)

Alma Wen (Gaithersburg, Maryland)

Mary Wong (Queens, New York)

Yungfi Wong (Long Island City, New York)

Diane Tang Woo (New York)

Wu Lao (Shanghai)

Alyce Wu (Los Angeles, California)

Jin Wu (Washington, D.C.)

Stanley and Vivian Wu (Moraga, California)

Xu Zhouyi (Shanghai)

Dongsheng Yan (Shanghai)

Linda Tsao Yang (Davis, California)

Marlene Yang (Foster City, California)

Peter Quai Yang (Hong Kong)

Richard Lin Yang (Shanghai)

T. C. and Joan Yao (Moraga, California)

Y. C. Yao (Beijing)

Taofu Ying (Hong Kong)

Matilda Young (San Francisco, California)

Beilin Woo Zia (Walnut Creek, California)

TO HELP FIND SHANGHAI exodus survivors, a corps of enthusiastic volunteers emerged serendipitously, with everyone querying families, friends, acquaintances, neighbors, coworkers, and random strangers for potential interview subjects. My sincere gratitude to all, many of whom were themselves children of Shanghai emigrants whose descendants now number in the many millions; my apologies to anyone I may have missed: Anthony Chan, Connie Chan, David Chan, Sue Chan, Ann Mei Chang, Dallas Chang, Claire Chao, Arthur Chen, Steve Cheng, Allan Chiang, Anthony Chiu, Renee Chow, Helen Doo, Maureen Fan, Kip Fulbeck, Gloria Holt Hartman, Kathy Hsiao, Jay Hsu, Lee Hsu, Wendy Hsu, Victor H. Hwang, M. Jean Johnston, Daphne Kwok, Jane Leung Larsen, Benson Lee, Kathy Wah Lee, Maya Lin, Wendy Lin, Andrea Liu, Betty Ming Liu, Jennifer Liu, Leo Martinez, Jeannie Park, Rachel Sha, Xiaohong Shao, Bing Shen, Eugenie Shen, George Sing, Amy Sommers, Benedict and Jane Tai, Minna Tao, Mi Ling Tsui, Rachel Wahba, Lulu Chow Wang, Alfred Wen, Andy Wong, Nancy Wong, Robin Wu, Tim Wu, Philip Yau, Albert Yee, Laura Wen-Yu Young, and Matilda Young.

This book might not have made the fragile transition from cherished idea to a real book project without the encouragement of journalists Martha Shirk, who first suggested I apply for a Fulbright to kickstart my research in China, and Yuen-Ying Chan, the director of Hong Kong University's Journalism and Media Studies Centre. I also received early support from feminist writer Robin Morgan; academics John Kuo Wei Tchen, formerly of New York University, now Rutgers University, Felix Guttierez of the University of Southern California, Barbara Bundy and Jeff Brand of the University of San Francisco, Dingli Shen of Fudan University, and Paul Levine of Shantou University; Ambassador Julia Chang Bloch; and journalist Julie Chao. With guidance from David Adams of the Institute of International Education, and the sponsorship of a professor at East China Normal University, I am most grateful for the Fulbright Scholar award that launched my research in Shanghai and Hong Kong.

Essential advice, information, and contacts for my research visits to China, Hong Kong, Taiwan, and elsewhere came from Anni Chung of Self-Help for the Elderly; Wang & Wang principals Laura Wen-Yu Young and Francis Wang; writers King-Kok Cheung, Stella Dong, William Poy Lee, Russell Leung, Shawna Yang Ryan, and Laura Tyson Li; China expert Diane Tang Woo; Sandy Pan and the St. John's University Alumni Association; Taiwanese advocates Anne Huang and Ho Chie Tsai; and visionary Rosalyn Koo, who introduced me to the McTyeire School for Girls alumnae and the Spring Bud Project of the 1990 Institute that educated one thousand girls in rural China. A number of organizations provided tremendous assistance to my research, including the Taipei Economic and Cultural Office in San Francisco, most especially press director Manfred Peng and senior press officer Janet Chang. I also thank the Organization of Chinese Americans; Museum of Chinese in America; Chinese Historical Society of America; Committee of 100's former president John Fugh, and its excellent staff: Alice Mong, An Ping, and Yong Lu, with special thanks to its members Richard King, Betty Lee Sung, Lulu Chow Wang, Frank Wu, Shirley Young; Association of Asian American Studies; Asian American Journalists Association; Chinese American Association of Rossmoor. Many thanks to Craig Chinn for connecting me to the annual reunion of the China National Aviation Corporation.

Invitations to lecture in China, Hong Kong, Taiwan, and Canada allowed me to cast a wider research net after my Fulbright fellowship ended; my gratitude goes to Richard Arnold at the Taipei American School; Wu Bing of the Beijing Foreign Studies University; Asia Society of Hong Kong; U.S.-China Educational Trust and Hon. Ambassador Julia Chang Bloch; New York University in Shanghai; and special thanks to Peter Herford, Yuen-Ying Chan, Ching-Ching Ni, and other professors at Shantou University in Guangdong for bringing me to teach in China a number of times over the course of writing this book. Historian Henry Yu, of St. John's College at the University of British Columbia, invited me to be a Distinguished Johannean Visiting Scholar and connected me to the college's oral history project involving St. John's University alumni in western Canada. I must also thank the Sea Change Residencies—Gaea Foundation in Provincetown, Massachusetts, for allowing me to be their first writer in residence, in a creative and LGBT-supportive atmosphere that opened my mind to the possibility of this book.

In Shanghai, my chief associate was a journalism and law graduate who brought her indispensable energy, dedication, and friendship to the research and translations. The gracious Lily Loh Lee, whose family exodus took her to Taiwan, Hong Kong, San Francisco, and back to Shanghai, lent her deep knowledge of China's culture to my research. Two extraordinary and thoughtful sisters who are third generation Shanghai natives of the Cantonese diaspora, became my good friends and invaluable guides to the city's folkways. Matilda Young, a former resident and Shanghai emigrant to Hong Kong and the United States, shared her knowledge, family story, and circle of friends, especially Dean Ho of Honolulu. Many other kind people assisted me in Shanghai in significant ways, including Tess Johnston, who made available her trove of historical books, documents, and wealth of knowledge. A leading sociologist with the Shanghai Academy of Social Sciences offered his knowledge and family's story. Thanks also to author Lynn Pan Ling; Amanda Miu; Vera Tsai Lee; and two lovely McTyeire alumnae who took me on a nostalgic tour of the Shanghai Number 3 Girls School, showing it to me as they had known it when they were girls. Richard Lin Yang provided extensive details of his exodus journeys and gave me a DVD of his documentary, *The China Chronicles*, about the flight of millions from China's coasts to its interior during the war with Japan. Other kind people in Shanghai include chef Olivia Wu; architect Anne Warr; Princeton alumni David Wu and Sam San-Kong Fang; the Explore Shanghai Heritage expatriate group, especially writer Barbara Koh, a generous daughter of the exodus.

In Hong Kong: my thanks to the Chinese University of Hong Kong vice chancellor Lawrence Lau and the Universities Service Centre for China Studies staff for naming me a research scholar with access to their excellent facilities. My carrel at the University Service Centre was near that of historian Suzanne Pepper, who loaned me the bound volumes from the 1950s of U.S. consular monitoring reports on Chinese media that she rescued from a dumpster. I am grateful to Eugenie

Shen, a child of the Shanghai exodus; historians Betty Peh-t'i Wei, John M. Carroll, Elizabeth Sinn, and sociologist Wong Siu Lun; law professor Lucetta Kam, who showed me the old sites of Shanghai refugees and exiles; Hong Kong's first Chief Executive, Tung Chee-hwa; Alice King; John Dolfin; Ann Marden; Ting Fong Lee of the Dui Hua Foundation; Tom Gorman of the American Chamber of Commerce; and numerous alumni of McTyeire, St. Mary's, Aurora, and Lester schools and of St. John's and Jiao Tong universities and others, several of which are listed previously as interview subjects.

In Taiwan: Academia Sinica historians Jiu-jung Lo and Chien-ming Yu generously met with me about issues faced by women in the post–civil war period, and thanks to Professor Lo for taking me to monuments to those who resisted martial law. Thanks also to Jean-Lien Chen, president of St. John's University in Taiwan, who welcomed me to a tour of her campus; artist Ya-Ping Lin, who introduced me to Old Taipei and military dependents' villages; Judge Herbert Ma; Anne Huang's sister Wei Lun, for taking me on an old train route to see the lives and culture of rural Taiwanese.

Elsewhere in China, thanks to Benedict and Jane Tai, who kindly hosted me in Beijing, and to my dear Shanghai-Cantonese friend who accompanied me to Wuxi and Changzhou in search of the area where Bing's birth family had lived.

I am grateful to many friends in academia who assisted me in countless ways. Besides those already mentioned, thanks go to scholars Mary Yu Danico, of California State Polytechnic University, Pomona; Wei Li, Arizona State University; Christopher Lee, University of British Columbia; Gregory Chow of Princeton University and Paula Chow, founding director of its International House; and several historians: Madeline Hsu at the University of Texas, Austin, who invited me to her conference on TransPacific China in the Cold War; Xiaojian Zhao, of the University of California, Santa Barbara; Gordon H. Chang, at Stanford University; Virginia Yans, professor emeritus at Rutgers University; Emily Honig and Gail Hershatter, of the University of California, Santa Cruz; Wen Hsin Yeh, of the University of California, Berkeley; Charlotte Brooks, Columbia University; Evelyn Hu DeHart, Brown University; Franklin Odo, Amherst College; John Cheng, Binghamton University; Wang Zheng, University of Michigan; Betty Lee Sung, professor emerita of City University of New York; Cindy Wong, City University of New York and College of Staten Island; and Philip and Sarah Choy, with the Chinese Historical Society of America.

A number of leading Chinese scholars met with me in China during my months as a Fulbright Scholar: with special thanks to a world-renowned scholar of the history of modern Chinese cities who gave me his demographic estimates of class breakdown in the Shanghai of the late 1940s to help gauge the potential size of the Shanghai exodus; and various scholars at East China Normal University; the Shanghai Academy of American Studies; Fudan University; a special conference on Hua ren, the Chinese diaspora; and the Su-Zhe (Kiangsu-Chekiang) associations of Hong Kong.

My gratitude goes to several accomplished people who translated various research materials into English: In addition to those previously noted are Maria Lee Koh; John Shing-chit Yu; Xenia Chiu and Gang Li, both of whom were students at the University of British Columbia; and a number of excellent student translators at Shantou University who shall remain anonymous in these sensitive times. Thanks also to Samantha Duarte and Gwendolyn S. Wells, research assistants for Mary Yu Danico at the Asian American Transnational Research Initiative of California State Polytechnic University, Pomona.

Certain libraries and archives served as veritable temples of knowledge for this book: Shanghai Main Library; Library of Congress; Shanghai Municipal Archives; Old China Hands Archive at California State University, Northridge, with its founder Robert Gohstand; Hoover Institution Library and Archives; National Archives and Records Administration in Washington, D.C., New York City, and San Bruno, California, and its archivist Marisa Louie; the Archives of the Episcopal Church in Austin, Texas; the microfilm and special collections of the Chinese University of Hong Kong and the University of Hong Kong; Regional Oral History Archives of the University of California, Berkeley, and its former director, Ann Lage; Museum of Chinese in America and Yue Ma, director of collections; Bob Hope Library Archives on Ellis Island and archivists George Tselos and Barry Moreno; CV Starr East Asian Library at the University of California, Berkeley; Old China Hands Reading Room Cafe in Shanghai; the Oakland Public Library's main branch periodicals room; and the San Francisco Maritime Museum and Archives.

Many friends and family members sustained me with their support and kindnesses in every way, and I owe them my heartfelt gratitude. Daniel Else, a former U.S. Navy officer and brothers Hoyt and Hugo Zia, former officers in the U.S. Marine Corps and U.S. Air Force, respectively, answered questions about military organization and warfare. Donna Kotake dug through boxes of old slides for a few that she took on the inside of Tilanqiao prison during a study tour of China eons ago. I received helpful feedback from Sally Lehrman, Teresa Moore, Venise Wagner, and Lisa Schoonerman, who read very early pages, as well as Kate Morris, M. Jean Johnston, and Linda Morris, who combed through later drafts. My sister Humane Zia read countless versions, giving unfailingly good suggestions, while her spouse, Kevin Else, provided excellent technical support. Steve Cheng, whose father was a stranded medical school graduate of St. John's University, gave me detailed notes with his keen insights. I must also thank Steve for encouraging me to file a Freedom of Information Act request for my father's FBI and INS files when Steve was producing Bill Moyers's *Becoming American: The Chinese Experience;* the files contained my parents' deportation hearings—and the INS decision not to deport because of the harm it would inflict on their young American-born children. Even in the depths of the Cold War and McCarthy hysteria, it was unthinkable to separate children from parents.

I owe tremendous thanks to my editor, Susanna Porter, whose infinite patience and wisdom guided me to find the right narrative; her brilliant, meticulous editing invariably made this book stronger. Gratitude always to Sydelle Kramer, my talented and knowledgeable literary agent, who gave crucial advice and support for this book. Many thanks also to Susanna's good-natured and omnicompetent associate editor, Emily Hartley.

Throughout the long journey of this book, my spouse, Lia, has been my greatest supporter, nurturer, cheerleader, and best friend, tolerating my absences for research and the necessary solitude for writing. She has read and reread every version of every draft with enthusiasm, giving me the gifts of her suggestions, encouragement, affection, and laughter. My gratefulness to you, Lia, knows no bounds.

WORDS CANNOT CONVEY THE esteem I hold for the book's central individuals—Annabel Annuo Liu, Benny Pan, Beilin Bing Woo, and Ho Chow, as well as Ho's wife, Theresa—who have spent countless hours with me, answering my intrusive questions and entrusting me to tell the truth of their joys and woes. Over the years, they have grown frail, and many more of their generation have passed away, including my mother, Bing, who died unexpectedly as my manuscript neared completion. To my sorrow, my dear mother and other brave *tao nan* did not live to see others find meaning from what they shared in this book. But their stories continue on. Even as I write this, Annabel Annuo Liu has penned an essay for her public radio station, drawing emotional parallels between her childhood separation from her family and the current-day hostilities against immigrants.

A professor in China told me that, in modern China, everyone's story is a tragedy. Unfortunately, the same may be said about those from many other regions of the world. My deepest appreciation goes to all who struggle to overcome the scars of exodus; their lives are cautionary tales that show why such tragedies of history must not be repeated.

Author's note: Because of shifting global politics and volatile sensitivities that could affect the well-being of some people, I have withheld the names of several individuals on whose excellent assistance and insights I relied. I remain grateful to one and all.

NOTES

ix   "Running away is" in "Special Issue on Running Away," *Lun Yu* [*Lùnyǔ bàn yuè kān:* Táo nàn zhuān kān] 173 (Mar. 16, 1949): 2376.

PROLOGUE

xvi   To the foreigners Peter Hibbard, *The Bund Shanghai: China Faces West*, 212–225, 271–274.

       Land and sovereignty Betty Peh-T'i Wei, *Shanghai: Crucible of China*, 20–45.

xvii   Scholars and journalists Sandra Burton, "Exodus of the Business Class: The Flight from Communism, 1949," *Time*, Sep. 27, 1999.

       These two groups comprised Zhang Zhongli (one of China's preeminent sociologists), interview with the author, the Shanghai Academy of Social Sciences, Dec. 14, 2007.

xx   "Ben Char" Interview with the author, May 6, 2010.

xxii   "After the baby" Marie Ristaino, *Port of Last Resort*, 254, 258–263.

       the *General Gordon* APL Holdings file, Pacific Maritime Museum archives. APL first chartered the *General Gordon*, which was built in 1944, on June 18, 1946.

xxiii   During the war *North China Daily News* (*NCDN*), Dec. 31, 1948.

xxiv   Only five months *NCDN*, Dec. 5, 1948.

       "Between two and" *NCDN*, Dec. 6, 1948.

       Communist gunners attacked *Shanghai Evening Post and Mercury* (*SEP*), Apr. 20, 1949.

xxv   The American President *SEP*, May 21, 1949.

       Elder Sister congratulated *NCDN*, May 20, 1949.

       Communist gunners narrowly *NCDN*, May 20, 1949.

       As soon as *SEP*, May 14, 1949.

       Only Alaska Airlines *NCDN*, May 20, 1949.

xxvi   Shanghai was a Bernard Wasserstein, *Secret War in Shanghai*, 2–3; Lynn Pan, *Shanghai Style*, 43.

       To the Communists Wen-hsin Yeh, *Shanghai Splendor*, 2–5.

       For China, that Wasserstein, *Secret War*, 1.

       When the war Arthur S. Lyman, *The China White Paper, August 1949*, x–xiii.

By late 1947 Ibid., 219, 256–261.

The outcome of Lloyd E. Eastman et al., *The Nationalist Era in China, 1927–1949*, 350–351.

xxvii   Nearly every family *St. John's Dial* and *Echo*, Dec. 7, 1948.

Yet with each *NCDN*, Nov. 12, 1948.

Some of Shanghai's Wong Siu-Lun, *Emigrant Entrepreneurs: Shanghai Industrialists in Hong Kong*, 3–7, 17–41.

xxviii Hong Kong's population Ibid., 3; Edvard Hambro, *The Problem of Chinese Refugees in Hong Kong*, 11–20.

In Taiwan, approximately A. Doak Barnett, report to Institute of Current World Affairs (ICWA), Oct. 15, 1954; Manfred Cheng, interview with the author, Taiwan Economic and Cultural Office, San Francisco, June 16, 2011; David M. Finkelstein, *Washington's Taiwan Dilemma, 1949–1950*, 110–111.

Many thousands of Lynn Pan, *Sons of the Yellow Emperor*, 178–218; Rose Hum Lee, "The Chinese Abroad," *Phylon* 17, no. 3 (3rd Qtr., 1956): 258–265.

CHAPTER 1: BENNY

3   Avenue Haig Huashan Lu.

4   Shanghai's foreign settlements Betty Peh-T'i Wei, *Shanghai: Crucible of China*, 20–103.

Though the boundaries Ibid.

6   German country club Wasserstein, *Secret War*, 1, 49–51.

a red band Ibid., 18; J.F.K. Miller, "The Rise and Fall of Nazi Shanghai," *That's Shanghai*, May 2009.

Soon he reached Christine Estève et al., *Lilongs—Shanghai*; Hanchao Lu, *Beyond the Neon Lights: Everyday Shanghai in the Early Twentieth Century*, 39–43, 138–166.

7   "The Japanese must" Frederic Wakeman, *Policing Shanghai: 1927–37*, 188–191.

Their island neighbor Eastman, *The Nationalist Era*, 116.

Frustrated Chinese leaders Ibid., 51.

8   But instead of Ibid., 4–9, 47.

But in recent Wasserstein, *Secret War*, 15; Wakeman, *Policing*, 277.

This new battle Eastman, *The Nationalist Era*, 119–120.

Five years earlier Harriet Sergeant, *Shanghai*, 187–193.

9   "Those planes have" Ibid., 296–308; Nancy Allison Wright, *Yankee on the Yangtze*, 166–170.

10 Tibet Road Xizang Zhong Lu.

Benny straightened Wei, *Shanghai*, 140–141.

If anyone would Wakeman, *The Shanghai Badlands*, 96.

Pan Zhijie was Wasserstein, *Secret War*, 7–9.

11 the Chinese were Wei, *Shanghai*, 51–63; Wakeman, *Policing*, xv–xvii.

The Chinese pilots Wakeman, *Policing*, 280.

Avenue Edward VII Yan'an Lu.

12   Benny's formal name would Lynn Pan, *Sons*, 10–12; H. P. Wilkinson, *The Family in Classical China*, 157–210.

   Just beyond the Sixian Deng, interview with the author; Hanchao Lu, *Beyond*, 39–43.

14   Some foreigners claimed Leo Ou-fan Lee, *Shanghai Modern*, 29–30; Wei, *Shanghai*, 231–232; *North China Herald*, May 27, 1911, as republished at earnshaw.com/shanghai-ed-india/tales/t-public01.htm, accessed Feb. 2, 2012.

   docks and godowns Nicholas R. Clifford, *Spoilt Children of Empire*, 42–43.

15   The Chinese compradors Wei, *Shanghai*, 123–127; Hanchao Lu, *Beyond*, 56–67.

16   And it was Edward Yihua Xu, "Religion and Education: St. John's University as an Evangelizing Agency" (master's diss., Princeton, 1994), 100–101.

   His father had Wei, *Shanghai*, 193.

18   the horror on Sergeant, *Shanghai*, 297–306.

19   Two of the Nancy Allison Wright, *Yankee on the Yangtze*, 168–170.

20   But no one Tingchang "T.C." Yao, interview with the author, May 14, 2010.

22   Avenue Joffre Huaihai Lu.

   Charlie and John Charlie Sie, interview with the author, Sep. 10, 2008.

   On the heels Wasserstein, *Secret War*, 17–18.

23   By December 1937 Eastman, *The Nationalist Era*, 119–123.

   Cut off from Frederic Wakeman and Wen-hsin Yeh, eds., *Shanghai Sojourners*, 4.

   Their gruesome massacre Eastman, *The Nationalist Era*, 120; Sergeant, *Shanghai*, 324.

CHAPTER 2: HO

27   In Changshu, the The Peabody Essex Museum has a thorough description of gentry life and a reconstructed multigenerational Chinese gentry house: yinyutang.pem.org/, last accessed Mar. 9, 2018.

29   Chinese lore is Judith Stacey, *Patriarchy and Socialist Revolution*, 34, 52–59; Christina K. Gilmartin et al., *Engendering China*, 47–68.

32   Weighing their options Sergeant, *Shanghai*, 188–191.

35   Medhurst Road Taixing Lu.

   Their house on Andrew David Field, *Shanghai's Dancing World*, 149, 197; Wakeman, *The Shanghai Badlands*, 14.

37   The Zhonghua Wen-hsin Yeh, *The Alienated Academy*, 120.

   Bubbling Well Road Nanjing Xi Lu.

   Avenue Foch Yan'an Lu.

39   Japanese secret police Wasserstein, *Secret War*, 8–11, 201; Sergeant, *Shanghai*, 323.

   In the early John B. Powell, *My Twenty-Five Years in China*, 334–335.

   Jessfield Road Wanhangdu Lu.

Chinese, rich or Lynn Pan, *Old Shanghai*, 96; Sergeant, *Shanghai*, 316; Christian Henriot and Wen-hsin Yeh, eds., *In the Shadow of the Rising Sun*, 116–132, 243–254.

CHAPTER 3: BING

43   There was no Hanchao Lu, *Beyond the Neon Lights*, 189–198.
The stove heated William Hinton, *Fanshen*, 37n.
44   The "1-2-8 invasion" Peter Harmsen, *Shanghai 1937*, 15–17; Wakeman, *Policing*, 188–191.
By 1935, when Jonathan D. Spence, *The Search for Modern China*, 403–424; John King Fairbank, *The Great Chinese Revolution*, 236–239.
48   Her mother in H. P. Wilkinson, *The Family in Classical China*, 149; Christina K. Gilmartin et al., *Engendering China*, 92–96.
54   She had a Lynn Pan, *Shanghai Style*, 25–32.
58   "These are not" Wakeman, *The Shanghai Badlands*, 85–88.

CHAPTER 4: ANNUO

59   The walls of George Wang and Betty Barr, *Shanghai Boy, Shanghai Girl*, 89–90.
patriotic Boy Scouts Frederic Wakeman and Wen-hsin Yeh, eds., *Shanghai Sojourners*, 124–125.
The Imperial Japanese Eastman et al., *The Nationalist Era*, 120, 134–135.
60   People rushed to Wei, *Shanghai*, 245.
By the end Harmsen, *Shanghai 1937*, 210–217.
61   During those ten Marie Bergère, *The Golden Age of the Chinese Bourgeoisie*, 227–241.
Annuo's parents epitomized Bergère, *Shanghai: Gateway to Modernity*, 147–165.
62   the Green Gang Brian Martin, *The Shanghai Green Gang*, 5–7, 10–43; Sergeant, *Shanghai*, 82.
businesses soared Nicholas R. Clifford, *Spoilt Children of Empire*, 257–275.
63   Chiang embarked on Sergeant, *Shanghai*, 68–94; Eastman, *The Nationalist Era*, 1–9.
"pact with the" Bergère, *Shanghai*, 195–199.
The gang's leader Ling Pan, *Old Shanghai: Gangsters in Paradise*, 16–17.
The "White Terror" Sergeant, *Shanghai*, 65–94.
Women sporting bobbed Wen-hsin Yeh, ed., *Becoming Chinese*, 346–347; Stella Dong, *Shanghai*, 184–185.
67   More than thirty *The China Chronicles: Exodus and Resistance*, directed by Yuan Min, exec. prod. Richard Lin Yang (2006; Canada Live News Agency, 2007), DVD.
"Kill all, loot" Spence, *The Search for Modern China*, 469; Hinton, *Fanshen*, 72.
68   southern supply route Barbara W. Tuchman, *Sand Against the Wind*, 234–240.

69   Rue Lafayette Fuxing Lu.
"**General Han Deqin**" Annabel Annuo Liu, interview with the author, May 17, 2007.

CHAPTER 5: BENNY

79   **Pro-Nationalists argued** Eastman, *The Nationalist Era*, 115, 136.
Tokyo had expected Ibid., 134.

80   **Chinese troops slowed** Ibid., 121–123; *The Battle of China*, directed by Frank Capra (1944; Office of War Information), accessed April 28, 2009, youtube.com/watch?v=m4Ebv-FzP60.
By early 1939 Eastman, *The Nationalist Era*, 117, map; 136.

81   **More than a million** *SEP*, Dec. 17, 1941.
So many of "Johanneans in Government Service," *Johannean* (1937), author's collection.

83   **In 1939, Pan** Wakeman, *Shanghai Badlands*, 96.
more than 150 Ibid., 25.
One particularly brazen Ibid., 59–64.

84   **Even Generalissimo Chiang** Martin, *The Shanghai Green Gang*, 80–81.
four hundred constables Wakeman, *Shanghai Badlands*, 96.
C. C. Pan even Ibid.

85   **76 Jessfield Road** Ibid., 58, 85; Wasserstein, *Secret War*, 24.

86   **Li Shiqun, reputed** Wakeman, *Shanghai Badlands*, 85.
An older St. John's Tao-Fu Ying, interview with the author, Oct. 6, 2008.

87   **Fu Xiaoan** Wakeman, *Shanghai Badlands*, 97.

88   **Wang Jingwei** Lynn Pan, *Old Shanghai*, 61–76.
Police Chief Pan Wakeman, *Shanghai Badlands*, 105.

89   **The elegant English-style** Zhang Yuanji, "40 Jessfield Road," Guangxi Normal University Publications Dept., Baidu, accessed Sep. 5, 2011. Translated for the author by John Yu.
British inspector scrawled "Private House Occupied by S.G.O.P.B. at 40 Jessfield Rd.," Police Report, Shanghai Municipal Police Investigation Files, 1947, RG 263, Microfilm Box 3, Roll 60, N332, National Archives, College Park, MD.

CHAPTER 6: BING

94   **Three Principles of** Henry Blair Graybill and You-kuang Chu, *The New China*, 355.

97   **"Blood and Soul"** Field, *Shanghai's Dancing World*, 203–204; Wakeman, *Shanghai Badlands*, 67–68.

101 **"tiger stove" shop** Lu, *Beyond the Neon Lights*, 102.
wartime price inflation Eastman, *The Nationalist Era*, 152–169; Henriot and Yeh, eds., *In the Shadow*, 122–132.
cronies and relatives Ibid., 134–138; Dong, *Shanghai*, 281–286.

102 **black markets popped** *NCDN*, Oct. 10, 1945; Bergère, *Shanghai*, 314.

103 **Marlene Yang** Interview with the author, Mar. 18, 2009.

CHAPTER 7: ANNUO

107   **a major riot** Wakeman, *Shanghai Badlands*, 55.

       a single egg Robert W. Barnett, "Starvation, Boom and Blockade in Shanghai," *Far Eastern Survey* 9, no. 9 (Apr. 24, 1940): 97–102; Henriot and Yeh, *In the Shadow*, 124–128; James R. Ross, *Escape to Shanghai*, 209.

108   **first four years** Henriot and Yeh, *In the Shadow*, 1–6; Poshek Fu, *Passivity, Resistance, and Collaboration*, 120–126; Ursula Bacon, *Shanghai Diary*, 113–117.

       Japan's military coordinated *NCDN, SEP, Hong Kong Standard* (*HKS*), and *New York Times* (*NYT*), Dec. 8–10, 1941; William C. McDonald III and Barbara L. Evenson, *The Shadow Tiger*, 208–216; Dong, *Shanghai*, 268.

109   **Gudao, Solitary Island** Fu, *Passivity, Resistance, and Collaboration*, 30–38, 120–126.

       Bridge House on Henry F. Pringle, *Bridge House Survivor*, 4–12.

112   **Avenue Pétain** Hengshan Lu.

114   **Waibaidu (Garden) Bridge** Sergeant, *Shanghai*, 315–316; James R. Ross, *Escape to Shanghai*, 205–208.

       128 bank employees Wakeman, *Shanghai Badlands*, 120–123; Theresa Chow, interview with the author, June 10, 2010.

115   **Rue Boissezon** Fuxing Xi Lu.

       Rosalyn Koo Interview with the author, July 23, 2007.

       Theresa Chen-Louie Interview with the author, May 21, 2010.

117   **Nationalists and Communists** Eastman, *The Nationalist Era*, 227–233.

CHAPTER 8: BENNY

120   **Students across Shanghai** Mary Lamberton and George C. Shen, *St. John's University—Shanghai 1879–1947*, 184; interviews by the author with numerous subjects, including Benny Pan, Nov. 10, 2012; Rosalyn Koo, July 23, 2007; Lo-Lo Zhang Pan, Aug. 24, 2007; Mary Ann Sun, May 22, 2008.

121   **private schools in** Wen-hsin Yeh, *Alienated Academy*, 284–287, tables 3–4.

       from Jessfield Park Lamberton and Shen, *St. John's University*, 183–184.

       Frank Kwok Interview with the author, Sep. 9, 2009.

122   **plain dormitory** Edward Yihua Xu, "Religion and Education: St. John's University as an Evangelizing Agency" (master's diss., Princeton, 1994), 149–151.

123   **a sandwich at** Benny Pan, interviews with the author, including on Mar. 3, 2010; Zoya Shlakis file, Series I, Box 1, Folder 4: Memories of Shanghai, Old China Hand Archives, California State University, Northridge.

       "Good manners mark" Xu, "Religion and Education," 33.

124   **even Japanese politicians** Wakeman, *Shanghai Badlands*, 112.

125   **C. C. Pan was** Ibid., 132–133; Wasserstein, *Secret War*, 129.

       William Zu Liang Sung Xu, "Religion and Education," 130; undated memorandum, "St. John's, Dr. T. M. Tang," RG 79-12, Archives of the Episcopal Church, Austin, TX.

126   **Chiang Kai-shek himself** Lily Soo-Hoo Sun, biography of Zu Liang (Wil-

liam) Sung, unpublished manuscript, 26–27; Mary Ann Sun, interview with the author, Feb. 11, 2011.

Sung called Benny's Lamberton and Shen, *St. John's University*, 203.

restore China's sovereignty Henriot and Yeh, *In the Shadow*, 253–262; H.L., "The End of Extraterritoriality in China," *Bulletin of International News* 20, no. 2 (Jan. 23, 1943): 49–56.

127 Jewish opera singer Ross, *Escape to Shanghai*, 85–88.

CHAPTER 9: BING

129 all Allied nationals Dong, *Shanghai*, 269–271.

Plenty of British Robert Bickers, *Empire Made Me*, 313–319.

131 He had plenty Wasserstein, *Secret War*, 135–140, 270–271; Ristaino, *Port of Last Resort*, 214.

Kristian received orders *SEP*, Dec. 17, 1941.

about twenty thousand Ristaino, *Port of Last Resort*, 98–108; Bergère, *Shanghai*, 296–297.

132 English-language papers Powell, *My Twenty-Five Years*, 342; Fu, *Passivity, Resistance, and Collaboration*, 30–38.

citizens of Allied Wasserstein, *Secret War*, 135–140.

seventy-six hundred Americans Ibid., 137.

CHAPTER 10: ANNUO

143 "Spies are everywhere" Henriot and Yeh, *In the Shadow*, 142; Wakeman, *Shanghai Badlands*, 135; Myra Souza dos Remedios, interview with the author, May 10, 2010.

"*baojia* snitches to" Wang and Barr, *Shanghai Boy, Shanghai Girl*, 150–152; "Shanghai—Counter-Espionage Summary," Aug. 12, 1945, Headquarters Office of Strategic Services, China Theater, author's collection, 5.

145 fleas infected with Spence, *The Search for Modern China*, 496.

149 where white rice Henriot and Yeh, *In the Shadow*, 143–146.

150 June 9, 1944 Wasserstein, *Secret War*, 256.

Chinese Curtiss Hawks Alexander Ludeke, *Weapons of World War II*, 218–275; Gregory Crouch, *China's Wings*.

154 Nellie Sung Tao Interview with the author, July 24, 2007.

CHAPTER 11: BENNY

156 Married men of Gail Hershatter, "Regulating Sex," in Wakeman and Yeh, *Shanghai Sojourners*, 145–167; Sergeant, *Shanghai*, 282–284.

158 one American bomb Dong, *Shanghai*, 279.

two hundred American Ibid.; Kenneth C. Liang collection, accessed Apr., 2008.

August 15, 1945 Dong, *Shanghai*, 279.

Chen Gongbo Fu, *Passivity, Resistance, and Collaboration*, 219; *NCDN*, Apr. 13, 1946.

159 Japanese military was Suzanne Pepper, *The Civil War in China*, 9–16; Eastman, *The Nationalist Era*, 308.

arrest C. C. Pan *Shanghai Herald,* Oct. 3, 1945.

160   "Confiscated from Puppets" *Shanghai Herald,* Apr. 3, 1946, Apr. 10, 1946; Pepper, *Civil War,* 16–24.

CHAPTER 12: HO

167   cabarets, gambling joints Field, *Shanghai's Dancing World,* 166–170.

168   one hundred thousand Harry S. Truman, *Memoirs,* vol. 2, 66; Pepper, *Civil War,* 9–12; Wasserstein, *Secret War,* 266.

169   Japanese and German officials Wasserstein, *Secret War,* 266.
The uncertainty stymied Ibid., 265.
U.S. Tenth Air Spence, *The Search for Modern China,* 484.
USS *Rocky Mount* Wasserstein, *Secret War,* 266.
more than one hundred thousand *NCDN,* Nov. 23, 1945, Jan. 1, 1946; Gail Hershatter, *Dangerous Liaisons,* 293–299.
American sailors, soldiers Dong, *Shanghai,* 281.

170   right-hand side *Shanghai Herald,* Dec. 31, 1945.

171   puppets and collaborators Pepper, *Civil War,* 37–40.
students who stayed Eastman, *The Nationalist Era,* 308–309.
"reconversion" training program Pepper, *Civil War,* 37–40.

172   students and workers Ibid., 38–39; Eastman, *The Nationalist Era,* 314.

173   marine had raped Eastman, *The Nationalist Era,* 54–58; Henriot and Yeh, *In the Shadow,* 359.

174   Jiao Da engineering Pepper, *Civil War,* 61.

175   terrible inflationary pressure *NCDN,* Nov. 23, 1948, Dec. 21, 1948; Eastman, *The Nationalist Era,* 309–314.
hundred yuan could Frank Dikotter, *The Tragedy of Liberation,* 18.
required foreign students Peter Kwong and Dusanka Miscevic, *Chinese America,* 237.

CHAPTER 13: BING

183   Nine hundred million Fairbank, *The Great Chinese Revolution,* 261–263.
five hundred thousand Eastman, *The Nationalist Era,* 294; David M. Finkelstein, *Washington's Taiwan Dilemma,* 23–24.
General George Marshall Eastman, *The Nationalist Era,* 297–305.
American soldiers grabbing Dong, *Shanghai,* 281.

184   Shanghai's local riders *SEP,* July 20, 1946, Oct. 9, 1946.
brokering a truce Dorothy Borg, "America Loses Chinese Good Will," *Far Eastern Survey* 18, no. 4 (Feb. 23, 1949): 37–45.
About $500 million Fairbank, *The Great Chinese Revolution,* 262–264; Hannah Pakula, *The Last Empress,* 556–561.
stream of carpetbaggers Pepper, *Civil War,* 16–24.

188   Avenue du Roi Albert Shanxi Nan Lu.

CHAPTER 14: HO

190   American GIs across R. Alton Lee, "The Army 'Mutiny' of 1946," *Journal of American History* 53, no. 3 (Dec. 1, 1966): 555–571.

Lo-Lo Zhang Pan Interview with the author, Aug. 24, 2007.

192   **more than three hundred** List of students on the *General Gordon*, 1947, Ho Chow papers, author's collection.

Ming Cho Lee Interview with the author, May 15, 2008.

CHAPTER 15: BENNY

201   **advice of Pan Da** Lamberton and Shen, *St. John's University*, 203; Xu, "Religion and Education," 130–133; undated memorandum, "St. John's, Dr. T. M. Tang," RG 79-12, Archives of the Episcopal Church, Austin, TX.

202   **grisly details of** Powell, *My Twenty-Five Years*, 335–338; Henry F. Pringle, *Bridge House Survivor*, 13–18.

"rather indifferent to religion" Xu, "Religion and Education," 156.

director, Grace Brady Lamberton and Shen, *St. John's University*, 188–189; Stephen Chun-Tao Cheng, "Remembering Ms. Grace Brady," *The Johanneans* (Oct. 2005); *The San Diego Union*, July 8, 1960.

205   **Ward Road** Changyang Lu.

Tilanqiao Prison, as "A History of Shanghai's Tilanqiao Prison," *That's Shanghai*, May 18, 2017, thatsmags.com/shanghai/post/18980/tbt-a-history-of-shanghai-s-tilanqiao-prison, last accessed Mar. 10, 2018.

206   **making mass arrests** *NCDN*, June 5, 1949, June 6, 1949; *NYT*, May 14, 1949.

Little Vienna, where *Shanghai Ghetto*, directed by Dana Janklowicz-Mann and Amir Mann (2002; Rebel Child Production, New Video Group, 2004), DVD.

208   **Dai Li himself** Benny Pan, interview with the author, June 9, 2014; Frederic Wakeman, *Spymaster*, 352.

209   **China National Aviation** Gregory Crouch, *China's Wings*, 381–383.

St. John's Dial Feb. 8, 1949, RG 30-2-23, Archives of the Episcopal Church, Austin, TX.

210   **Richard Lin Yang** Interview with the author, Oct. 15, 2007.

CHAPTER 16: ANNUO

216   **important military victories** Eastman, *The Nationalist Era*, 330–332.

217   **"'whites-only' policy"** Laura Madokoro, *Elusive Refuge*, 104–115; "White Australia Policy Begins," National Museum Australia, nma.gov.au/online_features/defining_moments/featured/white_australia_policy_begins, last accessed Jan. 10, 2018.

Big Four ruling Parks M. Coble, Jr., *The Shanghai Capitalists*, 255.

"A plane dispatched" Pakula, *Last Empress*, 556–557.

CHAPTER 17: BING

227   **U.S. Congress had** Madeline Y. Hsu, "The Disappearance of America's Cold War Chinese Refugees, 1948–1966," *Journal of American Ethnic History* 31, no. 4 (Summer 2012): 16; Richard Ferree Smith, "Refugees," *Annals of the American Academy of Political and Social Science* 367 (Sep. 1966): 44–46.

228   **"only a hundred and five Chinese"** Mae M. Ngai, "Legacies of Exclusion:

Illegal Chinese Immigration during the Cold War Years," *Journal of American Ethnic History* 18, no. 1 (Fall 1998): 3–35; Richard Ferree Smith, "Refugees," *Annals of the American Academy of Political and Social Science* 367 (Sep. 1966): 44–46.

229   sack of rice Spence, *The Search for Modern China*, 502.

August 19, 1948 Ibid., 520.

230   ordered citizens to hand over Wei, *Shanghai*, 261–262; Dong, *Shanghai*, 287–289.

went too far Ibid.; Pakula, *Last Empress*, 559–561.

231   As hyperinflation careened Colin D. Campbell and Gordon C. Tullock, "Hyperinflation in China, 1937–49," *Journal of Political Economy* 62, no. 3 (June 1954): 236–245.

spend their pay "Shanghai's Buying," *Life*, Nov. 15, 1948; Charles P. Gilson Memoranda, Oct. 26, 1948, Nov. 2, 1948, Records of the Treasurer, RG 64-128-13 and RG 64-128-14, Archives of the Episcopal Church, Austin, TX.

Shanghai's wealthy capitalists Wong Siu-lun, *Emigrant Entrepreneurs*, 16–25.

232   Marshall, having witnessed Arthur S. Lyman, "US Aid to the GMD, Statement to Committees on Foreign Affairs and Foreign Relations, US Congress," February 20, 1948, in *The China White Paper*, 382–383.

imposed martial law *NCDN*, Nov. 12, 1948.

"Removed by censor" Noel Barber, *The Fall of Shanghai*, 110–111.

China's entire treasury Ibid., 78.

China's greatest art Aschwin Lippe, "Hidden Treasures of China," *The Metropolitan Museum of Art Bulletin* 14, no. 2 (Oct. 1955): 54–60; Chia-feng Wang, "Adventures of the Treasures," *Kuang-hua-tsa-chih* [*Sinorama Monthly*], Aug. 1985.

toothpaste, screws—anything Shanghai confidential office memorandum from Taipei deputy mayor Chen Cheng, April 29, 1949, Q1-7-563, Shanghai Municipal Archives, accessed April 2008. Translated for the author by Emily Xuxuan Xu.

By November 1948 *NCDN*, Nov. 12, 1948.

233   MOTORCARS, APARTMENTS, CHEAP *NCDN*, Dec. 2, 1948.

235   ten-foot wooden *SEP*, Apr. 20, 1949.

CHAPTER 18: HO

243   Back in 1946 *NCDN*, Dec. 17, 1948, Dec. 24, 1948.

244   Ho's letters from Ho Chow papers, trans. by Emily Xuxuan Xu, author's collection.

245   called China Motors Ho Chow, interview with the author, July 11, 2007.

253   the last gasps Eastman, *The Nationalist Era*, 342–350.

255   landlords were being Spence, *The Search for Modern China*, 517.

Norwegian missionaries observed Odd Arne Westad, *Decisive Encounters*, 134.

256   great flight out *SEP*, Apr. 26, 1949, Apr. 30, 1949, May 2, 1949; Charles P.

Gilson Memorandum to Earl Fowler, RG 79-12, Archives of the Episcopal Church, Austin, TX.

256 CHIANG RELINQUISHES POST *NYT*, Jan. 22, 1949.

257 With Chiang's resignation Eastman, *The Nationalist Era*, 350–352.

259 Communists had swept Spence, *The Search for Modern China*, 510–513.

260 mayor, K. C. Wu *NCDN*, Apr. 1, 1949.

261 April 21, 1949 *SEP*, Apr. 21, 1949.
     "their Stalingrad" with *NYT*, May 19, 1949.
     mounted machine guns *NYT*, May 1, 1949, May 2, 1949.
     summarily executed dissenters *NCDN*, Apr. 2, 1949, May 12, 1949; *NYT*, May 8, 1949.
     warnings to evacuate *NCDN*, Apr. 26, 1949, Apr. 29, 1949.
     Operation Flying Dragon Jewish Telegraphic Agency, "Daily News Bulletin," May 20, 1949.

262 business as usual *NYT*, June 5, 1949.

CHAPTER 19: BENNY

265 martial law imposed Dong, *Shanghai*, 291–292.
     A strict curfew *NCDN*, May 26, 1949.

266 Shanghai universities shut *China Press*, Apr. 28, 1949; *SEP*, Apr. 28, 1949.
     On May 24 *NCDN*, May 25, 1949.
     few blocks away Ibid.
     the next morning *NCDN*, May 26, 1949.

267 only opposition arose *NCDN*, May 27, 1949; newsreel footage exhibit, Shanghai General Post Office Museum, viewed Jan. 3, 2008.
     "People's Liberation Army" *NYT*, May 27, 1949.

268 two thousand Red Army *NCDN*, June 5, 1949.
     Other Nationalist troops *SEP*, May 25, 1949.
     in wild celebration *NCDN*, May 26, 1949; *NYT*, May 27, 1949.
     the *yang ko* Ibid.; Sam Tata, *Shanghai 1949: The End of an Era*, 122–141, images 66–75.

269 the women's dormitory Confidential letter, RG 79-12, Archives of the Episcopal Church, Austin, TX.
     an underground Communist Tao-Fu Ying, interview with the author.
     pro-Communist campus "St. John's University," p. 82, RG 79-12, Archives of the Episcopal Church, Austin, TX.

270 Marshal Chen Yi *NYT*, June 5, 1949.
     Thousands of mines *NCDN*, June 5, 1949.
     the renminbi *NCDN*, May 24, 1949, June 5, 1949.
     With much fanfare *NCDN*, May 27, 1949.
     shut down the vice Field, *Shanghai's Dancing World*, 263.

271 attacks on Shanghai *NCDN*, June 24, 1949, July 22, 1949; *NYT*, June 30, 1949.
     Nationalist plane mistakenly *NCDN*, June 24, 1949.

272 Dr. Tu Yu-Ching Lamberton and Shen, *St. John's University*, 340.
     Communist government swiftly Barber, *The Fall of Shanghai*, 174–179, 192.

CHAPTER 20: HO

279   **Immigration and Naturalization Service** Ho Chow papers, author's collection.

280   **sympathetic Americans wrote** *NCDN*, Dec. 31, 1948; National Archives and Records Administration (NARA), RG 85, No. 56234/455.

281   **Chinyee** Interview with the author, Dec. 5, 2007.
    Chinese Students Club Confidential INS file, NARA, RG 85, No. 56324/950, Box 243.
    Chinese Students' Christian "Chinese Students' Christian Association," NARA, RG 85, folder 56292/617; Peter Kwong and Dusanka Miscevic, *Chinese America*, 221–222.

282   **named Paul Lin** "Proposed Course of Action Relative to Investigation of Questionable Chinese Student Organizations," Feb. 20, 1950, and "Subversive Activity of Dr. Paul Ta-kuang Lin," Jan. 25, 1950, NARA, RG 85, No. 56292/617.
    Dr. Paul Chih Meng "Chinese Students in the United States and Their Communistic Affiliations and Activities," July 19, 1950, NARA, RG 85, No. 56292/617.

283   **debate ensued in Washington** "INS Views on Bill to Permit Chinese Students to Remain in US for Three Years," NARA, RG 85, No. 56190/93.
    Maria Lee Koh Interview with the author, Oct. 28, 2009.

285   **powerful Americans claimed** Ellen Schrecker, *Many Are the Crimes*, 376–377; David E. Kaplan, *Fires of the Dragon*, 112; John Dower, *War Without Mercy*, 309.

286   **all Chinese were** Renqiu Yu, *To Save China, To Save Ourselves*, 182–191; Cindy I-Fen Cheng, *Citizens of Asian America*, 149–157.
    Madame Chiang Kai-shek Pakula, *Last Empress*, 626–632, 650–656.
    being a lesbian Jonathan Fenby, *Chiang Kai-shek*, 397.
    apartment on Fifth Ibid., 627n.

287   **Jack Tang, the** Interview with the author, Sep. 14, 2007; Jack Chi-chien Tang, oral history conducted by Carolyn Wakeman, 1999, "The Textile Industry and the Development of Hong Kong, 1949–1999," transcript, UC Berkeley Regional Oral History Archives, 2003, 28–31.
    clamoring to return "Proposed Mass Movement of Resident Chinese Back to China," NARA, RG 85, No. 56240/732.

288   **State Department established** "Reports from State Dept. re: Chinese Students Intending to Depart from United States," NARA, RG 85, No. 56324/395.
    letters came from "Proposed Mass Movement of Resident Chinese Back to China," NARA, RG 85, No. 56240/732.
    about one hundred "Reports from State Dept. re: Chinese Students Intending to Depart from United States," NARA, RG 85, No. 56324/395.

290   *WAI SHENG REN* Dominic Meng-Hsuang Yang and Mau-kuei Chang, "Understanding the Nuances of *Waishengren*," *China Perspectives* 83 (2010): 110–114.

290 Nationalist secret police Charlotte Brooks, *Between Mao and McCarthy*, 114–119; Yu, *To Save China*, 183–184; Kaplan, *Fires of the Dragon*, 112–116.

CHAPTER 21: ANNUO

294 Four hundred years Yu-Shan, "Formosa under Three Rules," *Pacific Historical Review* 19, no. 4 (Nov. 1950): 397–407; Harry Alverson Franck, *Glimpses of Japan and Formosa*, 141–147.
     China had ceded Ibid., 48–52.

295 Upon Japan's surrender Ibid., 52–55.
     February 28, 1947 Allan J. Shackleton, *Formosa Calling*, 45–68; George H. Kerr, *Formosa Betrayed*, 239–248; Finkelstein, *Washington's Taiwan Dilemma*, 61–67.
     more than a million Mahlon Meyer, *Remembering China from Taiwan*, 4–8.

297 entire Nationalist government Fenby, *Chiang Kai-shek*, 494–498; Finkelstein, *Washington's Taiwan Dilemma*, 71–73, 169–172.
     vigilant against the *NCDN*, May 3, 1949.

302 constant state of *NCDN*, May 24, 1949; United Press International, May 1, 1949.
     the White Terror Laura Tyson Li, *Madame Chiang Kai-Shek*, 344–348; Meyer, *Remembering China from Taiwan*, 3; Elizabeth Converse, "Formosa: Private Citadel?" *Far Eastern Survey* 18, no. 21 (Oct. 19, 1949): 249–250; Hong-zen Wang, "Class Structures and Social Mobility in Taiwan in the Initial Postwar Period," *China Journal* 48 (July 2002): 68, 77.

303 China Aid Act of Lyman, *China White Paper*, 408; Finkelstein, *Washington's Taiwan Dilemma*, 31.
     Theresa Chen-Louie Interview with the author, May 21, 2010.

304 General Bai Chongxi Eastman, *The Nationalist Era*, 352.
     Pai Hsien-yung Interview with the author, Nov. 29, 2010.

307 ["The United States does"] Bevin Alexander, *Korea: The First War We Lost*, 18.

308 China lobby roundly Finkelstein, *Washington's Taiwan Dilemma*, 264–270.
     vise of martial law Cheng, "The Formosa Triangle," 801–803; Kerr, *Formosa Betrayed*, chap. 20.
     On March 1, 1950 Finkelstein, *Washington's Taiwan Dilemma*, 295–297.
     on Green Island Ibid.; Shawna Yang Ryan, *Green Island*.
     "We Taiwanese have" Peter P. C. Cheng, "The Formosa Triangle," *Asian Survey* 7, no. 11 (Nov. 1967): 800.

309 urban residential sectors Hsinchu Museum of Military Dependents Village, Hsinchu city, Taiwan; military village restoration and museum, 44 South Village, Taipei.
     "retake the mainland" Meyer, *Remembering China from Taiwan*, 44–50.
     President Chiang was Eastman, *The Nationalist Era*, 352.
     bombers to attack Shanghai Ibid., 292–295.

CHAPTER 22: BING

311   Chinese Exclusion Act of 1882 *American Experience,* "Chinese Exclusion
      Act," directed by Ric Burns and Li-shun Yu, produced by Steeplechase
      Films, aired on May 29, 2018, on PBS; ricburns.com/film/the-chinese-
      exclusion-act; caamedia.org/blog/2017/03/13/chinese-exclusion-act-a-
      new-film-about-a-19th-century-law-with-21st-century-lessons/, accessed
      Mar. 3, 2018.

315   many Chinese were Erika Lee, *The Making of Asian America,* 96–99.

316   lengthy imprisonment with Ibid.; "Immigrant History," Angel Island Im-
      migration Station Foundation, aiisf.org/education/station-history/life-
      on-angel-island, last accessed Jan. 7, 2018.

318   most influential organizations Brooks, *Between Mao and McCarthy,*
      16–22.

320   Catholic priest, Reverend Margaret Soong, interview by author, June 11,
      2009.

CHAPTER 23: DOREEN AND BENNY

329   boss and benefactor Ellis N. Tucker, confidential letter, June 12, 1948,
      RG 79-12, Archives of the Episcopal Church, Austin, TX.
      Nationalist forces continued *NCDN,* June 30, 1949, July 22, 1949; Pepper,
      Civil War, 392, 401.
      from the Soviets Han Suyin, *The Morning Deluge,* 502–524.

330   Avenue Pétain mansion Anne Warr, *Shanghai Architecture,* 130–131.
      taken millions of dollars Dong, *Shanghai,* 289.
      misused diplomatic passports *NYT,* Sep. 23, 1947, Oct. 6, 1947.
      Communists had captured *NYT,* May 29, 1949.
      backlogged cases of Pepper, *Civil War,* 386–390; "Kill Nice!" *Time,* May 21,
      1951.

331   Hefty taxes and Pepper, *Civil War,* 394–400; A. Doak Barnett, "Letter on
      Economic Crisis," reports to the ICWA, Sep. 14, 1949, 6–9, icwa.org,
      accessed Apr. 16, 2007.
      businessmen were leaping Barber, *The Fall of Shanghai,* 223–224; Myra
      Souza dos Remedios, interview with the author, May 10, 2010.
      St. John's University "p. 82," RG 79-12, Archives of the Episcopal Church,
      Austin, TX.

332   revolutionaries organized rallies Odd Arne Westad, *Decisive Encounters,*
      130–136.
      a million landlords Spence, *The Search for Modern China,* 517.
      China National Aviation Wright, *Yankee on the Yangtze,* 260–272.

333   Republic of China Brooks, *Between Mao and McCarthy,* 97–98; Gordon H.
      Chang, *Fateful Ties,* 197–202; Gregor Benton, *The Hongkong Crisis,* 14.

334   never been restrictions Laura Madokoro, *Elusive Refuge,* 38–41; Hu Yueh,
      "The Problem of the Hong Kong Refugees," *Asian Survey* 2, no. 1 (Mar.
      1962): 30–32; Gregory Chow, *China's Economic Transformation,* 26.

336   a million Chinese Edvard Hambro, *The Problem of Chinese Refugees in*

Hong Kong, 13, table 4; Maduro, *Elusive Refuge*, 35–37; Benton, *The Hong-kong Crisis*, 13.

337 **agitators would stir** Leo F. Goodstadt, *Uneasy Partner*, 40–41.

339 **hawkers shouting headlines** *HKS*, Oct. 13, 1949, Oct. 22, 1949; George Shen, "Media and Communications Networks in Hong Kong," in Albert H. Yee, *Wither Hong Kong?*, 190–192.

340 **Hong Kong natives** Myra Souza dos Remedios, interview with the author, May 10, 2010; Hambro, *The Problem of Chinese Refugees*, 63–65.

     wrapping their leftovers Kenneth On-wai Lan, "Rennie's Mill: The Origin and Evolution of a Special Enclave in Hong Kong" (PhD diss., University of Hong Kong, 2006), 12.

     opposed large-scale relief Madokoro, *Elusive Refuge*, 32–46; Hambro, *The Problem of Chinese Refugees*, 36–40; Chi-Kwan Mark, "The 'Problem of People': British Colonials, Cold War Powers, and the Chinese Refugees in Hong Kong, 1949–62," in *Modern Asian Studies*, 2–3.

CHAPTER 24: ANNUO

343 **June 25, 1950** Spence, *The Search for Modern China*, 524–529.

     arbitrarily divided Korea Han Suyin, *The Morning Deluge*, 525–546.

     North Korea had Bevin Alexander, *Korea: The First War We Lost*, 2–3.

344 **President Truman made** Ibid., 36–37, 44–45.

     "thirty-three thousand Nationalist soldiers" Pakula, *Last Empress*, 601; Finkelstein, *Washington's Taiwan Dilemma*, 334.

     The U.S. Navy was Finkelstein, *Washington's Taiwan Dilemma*, 333.

     provide \$300 million Chi Wang, *The United States and China since World War II*, 40; George Kerr, *Formosa Betrayed*, chap. 20.

     Within a few years Ibid.; Neil H. Jacoby, "An Evaluation of U.S. Economic Aid to Free China, 1951–1965," Jan. 1966, Bureau for the Far East, Agency for International Development, Dept. of State, pp. 7–10, pdf.usaid.gov/pdf_docs/PNAAK054.pdf, accessed Mar. 16, 2015.

346 **about 30 percent** Theresa Chen-Louie, interview with the author, May 21, 2010.

348 **open feud between** Alexander, *Korea: The First War We Lost*, 176.

349 **March 24, 1951** Ibid., 407.

CHAPTER 25: HO

351 **Alger Hiss was** Schrecker, *Many Are the Crimes*, 163–165.

     "psychopathic personalities," and Bill Ong Hing, *Defining America through Immigration*, 74.

352 **China Area Aid** Richard Ferree Smith, "Refugees," 44–46; Madeline Y. Hsu, "The Disappearance of America's Cold War Chinese Refugees," *Journal of American Ethnic History* 31, no. 4 (Summer 2012): 16–21; Madeline Y. Hsu, *The Good Immigrants*, 122–127.

     Communist China entered Spence, *The Search for Modern China*, 528–531.

353 **to rain napalm** Alexander, *Korea: The First War We Lost*, 456–457, images 470–473.

use nuclear warheads Ibid., 258.

Several dozen stranded "Letter to Senator McCloy," Oct. 26, 1951, NARA, RG 85, No. 56324/797.

Others posted anonymous "Letter from Chinese Students Association in America," Aug. 20, 1951, NARA, RG 85, No. 56234/950.

Qian Xuesen Iris Chang, *Thread of the Silkworm*, x–xvii.

354   "lightning raids" in *Bedford* (Pa.) *Gazette*, Feb. 1, 1951; *The Cincinnati Enquirer*, Feb. 1, 1951; *The Terra Haute Tribune*, Jan. 1, 1954.

"Confession Program" was Peter Kwong and Dusanka Miscevic, *Chinese America*, 223–226.

John F. Boyd Memorandum to W. F. Kelly, "Inspection of Chinese Aliens at Port of New York," Jan. 4, 1952, NARA, RG 85, No. 56314/932, 5.

357   fall of 1951 Hsu, "The Disappearance of America's Cold War Chinese Refugees," 6.

CHAPTER 26: BING

362   Times Square—Chin Lee's Grace Lee Boggs, *Living for Change*, 6–9.

364   New York's Chinatown Brooks, *Between Mao and McCarthy*, 5–6; Peter Kwong, *Chinatown, NY: Labor and Politics*, 131–147.

368   CAN THESE TWO *Argus*, Jan. 10, 1951.

371   FBI conducted raids Yu, *To Save China*, 185–187.

375   American children FBI FOIA files, author's collection.

written numerous articles Ibid.

CHAPTER 27: BENNY

379   root out Rightists A. Doak Barnett, "Letter on the Chinese Communist Movement," reports to the ICWA, ADB–34, Sep. 8, 1949, 1–10.

his wife, Mary Mary Wang, interview with the author, Sep. 21, 2008.

Vem Chuang Interview with the author, May 6, 2010.

beggars, prostitutes, black Pepper, *Civil War in China*, 405–407.

prices for tickets Ibid., 394–398.

381   nothing to fear Bill Chen, Shanghai Overseas Returned Scholars Association, interview with the author, Feb. 2, 2008.

more worried letters Letters to Charles P. Gilson, RG 64-128, Archives of the Episcopal Church, Austin, TX.

Sisters of Loretto Patricia Jean Manion, SL, *Venture Into the Unknown*, 312–316.

unexpected government assessment Letter to James E. Whitney, Aug. 20, 1951, RG-135-2-5, Archives of the Episcopal Church, Austin, TX.

letter by Premier Zhou Enlai Letter in Chinese and English, pp. 1–3, RG 275-1-1, Archives of the Episcopal Church, Austin, TX; Philip L. Wickeri, ed., *Christian Encounters with Chinese Culture*.

forbade employers to Randall Gould, "Shanghai during the Takeover," *Annals of the American Academy of Political and Social Science* 277 (Sep. 1951): 184–187; Barber, *The Fall of Shanghai*, 189–190; Pepper, *Chinese Civil War*, 396, 403–404.

382   **Some Chinese soldiers** LTC Patrick A. Reiter, "Initial Communist Chinese Logistics in the Korean War," quartermaster.army.mil/oqmg/professional_bulletin/2004/Autumn04/Initial_Communist_Chinese_Logistics_in_the_Korean_War.htm, accessed Apr. 3, 2016.

   Chairman Mao had Mao Zedong, "Analysis of the Classes in Chinese Society," in *Selected Works*, 1:13.

   "Campaign to Suppress" Spence, *The Search for Modern China*, 535–536.

   "Conference of Christian" Mimeographed report, "Conference of Christian Institutions," Apr. 1951, pp. 79–81, Archives of the Episcopal Church, Austin, TX.

   a bishop, Francis Article, *Ta Kung Pao*, Apr. 24, 1951, translated, RG 275-1-3, Archives of the Episcopal Church, Austin, TX.

383   **"black imperialist university"** Lamberton and Shen, *St. John's University*, 260.

   "Three-Self Patriotic" Mimeographed report, "Conference of Christian Institutions," Apr. 1951, pp. 79–81, Archives of the Episcopal Church, Austin, TX.

384   **against Rightist thinking** A. Doak Barnett, letter on "Five Anti Campaign I: Nationwide Campaign," reports to the ICWA, ADB-1952-2, July 29, 1952, 1–7.

   finally shut down Spence, *The Search for Modern China*, 534.

   Sisters of Loretto Patricia Jean Manion, SL, *Venture Into the Unknown*, 327–328.

   McTyeire School for McTyeire Alumni Association, *Telling Women's Lives: In Search of McTyeire, 1892–1992,* 1992; Shanghai No. 3 Girls' High School, "The 120 Anniversary Celebration," program booklet, 2012, 4.

   St. John's University Lamberton and Shen, *St. John's University*, 261–263.

385   **Three Anti campaign** Barnett, letter on "Five Anti Campaign II: The Campaign in Shanghai," reports to the ICWA, ADB-1952-3, July 31, 1952, 1–7.

CHAPTER 28: DOREEN

388   **Moller Shipping Line** Sargeant, *Shanghai*, 107–108.

389   **Isabel Chao** Interview with the author, Sep. 15, 2007.

392   **Diane Tang Woo** Interview with the author, Aug. 21, 2007.

   George Shen Interview with the author, Oct. 1, 2010.

   Ronald Sun Interview with the author, Mar. 3, 2007.

   Valentin Chu Interview with the author, Apr. 12, 2007.

   Ben Char Interview with the author, May 6, 2010.

394   **textile mills and** Wong, *Emigrant Entrepreneurs*, 43–53.

395   **Hong Kong's gold** Leo F. Goodstadt, *Uneasy Partners*, 197–204; Caroline Courtauld and May Holdsworth, *The Hong Kong Story*, 63–69.

396   **shantytowns of Diamond** Feng Chi-shun, *Diamond Hill*.

   Matilda Young Interviews with the author, June 27, 2007, Aug. 26, 2010.

   Sydney Chang Interviews with the author, Feb. 9, 2008, Feb. 10, 2008.

   thousands of Nationalist Dominic Meng-Hsuang Yang, "Humanitarian Assistance and Propaganda War: Repatriation and Relief of the Nationalist Refugees in Hong Kong's Rennie's Mill Camp, 1950–1955," *Journal of Chinese Overseas* 10, no. 2. (Nov. 2014): 165–196.

397   **Shek Kip Mei** Chi-shun Feng, *Diamond Hill*, 73; Albert H. Yee, *Wither Hong Kong?*, 140–143; Courtauld and Holdsworth, *The Hong Kong Story*, 71; "The Hong Kong Story," Permanent Collection, Hong Kong Museum of History.

CHAPTER 29: ANNABEL ANNUO

399   **"good citizen" test** Peter Kwong and Dusanka Miscevic, *Chinese America*, 242–244; Ying-Ying Chang, interview with the author, Oct. 18, 2010.

CHAPTER 30: BENNY

408   **Hundred Flowers Campaign** Spence, *The Search for Modern China*, 563–573. **people north of** Emily Honig, *Creating Chinese Ethnicity*, 1–5.

409   **"struggle sessions,"** Benny Barnett, letter on "Five Anti Campaign I: Nationwide Campaign," reports to the ICWA, ADB-1952-2, July 29, 1952, 1–7; Nien Cheng, *Life and Death in Shanghai*, 96–122.

410   **Great Proletarian Cultural** Fairbanks, *The Great Chinese Revolution*, 316–333; Spence, *The Search for Modern China*, 613.

411   **Red Guards broke** Nien Cheng, *Life and Death in Shanghai;* Fairbanks, *The Great Chinese Revolution*, 335–341.

EPILOGUE

415   **nearly one in** Alexander, *Korea*, 483.
       Hong Kong, dependent Wong, *Emigrant Entrepreneurs*, 2–4; Patrick Yeung, "Trade Ties between Hong Kong and Mainland China," *Asian Survey* 10, no. 9 (Sep. 1970): 821–824.
       McCarthy's reign of Schrecker, *Many Are the Crimes*, xviii–xx.

416   **The resulting void** Ibid., 368.
       Department of Defense "Projects in Contemporary Cultures, China," G21-G31, "Chinese Political Character, 1950–52," G62-G63, "Human Ecology-China, 1954–1961," G94-G114, Margaret Mead Papers, Manuscript Division, Library of Congress.

417   **the "model minority"** Hsu, *The Good Immigrants*, 236–242, 248–249; Brooks, *Between Mao and McCarthy*, 197, 217; Cheng, *Citizens of Asian America*, 64–67, 88.

418   **Mi Ling Tsui** Interview with the author, Sep. 6, 2007; Charles N. Li, *The Bitter Sea*, 156–164.

419   **Richard King** Interview with the author, Mar. 31, 2017.

427   **Florence Lin** Interview with the author, Oct. 2, 2013.
       Cecilia Chiang Interview with the author, Mar. 30, 2016.

SELECTED
BIBLIOGRAPHY

ARCHIVES AND MANUSCRIPT COLLECTIONS

Chinese University of Hong Kong, University Services Centre
Episcopal Church Archives
Hong Kong University Special Collections
Hoover Archives, Stanford University
Library of Congress
National Archives and Records Administration, Washington, D.C. (NARA); San Bruno, CA; New York, NY
Old China Hand Archives, California State University, Northridge
Princeton University East Asian Library
San Francisco National Maritime Museum Library
Shanghai Library Biblioteca Zi-Ka-Wei (Xujiahui)
Shanghai Main Library
Shanghai Municipal Archives
St. John's University, Taipei
University of British Columbia, St. John's College, Vancouver, BC
University of California, Berkeley, Berkeley Art Museum, Pacific Film Archives
University of California, Berkeley, C. V. Starr East Asian Library
University of California, Berkeley, Regional Oral History Archives

DISSERTATIONS AND THESES

Lan, On-wai, Kenneth. "Rennie's Mill: The Origin and Evolution of a Special Enclave in Hong Kong." PhD diss., University of Hong Kong, 2006.
Li, Robin Anne. "'Being Good Chinese': Chinese Scholarly Elites and Immigration in Mid-Century America." PhD diss., University of Michigan, 2006.
Lin, Han-sheng. "Wang Ching-wei and the Japanese Peace Efforts." PhD diss., University of Pensylvania, 1967.
Xu, Edward Yihua. "Religion and Education: St. John's University as an Evangelizing Agency." PhD diss., Princeton University, 1994.

FILMS AND VIDEOS

The Battle of China. Directed by Frank Capra. 1944; Office of War Information. Accessed April 28, 2009. youtube.com/watch?v=m4Ebv-FzP6o.

China: A Century of Revolution. Directed and produced by Susan Williams. Part 1, "China in Revolution, 1911–1949," 1989. Part 2, "The Mao Years, 1949–1976," 1994. Part 3, "Born Under the Red Flag, 1976–1997," 1997. Winstar, 2001. VHS.

The China Chronicles: Exodus and Resistance. Directed by Yuan Min. Richard Lin Yang, executive producer. 2006; Canada Live News Agency Inc., 2007. DVD.

The Crossing II. Directed by John Woo. 2015; Beijing Galloping Horse Group, 2015. DVD.

Empire of the Sun. Directed by Steven Spielberg. 1987; Warner Bros. Pictures, 2006. DVD.

Finding Kukan. Directed by Robin Lung. 2017; Nested Egg Productions, 2018. DVD.

Legendary Sin Cities: Shanghai. Directed by Marrin Canell and Ted Remerowski. 2006; Demi-Monde Productions, 2012. DVD.

Lust, Caution. Directed by Ang Lee. 2007; River Road Entertainment, 2007. DVD.

Shanghai Exodus: Incredible Stories from the Caucasians Who Grew Up in China. 2010; China Light Media Foundation, 2011. DVD.

Shanghai Ghetto. Directed by Dana Janklowicz-Mann and Amir Mann. 2002; New Video Group, 2004. DVD.

The White Countess. Directed by James Ivory. 2005; Merchant Ivory Productions, 2006. DVD.

Zuflucht in Shanghai: The Port of Last Resort. Directed by Joan Grossman and Paul Rosdy. 1998; Pinball Films, 2012. DVD.

GOVERNMENT DOCUMENTS

Bound Copies of U.S. Consular (HK) Compiled Internal Reports, 1952–1957. Suzanne Pepper Private Collection. University Service Centre for China Studies, Chinese University of Hong Kong.

British Colonial Yearbooks, 1950–1977.

Hambro, Edvard. *The Problem of Chinese Refugees in Hong Kong: Report submitted to the United Nations Commissioner for Refugees*. Leyden, Holland: A. W. Sujthoff, 1955.

Jacoby, Neil H. "An Evaluation of U.S. Economic Aid to Free China, 1951–1965." January 1966. Bureau for the Far East, Agency for International Development, Department of State. Accessed March 16, 2015. pdf.usaid.gov/pdf _docs/PNAAK054.pdf.

"Shanghai-Counter-Espionage Summary," August 12, 1945. Headquarters Office of Strategic Services, China Theater. Author's collection. pp. 1–27.

INTERVIEWS

The full list of interviewees can be found in the acknowledgments. All interviews cited were conducted by the author unless otherwise noted. For Ho Chow, Theresa Junlin Chow, Annabel Annuo Liu, Benny Pan, and Bing Woo, dozens of interviews and conversations took place with each over a period of twelve years.

JOURNAL ARTICLES AND SERIAL REPORTS

Ahlers, John. "Shanghai at the War's End." *Far Eastern Survey* 14, no. 23 (Nov. 1945): 329–333.

Barnett, A. Doak. "The Economy of Formosa: Progress on a Treadmill." *American Universities Field Staff Reports* (New York, Oct. 15, 1954).

————. Reports to Institute of Current World Affairs. Multiple. icwa.org.

Barnett, Robert W. "Shanghai Rice Anomaly," *Far Eastern Survey* 10, no. 13 (July 1941): 146–148.

————. "Starvation, Boom and Blockade in Shanghai." *Far Eastern Survey* 9, no. 9 (Apr. 24, 1940): 97–102.

Borg, Dorothy. "America Loses Chinese Good Will." *Far Eastern Survey* 18, no. 4 (Feb. 23, 1949): 37–45.

Campbell, Colin D., and Gordon C. Tullock. "Hyperinflation in China, 1937–49." *Journal of Political Economy* 62, no. 3 (June 1954): 236–245.

Chen, Ta. "Migration." In "Supplement: Population in Modern China." *American Journal of Sociology* 52 (1947): 57–71.

Cheng, Peter P. C. "The Formosa Triangle: A Formosan's View." *Asian Survey* 7, no. 11 (Nov. 1967): 791–800.

Converse, Elizabeth. "Formosa: Private Citadel?" *Far Eastern Survey* 18, no. 21 (Oct. 19, 1949): 249–250.

Cope, Elizabeth W. "Displaced Europeans in Shanghai." *Far Eastern Survey* 17, no. 23 (Dec. 1948): 274–276.

Gould, Randall. "Shanghai during the Takeover." *Annals of the American Academy of Political and Social Science* 277 (Sep. 1951): 182–192.

Gruenberger, Felix. "The Jewish Refugees in Shanghai." *Jewish Social Studies* 12, no. 4 (Oct. 1950): 329–348.

Han, Yu-Shan. "Formosa under Three Rules." *Pacific Historical Review* 19, no. 4 (Nov. 1950): 397–407.

Henriot, Christian. "Shanghai and the Experience of War: The Fate of Refugees." *European Journal of East Asian Studies* 5 (2006): 215–245.

H.L. "The End of Extraterritoriality in China." *Bulletin of International News* 20, no. 2 (Jan. 23, 1943): 49–56.

Hsu, Madeline Y. "The Disappearance of America's Cold War Chinese Refugees, 1948–1966." *Journal of American Ethnic History* 31, no. 4 (Summer 2012): 12–33.

Huang, Andrew C. "The Inflation in China." *Quarterly Journal of Economics* 62, no. 4 (Aug. 1948): 562–575.

Kerr, George. "Formosa's Return to China." *Far Eastern Survey* 16, no. 18 (Oct. 1947): 205–208.

Ku, Agnes S. "Immigration Policies, Disclosures, and the Politics of Local Belonging in Hong Kong (1950–1980)." *Modern China* 30, no. 3 (July 2004): 326–360.

Lee, R. Alton. "The Army 'Mutiny' of 1946." *Journal of American History* 53, no. 3 (Dec. 1, 1966): 555–571.

Lee, Rose Hum. "A Century of Chinese and American Relations." *Phylon* 11, no. 3 (1950): 240–245.

————. "The Chinese Abroad." *Phylon* 17, no. 3 (3rd Qtr. 1956): 257–270.

————. "Chinese Dilemma." *Phylon* 10, no. 2 (1949): 137–140.

————. "The Stranded Chinese in the United States." *Phylon Quarterly* 19, no. 2 (1958): 180–194.

Ling, Huping. "A History of Chinese Female Students in the United States, 1880s–1990s." *Journal of American Ethnic History* 16, no. 3 (Spring 1997): 81–109.

Mark, Chi-Kwan. "The 'Problem of People': British Colonials, Cold War Powers, and the Chinese Refugees in Hong Kong, 1949–62." *Modern Asian Studies* 41, no. 6 (Nov. 2007): 1145–1181.

Mitter, Rana. "Classifying Citizen in Nationalist China during World War II, 1937–1941." *Modern Asian Studies* 45, no. 2 (2011): 243–275.

Murphy, Rhoads. "The Food Supply of Shanghai." *Far Eastern Survey* 17, no. 11 (June 1948): 133–135.

Pelcovits, N. A. "European Refugees in Shanghai." *Far Eastern Survey* 15, no. 21 (Oct. 1946): 321–325.

Selwyn-Clarke, Hilda. "Hong Kong Dilemma." *Far Eastern Survey* 16, no. 1 (Jan. 1947): 5–8.

Smith, Richard Ferree. "Refugees." *Annals of the American Academy of Political and Social Science* 367 (Sep. 1966): 44–46.

Tamagna, Frank M. "Financial Problems in China's War and Postwar Economy." *Pacific Affairs* 15, no. 3 (Sep. 1942): 325–344.

Wang, Chia-feng. "Adventures of the Treasures." *Kuang-hua-tsa-chih* [*Sinorama Monthly*], Aug. 1985.

Wang, Hong-zen. "Class Structures and Social Mobility in Taiwan in the Initial Postwar Period." *China Journal* 48 (July 2002): 55–85.

Wright, Quincy. "The End of Extraterritoriality in China." *American Journal of International Law* 37, no. 2 (Apr. 1943): 286–289.

Yang, Dominic Meng-Hsuang. "Humanitarian Assistance and Propaganda War: Repatriation and Relief of the Nationalist Refugees in Hong Kong's Rennie's Mill Camp, 1950–1955." *Journal of Chinese Overseas* 10, no. 2 (Nov. 2014): 165–196.

————. "Rennie's Mill: Origin and Transformation of 'Little Taiwan' in Hong Kong, 1950s–1970s." *Taiwan Historical Research* 18, no. 1 (Mar. 2011): 133–183.

Yang, Dominic Meng-Hsuang, and Mau-kuei Chang. "Understanding the Nuances of *Waishengren*." *Perspectives* 3 (2010): 109–122. Accessed January 27, 2012. journals.openedition.org/chinaperspectives/5310.

Yeung, Patrick. "Trade Ties between Hong Kong and Mainland China." *Asian Survey* 10, no. 9 (Sep. 1970): 820–829.

Yueh, Hu. "The Problem of the Hong Kong Refugees." *Asian Survey* 2, no. 1 (Mar. 1962): 28–37.

NEWSPAPERS, PERIODICALS, AND SERIALS

Argus (Melbourne, Aus.)
China Press
Hong Kong Standard (*HKS*)
Life magazine
Lun Yu
The New York Times (*NYT*)
North China Daily News (*NCDN*)
Shanghai Evening Post and Mercury (*SEP*)
Shanghai Herald
Shanghai Times
Shen Bao
South China Morning Post (*SCMP*)
St. John's Dial and *Echo*
That's Shanghai magazine
Time magazine
Chiao Tung (Jiao Tong) University Yearbooks
McTyeire School Yearbooks, No. 3 Shanghai Girls' School Library stacks, including McTyeire Alumnae Association, *Telling Women's Lives: In Search of McTyeire, 1892–1992*, 1992, and Shanghai No. 3 Girls' High School, "The 120 Anniversary Celebration," program booklet, 2012, 4.
St. John's University Yearbooks
St. John's University Alumni Association (SJUAA) chapter newsletters

ORAL HISTORIES AND MEMOIRS

Callahan, Lee Hsu. *Setting an Example: Memoirs of Hsu Chang Ling Nyi*. Orinda, CA: Self-published, 2004.
Chao, Isabel Sun, and Claire Chao. *Remembering Shanghai: A Memoir of Socialites, Scholars and Scoundrels*. Honolulu: Plum Brook, 2017.
Kador, John, and the Wang Family. *The Road We Have Traveled: As Remembered by Mary and Kenneth Wang*. Lyme, CT: Greenwich Publishing Group, 1997.
———. *Yoh-Han Pao: Navigating the Noble Road*. Lyme, CT: Greenwich Publishing Group, 2006.
Liu, Annabel Annuo. *My Years as Chang Tseng*. Self-published, 2012.
———. *Under the Towering Tree: A Daughter's Memoir*. Self-published, 2014.
———. *When Chopsticks Meet Apple Pie: Cross-Cultural Musings on Life, Family, and Food*. Self-published, CreateSpace, 2016.
Sung, Lily Soo-Hoo. Unpublished biography of Zu Liang (William) Sung, last modified April 2004.
Tang, Jack Chi-chien. Oral history conducted by Carolyn Wakeman, 1999. "The Textile Industry and the Development of Hong Kong, 1949–1999." Transcript. UC Berkeley Regional Oral History Archives, 2003.
Wang, Duncan K., et al. *The Chow Family*. Self-published, 2006.

PRIVATE COLLECTIONS

Benny Pan papers and photos
Diane Tong Woo papers and photos
Ho Chow personal archive
Kenneth C. Liang St. John's University personal archive
Margaret Soong papers and photos
Maria Lee Koh papers and photos
Philip Choy Collection
Valentin Chu papers and photos
William Yukon Chang interviews with Stella Dong, transcripts
Zia family papers and photos

BOOKS

Alexander, Bevin. *Korea: The First War We Lost.* New York: Hippocrene, 1986.

All About Shanghai: The 1934–35 Standard Guide Book. Reprint, Hong Kong: Earnshaw Books, 2008.

Allan, Ted, and Sydney Gordon. *The Scalpel, the Sword.* Toronto: McClelland & Stewart, 1971.

Bacon, Ursula. *Shanghai Diary: A Young Girl's Journey from Hitler's Hate to War-Torn China.* Santa Cruz, CA: M Press, 2004.

Baker, Barbara, ed. *Shanghai: Electric and Lurid City.* New York: Oxford University Press, 1998.

Ballard, J. G. *Empire of the Sun.* New York: Simon & Schuster, 2005.

———. *Miracles of Life.* New York: Liveright, 2013.

Barber, Noel. *The Fall of Shanghai.* New York: Putnam Pub Group, 1979.

Barlow, Tani E., and Donald M. Lowe. *Teaching China's Lost Generation: Foreign Experts in the People's Republic of China.* San Francisco: China Books & Periodicals, 1987.

Beers, Burton F. *China in Old Photographs 1860–1910.* New York: Scribner, 1981.

Belden, Jack. *China Shakes the World.* New York: Monthly Review Press, 1970.

Benton, Gregor. *The Hongkong Crisis.* London: Pluto Press, 1983.

Bergère, Marie. *The Golden Age of the Chinese Bourgeoisie, 1911–1937.* Cambridge: Cambridge University Press, 2009.

———. *Shanghai: China's Gateway to Modernity.* Translated by Janet Lloyed. Stanford, CA: Stanford University Press, 2009.

Bickers, Robert. *Empire Made Me: An Englishman Adrift in Shanghai.* New York: Columbia University Press, 2004.

Birns, Jack, Carolyn Wakeman, et al. *Assignment Shanghai: Photographs on the Eve of Revolution.* Berkeley, CA: University of California Press, 2003.

Bix, Herbert P. *Hirohito and the Making of Modern Japan.* New York: Harper-Collins, 2000.

Boggs, Grace Lee. *Living for Change.* Minneapolis: University of Minnesota Press, 1998.

Bramsen, Christopher Bo. *Peace and Friendship: Denmark's Official Relations with China 1674–2000.* Copenhagen: Nordic Institute of Asian Studies, 2000.

Brook, Timothy. *Collaboration*. Cambridge, MA: Harvard University Press, 2007.

Brooks, Charlotte. *Alien Neighbors, Foreign Friends: Asian Americans, Housing, and the Transformation of Urban California*. Chicago: University of Chicago Press, 2009.

—————. *Between Mao and McCarthy: Chinese American Politics in the Cold War Years*. Chicago: University of Chicago Press, 2015.

Buck, Pearl S. *Pavilion of Women*. New York: John Day, 1946.

Campbell, John, ed. *The Experience of World War II*. New York: Oxford University Press, 1989.

Carroll, John M. *Edge of Empires: Chinese Elites and British Colonials in Hong Kong*. Hong Kong: Hong Kong University Press, 2005.

Chamberlain, Jonathan. *King Hui: The Man Who Owned All the Opium in Hong Kong*. Hong Kong: Blacksmith Books, 2010.

Chang, Eileen. *Love in a Fallen City*. Translated by Karen S. Kingbury. New York: New York Review of Books, 2007.

—————. *Lust, Caution: The Story*. Translated by Julia Lovell. New York: Anchor Books, 2007.

—————. *Written on Water*. Translated by Andrew F. Jones. New York: Columbia University Press, 2005.

Chang, Gordon H. *Fateful Ties: A History of America's Preoccupation with China*. Cambridge, MA: Harvard University Press, 2015.

Chang, Iris. *Thread of the Silkworm*. New York: Basic Books, 1995.

Chang, Jung. *Wild Swans: Three Daughters of China*. New York: Simon and Schuster, 1991.

Chang, Jung, and Jon Halliday. *Mao: The Unknown Story*. New York: Anchor, 2006.

Chang, Kang-i Sun, and Haun Saussy, eds. *Women Writers of Traditional China: An Anthology of Poetry and Criticism*. Palo Alto, CA: Stanford University Press, 2000.

Chang, Leslie. *Beyond the Narrow Gate*. New York: Dutton, 1999.

Chao, Eveline. *Niubi! The Real Chinese You Were Never Taught in School*. New York: Plume, 2009.

Chao, James S. C. *Sixth Reunion Record of the Chiao-Tung University Alumni Association in America (CTUAAA)*. New York: CTUAAA, 1990.

Chen, Kaiyi. *Seeds from the West*. Chicago: Imprint Publications, 2001.

Chen, Yuan-tsung. *Return to the Middle Kingdom*. New York: Union Square Press, 2008.

Cheng, Cindy I-Fen. *Citizens of Asian America: Democracy and Race during the Cold War*. New York: NYU Press, 2013.

Cheng, Naishan. *The Banker*. Translated by Britten Dean. San Francisco: China Books and Periodicals, 1993.

Cheng, Nien. *Life and Death in Shanghai*. New York: Grove Press, 1986.

Chi, Pang-yuan, and David Der-Wei Wang, eds. *The Last of the Whampoa Breed*. New York: Columbia University Press, 2003.

Chin, Tsai. *Daughter of Shanghai*. New York: St. Martin's Press, 1989.

Chinese Satire and Humour: Selected Cartoons of Hua Junwu (1955–1982). Beijing: New World Press, 1989.

Ching, Leo T. S. *Becoming Japanese: Colonial Taiwan and the Politics of Identity Formation*. Berkeley, CA: University of California Press, 2001.

Chow, Gregory. *China's Economic Transformation*. Hoboken, NJ: Wiley-Blackwell, 2007.

Chu, Samuel C., ed. *Madame Chiang Kaishek and Her China*. Norwalk, CT: East Bridge, 2005.

Chu, Valentin. *Ta Ta, Tan Tan: The Inside Story of Communist China*. New York: W. W. Norton, 1963.

Clifford, Nicholas R. *Spoilt Children of Empire: Westerners in Shanghai and the Chinese Revolution of the 1920s*. Hanover, NH: Middlebury College Press, 1991.

Coates, Austin. *China Races*. Quarry Bay, China: Oxford University Press (China), 1984.

Coble, Parks. *The Shanghai Capitalists*. Cambridge, MA: Harvard University Asia Center, 1986.

Collins, Larry, and Dominique LaPierre. *Is Paris Burning?* New York: Simon & Schuster, 1965.

Courtauld, Caroline, and May Holdsworth. *The Hong Kong Story*. Hong Kong: Oxford University Press, 1997.

Crouch, Gregory. *China's Wings: War, Intrigue, Romance, and Adventure in the Middle Kingdom During the Golden Age of Flight*. New York: Bantam, 2012.

Dardess, John W. *Confucianism and Autocracy: Professional Elites in the Founding of the Ming Dynasty*. Berkeley, CA: University of California Press, 1983.

Darman, Peter. *World War II Stats and Facts*. New York: Fall River Press, 2009.

Deng, Ming, ed. *Survey of Shanghai 1840s–1940s*. Shanghai: Shanghai People's Fine Arts Publishing House, 1992.

Dikotter, Frank. *The Tragedy of Liberation: A History of the Chinese Revolution 1945–1957*. New York: Bloomsbury Press, 2013.

Dong, Stella. *Shanghai: The Rise and Fall of a Decadent City*. New York: Perennial, 2001.

Dower, John W. *War without Mercy: Race and Power in the Pacific War*. New York: Pantheon, 1987.

Eastman, Lloyd E., Jerome Ch'en, Suzanne Pepper, and Lyman P. Van Slyke. *The Nationalist Era in China, 1927–1949*. Cambridge: Cambridge University Press, 1991.

Eisfelder, Horst "Peter." *Chinese Exile: My Years in Shanghai and Nanjing*. Caulfield South, Australia: Ayotaynu Foundation, 2004.

Elegant, Robert. *Pacific Destiny: Inside Asia Today*. New York: Avon Books, 1991.

Emigranten Adressbuch fuer Shanghai: Mit einem Anhang Branchen-Register. Shanghai: Old China Hand Press, 1995.

Esherick, Joseph W. *Ancestral Leaves: A Family Journey through Chinese History*. Berkeley, CA: University of California Press, 2011.

Esherick, Joseph W., ed. *Lost Chance in China: The World War II Dispatches of John S. Service*. New York: Vintage Books, 1975.

Estève, Christine, et al. *Lilongs—Shanghai*. Shanghai: Tongji University and Heritage Foundation, 2010.

Fairbank, John King. *The Great Chinese Revolution, 1800–1985*. New York: Harper & Row, 1986.

Fairbank, Wilma, and Jonathan Spence. *Liang and Lin: Partners in Exploring China's Architectural Past*. Philadelphia: University of Pennsylvania Press, 2008.

Fay, Peter Ward. *Opium War, 1840–1842: Barbarians in the Celestial Empire in the Early Part of the Nineteenth Century and the War by Which They Forced Her Gates Ajar*. Chapel Hill, NC: University of North Carolina Press, 1975.

Fenby, Jonathan. *Chiang Kai-shek: China's Generalissimo and the Nation He Lost*. New York: Carroll & Graf, 2003.

Feng Chi-shun. *Diamond Hill: Memories of Growing Up in a Hong Kong Squatter Village*. Hong Kong: Blacksmith Books, 2009.

Field, Andrew David. *Shanghai's Dancing World: Cabaret Culture and Urban Politics, 1911–1954*. Hong Kong: The Chinese University Press, 2011.

Finkelstein, David M. *Washington's Taiwan Dilemma, 1949–1950: From Abandonment to Salvation*. Annapolis, MD: Naval Institute Press, 2014.

Foght, Harold Waldstein, and Alice Mabel Robbins Foght. *Unfathomed Japan*. New York: Macmillan, 1928.

Franck, Harry Alverson. *Glimpses of Japan and Formosa*. New York: Appleton-Century, 1939.

Fu, Poshek. *Passivity, Resistance, and Collaboration: Intellectual Choices in Occupied Shanghai 1937–1945*. Palo Alto, CA: Stanford University Press, 1997.

Fu, Poshek, ed. *China Forever: The Shaw Brothers and Diasporic Cinema*. Champaign, IL: University of Illinois Press, 2008.

Fu, Poshek, and David Desser, eds. *The Cinema of Hong Kong: History, Arts, Identity*. Cambridge: Cambridge University Press, 2002.

Fulcher, Helen M., and Michael C. McCracken. *Mission to Shanghai: The Life of Medical Service of Dr. Josiah C. McCracken*. New London, NH: Tiffin Press, 1995.

Gao, Wenqian. *Zhou Enlai: The Last Perfect Revolutionary*. Translated by Peter Rand. New York: Public Affairs, 2007.

Gilmartin, Christina K., Gail Hershatter, Lisa Rofel, and Tyrene White. *Engendering China: Women, Culture, and the State*. Harvard Contemporary China Series. Cambridge, MA: Harvard University Press, 1994.

Ginsbourg, Sam. *My First Sixty Years in China*. Beijing: Foreign Language Press, 2003.

Goodstadt, Leo F. *Uneasy Partners: The Conflict Between Public Interest and Private Profit in Hong Kong*. Hong Kong: Hong Kong University Press, 2005.

Goutiere, Peter J. *Himalayan Rogue: A Pilot's Odyssey*. Paducah, KY: Turner Publishing, 1994.

Graybill, Henry Blair, and You-kuang Chu. *The New China*. New York: Ginn, 1930.

Green, Barbara, and Tess Johnston. *Shanghai Walks*. Shanghai: Old China Hand Press, 2007.

Hahn, Emily. *The Soong Sisters*. New York: Doubleday, Doran, 1943.

Han, Bangqing, and Eileen Chang. *The Sing-Song Girls of Shanghai*. New York: Columbia University Press, 2007.

Han Suyin. *Destination Chungking*. New York: Panther Books, 1973.

———. *The Morning Deluge: Mao Tsetung and the Chinese Revolution, 1893–1954*. New York: Little Brown, 1972.

Harmsen, Peter. *Shanghai 1937: Stalingrad on the Yangtze*. Havertown, PA: Casemate, 2013.

Henriot, Christian, and Wen-hsin Yeh. *In the Shadow of the Rising Sun*. Cambridge: Cambridge University Press, 2009.

Hershatter, Gail. *Dangerous Liaisons: Prostitution and Modernity in Twentieth-Century China*. Berkeley, CA: University of California Press, 1997.

Hing, Bill Ong. *Defining America Through Immigration Policy*. Philadelphia: Temple University Press, 2012.

Hinton, William. *Fanshen: A Documentary of Revolution in a Chinese Village*. New York: Random House, 1966.

———. *Iron Oxen: A Documentary of Revolution in Chinese Farming*. New York: Vintage Books, 1970.

Hong Kong Annual Report 1977. Hong Kong Government Press, 1978.

Honig, Emily. *Creating Chinese Ethnicity*. New Haven, CT: Yale University Press, 1992.

———. *Sisters and Strangers: Women in the Shanghai Cotton Mills, 1919–1949*. Palo Alto, CA: Stanford University Press, 1992.

Hsu, Madeline. *The Good Immigrants: How the Yellow Peril Became the Model Minority*. Princeton, NJ: Princeton University Press, 2015.

Huaihai Lu: A Centennial Celebration, Its History in Words and Pictures. Shanghai: Shanghai Municipal Archives, 2006.

Huang, Wenguang. *The Little Red Guard: A Family Memoir*. New York: Riverhead Books, 2012.

Johnston, Tess. *Permanently Temporary: From Berlin to Shanghai in Half a Century*. Hong Kong: Old China Hand Press, 2010.

Johnston, Tess, and Deke Erh. *Frenchtown Shanghai*. Shanghai: Old China Hand Press, 2000.

Kao, George, ed. *Chinese Wit & Humor*. New York: Sterling Publishing, 1974.

The Kaohsiung Tapes. Seattle, WA: International Committee for Human Rights in Taiwan, 1981.

Kaplan, David E. *Fires in the Dragon: Politics, Murder, and the Kuomintang*. New York: Atheneum, 1992.

Kerr, George H. *Formosa Betrayed*. New York: Houghton Mifflin, 1965. Online version accessed 2008.

Knight, Michael, and Dany Chan. *Shanghai: Art of the City*. San Francisco: Asian Art Museum, 2010.

Knopf Map Guide: Shanghai. New York: Knopf, 2005.

Koehn, Peter, and Xiao-Huang Yin. *The Expanding Roles of Chinese Americans in U.S.-China Relations*. New York: Routledge, 2015.

Koo, Julianna, and Genevieve Young. *109 Springtimes: My Story*. Self-published.

Krasno, Rena. *Once Upon a Time in Shanghai: A Jewish Woman's Journey through the 20th Century China*. Beijing: China Intercontinental Press, 2008.

————. *Strangers Always: A Jewish Family in Wartime Shanghai*. Berkeley, CA: Pacific View Press, 1992.

Kung, S. W. *Chinese in American Life: Some Aspects of Their History, Status, Problems, and Contributions*. Seattle: University of Washington Press, 1962.

Kwong, Peter. *Chinatown, NY: Labor and Politics*. New York: New Press, 2001.

Kwong, Peter, and Dusanka Miscevic. *Chinese America: The Untold Story of America's Oldest New Community*. New York: New Press, 2005.

Lamberton, Mary, and George C. Shen. *St. John's University—Shanghai 1879–1947: The Fourth World Reunion of Johanneans*. N.p.: St. John's University Alumni Association, 1988.

Lattimore, Owen. *The Making of Modern China: A Short History*. New York: W. W. Norton, 1944.

Lau, Theodora. *The Handbook of Chinese Horoscopes*. London: Souvenir Press, 1986.

Lee, Erika. *The Making of Asian America: A History*. New York: Simon & Schuster, 2015.

Lee, Gus. *Chasing Hepburn: A Memoir of Shanghai, Hollywood, and a Chinese Family's Fight for Freedom*. New York: Three Rivers Press, 2004.

Lee, Leo Ou-Fan. *Shanghai Modern*. Cambridge, MA: Harvard University Press, 1999.

Lee, Lillian. *The Last Princess of Manchuria*. New York: William Morrow, 1992.

Legge, James, ed. *Confucian Analects, Great Learning, and Doctrine of the Mean*. Beijing: The Commercial Press, 1971.

Lew, Ling. *The Chinese in North America: A Guide to Their Life and Progress*. Los Angeles: East-West Culture Publishing Association, 1949.

Li, Charles N. *The Bitter Sea: Coming of Age in a China Before Mao*. New York: Harper Perennial, 2009.

Li, Laura Tyson. *Madame Chiang Kai-Shek: China's Eternal First Lady*. New York: Grove Press, 2007.

Li, Lillian M. *China's Silk Trade: Traditional Industry in the Modern World, 1842–1937*. Harvard East Asian Mongraphs (Book 97). Cambridge, MA: Harvard University Asia Center, 1981.

Li, Weiguo, ed. *Shanghai Famous Streets*. Shanghai: Shanghai People's Publishing House, 2006.

Li Zhisui. *The Private Life of Chairman Mao*. New York: Random House, 1996.

Lin, Florence. *Florence Lin's Chinese Regional Cookbook*. New York: Dutton, 1975.

Lin, Julia C., ed. and trans. *Twentieth-Century Chinese Women's Poetry: An Anthology*. New York: Routledge, 2009.

Lin, Jung-Tai, and Johnny Lin. *Who Was Bao-Xiang?* Translated by Joann Lin Oshima. Self-published, 2003.

Lip, Evelyn. *Chinese Beliefs and Superstitions*. Singapore: Graham Brash, 1988.

Liu, Shaw-Tong. *Out of Red China*. New York: Duell, Sloan and Pearce, 1953.

Loh, Ying Hwa. *The Face of China*. Hong Kong: Sum Shing Printing, 1959.

Lord, Bette Bao. *Legacies: A Chinese Mosaic*. New York: Knopf, 1990.

————. *Spring Moon*. New York: Harper & Row, 1981.

Louie, David Wong. *The Barbarians Are Coming*. New York: Putnam, 2000.

Lu, Han Chao. *Beyond the Neon Lights: Everyday Shanghai in the Early Twentieth Century*. Berkeley, CA: University of California Press, 2004.

Lu, Yuanmin. *Suzhou Creek*. Shanghai: Shanghai Culture Publishing House, 2000.

Ludeke, Alexander. *Weapons of World War II*. Bath, UK: Parragon, 2012.

Lyman, Arthur S. *The China White Paper, August 1949*. Palo Alto, CA: Stanford University Press, 1967.

Macciocchi, Maria Antonietta. *Daily Life in Revolutionary China*. New York: Monthly Review Press, 1972.

Mackinnon, Stephen R., and Oris Friesen. *China Reporting: An Oral History of American Journalism in the 1930s and 1940s*. Berkeley, CA: University of California Press, 1987.

Madany, Yvette Ho. *Shanghai Story Walks*. Hong Kong: Earnshaw Books, 2009.

Madokoro, Laura. *Elusive Refuge: Chinese Migrants in the Cold War*. Cambridge, MA: Harvard University Press, 2016.

Mah, Adeline Yen. *Chinese Cinderella: The True Story of an Unwanted Daughter*. New York: Dell, 1999.

————. *Falling Leaves: The True Story of an Unwanted Chinese Daughter*. New York: John Wiley & Sons, 1998.

Manion, Patricia Jean, SL. *Venture Into the Unknown: Loretto in China 1923–1998*. St. Louis: Independent, 2006.

Mao Zedong. *Selected Readings from the Political Works of Chairman Mao*. Beijing: Foreign Languages Press, 1967.

Martin, Brian. *The Shanghai Green Gang: Politics and Organized Crime, 1919–1937*. Berkeley, CA: University of California Press, 1996.

Mau, Edward Seu Chen. *The Mau Lineage*. Honolulu: Hawaii Chinese History Center, 1989.

McDonald, William C., III, and Barbara L. Evenson. *The Shadow Tiger: Billy McDonald, Wingman to Chennault*. Birmingham, AL: Shadow Tiger Press, 2016.

Meng, Chih. *Chinese American Understanding*. New York: China Institute in America, 1981.

Meskill, Johanna, and Margarete Menzel. *A Chinese Pioneer Family: The Lins of Wu-feng Taiwan, 1929–1995*. Princeton, NJ: Princeton University Press, 1979.

Meyer, Mahlon. *Remembering China from Taiwan: Divided Families and Bittersweet Reunions after the Chinese Civil War*. Hong Kong: Hong Kong University Press, 2012.

Mitter, Rana. *Forgotten Ally: China's World War II, 1937–1945*. New York: Mariner Books, 2013.

Mones, Nicole. *Night in Shanghai*. New York: Houghton Mifflin Harcourt, 2014.

Mu, Fu-Sheng. *The Wilting of the Hundred Flowers*. New York: Praeger, 1962.

Namioka, Lesley. *China: A Traveler's Companion*. New York: Vanguard Press, 1985.

Ngai, Mae M. *The Lucky Ones: One Family and the Extraordinary Invention of Chinese America*. New York: Houghton Mifflin Harcourt, 2010.

Oakes, Vanya. *White Man's Folly*. New York: Houghton Mifflin, 1943.

Pa Chin. *Family*. Translated by Sidney Shapiro. Prospect Heights, IL: Waveland Press, 1972.

Pai, Hsien-yung. *Crystal Boys*. San Francisco: Gay Sunshine Press, 1989.

———. *Taipei People*. Translated by George Kao. Hong Kong: Chinese University Press, 2000.

Pakula, Hannah. *The Last Empress: Madame Chiang Kai-shek and the Birth of Modern China*. New York: Simon & Schuster, 2010.

Pan Ling. *In Search of Old Shanghai*. Hong Kong: Joint Publishing, 1986.

———. *Old Shanghai: Gangsters in Paradise*. Singapore: Heinemann Asia, 1985.

Pan, Lynn. *Shanghai: A Century of Change in Photographs*. Hong Kong: Hai Feng, 1991.

———. *Sons of the Yellow Emperor*. New York: Kodansha USA, 1994.

———. *Tracing It Home: Journeys around a Chinese Family*. London: Secker & Warburg, 1992.

Pan, Philip P. *Out of Mao's Shadow*. New York: Simon & Schuster, 2008.

Pan, Stephen Chao-ying. *China Fights On: An Inside Story of China's Long Struggle against Our Common Enemies*. New York: Fleming H. Revell, 1945.

Peng, Ming-min, and George Kerr. *A Taste of Freedom*. Upland, CA: Taiwan Publishing, 1994.

Pepper, Suzanne. *Civil War in China: 1945–1949*. Berkeley, CA: University of California Press, 1980.

Perry, Elizabeth. *Shanghai on Strike: The Politics of Chinese Labor*. Palo Alto, CA: Stanford University Press, 1995.

Perry, Elizabeth, and Li Xun. *Proletarian Power: Shanghai in the Cultural Revolution*. Boulder, CO: Westview Press, 1997.

Powell, John B. *My Twenty-Five Years in China*. New York: Macmillan, 1945.

Prange, Gordon W. *At Dawn We Slept: The Untold Story of Pearl Harbor*. New York: Penguin Books, 1982.

Prange, Gordon W., and Donald M. Goldstein. *Pearl Harbor: The Verdict of History*. New York: Penguin Books, 1991.

Pringle, Henry F. *Bridge House Survivor: Experiences of a Civilian Prisoner of War in Shanghai and Beijing 1942–1945*. Hong Kong: Earnshaw Books, 2010.

Pye, Lucian W. *Warlord Politics*. New York: Praeger, 1971.

Rabushka, Alvin. *The New China: Comparative Economic Development in Mainland China, Taiwan, and Hong Kong*. San Francisco: Pacific Research Institute for Public Policy, 1989.

Rankin, Mary Backus. *Early Chinese Revolutionaries: Radical Intellectuals in Shanghai and Chekiang, 1902–1911*. Cambridge, MA: Harvard University Press, 1971.

Ristaino, Marie. *Port of Last Resort: The Diaspora Communities of Shanghai*. Palo Alto, CA: Stanford University Press, 2003.

Roberts, Priscilla, and John M. Carroll, eds. *Hong Kong in the Cold War*. Hong Kong: Hong Kong University Press, 2016.

Ross, James R. *Escape to Shanghai: A Jewish Community in China*. New York: Free Press, 1993.

Rowan, Roy. *Chasing the Dragon: A Veteran Journalist's Firsthand Account of the 1949 Chinese Revolution*. Guilford, CT: Lyons Press, 2004.

Rutter, Owen. *Through Formosa: An Account of Japan's Island Colony*. London: TF Unwin, 1923. Digitized 2007.

Ryan, Shawna Yang. *Green Island*. New York: Knopf, 2016.

Schell, Orville, and Joseph Esherick. *Modern China: The Story of a Revolution*. New York: Knopf, 1972.

Schram, Stuart. *Chairman Mao Talks to the People: Talks and Letters: 1955–1971*. New York: Pantheon, 1974.

———. *The Political Thought of Mao Tse-tung*. New York: Praeger, 1971.

Schrecker, Ellen. *Many Are the Crimes: McCarthyism in America*. Princeton, NJ: Princeton University Press, 1998.

Schuman, Julian. *Assignment China*. Beijing: Foreign Languages Press, 2004.

Schurmann, Franz. *Ideology and Organization in Communist China*. Berkeley, CA: University of California Press, 1966.

Seagrave, Sterling. *The Soong Dynasty*. New York: Harper Perennial, 1986.

See, Lisa. *Dreams of Joy*. New York: Random House, 2011.

———. *Gold Mountain*. New York: St. Martin's Press, 1995.

———. *Shanghai Girls*. New York: Random House, 2010.

Sergeant, Harriet. *Shanghai: Collision Point of Cultures 1918/1939*. New York: Crown, 1990.

Shackleton, Allan J. *Formosa Calling: An Eyewitness Account of the February 28, 1947 Incident*. Upland, CA: Taiwan Publishing, 1998.

Shapiro, Sidney. *Jews in Old China: Studies by Chinese Scholars*. New York: Hippocrene Books, 1984.

Shaw, Antony. *World War II: Day by Day*. London: Chartwell Books, 2010.

Shimer, Dorothy Blair, ed. *Rice Bowl Women: Writings by and about the Women of China and Japan*. New York: New American Library, 1982.

Smedley, Agnes. *Portraits of Chinese Women in Revolution*. New York: The Feminist Press, 1976.

Smith, Lloyd A. *Hong Kong*. Hong Kong: Longmans, Green, 1962.

Snow, Helen Foster. *My China Years*. New York: William Morrow, 1984.

Snow, Lois Wheeler. *Edgar Snow's China*. New York: Random House, 1981.

Snow, Philip. *The Fall of Hong Kong: Britain, China and the Japanese Occupation*. New Haven, CT: Yale University Press, 2003.

Soong, Irma Tam. *Chinese-American Refugee: A World War II Memoir*. Honolulu: Hawaii Chinese History Center, 1984.

Spence, Jonathan D. *The Chan's Great Continent: China in Western Minds*. New York: W. W. Norton, 1999.

———. *China Helpers: Western Advisers in China, 1620–1960*. London: Bodley Head, 1969.

————. *Emperor of China*. New York: Vintage, 1988.

————. *The Memory Palace of Matteo Ricci*. New York: Penguin Books, 1985.

————. *The Search for Modern China*. New York: W. W. Norton, 1991.

Stacey, Judith. *Patriarchy and Socialist Revolution in China*. Berkeley, CA: University of California Press, 1984.

Steiner, Fusang. *The Chinese Who Built America*. New York: Harper & Row, 1979.

Stokesbury, James L. *A Short History of the Korean War*. New York: William Morrow, 1988.

Tan, Amy. *The Bonesetter's Daughter*. New York: Ballantine Books, 2002.

————. *The Kitchen God's Wife*. New York: G. P. Putnam's Sons, 1991.

————. *The Valley of Amazement*. New York: HarperCollins, 2013.

Tata, Sam. *Shanghai 1949: The End of an Era*. London: B. T. Batsford, 1989.

Taylor, John Russell. *Strangers in Paradise: The Hollywood Emigres, 1933–1950*. New York: Holt, Rinehart and Winston, 1983.

Truman, Harry S. *Years of Trial and Hope, 1946–1953*. Vol. 2 of *Memoirs*. London: Hodder & Stoughton, 1956.

Tsao, Christina Ching. *Shanghai Bride: Her Tumultuous Life's Journey to the West*. Hong Kong: Hong Kong University Press, 2005.

Tuchman, Barbara W. *Sand Against the Wind: Stilwell and the American Experience in China 1911–45*. New York: Macmillan, 1971.

Van Luyn, Floris. *Floating City of Peasants: The Great Migration in Contemporary China*. New York: New Press, 2008.

Wakeman, Frederic. *Policing Shanghai: 1927–37*. Berkeley, CA: University of California Press, 1995.

————. *The Shanghai Badlands: Wartime Terrorism and Urban Crime, 1937–1941*. Cambridge: Cambridge University Press, 2002.

————. *Spymaster: Dai Li and the Chinese Secret Service*. Berkeley, CA: University of California Press, 2003.

Wakeman, Frederic, and Wen-hsin Yeh. *Shanghai Sojourners*. New York: Routledge Curzon, 1995.

Waley, Arthur. *The Opium War Through Chinese Eyes*. Palo Alto, CA: Stanford University Press, 1958.

Wang, Anyi. *The Song of Everlasting Sorrow*. Translated by Michael Berry and Susan Chan Egan. New York: Columbia University Press, 2008.

Wang, Chi. *The United States and China since World War II: A Brief History*. London: Routledge, 2013.

Wang, George, and Betty Barr. *Shanghai Boy, Shanghai Girl*. Hong Kong: Old China Hand Press, 2002.

Warner, John. *Fragrant Harbour: Early Photographs of Hong Kong*. New York: Hippocrene Books, 1980.

Warr, Anne. *Shanghai Architecture, Architecture Guides*. Balmain, NSW, Australia: Watermark Press, 2008.

Wasserstein, Bernard. *Secret War in Shanghai*. New York: Houghton Mifflin Harcourt, 1999.

Watson, Rubie S., and Patricia Buckley Ebrey. *Marriage and Inequality in Chinese Society*. Berkeley, CA: University of California Press, 1991.

Wei, Betty Peh-T'i. *Old Shanghai: Images of Asia*. Hong Kong: Oxford University Press, 1993.

———. *Shanghai: Crucible of China*. Hong Kong: Oxford University Press, 1988.

Westad, Odd Arne. *Decisive Encounters: The Chinese Civil War, 1946–1950*. Stanford, CA: Stanford University Press, 2003.

Wheelwright, E. L., and Bruce McFarlane. *The Chinese Road to Socialism: Economics of the Cultural Revolution*. New York: Monthly Review Press, 1971.

Wickeri, Philip L., ed. *Christian Encounters with Chinese Culture*. Hong Kong: Hong Kong University Press, 2015.

Wilkinson, H. P. *The Family in Classical China*. Taipei: Ch'eng Wen, 1974.

Wong Siu-Lun, *Emigrant Entrepreneurs: Shanghai Industrialists in Hong Kong*. Hong Kong: Oxford University Press, 1988.

Wood, Frances. *The Lure of China: Writers from Marco Polo to J. G. Ballard*. San Francisco: Long River, 2009.

Wright, Nancy Allison. *Yankee on the Yangtze: Romance and Adventure Follow the Birth of Aviation*. Self-published, 2011.

Wu, Ellen D. *The Color of Success: Asian Americans and the Origins of the Model Minority*. Princeton, NJ: Princeton University Press, 2014.

Wu, Emily, and Larry Engelmann. *Feather in the Storm*. New York: Anchor, 2008.

Wu Liang. *Old Shanghai: A Lost Age*. Beijing: China Press, 2006.

Xu Xixian and Xu Jianrong. *A Changing Shanghai*. Shanghai: Shanghai People's Fine Arts Publishing House, 2004.

Yatsko, Pamela. *New Shanghai: The Rocky Rebirth of China's Legendary City*. New York: Wiley, 2004.

Ye Zhaoyan. *Nanjing*. New York: Anchor, 2004.

Yee, Albert H. *Wither Hong Kong?* Lanham, MD: University Press of America, 1999.

Yeh, Catherine. *Shanghai Love: Courtesans, Intellectuals, and Entertainment Culture, 1850–1910*. Seattle: University of Washington Press, 2006.

Yeh, Wen-hsin. *The Alienated Academy: Culture and Politics in Republican China, 1919–1937*. Harvard East Asian Monographs. Cambridge, MA: Harvard University Asia Center, 2000.

———. *Shanghai Splendor: Economic Sentiments and the Making of Modern China, 1843–1949*. Berkeley, CA: University of California Press, 2008.

Yeh, Wen-hsin, ed. *Becoming Chinese: Passages to Modernity and Beyond*. Berkeley, CA: University of California Press, 2000.

Yu, Renqiu. *To Save China, To Save Ourselves: The Chinese Hand Laundry Alliance of New York*. Philadelphia: Temple University Press, 1992.

Yue, Meng. *Shanghai and the Edges of Empires*. Minneapolis: University of Minnesota Press, 2006.

Zhang, Yingjin. *Cinema and Urban Culture in Shanghai, 1922–1943*. Palo Alto, CA: Stanford University Press, 1999.

Zhang, Zhongli, et al. *The Swire Group in Old China*. Shanghai: Shanghai People's Publishing House, 1990.

PHOTO CREDITS

361 © Ho and Theresa Chow
365 © Helen Zia
373 © Helen Zia
380 © Jack Birns, courtesy of Harriet Birns Kellner
390 © Chan Pan family
401 © Annabel Annuo Liu
407 © Benny Pan

INDEX

Page numbers in *italics* refer to photographs.

PHOTO: © BOB HSIANG PHOTOGRAPHY

HELEN ZIA is the author of *Asian American Dreams: The Emergence of an American People*, a finalist for the Kiriyama Pacific Rim Book Prize (Bill Clinton referred to the book in two separate Rose Garden speeches). Zia co-authored, with Wen Ho Lee, *My Country Versus Me*, which reveals what happened to the Los Alamos scientist who was falsely accused of being a spy for China in the "worst case since the Rosenbergs." She is also a former executive editor of *Ms.* magazine. The daughter of immigrants from China, Zia is a Fulbright Scholar and a graduate of Princeton University's first coeducational class. She has received an honorary doctorate of humane letters from the University of San Francisco and an honorary doctor of laws degree from the City University of New York School of Law for bringing important matters of law and civil rights into public view.

helenzia.com

Facebook.com/realHelenZia

ABOUT THE TYPE

This book was set in Fournier, a typeface named for Pierre-Simon Fournier (1712–68), the youngest son of a French printing family. He started out engraving wood-blocks and large capitals, then moved on to fonts of type. In 1736 he began his own foundry and made several important contributions in the field of type design; he is said to have cut 147 alphabets of his own creation. Fournier is probably best remembered as the designer of St. Augustine Ordinaire, a face that served as the model for the Monotype Corporation's Fournier, which was released in 1925.